Twentieth Century
For Dummies

MW01006089

The Big Events of the Twentieth Century

1901	Twentieth century starts
	Death of Queen Victoria
1904	Russo–Japanese War
1905	First Russian Revolution
1911	Chinese monarchy overthrown
1914–18	First World War
1917	Russian Revolution
1919	Treaty of Versailles and creation of the League of Nations
1929	Wall Street Crash
1930–39	The Depression
1933	Adolf Hitler comes to power in Germany
1934–38	Purges and terror in Russia
1936–39	Spanish Civil War
1937	Japanese invade China
1938	Munich crisis
1939–45	Second World War
1941	Japanese attack Pearl Harbor
1945	Atom bomb dropped on Hiroshima
	United Nations founded
1946–1989	Cold War
1947	India and Pakistan gain independence
1948	State of Israel founded
	Apartheid introduced in South Africa
1949	Communist take-over in China
1950–53	Korean War
1954	Battle of Dien Bien Phu ends French rule in Indo-China
1954–62	Algerian War
1956	Hungarian uprising
	Suez crisis

The Big Events of the Twentieth Century (continued)

1957	European Economic Community founded
	Ghana gains independence
1960–64	Crisis in Congo
1962	Cuban missile crisis
1963	Martin Luther King gives his 'I have a dream' speech
	President John F. Kennedy assassinated
1964–73	Vietnam War
1966–69	Cultural Revolution in China
1967	Six Day War
1969	Moon landing
1970–75	War in Cambodia
1973	Military coup in Chile
	Yom Kippur War
	Watergate scandal in the USA
1978	Iranian revolution
1979–89	Soviet occupation of Afghanistan
1980	State of Zimbabwe established
1980–88	Iran–Iraq War
1985	Gorbachev comes to power in the Soviet Union
1989	Fall of the Berlin Wall
1990–91	First Gulf War
1991	Collapse of the Soviet Union
1991–99	Civil wars in former Yugoslavia
1993	Oslo Accords for peace in the Middle East
	Nelson Mandela becomes president of South Africa
1994–96	War in Chechnya
1994	Genocide in Rwanda
2000	George W. Bush declared US president

Twentieth Century History

FOR

DUMMIES®

Twentieth Century History FOR DUMMIES®

by Dr Sean Lang

John Wiley & Sons, Ltd

Twentieth Century History For Dummies®

Published by
John Wiley & Sons, Ltd
The Atrium
Southern Gate
Chichester
West Sussex
PO19 8SQ
England

E-mail (for orders and customer service enquires): cs-books@wiley.co.uk

Visit our Home Page on www.wiley.com

For general information on our other products and services, please contact our Customer Care Department within the U.S. at 800-762-2974, outside the U.S. at 317-572-3993, or fax 317-572-4002.

For technical support, please visit www.wiley.com/techsupport.

Wiley also publishes its books in a variety of electronic formats. Some content that appears in print may not be available in electronic books.

British Library Cataloguing in Publication Data: A catalogue record for this book is available from the British Library

ISBN: 978-0-470-51015-5

Printed and bound in Great Britain by Bell & Bain Ltd, Glasgow

10 9 8 7 6 5 4 3 2 1

WILEY

About the Author

Dr Sean Lang is the author of *British History For Dummies* and *European History For Dummies*. He lectures in history at Anglia Ruskin University and also teaches for the University of Cambridge Department of Continuing Education. He studied history at Oxford and has taught it in schools and colleges for the past twenty-five years. He has written textbooks and resource packs for A-level history and is co-editor of *Twentieth Century History Review*. He has been an A-level examiner and acted as adviser on history teaching to both government and opposition, as well as to the Council of Europe. He is Honorary Secretary of the Historical Association and has appeared frequently on radio and television talking about history.

Author's Acknowledgements

I must thank my editors at John Wiley, Steve Edwards and Sam Spickernell, who have shown more patience with my delays than I would have shown with my delays. The biggest thanks go, as ever, to my wife Lorna and our girls, Emily, Kate, and Imogen. Yes, girls, Dad's written another book, so there might be buns for tea!

Publisher's Acknowledgements

We're proud of this book; please send us your comments through our Dummies online registration form located at www.dummies.com/register/.

Some of the people who helped bring this book to market include the following:

Acquisitions, Editorial, and Media Development

Project Editor: Steve Edwards

Content Editor: Nicole Burnett

Development Editor: Tracy Barr

Copy Editor: Kate O'Leary

Proofreader: Helen Heyes

Technical Editor: James Vaughan

Commissioning Editor: Samantha Spickernell

Publisher: Jason Dunne

Executive Project Editor: Daniel Mersey

Cover Photos: © GettyImages/ World Perspectives

Cartoons: Ed McLachlan

Composition Services

Project Coordinator: Erin Smith

Layout and Graphics: Reuben W. Davis, Alissa D. Ellet, Melissa K. Jester, Christine Williams

Proofreader: Caitie Kelly

Indexer: Claudia Bourbeau

Brand Reviewer: Rev Mengle

Contents at a Glance

Table of Contents

Introduction

One day in the early 1970s I was watching an item on a children's television programme. The presenters had got hold of a newspaper from the 1920s and were looking at articles imagining what life would be like in the future – specifically, in the 1970s. They imagined we'd all be living in sleek towers soaring into the sky and driving cars that flew, though the illustration, showing a Model T Ford with wings, didn't inspire much confidence. My grandmother, who was watching the programme with me, was a bit put out. 'They're talking about the 1920s as if they were ancient history!' she said, indignantly. Which had me puzzled, because that's exactly what I thought they were!

Now, you could see that incident as a little illustration of different age perspectives. My grandmother was born in 1900 so the 1920s were her twenties, and you always think they were only yesterday. But this story also tells us something about the century itself. Wondering what the future will be like is a very twentieth-century thing to do – after all, in the Middle Ages no one thought it would be so very different from the present. The comics I read as a child used to carry pieces about the Future and their vision wasn't so very different from that 1920s newspaper: By the year 2000 we'd all be – you've guessed it! – living in sleek towers and whizzing around in flying cars. Oh, and wearing *Star Trek*-style outfits in all weathers too.

Now, all centuries think of themselves as modern, but the twentieth century went further: It was the *futuristic* century. The pace of technological change was bewildering. Even in the days of the electric telegraph at the start of the century, no one could have believed that by the end of it people would be beaming instant messages to each other via space. *And thinking nothing of it*. Yet in many ways the twentieth century was no different from any other. It's not just that people still fell in love or laughed or cried. Future-gazers didn't expect that by the year 2000 people would still be starving in Africa while the rest of the world had too much to eat, or that whole communities would set out to massacre their neighbours with guns or machetes, or that millions of people would live in poverty, sheltering under road bridges or on fetid rubbish dumps on the outskirts of hi-tech cities. Or that the world would be pole-axed with grief because of the death of a princess.

No, my friends, the history of the twentieth century will surprise you. You'll find tragedy and horror, but you'll also find tremendous advances in the cause of humanity.

About This Book

This book is called *Twentieth Century History For Dummies*. That title needs a word of explanation. Historians like arranging history in centuries, mainly because a period of a hundred years has a nice round feel to it, but that approach is always a bit arbitrary: Things don't always change dramatically from one century to another (do you feel so very different when you wake up on your birthday? Apart from the hangover, I mean). Some historians talk of the twentieth century as if it *really* started in 1914 when the First World War broke out and some like to wrap it up with the fall of the Berlin Wall in 1989. But you've paid good money for this book and I'm not going to short-change you. In fact, I'm going to give you a bit extra. This book takes you from the end of the nineteenth century right the way through to the Millennium and a little bit beyond. Not too far beyond, because we're only just into the twenty-first century as I write this, but enough to round off the story.

If you're going to write the history of the twentieth century you've got to think global because that's how the century thought. When the century opened the world was dominated by global empires and when it ended it was dominated by global corporations, and the two wars which shaped the period in-between were both called world wars. In 1900 travel was an adventure for the rich but by 2000 people of all social classes were hopping on planes and jetting off around the world. To some extent, therefore, any history of the twentieth century is bound to be a history of the world.

But writing truly global history isn't easy. For much of the century the drive behind world events came from Western leaders, and Western culture certainly came to dominate the world (though Islamic culture made an impressive stand against it). So you'll find that the first half of this book is rather dominated by the doings of Western countries dragging the rest of the world behind them. Once you get past the Second World War, however, a different story emerges: Countries in other parts of the world gained their independence and began to follow their own courses of action. Lastly, the title says this book is for dummies. As you probably know, this book is part of the successful *For Dummies* series, but don't get the wrong idea: I don't think you're a dummy. How could I? You bought my book. But all of us can feel like a dummy in front of something we know nothing whatever about. The twentieth century isn't going to be quite like that, because you're bound to know *something* about it, but knowing a few odd bits can be almost as bad as knowing nothing at all, especially if you don't know how they connect or what the overall picture is. The trouble is that some books can be so off-putting, or use such technical language, or just not bother to explain things that you end up *feeling* like a dummy. This book will not do this. You may feel like a dummy when you pick it up, but you won't by the time you put it down. And, hopefully, you'll have enjoyed it too.

Conventions Used in This Book

The most obvious convention I follow is to use standard dating: 1900, 1914, 1939, and so on. You might think 'So what?' but not everyone sees history that way. You might read that the Battle of Kursk, a huge tank battle between the Germans and the Russians, took place in the year 1943, and so it did in the normal way of dating. But in the Islamic calendar it took place in the year 1362 and in the Hebrew calendar it was in 5703. Confusing. In this book, I use the form of dates in most common use, from the Gregorian calendar drawn up in the sixteenth century by Pope Gregory XIII after whom it is named. Some people like to shy away from this calendar's Christian origins by adding the letters 'CE' after dates, to stand for 'Common Era'. But since history has no common era this idea has never seemed very sensible to me. No, the nearly-universal use of the Gregorian calendar is just another reminder that, for much of the twentieth century, the world was dominated by the West. Get over it. You can decide whether or not this was a good thing when you've read a bit more of the book.

Speaking of dates, not everyone knows that the twentieth century began on 1 January 1901 and soldiered on until the end of 2000. If you're wondering why 1900 isn't considered part of the twentieth century, remember that centuries are numbered from the notional date of the birth of Jesus Christ. Because there wasn't a year 0, the first set of hundred years is numbered 1–100, the second century from 101–200, the third century 201–300, and so on, with every century beginning with a year ending in 01 and ending at the end of a year ending in 00. That means that 1901 was the first year of the twentieth century, and the twenty-first century began on 1 January 2001. But of course people always get the decorations out when the numeral at the start of the date changes, as it did in 1900 and 2000. Trying to explain to them why 1900 and 2000 weren't the first years of either century but the last years of the previous ones is pointless: You'll just have to bathe in the warm glow of knowing you're right and go out and buy an anorak.

Names are the other issue. Names matter but place names and even people's names often change, which can make things difficult for the poor old historian. The Russian city of St Petersburg was known as Petrograd, Leningrad, and then St Petersburg again at different points in the century. Some cities changed names according to which country they ended up in: For the first half of the century, for example, the Polish city of Gdansk was a German city called Danzig. Some cities deliberately changed their name to wipe out memories of the past: Salisbury in Rhodesia became Harare in the independent state of Zimbabwe, Saigon in South Vietnam became Ho Chi Minh City, Chemnitz in Germany became Karl-Marx Stadt and then changed back to Chemnitz after the fall of communism. Countries changed their names: Ceylon became Sri Lanka, Burma became Myanmar. And sometimes the whole system of spelling changes: We used to write about how Mao Tse-tung defeated the Kuomintang to seize power in Peking; now we say that Mao Zedong defeated the Guomindang to seize power in Beijing. But sometimes people get confused and mix old and new spellings on the same page.

In this book I try to use the names and forms in use at the time – so I refer to Abyssinia in the thirties but Ethiopia in the 1980s, and Peking and Mao Tse-tung until the 1980s when the general usage changed.

Foolish Assumptions

You might have made some foolish assumptions about me; I hope I haven't made too many about you.

I'm assuming:

- ✔ You've probably heard of the most important figures of the century, such as Lenin or Gandhi, but don't know much about them
- ✔ You're interested to know a bit about the twentieth century but you don't want to get bogged down in a lot of boring detail
- ✔ You don't usually buy history books if you can help it
- ✔ You haven't got much time

If this is you, then smile: Your trip through the twentieth-century's major people and events will be clear and painless and as short or long as you care to make it. You may end up learning more than you bargained for, in fact I hope you do, but I won't pile too many details on you.

Ah, but you may be thinking in terms of someone else. Perhaps you've got a relative or a friend who is learning history at college and needs help. Perhaps you are that relative or friend. Perhaps someone has set you an essay.

If so, then this book is the place to start. It will give you a road map, tell you how the land lies, and what the dangers are. If you need to know a lot about the Mexican Revolution or Sukarno's regime in Indonesia or about the Cold War and you need to know it now, then starting here will make the rest of your reading a whole lot easier to understand. This book is your friend.

But what about you? Perhaps you're assuming:

- ✔ This book will have lots of dates
- ✔ This book will have exercises and tests for you to do
- ✔ You have to read this whole book

Wrong! You'll find dates where they're useful, which is what dates are for. You won't find any tests or exercises because this book aims to help you learn, not to make you feel small. And you don't have to read all the book. You don't have to read all of every chapter. I've written it so you can home straight in on the bits you want. Okay, you might need to check some bits elsewhere, and I've indicated where doing so might be helpful, but always remember: This book is here to serve you, not you to serve it.

One last very foolish assumption. You might be thinking:

    ✔ History is heavy

Read on: I think you'll be surprised.

How This Book Is Organised

I've divided the book into chapters which deal with major themes, and the chapters are grouped into four parts. (The fifth one, the Part of Tens, is a bit different and doesn't fit into the overall historical structure. But it is rather fun.) The overall approach is chronological, that is, I've tried to talk about things in the historical order in which they happened. But not always. For example, I deal with the Russian Revolution and the spread of communism in the 1920s and 1930s in Chapter 4 and then Chapter 5 deals with the growth of fascism, even though they were happening at the same time. Parts III and IV also overlap a bit. The Cold War started in the 1940s and carried on right through to the 1980s, so putting it all into Part III so you can get a sense of the whole story makes sense. If I do put everything from those years into Part III, however, it makes that part very large while Part IV only has the 1990s to deal with. So Part III concentrates on issues relating to the Cold War and to the end of Europe's worldwide empires, while Part IV looks at some of the issues which weren't resolved by 1989, and which were still keeping the world's leaders awake at night by the Millennium.

Part I: The Great War Years: 1900–19

This part looks at the first two decades of the century, which were dominated by the Great War. I start by looking at some of the issues left over from the end of the nineteenth century – centuries always take a bit of time to hand on to their successors – and at how quarrels among Europeans turned into a nightmarish global conflict. Europe's worldwide empires were at the height of their power then, but that situation would soon be changing.

These were also the years of amazing technological changes. Motor cars had been expensive playthings for the rich; thanks to Henry Ford they were rapidly becoming must-haves for everyone. Within a few years of the Wright brothers' first flight at Kitty Hawk, men were taking to the air, crossing the English Channel, and soon learning how to fix guns to their planes and shoot each other down. Telecommunications were taking off, thanks to pioneering work in wireless radio, so that not even a ship at sea need be out of touch with the world. These were exciting years, but dangerous ones.

Part II: The Years of the Great Dictators: 1919–45

The First World War shocked the world to its foundations. The old order had led the world into chaos, and would never enjoy people's confidence in the same way again. Nationalist movements were getting going in Asia and Africa, beginning to challenge the West's claim to rule the rest of the world. And the working people of the world were challenging the right of the middle classes to rule them.

The Russians led the way when they tore down their imperial regime and set up the world's first communist state. Many people around the world were excited and expected their own countries to follow Russia's example. Even when the Russian experiment turned into a nightmare of famine and brutal dictatorship, many communists stayed loyal to their ideals. But others rejected communism and turned instead to fascism, which was developed in Italy as a sort of socialist movement but in military uniform. Adolf Hitler, the German dictator, was the most notorious leader. His drive to make Germany the greatest state in the world led to the Second World War, which was even longer and more destructive than the first. At the end of it, Germany was crushed and the might of the old great powers was shattered.

Part III: The Divided World: 1945–89

This part deals with the age of the Superpowers. The United States and the Soviet Union had crushed Hitler together, but they soon became enemies. Each side suspected the other of planning to take over the world, and each side gathered allies and weapons. Nuclear weapons. By the 1950s the world was divided into two hostile blocs of terrifying power. The Cold War was a period of paralysing fear that the next international crisis could mean the end of the world.

On a brighter note, the rest of that world began finally to get its voice heard. As Europe's worldwide empires finally collapsed, sometimes peacefully, more often very bloodily, new states emerged in Africa and Asia and began to take their places in the councils of the world. But hopes that independence would lead to international peace and prosperity didn't last long: Many of these new states proved poor and corrupt, and soon got dragged into the Cold War. One of them, Vietnam, was the scene for America's twentieth-century nightmarish war.

And then, suddenly, the Cold War ended. All that was required apparently was a new leader in Russia and a more open attitude in Washington. Borders opened and Berlin's infamous wall was torn down. This part explains why.

Part IV: To the Millennium

Not all problems were solved when the Cold War ended. For some areas, like Europe, it produced a whole set of new problems. Incredibly, the 1990s saw horrific tribal killing in Yugoslavia and in Rwanda. In the Middle East, the long battle between Israel and its Arab neighbours carried on as before, only now it grew as the West increasingly identified militant Islam as its new enemy. Only a matter of months into the new millennium Islamic terrorists launched a devastating attack that destroyed the World Trade Center in New York: This event was probably the twentieth century's biggest legacy to the twenty-first.

This period wasn't all bad. The last decades of the century saw breathtaking developments in communications and technology, as the world discovered the World Wide Web. Advances in medicine made it possible to treat increasing numbers of diseases. But AIDS appeared in the 1980s, sweeping through the world like a medieval plague and devastating Africa. And as the century ended, our technological advances themselves seemed to put the future of the planet at deadly risk.

Part V: The Part of Tens

Time to cheer up. If the century's doom and gloom is getting too much for you, have a look in here and discover my thoughts about the century's highs and lows. Not just the serious stuff: Which were the century's most important films? What were the century's most iconic moments? And were men's flares really the century's worst idea?

The Part of Tens is always the most fun part to write; you should find it fun to read, too.

Icons Used in This Book

At different points in the book you'll see little icons that highlight particular points. This is what they mean:

 Sometimes something that happened in the past has a direct link with today. It might be the origin of something we're familiar with, or it might explain why we do things the way we do. Where you see this sign you'll find one of these direct links between yesterday and today.

 Beware: Historians disagree. Not (usually) about dates or events but they can disagree violently about how we should understand the past. Was Stalin just a bloodthirsty tyrant or was he the direct product of the Russian Revolution? Did President Truman need to authorise dropping the atomic bomb on Japan? Was Indian independence rushed through too quickly? These are important issues, often with major consequences, and historians can get surprisingly heated when debating them. This symbol indicates where significant debates have sprung up, so you'll know how you stand if you decide to look into the issue further.

 We may not know much about history, but at least we like to think we know some things. The trouble is, some of the things we think we know turn out not to have happened in the way we thought at all. We all like our myths, but part of a historian's job is to check facts and doing so inevitably means a lot of myth-busting. If you hate having your illusions shattered, you may want to steer clear of this icon, but if you can take it, read and be amazed.

 You'll see this icon where I mention a significant point that you need to bear in mind, especially if you are to understand something that comes later. Of course the good thing about this book is that if you forget what it is you are supposed to remember you can always look for the Remember icon.

 Or, to put it another way, Fancy That! Here I point out some of the enormous technological advances that have been made in the twentieth century and how they have affected events. Some, such as telecommunications, have been entirely to the good; others, like flamethrowers or Agent Orange, have not.

 Not to be confused with Technological Breakthroughs! Here I explain some technical terms or ideas as they arise. If you want detail, this is where to look. Or, you can skip these sections and carry on with the story. No one will know.

Part I
The Great War Years: 1900–19

'I'm not looking forward to the releasing
of the balloons.'

In this part . . .

The Great War (1914–18) dominated the first two decades of the century. Long before it broke out people talked excitedly or apprehensively of the coming war, as if they were waiting for a thunderstorm to clear the air. No one imagined how long or appallingly destructive this 'thunderstorm' would prove.

The world that entered the twentieth century was that of the white man. Half the globe, including nearly the whole African continent, was ruled from Europe. The whole world seemed shaped by Western ideas and Western principles; increasingly, it even wore Western clothes. The new century seemed set to mark the final triumph of the West. The Great War put an end to that idea.

To many people the twentieth century appeared to herald a new age of science and technology, when human beings would show how they could apply their minds to the happiness and progress of humankind. These years certainly saw great advances in medicine and technology. But they also saw scientific ideas applied to cruelty, death, and destruction.

These were the catastrophic opening years from which the twentieth century never fully recovered.

Chapter 1

Overview of a Century

*T*he twentieth century saw more change in a shorter time than any other period of human history. By the time the century ended people were flying regularly, sending instant messages by e-mail or text, slipping mobile phones into their pockets, and communicating with any corner of the world in seconds. What was everyday life to millions of people (okay, millions of people in rich countries) was the stuff of dreams at the start of the century. Yet many things seemed hardly to have changed at all: wars still broke out, famine still struck, and the gulf between rich and poor seemed as wide as ever. This chapter introduces you to the twentieth century and looks at some of the themes you can explore in the rest of the book.

When (and How Long?) Was the Twentieth Century?

The twentieth century officially started on 1 January 1901 and carried on until the end of 2000. But centuries aren't just groupings of dates; they're periods that historians reckon had some unique flavour or theme. The nineteenth century had a particular mindset and outlook that was quite different from the way people thought in the eighteenth century and different again from the way people thought in the twentieth. Often these changes in thinking were linked to a big event that forced people to re-examine their ideas.

The end of history is nigh! Or is it?

In 1990, as the communist bloc was crumbling before the eyes of the world, the American historian Francis Fukuyama published an article, later expanded into a book, in which he declared that the world had finally reached the 'End of History'. That's quite a claim and very bad news for those of us who depend on it for a living. But hang on: How can you possibly end history? History goes on whether we like it or not. So what was Fukuyama on about?

Fukuyama had gone back to a nineteenth-century German philosopher, largely forgotten nowadays, called Friedrich Hegel. Hegel taught that human affairs – that is, the events that drive history – operate in much the same way as forces in the natural world: You have one force coming one way challenged by a different force coming the opposite way. They clash, an almighty bang happens, and when the dust has settled a new force emerges, dusts itself down, and sets off in a new direction, until it's met by a different force coming the opposite way – you get the idea. In other words, conflict makes the world go round. This pattern of force and counter-force is called *dialectic* or, specifically, 'Hegelian dialectic' – a useful phrase to use at parties if you want the room to yourself.

Hegel's most famous follower was Karl Marx. Marx worked Hegel's ideas out simply: The first force is the bosses, the force coming the opposite way is the workers, the clash will be the great revolution, and out of that will emerge a new

force going in its own direction, which will be a workers' democratic republic. *Class* conflict, said Marx, is what makes the world go round. And for some two hundred years, you could argue, it did. The Cold War, which pitted the communist (that is, Marxist) countries against the capitalist countries, seemed to prove Hegel's (and Marx's) point very well. The only trouble was that when the revolution finally came, it was the *communist* countries, not the capitalist ones, that fell. The people tore down the communist regimes, declared democracy, and immediately started opening links and ties with the West. Not only was the Cold War over, but the West had won. More to the point, there was no one around who could challenge the US and its allies. Or, in Hegelian terms, no counter-force existed: The liberal-democratic West could set off in its new direction in full confidence that it had overcome every enemy it was ever likely to face. Hegelian dialectic had finally run out of counter-forces: History, as Fukuyama put it, was henceforth at an end. His book sold well.

Until 9/11. A new counter-force had arrived on the scene to challenge the might of America: Militant Islam. It's far too soon to say what new direction will emerge from that clash, but it persuaded Professor Fukuyama to revise his opinions. Maybe history isn't over after all: We've got a few more forces and counter-forces to go through yet. That strange sound you can hear in the distance is Friedrich Hegel having the last laugh.

Centuries aren't determined by years, but by pivotal events. For this reason, they can be 'long' (going beyond the span of a hundred years) or 'short' (starting and finishing inside their chronological span). Consider these examples:

> ✔ **The seventeenth century:** Historians like to say that the eighteenth century, which 'ends' with the French Revolution in 1789, only really 'began' in 1714 when King Louis XIV of France died. That makes the eighteenth century only seventy five years long!

✔ **The nineteenth century:** Most historians would say that the nineteenth century started with the outbreak of the French Revolution (if you're not sure what *that* was, see *European History For Dummies* (Wiley)). But that started in 1789. And if the nineteenth century *really* began with the French Revolution, when did it end? No great earth-shattering event occurred in 1900 to make people spill their coffee and say, 'Oh well, there goes the century'; but fourteen years later there certainly was, when the First World War broke out. So historians often like to talk of a 'long nineteenth century' from the French Revolution in 1789 to the First World War in 1914 and forget the maths.

So when should we date the twentieth century? Is it a 'long' century or a 'short' one? If we take the First World War as the point when the nineteenth century really ended and the world changed fundamentally, then 1914 becomes our start date, and most historians would go along with that.

Not all historians agree with this beginning date. Some argue that the twentieth century started with the Russian Revolution in October 1917. Others say the century began when Queen Victoria died on 22 November 1901. Others say the century *really* started in 1905 when Einstein published his *General Theory of Relativity*, or in 1918 when Marie Stopes published *Married Love* and made family planning possible, or in 1903 with the Wright Brothers' first powered flight. Or you could just take the mathematical view and say the century began on 1 January 1901!

If saying when the twentieth century began is difficult, just as tricky is saying when it ended. If we leave aside the mathematical date, 31 December 2000, then we have two serious contenders:

✔ **9 November 1989:** The Berlin Wall coming down symbolised the end of the Cold War (though strictly speaking the Cold War had ended the year before). People knew that the world would never be the same again and they were right.

✔ **11 September 2001:** The attacks on the United States on 11 September 2001 were so bewildering that they never got a real name: At first people just referred to 'the events of 11 September', as if a minor scuffle had occurred in the street, and then everyone settled on '9/11'. People knew that the world had changed at that pivotal moment, and again, they were right.

Which of these two dates marked the turning point when the twentieth century ended and the twenty-first got going? That will be for historians of the future to judge. In this book, I take the story just into the new century, to the 9/11 attacks on the USA. That's when the 21st century really got going.

Characterising the Twentieth-Century World

At the start of the century the world was essentially divided into two parts: Advanced industrial countries in Europe, North America, and Japan, and vast areas of the globe, including most of Asia and almost the entire continent of Africa, which *belonged* to them as colonies. Some countries came into a third category of independent nations, for example China and the nations of South America, which didn't belong to anyone else, but in fact were so heavily dependent on the industrialised countries that they may just as well have been colonies. So what, exactly, was the twentieth-century world? And to what extent did people of the twentieth century think in terms of a single 'world'?

All together now: A world government (of sorts)

The world seemed to get its act together after the Great War (1914–18). For the first time in history a sort of world government actually existed: The *League of Nations*. The League met in Geneva, with nations from all over the world represented equally, and was supposed to lay down international law and solve disputes between nations by common agreement. The League did achieve some very important breakthroughs, such as banning the use of lead in paint and establishing a proper law of the sea, but its political work proved a flop. Some major nations stayed out of the League, and those that joined took no notice of it when it suited them. Above all, the League didn't represent those parts of the world that were ruled as colonies – most of Africa and Asia, in other words. The League proved totally unable to stop aggressive nations plunging the world into the Second World War. But the *idea* of a world government didn't go away.

After the Second World War the nations of the world had another go at setting up a world government. This time it was called the United Nations and it met in New York. Unfortunately, the UN was immediately paralysed by the Cold War, the name given to the period of icy tension between the capitalist West and the communist world that lasted from the 1940s to the 1980s. The UN has sent armed peacekeeping missions into various world troublespots, but hasn't always been able to prevent wars, massacres, and atrocities.

'First World, Third World' – What happened to the 'Second World'?

'Third World' was never a satisfactory term, not least because people were often unsure what the first two worlds were. Other phrases were tried: First 'Undeveloped World', then, in case that term seemed a bit harsh, 'Under-developed World', and, more encouragingly, 'Developing World'. In the 1980s a special commission on poverty in the 'Third World' headed by the former German Chancellor Willi Brandt recommended referring to the rich countries as 'the North' and the world's poorer countries as 'the South', which made geographical sense up to a point (though it meant wealthy Australia and New Zealand found themselves allocated to the North. Strewth!). But even this terminology has its limits. After the end of the Cold War the world learned that some former communist 'northern' countries like Bulgaria and Romania lived in conditions as bad as some 'southern' or Third World countries. And what about big 'Third World' or 'Southern' countries like India and China, which by the end of the century were well on their way to becoming economic superpowers, yet had problems of poverty every bit as bad as the poorest African countries?

Three worlds in one: First, third, and non-aligned

In 1955, when the Cold War seemed to be heading towards nuclear disaster, the leaders of many of the nations who had recently gained independence from the European colonial powers met at Bandung in Indonesia and declared themselves the 'non-aligned' world – that is, they were not allied to either side in the Cold War. In fact, most of them tended to sympathise with the communist bloc on a my-former-colonial-ruler's-enemy-is-my-friend basis, but the fact remained that the world now seemed to be divided into *three* camps: Capitalist, communist, and non-aligned.

By the 1960s, after most of Africa had gained its independence from the Europeans, one fact began to become crystal clear about this non-aligned world: many of the countries in it were economic disaster areas. Many of these new nations had to borrow huge sums of money to combat famine and disease and they were expected to repay at interest. As a result, this debt-ridden 'third world' became a by-word for poverty, hunger, corruption, and, all too often, dictatorship and war.

Connecting through technology

During the last thirty or so years of the twentieth century, technology brought the world closer. The Internet and the World Wide Web created an international communications system that helped people get in touch with each other and feel part of the same world. You could log onto a gaming site in your front room and find yourself playing against someone from the other side of the world. While sending a letter abroad had once meant buying special lightweight air mail paper and a colourful stamp and feeling rather exotic at the post office, now you could e-mail someone on the other side of the world in the time it took to e-mail your colleague at the next desk.

Save the world!

The issue that did most to give a truly global sense of togetherness wasn't a political ideology but a growing realisation that if we didn't all learn to act together, we were likely to destroy the planet we all live on.

Environmental groups started campaigning in the 1960s and 1970s to save endangered animal species, but by the 1980s they were turning their attention to the appalling damage being created by industrial pollution. Because pollution doesn't respect borders, countries *had* to start thinking and acting together to defend their common global interests.

By the 1990s, environmentalists were raising the alarm about changes to the climate caused by the release of carbon gases into the atmosphere. These gases are emitted from objects common to life in the West, such as refrigerators, cars, and aeroplanes. Making the situation worse was the destruction of vast areas of rainforest – particularly the steady destruction for economic and political reasons of the Amazon rainforest – that would normally absorb these 'greenhouse gases'. It was no good the Brazilian government arguing that what was happening to the Amazon was an internal matter: The destruction had implications for *everyone*.

Sometimes global problems can seem too big for any of us to do much about, but environmentalists have a good slogan which reminds us that we're all part of one world: *Think globally – Act locally*.

Ch-ch-ch-changes!

A lot changed during the twentieth century, including a few things that people used to think would go on for ever. The poet Thomas Hardy wrote about a man ploughing his fields, following his horse as men had done for centuries and would do for ages to come: He hadn't reckoned on tractors, though. So many basics of life – farming, childbirth, travelling, sitting at home in the evening – went through such huge changes that it is often hard to believe that the 1900s and the 1990s were less than a hundred years apart.

From monarchs . . .

The twentieth century saw some major changes in leadership. In 1900, most of the world's major states, and quite a few of the smaller ones, were ruled by monarchs. Even states that had got rid of their kings, such as France, the USA, or the states of South America, often treated their presidents as if they were royalty.

However, monarchs didn't enjoy anything like the power and authority their ancestors had possessed. The British monarchs and the German emperors had to work with elected parliaments which laid down strict limits on royal power; the Russian and Chinese emperors and the Turkish sultan all claimed to have total power over their subjects but soon found that in fact they didn't: All of them were forced to grant their people an elected parliament. The appalling destruction of the First World War made many people lose faith in the monarchs who had led them into it. After the war, revolution broke out in many of the countries that had fought in it, and many monarchs had to flee for their lives. But all too often the new democratic politicians proved incapable of dealing with the serious problems the new republics faced. The people didn't necessarily want the old monarchs back, but they did want rulers who could promise to restore order. Cue the dictators.

. . . to dictators

If you've lived all your life in a democratic country, it can be quite a shock to realise how unusual you are. In the second half of the twentieth century dictatorship was the *usual* form of government in most of the world. Most African countries were dictatorships and so were most South American ones. In Chile, the democratically elected government was overthrown by an American-backed coup in 1973 and the Chilean president, Salvador Allende, was murdered. Brutal dictatorships operated at various times in Indonesia, in North Korea (and, you could argue, in South Korea too), in Iraq and Syria, in Iran, in Afghanistan, as well as in the Soviet bloc in eastern and central Europe. Post-war Spain, Portugal, and Greece all went through military rule and had to establish themselves as fully democratic countries before they could even think of applying to join the European Union. The following sections identify some of the century's most influential dictators.

Vladimir Ilyich Lenin (1870–1924)

When the Russians overthrew their tsar in February 1917, the new government was supposed to set up a democratically elected parliament, but instead the Bolsheviks (communists), led by Vladimir Ilyich Lenin, overthrew the Russian government and took power themselves. Lenin said that democratic elections were just a middle-class ploy to fool people into thinking their opinions mattered; real democracy, he said, lay in setting up the *dictatorship of the proletariat* – that is, all power to the workers. (You can find out more about the Russian Revolution and Lenin in Chapter 4.)

After Lenin died in 1924, he became venerated almost like a saint, which was ironic because he'd abolished religion in Russia. His body was embalmed and put on show in Moscow and his possessions were regarded virtually as holy relics. Russians invoked his name and guidance before doing almost anything, from building a bridge to doing their homework. This phenomenon was known as the *cult of personality*.

Josef Stalin (1879–1953)

As soon as Lenin was dead, the Bolshevik leaders all started plotting against each other. The man who won was Josef Stalin, and he set up a cult of his own personality even bigger than Lenin's. The only free debate allowed in Russia was over who could come up with the best praise for Stalin. What made this situation worse was that while everyone was calling Stalin the father of the country who looked after everyone, the reality was that his secret police were rounding up people in their thousands and sending them to labour camps. See Chapter 4 for more on Stalin.

Benito Mussolini (1883–1945)

Italian dictator Benito Mussolini was the first ruler outside Russia to copy Lenin's style of dictatorship. Mussolini seized power in 1922, saying he would save Italy from anarchy and communism. Instead he took all power into his own hands, had anyone who opposed him killed, and persuaded the Italian people to hail him as their leader, or *il Duce* in Italian.

Mussolini saw himself as a new Caesar who would restore Italy's ancient days of glory. He borrowed many details from the Romans, including the raised arm salute and a desire to conquer the Mediterranean world. For the symbol of his new party, Mussolini borrowed an ancient Roman symbol of a bundle of rods bound together around an axe to symbolise the strength and authority that come from unity. This symbol was called the *fasces*, which is simply the Latin word for 'rods', so Mussolini's regime became known as *fascism*. (To find out more about the Romans , see *The Romans For Dummies* (Wiley)).

Mussolini didn't just seize power in Italy; he established a new type of rule known as *Totalitarianism*. This idea holds that the State is all important and the individual isn't. Everything belongs to the State and should be run by the State and anyone who stands out against this idea is an Enemy of the State and must be crushed. In theory, 'the State' and 'the People' were the same thing; in reality the State meant the government and the people had to do what they were told. The leader or *dictator* (another term the Italians got from the Romans) embodied the State and therefore in theory he embodied the People. Which was just a neat way of saying that if you opposed the leader you were, by definition, an Enemy of the People and should be destroyed.

At first Mussolini seemed to be so successful that his style of leadership caught on and soon fascist-style leaders popped up all round the world. Fascist-style regimes sprouted in South America, across central and eastern Europe, in China, and in Japan. Mussolini's most fervent admirer, however, was the man who would give dictatorship a permanently bad name, Adolf Hitler. See Chapter 5 for more on Mussolini (and Hitler).

Adolf Hitler (1889–1945)

Hitler showed there wasn't much anyone could teach him about how to run a dictatorship. Not only did he have his opponents murdered, take all of German life under the control of the State, and set up a secret police force to keep everyone under observation, but he so captivated the German people that he turned this most cultured of European nations into a gang of racist thugs. He set up a huge industrial programme dedicated to finding and killing every Jew and gypsy in Germany, and later in the whole of Europe. Germany was a chilling illustration of what a dictator can do if he really sets his mind to it.

Hitler led Germany into the disastrous Second World War, which killed millions around the world and utterly destroyed his beloved country. When the dust had settled, people were determined that never again should power lie in the hands of tyrannical megalomaniacs like Mussolini and Hitler. That was the intention, at any rate, but it didn't quite work out.

Mao Zedong (1893–1976)

Chinese communist leader, Mao Zedong, who seized power in 1949, set up a cult of personality every bit as ruthless and disastrous as anything Mussolini or Stalin had run. Mao even pretended to welcome criticism: 'Let a Thousand Flowers bloom!' he declared in the 1960s, encouraging people to come forward and express their views openly. They did, and he had them arrested. See Chapter 16 for more on Mao.

Pol Pot (1928–98)

One of the most tragic examples of dictatorship occurred in Cambodia. Pol Pot, leader of the communist *Khmer Rouge*, seized control of Cambodia in 1975 and immediately declared it 'Year Zero': Cambodia would start again, from scratch. Pol Pot ordered everyone – *everyone* – out of the cities and into the countryside to till the land alongside the peasants. Doctors, teachers, and anyone with any degree of learning were regarded as an enemy of the people and shot. Pol Pot had whole villages wiped out. Thousands and thousands of Cambodians were shot and their bodies left to rot in what became known as the 'killing fields'. No one knows exactly how many Cambodians were massacred before Pol Pot's murderous regime was finally overthrown in 1979. See Chapter 14 for more on Pol Pot.

Nineteen Eighty-Four

In 1949 the British writer George Orwell produced *Nineteen Eighty-Four,* a chilling vision of an England under the heel of the ruthless dictatorship of 'Big Brother'. It was a bleak world, in which the secret 'Thought Police' prevented people thinking for themselves and telescreens watched what people were doing and saying at home. You could be arrested for 'thoughtcrime' and language was manipulated into something called 'newspeak' so you couldn't even have the words with which to voice dissent. (Originally Orwell wanted to call it *Nineteen Forty-Eight* but his publishers thought that was a shade too

pessimistic so he reversed the figures to get *Nineteen Eighty-Four.*)

Of course, when the real 1984 arrived and turned out to be a year much like any other, people decided 'Panic over – George got it wrong'. Even the Soviet Union soon started unravelling. But many aspects of Orwell's vision of the future remain true, even if not quite the way he envisaged: Thanks to microchip technology and genetic records the State *can* keep tabs on every aspect of our lives. So can many multinational corporations. Even Orwell didn't anticipate that.

African dictators

Africa produced a series of grotesque dictators in the last decades of the century, including:

- ✔ **President Mobutu of Zaire**, who seized power in a military coup in 1965 and amassed an enormous fortune for himself while his country grew steadily poorer.

- ✔ **President Idi Amin of Uganda**, who seized power in a military coup in 1971, expelled the country's Asian population, and set about murdering thousands of Ugandans, including many schoolchildren. He was eventually overthrown in 1979.

- ✔ **Emperor Jean-Bedel Bokassa of the Central African Empire** (otherwise known as the Central African Republic), who seized power in a military coup (do you see a pattern here?) in 1965 and declared himself President. His regime became steadily more bizarre thanks to his deep Napoleon fixation. In 1977, he declared the country an Empire and staged a massive coronation ceremony based exactly on Napoleon's in 1804. It cost a small fortune while his people were some of the poorest in Africa. When schoolchildren protested against the uniforms he was making them wear (and pay for) he ordered his troops to kill them. He was overthrown in a coup in 1979.

Two cheers for democracy?

Democratic regimes can rarely compete with dictatorships on the glamour front: Democracy tends to run to balding middle-aged men in suits rather than eccentrics in uniform, but its had its fair share of successes. The

Western democracies were on the winning side in the Second World War (though so too was the highly undemocratic Soviet Union, don't forget), and they also saw out and won the Cold War. Perhaps more importantly, democratic ideas have taken hold around the world so that even dictatorships have to *pretend* to be operating democratically. The 1980s saw a series of popular risings for democracy that overturned the dictatorships in Argentina, the Philippines, Haiti, and then across eastern Europe. Even South Africa dismantled its racist apartheid regime and allowed democracy; in 1994 thousands of black South Africans queued for hours to have the chance to cast their vote for the first time in their lives.

Even so, the world was very far from being fully democratic by the time the century ended. Some dictators managed to stay in power; some democratic countries seemed to have trouble living up to their own ideals. Italian politics became notorious for corruption and instability, much of it down to Italy's particular form of democratic structure. France's democracy seemed very shaky during the crises of the 1960s. Even American democracy was tainted, first by President Nixon's involvement in the Watergate scandal, next by sex scandals involving democratic darling Bill Clinton, and in 2000 by extraordinary scenes in the presidential election which seemed to suggest the sophisticated voting system in Florida had broken down and that the wrong candidate was declared President.

More worryingly, some groups even denied that democracy was necessarily the best way to rule. In particular, some religious groups argued that if democracy allowed people the freedom to deny and attack their religious faith, then democracy was not as good as it was cracked up to be. And the spectacle of democratic countries appearing to *force* democracy on countries like Vietnam or Iraq tarnished democracy's reputation for many people.

A violent century

Thinking that as time progresses, people become more civilized and humane in the way they treat each other is natural. Natural, but wrong. The twentieth century saw some really inventive thinking in how to harm people.

✔ **Bigger and bigger bombs:** Blowing people up is a very old idea, but the twentieth century came up with ways of doing it on a much bigger scale than ever before. Artillery bombardments in France and Belgium in the First World War were so enormous that they could be heard in London. Then the Second World War perfected ways of dropping bombs from aircraft to destroy whole cities, a technique that reached its destructive height with the atom bombs dropped on Hiroshima and Nagasaki. Then came the hydrogen bomb, hundreds of times more destructive than the atom bomb, and then instead of planes dropping nuclear bombs, the boffins worked out how to attach nuclear warheads to missiles that could take off at the press of a button and travel from one continent to another.

✔ **Chemical warfare:** People have long used contaminated material to hurt their enemies, but the twentieth century really took to this ghastly way of fighting. Both sides in the First World War used poison gas, and Mussolini used it against the Abyssinians. In the Second World War it was used to murder millions of people in concentration camps. The Americans used a burning chemical jelly called *Napalm* against villages in the Vietnam War, as well as an acid called *Agent Orange* to destroy forest vegetation. President Saddam Hussein used gas to murder thousands of Iraqi Kurds in the 1980s. And by the 1990s all major nations, and quite a few less major ones, had huge stockpiles of nerve gas and biological and chemical weapons.

✔ **Terrorism:** The twentieth century was *the* century of terrorism, which means making people so afraid of you that they'll do whatever you want them to. The most effective way to scare people is to kill *randomly*, so no-one can feel safe. Significant terrorist campaigns occurred in Russia before the revolution, in Palestine in the 1930s, in colonial Africa, in the Middle East, South America, the Caribbean, and western Europe. Can terrorism work? Yes, it can: It forced a number of countries to change their policies and many terrorist leaders went on to become political leaders. But not always: Governments have learned a lot about how to fight terrorism, especially by using informers.

✔ **Knives:** The twentieth century found new ways of using this simple old weapon, with global implications, and at the end of the century the humble knife was the most successful weapon of mass murder. Stabbing never went out of fashion on the streets, but in the 1990s knives and machetes were used in the mass killings in Rwanda, when Hutus turned on their Tutsi neighbours and literally hacked them to death. A few years later, the 9/11 hijackers used knives to take over the planes they then flew into the World Trade Center and the Pentagon.

Old faiths, new beliefs – Christianity

The nineteenth century, at least in the Western world, was a great age of religious faith. Everyone expected the twentieth century to be very different, especially after the appalling suffering of the First World War left many people questioning how a loving God could allow it to happen. But in fact religion turned out to be a very important factor in world history, that no ruler, however powerful, could afford to ignore.

God is dead! (Or so they say)

When the century started, the smart thinking was suggesting that God was dead: The new go-ahead techno age would have no need for superstition and archaic ritual. None of the new beliefs that people were turning to – communism and fascism – had any time for religion. The Nazis claimed to be standing up for Christian civilization, but in reality, they persecuted anyone who actually believed in God and did their utmost to destroy the Jewish religion completely. Communist regimes in Russia and China closed down churches and arrested anyone who preached belief in God. When someone once pointed out to Stalin that he should be careful of offending the pope, he snorted and asked sneeringly, 'How many divisions has the pope?'

In the Communist bloc

Across the communist bloc, people held to their religious faith as a way of resisting the regime. The election of Polish Cardinal Karol Wojtyla as Pope John Paul II in 1978 had an immediate impact in Poland and encouraged the Poles to resist the communist regime. Churches played an important role in encouraging anti-communist resistance in East Germany and Czechoslovakia as well.

In South American countries

Religion could also work *alongside* socialists and communists. In South America, many Catholic priests were shocked at the way the rich kept down and exploited the poor; many workers had to live in shanty towns while their bosses lived in luxury villas. Priests preached a revolutionary style of Christianity called *Liberation Theology*. Archbishop Oscar Romero of El Salvador spoke out against the harsh military regime that had taken control of the country, and called for human rights to be restored and for safeguards for the poor. In 1980, he was assassinated while saying Mass in his cathedral; most people agree that the murder was carried out on behalf of the military government. Chapter 13 has more on the conflicts in Latin America.

Christianity and civil rights

Archbishop Desmond Tutu of Cape Town won respect from around the world for the way he stuck to the Christian gospel in his condemnation of the apartheid regime in South Africa. The leading American Civil Rights campaigner, Dr Martin Luther King, was a Baptist preacher whose Christian faith lay at the heart of his campaigns against racial segregation in the American South; his experience as a preacher made him a very powerful political orator.

King and Tutu both preached non-violent resistance to oppression and they got that idea from another religious leader, Mohandas Gandhi, known as the Mahatma ('Great Soul'), who led Indian resistance to British rule over India. Gandhi was a devout Hindu who rejected violence and believed that British violence undermined their moral position, so he provoked as much of it as he could. And he was right – world opinion decided that a government that had to use so much violence to enforce its authority didn't deserve that authority in the first place.

Not all twentieth-century Christians believed in non-violence. Catholics and Protestants in Northern Ireland bombed and shot each other, sometimes in churches; in America, the Ku Klux Klan claimed to be defending Christian values as it attacked black Americans and fire-bombed their churches; and in Lebanon, Christian militia carried out an appalling massacre of Palestinians in two camps, Sabra and Chatila, in 1982.

Old faiths, new beliefs – Islam

While Christianity seemed to adapt very successfully to the twentieth century, Islam seemed to be stuck in the Middle Ages: It hardly played any role in political events until the last quarter of the century. Even in their long wars with Israel, the Arab states were fighting more for land and national pride than for Islam. In fact, the Arab world seemed to be becoming more westernised and secular. By the 1960s and 1970s, many Arab states were immensely rich, thanks to their oil reserves, and 'oil sheikhs' splashed their money around in the casinos and luxury hotels of the West.

Iran: Reviving Islam

The westernising of the Arab world came to an abrupt halt in January 1979 when the Iranians rose up and finally got rid of the corrupt and tyrannical regime of the Shah. While they were celebrating, an elderly Islamic leader called Ayatollah Ruhollah Khomeini arrived back in Tehran from exile in Paris. Khomeini had visions for Iran, and Western influence and culture did not feature in them. He set about making Iran a strictly Islamic state, with harsh punishments for anyone who offended against Islam's strict moral codes. Women were forced to stop wearing Western clothes and adopt full Islamic dress. They also had to accept traditional Islamic restrictions on what they were allowed to say and do. Violently anti-American, Ayatollah Khomeini called America 'the Great Satan' and his supporters attacked the American embassy in Tehran and took its staff hostage.

Just whose side are these guys on?

If the Muslims in Iran were anti-American, they must be pro-Soviet, right? That's what the Russians thought, but they were wrong. Muslims hated atheistic communism too, so when the Soviet Union invaded Afghanistan in 1979, the Muslim *mujaheddin* fought back – and won. 'They're anti-Soviet: They must be on our side!' thought the Americans. Wrong again. After the Russians had gone, the mujaheddin set up an Islamic government in Afghanistan run by a student group known as *taliban*, who hated America and helped plan the 9/11 attacks in 2001.

When the Islamic revolution broke out in Iran both the Americans and the Russians were still thinking in old-fashioned Cold War terms of East v. West. The militant Muslims were thinking in *religious* terms, of God v. Satan, and Satan could be Western secular society or godless Russian communism. Muslim extremists hated American support for the state of Israel, but even more they hated American presence and influence in the Muslim world, especially in Saudi Arabia, home of Islam's holiest shrines. See Chapter 17 for more about how the dangerous conflict in the Middle East developed.

Islam in the West

After Europe's worldwide empires collapsed, many people from the former colonies moved to the West in search of a better life, so some Western countries gained substantial Muslim populations. As the new generation of Muslims went to school and grew up in Western culture, most people in the West thought their Muslim neighbours were just as liberal and relaxed about religion as they were. So it came as a shock when Western Muslims, especially young people, started supporting the most extreme voices coming out of the Middle East. Some supported terrorist attacks on Western targets; some even helped carry them out. Most Muslims condemned such violence, but the fact that some could launch terrorist attacks showed that there were serious issues to address about relations between Western society and Islam by the time the century ended.

Mars, Venus, and their kids in the twentieth century

For centuries, men had ruled and women had followed. Not any more. Twentieth-century women wanted a bigger role in society and men had to change their attitudes pretty sharpish. Young people changed too. They weren't so ready to do everything their parents told them to. The twentieth century was the Age of the Teenager.

This is a man's world

The nineteenth century had been very much a man's world: Men ruled the home and the world, women had to submit to their will. People in the industrialised West liked to accuse other cultures of oppressing their womenfolk, but Western society could be just as oppressive. Fashion dictated that well-born women should wear suffocating corsets (no wonder Victorian women were always fainting) and stay at home looking decorative, while the man of the house was out at work. Working-class women were expected to do manual work, but they got paid less for it than men.

Nevertheless, attitudes were changing. The idea that men and women should have equal rights was gathering pace as women gained access to higher education and to professions such as medicine and teaching. As cities expanded, shops, offices, and telephone exchanges all provided employment for young women looking for an income and a bit of independence. New Zealand and Finland even managed to grant women the vote without shaking the foundations of civilisation, but other countries needed a bit more persuasion. Britain and America only conceded female suffrage after the First World War, French women didn't get the vote until 1944, and Swiss women had to wait until the 1970s.

Communist countries boasted that they treated men and women equally, though all too often this just meant that women had to do a day's work in the factory alongside the men before doing all the cooking and cleaning when they got home in the evening.

Girl power

The big changes for women started in the 1960s with what was then called 'Women's Liberation', or 'Women's Lib' for short. It began in the USA with campaigns in favour of abortion and against the general stereotype of women as bimbos or airheads; The movement also demanded that the authorities take rape and violence against women much more seriously. The most radical feminists symbolically burned their bras, which increased male interest in the movement considerably.

The women's movement made real progress in the Western world, getting sex discrimination outlawed, securing tougher laws on sexual violence, and getting women into male-only work, from bus driving to politics. But by 2000, much still remained to do. In many areas of work, women found they were prevented from reaching the top by a 'glass ceiling', a barrier of prejudice which wasn't apparent when you first started work but was when you tried to rise higher.

Meanwhile, what about men? By the 1990s, they were under pressure to become 'new men', eating quiche, being there when their children were born, and doing the washing up. Some men took to going off together deep into the woods at weekends to bond and get in touch with their primaeval masculinity, but they had to be back in time to pick up the children.

Making whoopee

People fell in love, got married, fell out, and got caught in the eternal triangle all through the twentieth century. Western countries eventually relaxed their attitudes towards gays and lesbians, though other countries, especially in Africa and the Islamic world, didn't. For most of the century having – or being – an 'illegitimate' child carried an enormous social stigma; many children born out of wedlock were taken away and their mothers were sometimes locked up in institutions. By the 1990s, the world had got more used to the idea of couples living together before marriage or even without getting married at all.

The 1960s and 1970s saw a huge shift in attitudes towards sex, especially among young people. The contraceptive pill was available from your local doctor, and you could get condoms from the chemist or even the supermarket. Of course sexual shenanigans had been going on throughout the century – terrible worries about sexual morality existed in the 1920s, every bit as fierce as anything the sixties had to offer – but it did *seem* as if people were being a lot more open about sex in the 1960s and 1970s than they had ever been before. Only with the advent of AIDS in the 1980s did people begin to exercise a bit of restraint.

A question of black and white

The twentieth century saw some of the most open and violent racial conflict in history. Some enormous advances were made, but saying that racism had been eradicated by the year 2000 wouldn't be true. What we probably can say is that the experiences of the twentieth century made it publicly unacceptable to hold the sort of racist views and make the sort of racist comments that, earlier in the century, were commonplace. Since racist acts always start with racist thoughts and ideas, perhaps that's more of an achievement than it looks.

The trouble with young people today . . .

Childhood used to stop at about fourteen, when young people started wearing adult clothes and going out to work; only the lucky few were able to stay on at school. That situation changed in the 1950s as young people in different countries stayed on longer in education and were able to get better-paid work at the end of it. The young person with money to spend was a new phenomenon and many companies moved in to sell to this exciting new market. Thanks to American capital and worldwide advertising, Levi jeans, casual shirts, Coca-Cola, and above all pop music became the common culture of teenagers around the world. Not very far below the surface was a flourishing subculture of drugs and sex. Older people shook their heads, banged on the ceiling with a broom, and wondered where it would all end.

Apart from a few ageing hippies, where it all ended was with all these groovy young people growing into grey-haired accountants with mortgages, reminiscing about Woodstock, worrying about what their own teenage children were getting into, and wondering where it would all end.

What will they think of next? *A scientific century*

If you wanted to sum up the difference between the twentieth century and all its predecessors, you'd have to look at science and technology. If you want a list of top inventions of the twentieth century, look at Chapter 22, but here's a very quick overview of the impact science had over the course of it:

  ✔ **Biologists** wasted time at the start of the century coming up with theories about racial hierarchies and eugenics, but thanks to chemists' discovery of DNA, the structure of living organisms, they've been able to work in the controversial field of genetic engineering and cloning.

✔ **Chemists** not only discovered DNA, but they led the field in working out effective remedies for infections and diseases. For the first time in history it was possible for most people to expect to overcome illnesses that would have killed off their ancestors.

✔ **Engineering** can chalk up the car and the aeroplane as the inventions which have transformed the lives of people the world over – though not always for the better, of course.

✔ **Electronics** has probably had the most immediate and widespread impact on the lives of everyone on the planet. Nowadays we just *expect* homes to have radios, television, hi-fi, Internet access, and mobile phones, and it's difficult to imagine a time when people didn't have them.

✔ **Medical science** benefited enormously from work in the other sciences, but one highly influential development was the cultivation of an entirely new branch of science, Psychology. Twentieth-century scientists explored the brain the way nineteenth-century travellers explored Africa, with the same sense of embarking on uncharted territory. Above all, this work allowed for proper recognition and treatment, for the first time in human history, of mental illness.

✔ **Physicists** were able to show the structure of matter and energy both on Earth and out in space, thus making it possible to create and harness nuclear power.

These advances came at a cost in terms of pollution and, more recently, changes in the climate. One thing we can be sure of: The twenty-first century will pick up the tab for the twentieth.

The More Things Change, the More They Are (Basically) the Same

'The fundamental things apply', goes the song in the film *Casablanca*, 'as time goes by'. And as time goes, a century, even one as full of incident and change as the twentieth century, isn't that long. Why, there are people who *lived* through all of it. So, before we start getting excited about all the changes the century saw, let's look at a few fundamentals that didn't change.

Not feeding the world: Famine

Food is one of the basics of human existence and nothing in the twentieth century changed that. Styles of eating changed enormously as mass production and fast food began to make their presence felt, but the *need* for food didn't change. Neither did famine. That for all the twentieth century's technology, it was still faced with disastrous famine is a sobering thought.

Contrary to popular misconceptions, famine is very rarely the result of a straightforward natural phenomenon such as a drought; natural factors are nearly always combined with human activity, usually war. Russia was the scene of horrific famine in the 1920s during the civil war that followed the Russian Revolution; the famines that regularly struck Africa through the century were nearly always the result of civil war, like in Biafra in the 1960s and Ethiopia in the 1980s. It seems incredible that over eighty years into the century it should still have been necessary to market a charity record calling on everyone to 'feed the world', but it was.

Home (not so) Sweet Home

As cities expanded in the nineteenth century, so city authorities had to build somewhere for all these new people to live. The trouble was, they generally went for the cheapest and dodgiest options, so that as the twentieth century dawned, millions of people around the world lived in filthy, crowded slums, whole families to a single room, with no sanitation and often ankle-deep in human waste. Many of them were still living in such conditions at the outbreak of the Second World War in 1939. The war destroyed so many homes in Europe and Asia that the post-war years were very busy for architects and builders the world over. But they couldn't keep up with a world population that didn't stop growing and moving about in search of work. In South America people lived on enormous rubbish heaps on the outskirts of the big cities; in Europe the homeless sheltered in cardboard boxes or slept in doorways; in Asia they slept in the street. Mumbai, India's hi-tech financial capital, boasts the largest slum in Asia, and if you take a taxi from the airport you'll spend most of your journey going through it.

War: What is it good for?

The twentieth century saw many attempts to outlaw war altogether, but none of them succeeded. Here are some of the most destructive wars of the century:

✔ **First World War:** People assumed the war would be intense and destructive but short. Well, they got the first two right. In fact the First World War, or 'Great War' as people called it at the time, was so appalling that many people could hardly believe the world would survive. They began to call the conflict 'the war to end all wars', mainly because they hoped it would. But it didn't.

When is a world war not a world war?

What should the world wars be called? That's not a silly question: Names matter and they haven't always been called the First and Second World Wars. At the time, people called the 1914–18 war the Great War, which summarises very neatly its symbolic importance for them: They'd have been very shocked if someone had told them that actually it was only the *first* world war! The war that broke out in 1939 didn't get called the Second World War until much later; at the time, people in Western countries tended to talk of the 'first and second German wars', while the Russians still refer to it as the 'Great Patriotic War', which suggests that the war was essentially about defending Russia, with a few unimportant sideshows in other parts of the world. More recently, historians outside the West have objected to the 'world war' label: They point out that the war may have involved Africans and Asians but only because their countries were European colonies and argue that it would be more accurate to talk of the 'European Civil Wars'. They have a point, though 'European Civil Wars' rather ignores Japan and America. Personally, I'll stick with 'World Wars', but feel free to disagree.

✔ **Second World War:** This one proved even more destructive than the First, with cities destroyed from the air and a death toll that ran into millions. When it ended, public opinion around the world demanded a more effective way of keeping peace in future.

After the First World War, US President Woodrow Wilson drew up plans for the League of Nations – a sort of world government which would make sure countries resolved their disputes peacefully instead of resorting to war. The League didn't work. After the Second World War, the United Nations was born, and every country in the world joined up. United Nations' peacekeeping troops have been sent into trouble spots all round the world, but they haven't been able to stop wars breaking out or spreading. You can read more about the UN and the League of Nations in the earlier section 'All together now: A world government (of sorts)'.

✔ **The Korean War:** While most think of wars as being between countries, the Korean War was different. In this case, the UN itself went to war, in 1950, with North Korea. The war lasted four years, cost an estimated half a million lives, and ended up with both sides back where they'd started.

Massacre and genocide constitute another grim phenomenon that continued right through the century. In the worst cases of the late twentieth century, like Bosnia and Rwanda, even the UN couldn't prevent wholesale massacre.

Chapter 2

Fin de Siècle – Wrapping Up the Nineteenth Century

. . . .

In This Chapter

▶ Braving the troubled states of Europe

▶ Surveying European empires

▶ Winding down the American West

▶ Considering Central and South America

▶ Encountering radical new ideas

. . . .

*T*he world didn't spring out of bed on 1 January 1901 completely different from the world that had gone to bed the night before. (If you're puzzled why I'm talking about 1901 and not 1900 see the Introduction.) Although the 1890s became known as the *fin de siècle* (which just means 'End of Century' but sounds better in French), the nineteenth-century way of doing things still had a few more years to run. Some historians don't see the twentieth century really getting going until the First World War broke out in 1914. So this chapter is about how the world wrapped up its unfinished business from the nineteenth century and slowly adapted to the exciting new twentieth century that was just beginning.

Europe: A Dangerously Unstable Continent

For all its wealth, culture, and industry, Europe had big problems and when these came to a head they would tear the world apart.

Britain: Tired of hope and glory?

Britain *looked* strong and confident at the end of the nineteenth century, but all the flag-waving hid a deep sense of unease. The British were aware of powerful new rivals like Germany and the United States; they also felt that they were losing their old touch. Poverty was worse than ever and the trade unions were more militant. The Irish were demanding self-government and women were demanding the vote. By 1900 many British people were convinced that they were no longer the sort of vigorous, manly people who had built their great empire.

The British could point to two apparently very different events to illustrate what had gone wrong:

- ✔ The Trial of Oscar Wilde, 1895
- ✔ The Boer War, 1899–1902

Oscar Wilde was tried and imprisoned for homosexual activity. To shocked British people, that such things should happen at all seemed bad enough, but Wilde's trial was one of a number of scandals in the 1890s that revealed a network of homosexual brothels and rent boys at the heart of London, some of them visited by high-ranking people. All this seemed to suggest that the British ruling classes had lost their sense of moral decency.

In the Boer War, Britain fought against two small south African states and should have won easily. Instead, the Boers outmanoeuvred the British, trapped them in small townships, and cut their troops to pieces. To add to Britain's humiliation, thousands of volunteers for the army proved to be medically unfit, and the Boers' guerrilla campaign forced the British to round up Boer civilians in concentration camps. World opinion supported the Boers and opinion at home divided between those who supported the war and those who thought it showed Britain resorting to barbaric methods. (See the section 'Britain and the Boers' later in this chapter for more on the Boer War.) By 1900, therefore, the British had a terrible feeling that their empire was about to go the same way as the Romans' – into terminal decline.

France: A troubled state

By the beginning of the twentieth century, France was vulnerable and politically divided. The French had lost a disastrous war with the Germans in 1871, in which the Germans had conquered the country and taken over the two border provinces of Alsace and Lorraine. The French felt deeply humiliated and longed for revenge. The Germans were no fools, though, and kept their army in tip-top condition to stop the French getting ideas. To make things worse, the defeat in 1871 opened up deep divisions within France. A left-wing group called the *communards* tried to seize power in Paris, and the right-wing government sent in the army to crush them. The French left never forgave the French right for what happened to the communards; the French right thought it showed that the French left were France's worst enemies.

Political divisions in France run deep to this day. During the Second World War, when France was occupied by the Germans (see Chapter 9), many French right-wingers thought the Nazis were less of a threat than French communists and actively collaborated with them.

Rifts opened up elsewhere, too. French people hoping to forget their troubles could sink their savings into the Panama Canal Company, hoping that engineer Ferdinand de Lesseps would follow up the profitable success of his Suez Canal. But that proved a bad move. The company went bust and was riddled with fraud. For extra grief, some of the company directors caught pocketing the cash were Jewish, so everyone just started blaming the Jews.

And if that wasn't enough to put any country in a funk, the French also had a controversial spy case to deal with. In 1894, a French army officer, Captain Alfred Dreyfus, was found guilty of passing military secrets to the Germans and was shipped off to the notorious penal colony on Devil's Island, French Guyana. Case solved – except that locking up Dreyfus didn't stop the flow of military secrets to Berlin. It became pretty clear that Dreyfus had been framed and should be released (an apology would have been nice, too), but the French army, the Church, and everyone else on the right said that Dreyfus was just trying to sully the good name of the army until the writer Emile Zola wrote a famous letter in the press headed 'J'Accuse!' ('I accuse!') saying that Dreyfus was being kept in prison only because he was Jewish. The case dragged on for years, splitting France down the middle. Dreyfus was finally acquitted in 1906, twelve years after his imprisonment.

Germany: Military correctness gone mad!

Germany seemed to be the European State Most Likely To Succeed in 1900. From a collection of small states, it had formed itself into a powerful united nation and rapidly gained an empire overseas. German society and politics were dominated by the army; on one famous occasion a Berlin shopkeeper had great fun dressing up as an army captain and finding that everyone did whatever he told them to do. But even the army couldn't stop the rise of the German socialist party. The German government tried to win the workers over by introducing social security and national insurance, but doing so made no difference. By 1914, the socialists were the largest party in the German parliament.

Russia – behind the times but itching for change

Russia is a huge country with its western part in Europe and vast eastern expanses in Asia. Russia's business end, however – government, industry, and all the major cities – was in the west. Russians still agonise about whether they belong to Europe or Asia, but in 1900 Russia's movers and shakers were all looking to the West.

Visiting Russia around the turn of the twentieth century was like going back to the Middle Ages. Russia was still made up of old-fashioned peasant villages and ruled by an all-powerful emperor, the tsar. It had no parliament, no elections, and millions of hungry people. Industry had taken root in only two cities, Moscow and the capital, St Petersburg, where the workers lived in appalling squalor and had to get by on the tiny wages their bosses paid them. If you were rich in Russia, life could be very pleasant, but if you were poor – and most Russians were – life was very harsh indeed. Making life worse, local police chiefs instituted anti-Jewish attacks known as *pogroms*. Many Russian Jews chose to get out and head for America.

Various people wanted change:

- ✔ Constitutional Democrats wanted a Western-style democracy
- ✔ Social Revolutionaries wanted a peasant-run state
- ✔ Communists, known as *Bolsheviks* (which means 'majority party' – even though they weren't!) wanted a workers' revolution and a worker-run state.

But it didn't look as if any of them would get what they wanted because Tsar Nicholas II had a highly efficient secret police known as the *Okhrana*, which kept files on potential revolutionaries and regularly locked them up. Most revolutionaries went into exile, though some stayed under cover and set an impressive record for assassinating major figures in Russian public life. Although life in Russia looked outwardly much as it always had been, people in the know realised that it would only take one set back – defeat in a war, for example – to spark off revolution.

And that scenario is exactly what happened. In 1904, Russia went to war with Japan over who should control Manchuria and Korea. The Russians thought the Japanese were an inferior Asiatic people who would be no match for the mighty Russian war machine. The Japanese proved them wrong. They encircled the Russian army and sank the Russian Pacific fleet, and when the Russians sent their Baltic Fleet half way round the world to deal with the Japanese, the Japanese sank that too. US President Theodore Roosevelt won the Nobel Peace Prize for brokering an agreement between the two sides, which gave Japan Korea, including the important naval base at Port Arthur, and told the Russians to pay the Japanese a large indemnity as well.

Being beaten by the Japanese brought home to the Russian people just how badly off their country was. The people demanded change, and a crowd of workers walked through the streets to the Tsar's palace, thinking he'd give it to them. When they arrived, the Tsar's soldiers opened fire. Before Nicholas knew what was happening (actually, it's doubtful if he ever knew what was happening), he had a revolution on his hands. The army mutinied and joined in with the protestors, and the workers set up their own parliament called a *soviet*. At which point, even Tsar Nicholas realised the time had come to do something. So he took a deep breath and agreed to grant Russia an elected parliament, known as a *duma*. Cheers and smiles all round. Unfortunately, Nicholas had no intention of letting the Duma do anything, so Russia's problems were only postponed, not solved.

Worldwide web: Europe and its empires

In 1900, the world was still dominated by the continent of Europe. Europe had developed industry ahead of the rest of the world, and the Europeans' superior technology had enabled them to conquer whole continents. They had long been settled in Asia, ruling India and Indo-China and much of the East Indies. Then, in the space of less than twenty years in the 1880s and 1890s, they took over the whole of Africa. This process was so undignified and unscrupulous that even at the time people called it the 'Scramble for Africa'.

What on earth did the Europeans want all these colonies *for*? Historians argue about this question a lot. Some argue that colonising was just about getting hold of economic resources, some say it was more about international rivalry, others say it was about missionary work and – of course – the Europeans' belief in their own racial superiority.

The peoples of Asia and Africa didn't just sit back and let the Europeans walk all over them: When they could, they hit back – hard. In 1879, a British force was slaughtered by the Zulus and the French were cut to pieces in Senegal. At the Battle of Adowa in 1896, the Abyssinians (modern-day Ethiopia) defeated the Italians so badly they gave up and went home. (The Italians didn't forget their humiliation at Adowa, though. Read Chapter 5 to see how Mussolini got his revenge.) The biggest blow to one of these European empires, however, came from other Europeans, the Dutch settlers ('Boers') of South Africa.

Britain and the Boers

The British Empire was vast. Something like a third of the surface of the globe, and a quarter of its population, was ruled from London. By the 1890s, British eyes were focused on Africa. Britons dreamed of an unbroken line of British territory from north to south. Only the Boers, Dutch descendents who had settled in South Africa in the seventeenth century, stood in the way.

Scouting for boys, guiding for girls

One Britisher who took the business of national decline seriously was Robert Baden-Powell. 'BP', as he insisted on being called, was a rather eccentric army officer who became a national hero when he defended the township of Mafeking against the Boers. Baden-Powell was impressed by the young lads who dodged the Boer shells to run errands and carry messages and decided they were just the right role model for the flabby layabouts lazing about the streets back home. In 1907, he held a camp for a group of working-class city boys, and he followed it up the next year with his famous handbook *Scouting for Boys*. Baden-Powell believed that with the sort of resilience and resourcefulness army scouts have, young people could rejuvenate the Empire. When the girls said 'What about us?' he set up the Girl Guides, named after a famous Indian army regiment, though they didn't get housework badges the way the girls did. The Scouts and Guides were devoted to developing character and promoting international peace and harmony. Some of the later organisations that sprang up in imitation of the Boy Scouts, such as the Hitler Youth or Mussolini's *Ballila*, had a rather different philosophy.

When large diamond mines turned up in the Transvaal, one of the two Boer republics, the Boers feared that the British would try to take over – and they were right. Thousands of Brits flocked to the Transvaal to work in the mines, and in 1895 a young British hothead called Dr Leander Starr Jameson led an armed raid into Boer territory in a failed attempt to launch a coup. When it turned out that the British government had known about the raid in advance – well, talk about scandal!

Transvaal President Paul Kruger decided to strike back. In 1899, the Boers invaded British territory, ran rings round the British forces, cut them to pieces in the Battle of Spion Kop, and cooped them up in three small townships, Ladysmith, Kimberley, and Mafeking. In the end, however, Britain's superior numbers told: The Brits raised the sieges, defeated the Boer armies, and took their towns. Mission accomplished? Er, no. The Boers switched to guerrilla tactics. The British commander, General Kitchener, tried to deal with the insurgency by fencing the land off and forcing the population to move into hastily set-up *concentration camps*. We're not talking gas chambers here, but so little thought had been given to basic hygiene and survival that the inmates started dying like flies, especially the children. The leader of the Liberal Opposition in Parliament denounced Kitchener's 'methods of barbarism'.

The Boer war showed that Britain was not as strong as she looked. It also raised an important moral question: How could European empires claim to be a superior civilisation if they were also capable of starving people to death in concentration camps?

Icy wastes

Towards the end of the nineteenth century polar exploration became a sort of obsession, an international race to get to the Pole – any Pole – before anyone else. In 1895 the Norwegian scientist Fridtjof Nansen got closer to the North Pole than anyone else had managed, until the Americans Robert Peary and Matthew Henson finally got there in 1909 using Inuit-style sledges and dogs. Or at least Peary said he got there, though some historians doubt it. Norwegian Roald Amundsen and Briton Robert Falcon Scott raced each other to the South Pole, with Amundsen ploughing ahead with his huskies and Scott bogged down with ponies trying to drag his supplies through the snow. Amundsen got to the South Pole first while, tragically, having reached the Pole second, Scott and all his team died on the way back. In 1914, British explorer Ernest Shackleton and his men were stranded trying to cross Antarctica, and Shackleton pulled off an amazing coup by getting them all back alive.

At one level polar exploration was about extending our knowledge of the world, just as space exploration was meant to be about science. But at another level it was about getting *your* flag there before anyone else's – much like the race to the moon, in fact.

The British liked to talk of their empire as a family, and some of its 'children' were growing up. Canada had been self-governing since 1867 and in 1901 the separate colonies in Australia united to become the self-governing Commonwealth of Australia. New Zealand got self-government in 1907 and the Union of South Africa, which combined the British and Boer territories, followed in 1910. If you were a cynic you might say that colonies could only become self-governing if they were largely white. And you'd be right.

Asia boxes back

China was a vast empire, but it was weak and corrupt and had been torn apart in the nineteenth century by rebellions and civil war. In the nineteenth century, Britain and France had forced China at gunpoint to open up to outside trade, mostly so that they could carry on pumping opium into the country. At the time, the Chinese government was led by the Dowager Empress Tzu-hsi, who loathed foreigners, especially missionaries. In 1900, she encouraged a young radical group, the Society of Harmonious Fists, known – inevitably – as the Boxers, to rise up and kill as many westerners as they could find. The westerners – British, French, German, Russian, as well as American and Japanese – retaliated by sending an extraordinary international force into China to crush the Boxers and force China to hand over more of its ports and open others up to Western trade; in 1905, the British even invaded Tibet. These events gave the Chinese a deep sense of grievance that lasted throughout the century.

Japan was one Asian nation that made sure it wasn't carved up by the Europeans or the Americans. When US Commodore Perry sailed into Nagasaki harbour in 1853, the Japanese quickly realised it was a case of westernise or die. In 1869, the Meiji Emperor overthrew the last of Japan's medieval war-lords, and Japan set about modernising itself in double-quick time, importing Western experts and techniques and turning Japan – especially its army and navy – into a modern, industrial power. By 1902, Japan was powerful enough for Britain, the leading naval power in the world, to choose Japan as its only ally. Two years later Japan went to war with Russia – and easily won.

More fun times in Europe

The opening decades of the century saw the powerful states of Europe itching to go to war with each other, like over-excited children needing to let off steam.

Love me, love my ally

At the end of the nineteenth century the European great powers squared up to each other in a set of rival alliances. In 1900, the two main alliances were:

- ✔ **The Triple Alliance:** Germany, Austria-Hungary, and Italy.
- ✔ **The Dual Alliance:** France and Russia.

But the situation wasn't quite as simple as that. Russia had a separate under-standing with Serbia, whose people shared a similar language and culture. Britain had stayed aloof from these European alliances (well, okay, no one had actually wanted her), but she signed an alliance with Japan in 1902, and signed *ententes* (agreements) in 1904 with France and in 1907 with Russia. In effect, Britain, France, and Russia were allies.

An alliance is an agreement which says, essentially, 'If someone attacks me, you come and help me and if someone attacks you, I'll come and help you.' The alliances had no room for negotiating or saying, 'Hey, we can sort this out.' In other words, any dispute between two European states, even over something relatively trivial, could easily drag the whole continent into a massive war. Which is exactly what happened.

The spectre of nationalism and the looming fight for the Balkans

When war did break out in Europe, it had one overriding cause: Nationalism. Nationalism is different from patriotism. If you're a patriot, you're proud of your country, cheer it at sports events, and generally feel that, the place may have its faults but, hey, it's home. Nationalism, by contrast, is about the people and their ethnic identity and their mystic ties to their homeland. European nationalists had spent the nineteenth century fighting to create nation states in Europe, each national group claiming that it had lived on its land for generations. That claim was all well and good until *another* ethnic group came along and said, 'Actually *we* have lived on that land for generations.' You can see why nationalism so often leads to wars.

Africa's Heart of Darkness

Joseph Conrad's novel *Heart of Darkness,* set in the Belgian Congo, tells of an expedition deep in the African jungle to find a European trader called Kurtz who has lost touch with reality. The story was based on the very real tales of cruelty that emerged from British reports about conditions in the Congo basin after the Belgians and the French had taken it over.

The French rubber and ivory trading companies and the representatives of King Leopold II of Belgium treated the Congolese as slaves in their own lands; the Belgians made a speciality of terrorising the local population by cutting off the hands of anyone who protested against the way they were being treated. As news of the atrocities began to leak out, despite the best efforts of the French and Belgians to hush it up, international opinion was outraged. In 1907 the French government imposed some control over the French companies; in 1908 the Belgian government took the Belgian Congo away from King Leopold. No one can doubt that conditions in the Congo were appalling, but some historians say that other Europeans thought that pointing the finger at the Belgians would help to divert attention from the way they treated their own African colonies.

As the new century dawned, the big nationalist trouble spot was southeastern Europe, the area known as the Balkans. In 1900, most of this area was ruled by the tottering Turkish Ottoman Empire. Although everyone confidently expected the Empire to collapse in the near future, in 1908 a group of nationalist officers called the *Young Turks* seized power and put some backbone into the Turkish government. If the Balkan nationalists wanted to declare independence from Turkey, they were going to have to fight for it.

Making matters worse, in 1908 the government of Austria-Hungary, another hybrid empire with lots of different nationalities within it, decided to move in and take over the Balkan province of Bosnia-Herzegovina. The Serbs, who wanted Bosnia-Herzegovina for themselves, were furious and looked for ways of kicking the Austrians out. It was one such attempt that led eventually to the First World War.

America: A Waking Giant

Europe's days of dominating the world were numbered. The twentieth century would see new states arising to enormous power and leaving the Europeans far behind. The first of these new powers was the United States. By 1900, the United States had only recently completed its westward expansion and American ports were filling with immigrants from Europe and Asia. But America's business leaders were wealthy and ambitious, and the United States was already conquering an empire in the Pacific and the Caribbean. American power would grow even more in the new century.

Sunset in the West

The wagon trains and railroads of the American West were just a few years away from the cars and highways of the twentieth century. The American government only declared the famous 'Frontier' in the West officially closed in 1890, the year the Sioux tribes in South Dakota launched their 'Ghost Dance' wearing special shirts they believed would turn the white soldiers' bullets to water. Sadly, when the soldiers moved in for the kill at Wounded Knee Creek their bullets proved all too solid as they massacred some 200 Sioux, including women and children. America's native peoples were going to have to enter the new century living in small, barren reservations. Some of them were able to make a living *playing* Indians in the early Hollywood movies, only a few years after they'd been attacking wagon trains for real!

The 'Old West' had never been quite as Americans liked to imagine it, but by 1900 the old days of gunslingers and rugged pioneers were over. If you've seen the film *Butch Cassidy and the Sundance Kid*, you'll remember the scene where they rob the Union Pacific Railroad. That happened (though not quite in the happy-go-lucky way we see it in the film) on 29 August 1900. It was in 1901 that Butch and Sundance (real name Harry Longabough) headed south for Argentina and Bolivia. They died in the famous shootout at San Vicente, Bolivia, on 3 November 1908, only six years short of the First World War. By the way, Butch and Sundance didn't go out in a blaze of glory the way they do in the film. Trapped by a Bolivian army detachment, they probably committed suicide. But hey, why let the facts get in the way of a good movie?

The American West was entering the twentieth century, settling down into an orderly group of states within the Union, with state capitals, governors, and highways – and some romantic memories.

Huddled masses: America's immigrants

While the heyday of the West was coming to a close, a new America was getting going in the East. Thousands of immigrants arrived each week from Europe. They came from Italy, Hungary, Scandinavia, Poland, Russia – wherever there was poverty or repression or both. Russian Jews, for example, came to America to escape violent police raids on their communities.

These immigrants, first greeted in New York harbour by the sight of the Statue of Liberty and her famous poem welcoming 'huddled masses yearning to breathe free', found themselves in the hands – and at the mercy – of tough, businesslike immigration officers in the infamous reception centre on Ellis Island. Those immigrants found to be diseased were held in quarantine or packed off on the next boat back; those who made it through wandered out into New York's poor tenements to start to build their new life.

Black tie at the White House

Americans who disliked immigrants from Europe still kept their bitterest hatred for America's oldest and most involuntary immigrant community, its black people. When President Theodore Roosevelt invited the black educational reformer Booker T. Washington to dinner at the White House in 1901, angry rioting broke out and 34 people were killed. The rioters couldn't abide the idea that the President of the United States should sit down to dinner on equal terms with a black man. In fact, Washington was a very moderate reformer: He thought America's black people should get themselves educated so they could fit in with the white way of doing things. But if you can't stomach a black man in the White House, I guess you're hardly going to care about his opinions. America was to see a lot more of this sort of bigotry as the new century got going.

Not all of these immigrants came from Europe. Large numbers of Chinese and Japanese arrived in San Francisco and other Californian ports, where their reception was much the same as on Ellis Island.

These immigrants had to start at the very bottom. They had little money and could often only get low-paid menial work. They had to live in crowded tenements where they were at the mercy of ruthless 'robber barons', industrialists who needed lots of cheap labour to fill their own pockets. Whole areas of American cities were colonised by the immigrants and you could walk the streets of New York's Lower East Side and hear almost every European language – except English.

Not all Americans were happy with their new neighbours, especially if they thought the immigrants were doing them out of a job (they weren't, but many Americans thought they were). Congress tried to halt Chinese immigration, essentially on racial grounds, and stopped the practice of contracting foreigners to work for very low pay on major construction projects without giving them the chance to look for other work. In 1903, Congress brought in new rules to control 'undesirable' immigrants. 'Undesirable' meant anyone of vaguely liberal opinions.

If you've got it, flaunt it! The age of the robber barons

In late nineteenth- and early twentieth-century America, real power lay in big business, not in the White House (so don't worry if you're a bit hazy on American presidents after Abraham Lincoln). There was money to be made in oil, steel, and coal, and a handful of *plutocrats* made a lot of it, partly by canny investments but mainly by working together in 'trusts' to keep prices high and wages low. John D. Rockefeller made his fortune in oil, J. Pierpoint Morgan in banking, and Andrew Carnegie, who'd started out as a penniless Scottish immigrant, in steel.

These *robber barons*, so called because they acquired their wealth by ravaging natural resources, exploiting workers, and cozying up to like-minded politicians, built massive palaces, collected priceless antiques or historic manuscripts, and held lavish parties for their super-rich friends. They founded museums or charitable institutions – Carnegie virtually sold up completely to devote his time and money to charity work – but they made dam' sure their names were attached to any building or institution they founded. Yet while the bosses of corporate America were living in luxury, the people who actually did the work that made them so rich were living in overcrowded tenements on tiny wages.

A new breed of politicians and journalists known as *progressives* started to attack the discrepancy between rich and poor and to expose the corporate corruption and sleaze behind those gleaming palace doors. The journalists got called 'muckrakers' for their pains – people who'd stop at nothing to dig the dirt – but in fact they were exposing serious flaws in the American Dream. Some politicians began to take up the causes the muckrakers were exposing.

Building an American empire

Strictly speaking, the Americans didn't approve of empire-building and never referred to their overseas possessions as 'colonies' but that's what they were. By 1903, the US had six colonies. If you're thinking that's a lot of colonies for a country that doesn't believe in them, you're right. A 'splendid little war' – the Spanish–American War – broke out in 1898 between the United States and the original European empire in America – Spain – and that event got the American-empire-building ball rolling.

By the 1890s, the Spanish Empire in the Caribbean and the Pacific was a far cry from its glory days in the sixteenth century (to find out about that period, see *European History For Dummies* (Wiley)). The Spanish government was weak and corrupt. Cuba had tried once to throw off Spanish rule and failed; then they had another go in 1898. American business, with an eye to the profits after the war, backed them.

The Spanish–American War was essentially a business enterprise fomented in the US press. US press baron William Randolph Hearst and his rival Joseph Pulitzer fuelled their cut-throat circulation war with ever more lurid tales of sadistic Spanish troops starving and torturing Cuban prisoners in concentration camps. When one reporter wired to Hearst, that no one actually seemed to be torturing anyone and the fighting seemed to be over, Hearst wired back: 'You furnish the pictures and I'll furnish the war.' And he did.

On 15 February 1898, the USS *Maine* blew up in Havana harbour in a massive explosion that killed 260 of her crew. To this day, no one knows how it happened, but Hearst said the Spanish did it, and the American public agreed with him. 'Remember the *Maine!*' they cried, forcing a reluctant President McKinley to declare war on Spain. The war lasted from April to August 1898.

The US army proved awesomely incompetent – except for the 'Rough Riders' led by one Colonel Theodore Roosevelt – but luckily for them, the Spanish were even worse. When the Americans sank the Spanish fleet, Spain gave in and handed over to the USA nearly all her remaining colonies in the Caribbean and Pacific: Puerto Rico, the Philippines (Filipinos tried to resist but were defeated when Americans captured their general, Emilio Aguinaldo, in 1901), and Guam. The Americans would've taken Cuba as well until they remembered they'd been fighting for Cuban independence. Oops.

Following are some of the other colonies America added to its belt and the circumstances under which they were acquired:

- ✔ **Wake Island, 1898:** America annexed this uninhabited Pacific island just in case it came in useful.

- ✔ **Hawaii, 1898:** American businessmen had invested so heavily in Hawaii that they virtually ran the islands' economy. When Queen Liliuokalani tried to remind them who was in charge, they arranged for her overthrow and in 1898, at the third time of asking, persuaded the US Senate to declare Hawaii a US territory.

- ✔ **Panama Canal Zone, 1903:** The French were making such a hash of building it that US President Theodore Roosevelt simply bought them out.

The Americans' success in taking over the Spanish Empire inspired another man who knew something about empires to appeal to the United States to 'take up the white man's burden' and take over from Britain as the leading imperial power of the new century. He was the British writer Rudyard Kipling, author of *Kim* and later of *The Jungle Book*. Kipling recognised that the great empire of the new century would be America. He was right.

Central and South America

Nationalism (see preceding section) had also taken root in Central and South America. Central America and the whole South American continent had once been ruled by Spain and Portugal, but by 1900 the Spanish and Portuguese had been sent packing and the continent was made up of independent states. 'Independent' didn't mean stable or secure, though. Nineteenth-century South America was notorious for its endless wars, revolts, and revolutions, for example:

✔ Chile had fought Peru and Bolivia between 1879–83 and taken land off both of them.

✔ In 1889, the Brazilians overthrew their monarchy and set up a republic.

✔ The Peruvians had a coup in 1895.

✔ In 1899, civil war broke out in Colombia and lasted until 1902.

If wars amongst themselves weren't bad enough, other countries – notably Britain and America – were also involved in the region. The British had invested heavily in South America but by 1900 the Americans were moving in fast, taking over the region's flourishing trade in fruit. American money supported right-wing rebels in Nicaragua and in 1909 US troops invaded and overthrew the government.

The 1909 US invasion of Nicaragua wasn't the last time the Americans intervened in Nicaraguan politics. In the 1980s, the government of US President Ronald Reagan used a secret arms deal with the Iranians to finance aid to the right-wing Contra rebels against the left-wing Sandanista government of Nicaragua. History doesn't necessarily repeat itself, but that's never stopped people trying!

But nothing compared to nineteenth-century Mexico. This poor country saw it all: Revolution, rebellion, war with the United States, invasion by France, and an Austrian Archduke who declared himself emperor before being overthrown and shot. In 1876, General Porfirio Diaz led a military coup and for the next 35 years ruled Mexico as a dictator. Diaz restored a bit of stability (military dictators do tend to do that) but at a price: No democracy, no opposition, and no concessions to the workers.

In 1910, Diaz, who was getting on a bit, decided to hold an election, just to show he could move with the times. He took the sensible precaution of having the main opposition leader, Francisco Madero, thrown into jail and, to be on the safe side, rigged the ballot as well. According to the official results, the whole country had voted for Diaz except for the immediate friends and family of Francisco Madero. Diaz started to draw up his big Thank-You-Really-You-Shouldn't-Have speech, when Madero from his prison cell denounced the election as a fraud and called on Mexicans to rise up in revolt. They did.

Diaz found himself under attack by a string of colourful revolutionaries, including Emiliano Zapata and Pancho Villa. In 1911, the rebels defeated the government troops, forced President Diaz into exile, and let Francisco Madero out of jail. Mexicans went back to the polls and this time Madero won. And they all lived happily ever after? Not a bit of it! See Chapter 3 to find out how Mexico's revolution got even bloodier.

Radical New Ideas

In some ways the world in 1900 seemed very stable. Class structures were in place over most of the globe, the rich seemed richer than ever, and in every half-way modernised country, a prosperous middle class was rapidly establishing itself, taking tea, going for walks on Sundays, and making sure the workers knew their place. That place was right down at the bottom of the social heap, whether it was peasants and rural labourers in the countryside or industrial workers in the cities.

All major cities had their slum areas where the poor lived in filthy, squalid, and unsanitary conditions. In 1902, the British philanthropist Charles Booth published his study on *Life and Labour of the People of London*, though many of his findings would also apply to other industrial cities around the world. Looking at workers in each trade in turn, Booth examined their living conditions and the patterns of migration that had brought them to the city in the first place. He argued that it was perfectly possible for poor people to live with dignity if they were provided with decent housing, access to health care, and security in their old age. Booth's ideas were taken up by the British socialist movement and had a major influence on socialist thinking around the world.

Smash the system!

Not everyone was prepared to wait around for governments to build workers' flats and introduce old age pensions. Many socialists thought that the answer to the poor conditions in which workers lived was to rise in revolution. They got their ideas from the writings of Karl Marx, a nineteenth-century German writer who had studied British industrial society in great detail and worked out how capitalist systems evolve – and collapse.

Marx thought that trying to introduce small-scale changes to make life a bit better for the workers was a waste of time: Doing so was just a way of keeping the workers quiet while the bosses enjoyed their wealth. He also believed that, because capitalism is so driven by the need to expand, economic and political power would eventually lie with an ever-smaller group of super-rich. The unfairness of this system would be so obvious that the poor exploited workers, who had produced the wealth in the first place, would rise up and take over. Not 'might' rise up or 'probably' will rise up, mind you: Marx believed that a revolution to overturn the capitalist system was *inevitable*. See Chapter 4 to see how Marx's ideas worked in practice.

A good head of state is a dead head of state

One alarming trend in political life at the end of the nineteenth century was an increasing tendency for heads of state to get assassinated. After Abraham Lincoln was shot in 1865, radicals and oddballs the world over seemed to think a day wasted that wasn't spent using some high-up person as target practice. US President James A. Garfield was shot in 1881 by a man with a grudge, the same year that Russian revolutionaries blew up Tsar Alexander II. In 1894, President Sadi Carnot of France was stabbed by an anarchist, and the same thing happened four years later to Empress Elizabeth of Austria. In 1900, anarchist assassins tried to shoot the Prince of Wales, killed King Umberto of Italy, and the following year killed US President William McKinley. In 1903, a group of very disgruntled army officers burst into the royal bedroom in Belgrade and shot dead the King and Queen of Serbia; three years later an anarchist group tried to blow up the King and Queen of Spain (on their wedding day, if you please), and in 1908 the King of Portugal and his son were assassinated in Lisbon. The following year Prince Ito of Japan was shot.

But it was the Russians who really had political assassination down to a fine art. In 1902, Russian revolutionaries shot the Minister of the Interior and two years later they shot his successor as well. In 1905, they blew up the Grand Duke Sergei, the tsar's uncle, and one of his closest advisers. Prime Minister Peter Stolypin cracked down so hard on dissident groups that 'Stolypin's necktie' became the grim nickname for the hangman's noose. So in 1911, the revolutionaries shot Stolypin as well. When the Archduke Franz Ferdinand of Austria and his wife were assassinated in Sarajevo by Serb nationalists in 1914, it just seemed like yet another high-profile assassination. No one could guess that this assassination would have much more serious consequences than any of the others. Go to Chapter 3 for more on the First World War.

Vladimir Ilyich Lenin led the revolutionary wing of the Russian Social Democratic (that is, socialist) Party (SDP). The SDP met in London in 1902 (they were all in exile to escape the tsar's secret police) and the party split in two, between Lenin's revolutionaries, who wanted immediate change, and those who wanted to wait for revolution, as Marx had said you should. Lenin called his followers *Bolsheviks*, which means majority party in Russian, which meant his opponents were now called *Mensheviks*, or minority party. Even though they were actually in the majority!

The Bolsheviks didn't just want revolution in Russia: They wanted it to spread around the world. An international communist association was created called the Second International (the First International had collapsed shortly after Marx had founded it back in 1864 because no one could agree on anything), and communists from different countries kept in regular touch with each other. Communists existed in industrialised countries all around the world, but most communist parties were only founded officially at the end of the First World War, after the Bolsheviks had seized power in Russia. Chapter 4 tells you what they did with the power they'd seized.

Out of the dolls' house

The nineteenth century had seen a great stirring among women agitating for the same opportunities that were open to men, and it soon became clear that this movement would grow even stronger in the new century. Women were active in all the nationalist and revolutionary groups, and in Western countries they were actively campaigning for the right to vote. New Zealand had already granted female suffrage and Finland followed suit in 1907, but most countries still held back. The famous British *Suffragette* movement was launched in 1904, and it linked with a similar campaign in the United States. Meanwhile, women were making huge advances in medicine and education: Universities and colleges were opening their doors to women, and Western women played a leading role in spreading the message of education and emancipation in Africa and Asia. Much remained to do, though: Not until 1902 did China formally ban the practice of binding girls' feet.

Changes in art, music, and literature

As if feminists, assassins, and socialists weren't enough to have to cope with (see previous section), as the new century got underway artists, writers, and musicians seemed to have lost the plot as well. Gone were the traditional forms, storylines, and images.

My four year old could do better than that! Modern art

In 1907, the art world was taken aback by a painting called *Les Demoiselles d'Avignon* (the Ladies of Avignon) by the young Spanish painter Pablo Picasso. What was so shocking wasn't the bold colours or the fact the women were nude, but the way two of the ladies were painted as if they'd been broken down into geometrical shapes. This new style was known as *Cubism*. Cubist painters like Picasso and Georges Braque were trying to make people look at the world around them in a new way, looking underneath the surface at its underlying shapes. Some painters went even further, painting shapes and lines without even trying to portray people or things as they really were. Vassily Kandinsky, who pioneered this abstract art, said that he got the idea from seeing a painting lying on its side and thinking it looked more interesting that way. Of course, most people just thought these modern artists' paintings looked wrong.

One young would-be artist scraping a living in Vienna could never get his head round these new ideas and preferred to paint simple watercolours of pretty views. He never made it as an artist, which is a shame really as it could have saved the world a lot of trouble. His name? Adolf Hitler.

The golden age of children's lit

If all this challenging literature was too much for you, you could take comfort in children's writing, which was entering a veritable golden age. In Britain alone, the new century brought Beatrix Potter's *The Tale of Peter Rabbit* (1902), J. M. Barrie's *Peter Pan* (1904), E. Nesbit's *The Railway Children* (1906), Rudyard Kipling's *Just So Stories*, and Kenneth Grahame's *The Wind in the Willows* (1908); while across the Atlantic in Canada, Miss

L. M. Montgomery published *Anne of Green Gables* in 1909. The Western world was creating something of a cult of childhood, with separate nurseries, professional nannies, and a whole literature of magazines and novels written specially for children. Sadly, many of the children who read it were just at the right age for the First World War when it broke out in 1914.

Music to my ears – not!

Things were changing in music, too. The Italian opera composer Giuseppe Verdi died in 1901, but Giacomo Puccini was still composing operas in the style opera-lovers were used to: *Madame Butterfly* was the big hit of 1900 and in 1904 he had another success with his opera-thriller *Tosca*. But in the dance world, some of the old rules were being challenged. The French composer Claude Debussy had composed an impressionist ballet in 1894, *L'Après Midi d'un Faun*, which painted a sort of sound picture by breaking all the usual rules of harmony. It was still hauntingly beautiful, though, which was more than could be said for the dissonant sounds being produced by Arnold Schoenberg and his musical chums in Vienna.

Schoenberg and others of his ilk completely turned their backs on the established rules of structure and harmony to explore new ways of conveying emotion and ideas through music. But the real outrage came in 1913 when the Russian composer Igor Stravinsky had his ballet *The Rite of Spring* produced in Paris. Set in pagan times, the ballet featured a wild dance set to clashing chords which assaulted the ears with sheer animal power. Stravinsky was trying to put across something of the raw energy and emotion of ancient Mother Russia, but the audience hated it. Not only did the ballet challenge every rule of decency and order, but it didn't produce one hummable tune either.

Both Picasso and Stravinsky and their followers caused controversy not just by breaking the rules but by turning to non-Western art and music for their inspiration. To educated people in the West, Western civilisation represented the highest level of technological advancement and moral precepts that humankind was capable of, so to turn to the art of the non-Christian peoples of Africa or Asia seemed to be a shocking renunciation of all the modern world stood for. Artists and musicians often said they were trying to express the feelings of the people, but the people by and large wanted nothing to do with modern art or music: They preferred old-time waltzes, or light opera, or – if they were really daring – the catchy ragtime tunes coming out of America's 'Tin Pan Alley'.

A good read – if you like racy stories!

The new century seemed to be bad news for literature. Oscar Wilde died in 1900 followed by Anton Chekhov (1904) and Henrik Ibsen (1906). Sherlock Holmes, on the other hand, came back from the dead. His creator, Sir Arthur Conan Doyle, had got so tired of the great detective that he'd killed him off, but such an outcry rose up around the world that in 1902 Conan Doyle brought out *The Hound of the Baskervilles* followed by a new set of adventures. Meanwhile, a mysterious French writer caused scandal with an account of a young woman's initiation into the arts of love; the scandal was even greater when it turned out the writer was a woman hiding behind a man's name and henceforth known as Colette. H. G. Wells, who had already made a name for himself with his disturbing vision of the future in *The Time Machine* in 1895, raised more eyebrows with his 1909 novel *Ann Veronica* about the need to loosen up public attitudes to love and sex. And the Irish playwright George Bernard Shaw was having fun with his successful plays attacking middle-class attitudes.

But even writers seemed to have caught the modernism bug. James Joyce's novel *Ulysses* about one day in the life of an ordinary Dubliner abandoned ordinary language and seemed to be written in gobbledegook. The 'Dada' poets did away with the normal rules of rhyme and rhythm and just picked words at random out of a hat. Many people, of all classes, felt that the arts had completely lost touch with ordinary people.

The Brave New World of Science and Technology

The 1900s witnessed some major breakthroughs in science and technology that would set the tone for the century that followed.

Visions of the future

The happening science at the start of the new century was physics. All the best brains seemed to be working on exactly what this matter is that makes up the world around us. A group of scientists got the century off to a good start with a remarkable series of discoveries that were to have enormous impact in the future:

At home with the Curies

If you ever got invited to tea with the Curies and couldn't cope with small talk about atomic particles, Polish nationalism was a very acceptable substitute. It was Marie Curie's main interest outside her scientific work. The Curies were a formidably intelligent pair – not many married couples share the Nobel Prize for Physics, as Pierre and Marie did in 1903. Working on humanitarian applications for radium meant Marie had to master a lot of chemistry, which she did so well that in 1911, five years after the death of her beloved Pierre in a road accident, she won another Nobel Prize, this one for Chemistry. That wasn't the end of the Curie family's involvement with Nobel Prizes: Their daughter Irene Joliot-Curie and her husband Frédéric won the Nobel Prize for Physics in 1935 for their work on artificial radioactivity. Sadly, Marie had died the year before. Still, all those prize certificates on the walls must have made a change from the usual family photos.

✔ **Max Planck** (1858–1947) was a German physicist who looked into why the radiation hot bodies give off doesn't flow steadily but seems to come out in spurts. Planck concluded that energy is released in small packets that he called *quanta*. His 'Quantum Theory' (from which we get the term 'quantum leap') had a big influence on the work of Albert Einstein.

✔ **Albert Einstein** (1879–1955) sought to use quantum theory in his work on the nature of matter. Taking the tram to his work in Zürich each day, the German-born Einstein noticed that the buildings he passed appeared tall and thin when the tram was moving but settled into their old shape when the tram stopped. Were his eyes deceiving him, or perhaps did those houses actually change shape? And why didn't they change shape for the people inside them? The answer was that, unlike the people in the houses, Einstein was moving past at speed, so to him the houses didn't just *look* thin: They actually *were* thin. Because of the speed and direction of the tram, Einstein was looking at the houses in a different combination of space and time from people outside the tram; or, to put it another way, the nature of space and time depend on where you are. Einstein put his ideas into his *Special Theory of Relativity* in 1905, followed in 1907 by his *General Theory of Relativity*, arguing that space and time change and as they do so, they affect matter – hence the thin houses. The only thing that doesn't change, Einstein said, is the speed of light.

Einstein's theory had a number of important implications. Firstly, it showed that Newton's laws of motion, including his famous law of gravity, did not apply everywhere, most obviously in space (if you're a bit hazy on Newton's Laws of Motion, see *British History For Dummies* (Wiley)). Secondly, Einstein suggested that matter itself is not fixed: It is made up of enormous concentrations of energy, even in the tiniest particles of matter. That meant that matter could be changed into energy – possibly a vast explosion of energy. And all sorts of ways of using vast explosions of energy exist, some of them peaceful, some not.

- **Ernest Rutherford** (1871–1937) worked out the structure of an atom – hence 'atomic' physics – in 1911.

- **Niels Bohr** (1885–1962), a Danish physicist, used quantum theory to draw up a model of the hydrogen atom.

- **Pierre and Marie Curie** (1859–1906; 1867–1934) identified the radioactive element within uranium and named it radium in 1902. But what can you do with it? Marie, a brilliant mathematician and physicist, set herself to working out the medical application of radium. She found it could be used to combat tumours; she also pioneered its use in x-rays.

The first Nobel Prizes were awarded in 1901. They were named after Alfred Nobel, a Swedish manufacturer who made his money from inventing dynamite and left it after his death, in 1896, to endow the famous prizes for physics, chemistry, medicine, literature, and peace. (Later, a Nobel Prize was established for Economics as well.) Establishing the prizes was a timely move, because the new century would be shaped by advances in science and technology that Mr Nobel could never have dreamt of. All the people in the preceding list were Nobel Prize winners.

In your dreams: Exploring the human mind

While some scientists were exploring the nature of matter (see preceding section) others were delving deep into the human mind:

- **Sigmund Freud** (1856–1939) lived in Vienna and virtually invented the science of psychoanalysis. In his famous book, *The Interpretation of Dreams* (1900), based on hundreds of interviews in which his subjects talked about their childhood and recounted their dreams, Freud theorised that dreams are messages from our subconscious revealing fears and thoughts that are usually kept hidden. He said that human consciousness can be divided into three parts, the *Id* (instinct), the *Ego* (sense of self), and the *Superego* (conscience and morality). Above all, Freud thought that sex was a powerful factor in determining behaviour, even if people were not aware of it and even in young children.

- **Carl Gustav Jung** (1875–1961) thought that Freud had simplified things too much and had allowed the sex to go to his head. Jung argued that male and female minds work in different ways (and who would disagree with that?) and that people are also influenced by the *Collective Unconscious* – a sort of mindset that is shared within a whole society – a bit like urban myths or believing the *Da Vinci Code*.

> ✔ **Ivan Petrovich Pavlov** (1849–1936) showed in 1902 that you could condition behaviour by controlling reflexes. He kept some dogs in his lab and rang a bell at feeding time. They got all excited and started drooling, but they did the same every time the bell rang, whether any food came or not. This suggested that behaviour and even instincts could be controlled – a lesson that some of the century's dictators would learn very well.

Bye bye, blacksmith – here comes the car

The nineteenth century had been the great age of steam and prestigious railways were still being built: Russia opened the famous Trans-Siberian Railway in 1904 in order to get its troops to the Far East quickly. For shorter distances, people still travelled in horse-drawn carriages. Motor cars had been invented, but they were slow, dirty, and very expensive. But that situation was about to change with Henry Ford's ideas about mass production. In 1903, Henry Ford set up his motor company in Detroit and put his ideas to work: Instead of a small team of craftsmen making a car, he broke each task down into its component parts, engaged cheap unskilled workers to perform each little bit of the process, and sent the cars round to them on a conveyor belt system. Instead of making a car, a worker stood in the same place and performed the same task over and over again. It was mind-numbingly boring, and Henry Ford made sure his workers had nothing to do with unions or any idea of workers' rights, but he paid them very well – his cars sold so cheaply and in such numbers that he could afford to. Ford's most famous car, the 'Model T', came off the assembly line in 1908. To keep the price down, it was only available in one colour – black – and very few variations in design were available. Since you could buy the car on hire purchase, paying in monthly instalments, Henry Ford had put cars within the pockets of millions of Americans.

Cars were soon changing the face of America and, as they spread to other countries, of the whole world. Out went the smithies and stables that horses needed and in came garages, petrol stations, hotels, holiday resorts, and even naughty nights out in the back of the car! Steel, rubber, and above all oil all boomed thanks to Henry Ford. To read about some of the impact Ford had, skip to Chapter 6.

Ford liked to claim that he had democratised travel, but the upper classes hadn't given up their hold on motoring yet. The year after Ford set up his company, Mr Rolls and Mr Royce founded their company, selling luxury cars to the very, very rich.

Disaster areas

Great disasters have always happened, but the twentieth century did seem to start with an awful lot of them. Maybe it was because the newspapers could report them so much more quickly. One of the most shocking happened on Martinique in 1902 when Mount Pele erupted, spewing out poisonous fumes that killed the entire population of the island's capital, St Pierre. Only one man survived, and that was because he was locked up in jail with no access to the outside. Mount Vesuvius erupted in 1906 and destroyed the town of Ottaiano, and an earthquake in India in 1905 left 10,000 people dead. Venice's bell tower suddenly collapsed in rubble in 1902, and the following year 578 people were killed at a New Year party in Chicago when the Iroquois Theater went up in flames. The most famous disaster, though, was the earthquake that hit San Francisco in 1906. It was followed by a firestorm that killed nearly a thousand people. It seemed incredible that a whole modern city could be so utterly destroyed by nature. The twentieth century would show that human beings were quite capable of doing the same thing.

Up, up, and away

People had been dreaming of flying since ancient times but the closest anyone had got to it by the nineteenth century was hot air ballooning, which is fun but not much good if you've got a meeting in New York on Tuesday. In December 1903, Orville and Wilbur Wright carried out their famous test flight at Kitty Hawk, North Carolina. They could only get airborne for a few seconds, and they had to lie down in the frame, but it was powered flight in a heavier-than-air structure.

Designers started working fast, trying to improve on the Wright brothers' design. Everyone agreed that a seat for the pilot would be nice. In 1909, a French aviator called Louis Blériot caused a sensation by flying over the English Channel. Everyone cheered and waved flags, but for anyone who stopped to think, Blériot had shown something very important: The sea was no longer a barrier. Control of the sea in the twentieth century would be by air.

Wireless connection

One of the most important technological breakthroughs of the twentieth century came on the coast of Newfoundland on a blustery day in December 1901. Italian engineer Guglielmo Marconi had set up a flimsy aerial at Poldhu in Cornwall which was transmitting the single letter 'S' in Morse code. Marconi crossed to Newfoundland and set up an aerial on a kite to try to receive the transmission. It took a long time, but eventually the 'beep-beep-beep' could be heard through the crackle and hiss. Marconi had sent a radio signal across the Atlantic.

The *Titanic:* A metaphor of the times

Historians sometimes use the famous story of the SS *Titanic* to illustrate the way in which the old nineteenth-century world was sailing steadily on, over-confident and arrogant, towards destruction in the First World War. *Titanic* was a British luxury liner which, like all liners at the time, segregated its passengers very strictly by social class. Poor passengers were kept below decks in steerage, well away from the incredible luxury in which the first-class passengers were enjoying their trip. Middle-class passengers went second class. Hidden away from all of them were the stokers and engineers keeping the enormous engines going. The ship was like a floating version of the Western class structure. The different shipping companies competed fiercely for the Blue Riband, awarded to the fastest ship to cross the Atlantic, and the White Star line had high hopes that *Titanic*, which they were already declaring 'unsinkable', would prove fastest of all. Just like the Western world and its leaders, the shipping owners were over-confident and took no notice of warnings. One of the company directors was on the ship for its tragic voyage and put pressure on the captain to go fast through the ice packs, even against his better judgement. Result: Disaster. The ship struck an iceberg and sank within hours. Something like 1,500 people drowned.

After the sinking people on both sides of the Atlantic were angry. They wanted to know why the ship had been sailing so fast and why there had been so few lifeboats. Quite a few of the richest passengers, including the White Star director, had got away, leaving the poorer passengers to drown. Some lifeboats had gone off only half-full and people in the lifeboats had stopped others from getting in. To socialists and Marxists, the *Titanic* disaster seemed to illustrate the class struggle openly. Two years later, in 1914, the Great War would finally destroy the confidence and luxury of the world of the *Titanic*.

Radio telegraphy wasn't new, but it had always worked along wires, which meant that huge coils of cable had to be laid along the ocean floor. Marconi showed that signals could be sent through the air. Distance was no problem and neither were natural barriers. For the first time it was even possible to communicate directly with a ship at sea. In 1910, the captain of a transatlantic liner sent a radio message to alert the police in London that the murderer Dr Crippen was sailing to Canada, so they were able to cross on a faster ship and arrest him when his ship docked.

Read all about it!

The newspapers got into the mass communications world, too. Newspapers were nothing new, but by the 1890s a handful of 'press barons', like Britain's Lord Northcliffe or William Randolph Hearst and Joseph Pulitzer in the United States, were making a fortune from mass-circulation papers aimed at the newly educated classes. These popular papers served up their news spiced with plenty of sensation, and getting the facts right was much less important than getting the sales figures up. This, er, noble standard of journalism is, I'm pleased to say, rigorously upheld by much of the popular press to this day.

Chapter 3

The Great War: 1914–18

The First World War, or *Great War* as it was known at the time, was so destructive and caused so much suffering that it shattered the participants' national pride and confidence in their leaders. The war saw fighting in Russia, Turkey, Arabia, Iraq, Palestine, China, East Africa, the South Atlantic, the Pacific, and the North Sea, as well as in the trenches of France and Belgium. The Great War introduced the world to such marvels of modern science as bombing from the air, submarine warfare, poison gas, and death by machine gun. Welcome to the twentieth century.

A Powder Keg: Events Leading to the Great War

For years before 1914, the Great Powers of Europe had been sizing up to each other, signing military alliances which said that if one of them was attacked, its allies had to help. A strong sense of tension persisted in Europe, like children needing to burn off energy. And the way nations burned off energy in those days, at least according to the theorists, was to have a good *war*.

That idea may seem a bit drastic, but it seemed self-evident to people at the time. Many of the wars in Europe over the decades preceding the twentieth century had been short and decisive, thanks to modern technology such as railways and rapid-fire rifles. Statesmen were confident that they could take on even their most powerful neighbours, use state-of-the-art weaponry and techno-gadgets to run rings round them, dictate a peace settlement, and be home in time for the victory parade and tea. So when the expected war finally broke out in late July 1914, people really did think it would all be over by Christmas.

However, Europe's leaders and generals had forgotten three important points:

- ✔ Just because countries had been beaten easily in the past didn't mean they would necessarily collapse so easily next time. France had lost badly to the Germans in 1871, but by 1914 it had recovered and was bent on revenge.

- ✔ All that technology would only win you a quick victory if you had it and your enemy didn't. No one had thought about what would happen if everyone had the latest hardware.

- ✔ Some recent wars had indeed been short, but others hadn't. The Crimean War (1854–56), the American Civil War (1861–65), and the Anglo–Boer War (1899–1902) had all been long wars, with appalling loss of life. Somehow, when war broke out in 1914, people didn't think that this war might follow the same pattern.

He started it! Regional disputes and old grudges

Before 1914 the Great Powers were caught up in a series of increasingly dangerous disputes:

- ✔ **France v Germany:** The Germans had defeated and humiliated the French back in 1871, besieging Paris and taking over two French border provinces, Alsace and Lorraine. The French wanted to get even; the Germans thought it might be a good idea to get their retaliation in first.

- ✔ **Britain v Germany:** The Germans had started building a massive battle fleet to challenge Britain's control of the seas. Both sides started building more and bigger battleships, especially the new Dreadnought type, heavily armoured and fast too – a rare combination.

- ✔ **Slavs v Turks:** The Turks still ruled most of the Balkans (south-eastern Europe) and the Balkan states wanted them out. Some of them wanted to set up a single Slav superstate, but which of them would control it?

- ✔ **Serbia (and friend) v Austria-Hungary (and friend):** The Serbs were hoping to set up a big Slav state (with them in charge, of course); their powerful neighbours, Turkey and Austria-Hungary, weren't having that. In 1908 the Austrians took over the Slav province of Bosnia-Herzegovina, which infuriated the Serbs because they'd wanted it. The Serbs turned to their friend, Russia, and the Austrians turned to their friend, Germany, and for a time it looked like war, until everyone saw sense and calmed down. Next time the world would not be so lucky.

This means war! PS Love to all the family

Britain's Queen Victoria had married her numerous offspring into most of the other royal houses of Europe. The three leading European monarchs in 1914, Kaiser Wilhelm II of Germany, Tsar Nicholas II of Russia, and the King-Emperor George V of Great Britain and India, were all first cousins and knew each other well.

Monarchs were still very important. Tsar Nicholas was an autocrat, a monarch with absolute power (in theory at any rate, though his ministers did most of the work); the German Kaiser helped decide policy and the war was actually sparked off when the Austrians got indignant because their heir to the throne was assassinated. But ultimately these monarchs weren't able to stop the drive towards war and even their close family kinship didn't stop them declaring war on each other.

Unfortunately, 1908 wasn't the last time little Bosnia-Herzegovina provoked an international crisis. When Yugoslavia fell apart in the 1990s, Bosnia-Herzegovina was the scene of some of the worst atrocities and mass killings the world had seen since the Second World War. Chapter 19 has the lowdown.

Germany: *We want a place in the sun*

The Germans had come from nowhere in the nineteenth century to create Europe's most formidable military and economic superpower. You might think that would be enough to be going on with, but the German Kaiser, Wilhelm II, wasn't satisfied. He had a massive inferiority complex about the British – he was half British himself – and convinced himself that they were behind a global conspiracy to exclude Germany from the top rank of Europe's Great Powers. Germany, he said, wanted its 'place in the sun'.

German ministers talked of *Weltpolitik* – making Germany the dominant power in the world. To achieve that position, Germany had to build up its army and navy and generally throw its weight around in international affairs. Germany wasn't just powerful, but dangerously unpredictable too. Ironically, the German government abandoned Weltpolitik and stopped building expensive battleships in 1913. But by then the damage to Germany's relations with the other Great Powers had been done.

Agreements and assignations affecting the rest of the world

Most of the world was part of one or other of the European empires, so that what happened in Europe would have an immediate impact in Africa, Asia, the Caribbean, and the Pacific whether they liked it or not. Africa and Asia provided the setting for some of the big diplomatic showdowns before the war:

- **Anglo–Japanese alliance, 1902:** Britain's only actual military alliance was with Japan. The Japanese agreed to keep an eye on Britain's possessions in the Far East.

- **Anglo–French entente, 1904:** Also known as the *entente cordiale*, this was, in theory, just an agreement between Britain and France about how they would divide up Africa, but the Germans always suspected there was a bit more to it than that. And they were right.

- **Morocco, 1905:** The Kaiser decided to test the new Anglo–French entente. He took a ship to Morocco, whose Sultan had recently accepted French control – sorry, protection – and made a speech saying that if the Sultan ever wanted any help kicking the French out, he only had to give Wilhelm a call. Result: International outcry, Britain stood by France, all the Great Powers met at Algeçiras (Spain) and told the Kaiser to keep his nose out of Morocco. Kaiser's conclusion: The entente cordiale is an Anglo–French military alliance. Told you so.

- **Anglo–Russian entente, 1907:** The Germans were busy sending military advisers to Turkey and planning a railway link from Berlin to Baghdad, so the British and Russians signed this agreement to share out Persia between them, leave Afghanistan alone – and keep the Germans out of the whole region.

- **Morocco, 1911:** A German gunboat, the *Panther*, sailed into the Moroccan port of Agadir, supposedly to defend German interests but really just to annoy the French. To the Germans' surprise it was the British who seemed ready to go to war if the Germans didn't pull out of Morocco. So the Germans very sensibly did.

- **Tripoli, 1911:** The Italians landed troops in Tripoli and took it away from the Turks. Why? The Italians thought no one would take them seriously if they didn't have a colony or two. They'd been badly beaten when they tried to conquer Abyssinia (Ethiopia) in the 1890s and Tripoli looked a bit easier. People still didn't take Italy very seriously though.

Apocalypse Now: The War Starts (1914)

When the Great War finally came, it came from the Balkans. The Balkans are the area of south-eastern Europe, which includes Greece, Bulgaria, and Serbia. In the 1900s most of the Balkans were still ruled by the sleazy and corrupt Turkish Empire. In 1908 a group of young nationalist army officers called the Young Turks seized control in Constantinople and injected a bit of backbone into the Empire, but even they couldn't stop what was about to happen in the Balkans:

- ✔ **Balkan War No. 1: Everyone attacks the Turks (1912):** All the Balkan states launched a fierce attack on the Turks and forced them out of the Balkans. All that remained of the once-mighty Turkish Empire in Europe was a little strip of land near Constantinople, which is still part of Turkey to this day.

- ✔ **Balkan War No. 2: Everyone attacks Bulgaria (1913):** No sooner had they beaten the Turks than all the Balkan states started arguing over territory. The squabbling culminated in a huge showdown between Bulgaria and all its neighbours. Bulgaria was pulverised. The Balkan states agreed their new national boundaries in the 1913 Treaty of London but the Bulgarians didn't forget what had happened and were on the look-out for revenge.

The shot heard around the world

Flush from beating the Turks and the Bulgarians, the Serbs were determined to get Bosnia-Herzegovina back off the Austrians (see the earlier section 'He started it! Regional disputes and old grudges' to find out why the Austrians had Bosnia-Herzegovina in the first place). On 28 June 1914, the Austrian Archduke and future emperor Franz Ferdinand visited the Bosnian capital Sarajevo with his wife to inspect the Austrian forces of occupation (that day was Franz Ferdinand's wedding anniversary. If only he'd settled for roses and a box of chocolates).

Unfortunately, 28 June was also the anniversary of the 1389 Battle of Kosovo and one of the most important days in the calendar for Serbs. For the Serbian nationalist terrorist gang the *Black Hand*, the date was too good a chance to miss. They slipped over the border to Sarajevo where one of them lobbed a bomb at the Archduke's car. It bounced off and exploded in the street. The bomber was caught and the others hastily tried to get out of town. One of them, Gavrilo Princip, was sitting at a café trying to look calm when, quite unexpectedly, the Archduke's car pulled up right in front of him, with the Archduke and his wife inside. Princip stepped up to the car and shot them both – dead.

The Austrian government was furious. They were sure the Serbian government was behind the plot and decided the time had come to crush Serbia once and for all. First, though, they checked with the Germans: Would they help if the Russians stood by the Serbs? The Germans, who didn't actually think the Russians would do anything, told the Austrians: 'Do what you have to: We'll stand by you.' This German promise became known as the 'blank cheque'. The Germans didn't know it, but they'd just guaranteed that this quarrel in a little corner of southern Europe would become a global war.

A rickety republic in China

China was still a medieval-style empire, with a child emperor and all power in the hands of his grandmother, the dowager empress Tz'u-hsi. Her idea of policy was essentially 'Change Nothing', so as soon as she died in 1908 the country fell apart, with different revolutionary groups all wanting to Change Everything but disagreeing about how. The man who stepped in to restore a bit of order was Dr Sun Yat-sen, a widely-respected medic who had very sensibly fled China for the USA one step ahead of the imperial police. In 1911 Sun declared a republic with himself as President; little Emperor Pu-Yi had to abdicate before bedtime. But trying to control China proved too much for Sun and within a few months he handed power over to a rather more military-minded tough guy called Yuan Shih-k'ai. Yuan closed down China's new democratic parliament and ruled China as a dictator. The Chinese soon got fed up with Yuan and in 1916 they rose up in arms against him. While the rest of the world was busy fighting and recovering from the Great War, China sank into civil war, famine, and massacre.

Ironically, Archduke Franz Ferdinand had been opposed to war with Serbia and tended to restrain those who wanted war. Now he was dead, no one could stop the hawks in the Austrian government.

Declarations of war

Following the assassination of their archduke, the Austrians sent the Serbian government a furious note, demanding an apology, telling them to hand the assassins over, and claiming the right to send the Austrian police into Serbia to look for them. The Serbs had forty-eight hours to reply. The Serbs were genuinely shaken by the assassination and agreed to nearly everything, just asking if they could talk about that point about the police. Not good enough, said the Austrians. And declared war.

Events moved very fast from that point, with declarations of war whizzing around like flyers:

- **28 July:** Austria-Hungary declared war on Serbia and immediately shelled the Serb capital, Belgrade.
- **30 July:** Russia mobilised its army, that is, got it ready for war.
- **31 July:** Germany told Russia to stand its army down. Russia took no notice.
- **1 August:** Germany declared war on Russia.
- **3 August:** Because their war plans were all based on the idea that they would have to fight Russia *and* France, Germany declared war on France. So:

✔ **4 August:** Following their famous *Schlieffen Plan*, or How To Invade France in Three Easy Lessons, which said the best way was to sneak in via Belgium, Germany invaded Belgium. But that move alarmed the British (it didn't exactly please the Belgians either), who told the Germans to clear out of Belgium, or else. The Germans didn't really believe the British were serious, but they were. So:

✔ **4 August (at midnight):** Britain declared war on Germany.

The declarations of war didn't stop there. Britain, France, and Germany all had colonies around the world, so they were suddenly all at war with each other as well. Australia, New Zealand, Canada, Newfoundland (which was separate from Canada in those days), and South Africa were all self-governing dominions within the British Empire, but they all took their lead from Britain and declared war on Germany and its allies, as did Britain's ally in the Far East, Japan. The war started in Europe but it quickly spread to the rest of the world.

All Not So Quiet on the Eastern and Western Fronts

You may have seen some of the well-known photographs of cheering crowds in different European cities in 1914 greeting the outbreak of war. If you look more closely, you'll see that they are mostly young office workers who loved the idea of a bit of excitement for once. The workers and agricultural labourers who'd be making up most of the world's armies were usually a bit more resigned about the conflict.

Hmm, so much for Plan A . . .

All the Great Powers had plans for war in 1914 but they all came unstuck. The Austrians' plan for defeating Serbia didn't work because they had to fight Russia as well and they didn't have enough men to do both. And the Serbs weren't the push-over the Austrians thought they would be either. Then the Austrians had a plan to invade Russian Poland from the south while the Germans marched in from the north with the intent that they could envelop the Russians who, the Austrians confidently expected, would be sitting around twiddling their thumbs. But the Germans were too worried about a Russian invasion of East Prussia to spare any men for invading Poland, and the Russians didn't actually send any men into Poland anyway.

The French plan for invading Germany had to be called off when the Germans got in first with their plan, called the *Schlieffen Plan* after the general who had

TECHNOLOGICAL BREAKTHROUGH

The technology of the First World War

The armies of 1914 had all the latest military technology. Rifles could fire ten bullets a minute and had a range of about a mile; they didn't give off any tell-tale smoke either. Machine guns could fire 400 bullets a minute, fed through on a long belt, though they weren't very portable and were better kept for defence. Artillery was accurate and deadly and the only real defence against it was to encase yourself in thick concrete forts or 'pill boxes' (so called because they looked like, er, pill boxes). However, once trench warfare started the artillery just stayed in one place firing shells at such a rate that the munitions factories at home couldn't keep up (see the section 'Stalemate in the west' later in this chapter for more on trench warfare). Many manufacturers cut corners, with the result that huge numbers of duds or – worse – shells blew up inside the gun.

Some of the most important technological developments on the western front had their origins in the American West. Barbed wire was developed in the 1860s as a cheap way of fencing off large areas of land for farming. The idea for tanks came from a new design of tractor with caterpillar tracks to go over rough terrain, patented in the USA in 1901. The new vehicles were originally to be called landships; 'tanks' was just a cover name but it stuck. So, at first, did most of the tanks. Not till the Battle of Cambrai in 1917 did tanks really show what they could do. Tanks didn't tip the scales in the First World War, but military tacticians were already taking careful notes in case there was a Second.

The First World War was also the first war to use aircraft. At first these were small one-seater planes used to spy out the land, but soon the planes acquired guns and started shooting each other down. The best 'aces' on each side became national heroes. The Germans also used enormous gas-filled airships called Zeppelins, which could travel much further than aeroplanes: They carried out the world's first aerial bombing raids, on London and other British towns. Zeppelin raids caused serious loss of life until the British worked out how to shoot them down with incendiary bullets. And when a Zeppelin caught fire and went down, it *really* went down.

devised it. The plan was to defeat France quickly and then concentrate on fighting Russia so that Germany didn't end up fighting a war on two fronts, against Russia in the east and France in the west. Guess what Germany ended up doing? Yes – fighting a war on two fronts, against Russia in the east and France (and Britain, and Belgium, and later the USA) in the west. Here's why.

The Schlieffen Plan was based on three assumptions. Each one turned out to be wrong:

- ✔ **Assumption 1:** Russia would take months to get its armies ready for war so there'd be time to defeat the French first. In fact, the Russians were ready in three weeks. Oops.

- ✔ **Assumption 2:** Going through Belgium would be a cake walk. In fact the Belgians and the British held the Germans up badly, messing up the Germans' timetable.

Crimes of war?

German soldiers going into Belgium were shocked when the locals shunned them as if they were monsters. People accused the Germans of all sorts of unspeakable acts, usually involving babies, nuns, and bayonets. Allied propaganda made the most of these stories of 'Hun' frightfulness to persuade people to join up. After the war, many of these stories were exposed as false or, at best, wildly exaggerated, which explains why so many people found it difficult to believe the tales coming out of occupied Europe in the Second World War. Recent historians have looked more closely at what happened in the territories the Germans occupied in 1914. They haven't found instances of babies or nuns being bayoneted, but they have found evidence of shootings and executions without trial. The Germans claimed these were legitimate reprisals for being fired on by non-uniformed *francs tireurs*, 'free shooters'; in later wars these people would be called resistance fighters, insurgents, or illegal combatants. In fact, the Germans were just acting much like any other army in any other war in the twentieth century. Or any century, come to that.

✔ **Assumption 3:** The Germans would sweep along the Channel coast and come up on Paris from behind, where the French wouldn't be expecting them. In fact, the Germans found they hadn't got time to go swanning along the Channel coast, at least not if they didn't want the French to cut them off from all contact with home. So they turned left out of Belgium and headed straight down to Paris. Which was exactly where the French were expecting them.

Stalemate in the west

As the Germans closed in on Paris, the French launched a massive counter-attack north of the River Marne. The Battle of the Marne was a huge German defeat (despite the fact that the Germans always liked to claim that they were never actually defeated in the First World War). The Germans had to retreat fast, and every time they tried to slip round the Allied lines, the French and British blocked them. Soon each side dug deep trenches to protect themselves from the machine guns and shells, so that neither side was able to move forward. The whole western front turned into two long lines of trenches that stretched all the way from the Swiss frontier to the English Channel. No one had ever seen anything like it.

The problem was how to break through the lines of trenches. Commanders tried sending men running over to seize the enemy's trenches, but long lines of men could just be mown down by machine guns. They tried shelling, firing thousands and thousands of shells, so that the landscape on the western front was blown into mud and craters and the whole place came to look like the surface of the moon. But men just dug themselves deeper into the earth and, in any case, even shelling couldn't destroy the barbed wire that ran along in front of each side's trenches.

If at first you don't succeed . . .the major assaults in the west

In 1915 both sides concentrated their efforts on other fronts. The Germans attacked in the east and the British and French attacked the Turks at Gallipoli (the sections 'The eastern front' and 'Disaster in the Dardanelles' tell you more about these campaigns). The Germans attacked the British positions around the Belgian town of Ypres and reduced it to rubble, but they weren't able to break through.

In 1916 the French and British planned a massive attack on the River Somme to overrun the German lines and break through into open country. Unfortunately, the Germans got their attack in first, on the French lines at Verdun. The French put up fierce resistance. 'They shall not pass!' declared General Pétain, the French general hurriedly brought in to take charge. Verdun saw a long, bitter battle with appalling casualties: The French called the road leading to the front the 'Sacred Way' because so many men went along it to their deaths. The Germans never did break through, but the French were fully occupied so the Somme attack was now down to the British.

The British attack on the Somme on 1 July 1916 was a disaster. The British had spent months planning it and a week shelling the German trenches, but on the day of the attack, the Germans just came up from their deep dug-outs and machine-gunned the advancing British soldiers, mowing them down like a scythe through corn. The British suffered *60,000* casualties, about 20,000 killed and 40,000 wounded. In *one* day. To get this fact in perspective, think about the impact a single soldier's death can have in news coverage of wars today.

The British learned the lessons of 1 July. By the time the battle ended in the autumn of 1916, Allied attacks were much more effective and the Germans had suffered crippling casualties. But the British still hadn't broken through.

. . .Try, try, try again: Using poison gases

If huge assaults couldn't break through the trenches, each side would have to find something else. In 1915 the Germans started using poison gas; the Allies acted shocked at first and then started using it themselves. Of course, if the wind changed direction you could end up gassing your own men and they frequently did. In 1916 the British introduced tanks, which scared the life out of the Germans – until most of those tanks broke down.

The eastern front

The Germans had much more success in the east. To everyone's surprise, not least their own, the Russians got their armies together quickly and sent them off, all smiling for the cameras, to smash their way through to Berlin. Unfortunately the Russian communications system was so bad – and so easy to hack in to – that the Germans had a fuller picture of the Russians' plans than the Russians did! The Germans surrounded one Russian army at the Battle of Tannenburg and annihilated it, then they attacked a second army and destroyed it at the Masurian Lakes: Many Russians drowned trying to escape. The situation was so serious that Tsar Nicholas II decided to take command himself. Which proved a *real* disaster for the Russians.

The Russians fought well against the Austrians, and after the disasters of 1914, they were even able to hold their lines against the Germans. In 1916, under General Alexei Brusilov, the Russians achieved what everyone had thought impossible – they broke through the Austrian trenches, captured thousands of prisoners, and advanced miles into Austrian territory. But even victorious offensives need food and ammunition to keep going, and the chaotic Russian supply system just couldn't cope. The attack petered out, the Germans sent help to their allies, and the Russians were driven back again. By the end of the Brusilov offensive the Russians had lost *one million* men. Thousands of Russian soldiers decided they'd had enough and headed for home, and can you blame them?

World Wide War

The First World War wasn't just fought on the eastern and western fronts: It quickly began to spread to other parts of the world.

You Italian? I got an offer you can't refuse

Italy was allied to Germany and Austria-Hungary in 1914, so she should have come into the war on their side, but the Italians held back. Not from principle but because, allies or no allies, the Austrians were their old enemies. So the British made the Italians an extremely interesting offer: Come over to our side and you can help yourself to Austrian land after the war. As a result, in 1915 Italy suddenly declared war on her own allies. Switching sides didn't do the Italians much good, though. They got into a long stand-off with the Austrians up in the Alps, until in 1917 they finally had their great showdown battle at Caporetto. And lost.

Beat your neighbour – Balkan style

The Bulgarians, Romanians, Greeks, and Turks had long been enemies and rivals, and the war gave them the chance to settle a few old scores. In the Balkan Wars of 1912–13, the Turks and Bulgarians had both lost a lot of land to Serbia and Romania, and they wanted revenge. So in 1915 the Turks joined the war on the side of Germany and Austria-Hungary. In 1916 Bulgaria followed suit. The Romanians joined in on the Allied side and immediately started fighting their old Bulgarian enemies.

The Austrians and their new Bulgarian allies were getting ready for a massive offensive to crush the Serbs, so as a distraction the British and French landed troops at Salonika in Greece. Which was a bit awkward as Greece wasn't actually in the war. The Greek king, Constantine I, protested, but his prime minister was secretly rather pleased: He wanted to join the winning side before it was too late. In 1915 the Austrians and Bulgarians did indeed crush Serbia, but the Serbs evacuated their army and sent it round to join the British and French at Salonika. In 1917 the Greeks decided it was safe to come down off the fence and declared war on Bulgaria, Turkey, Germany, and Austria-Hungary.

The Salonika front proved a long and slow campaign, but eventually, in 1918, the Allies managed to break through, defeat Bulgaria, capture Constantinople, and force the Turks to surrender.

Turkey – the not-so-sick man of Europe

The old Turkish Ottoman Empire had been in decline for so long, with a long line of weak and corrupt rulers, that many people simply wrote the Turks off as losers. The Tsar of Russia had once referred to Turkey as 'the Sick Man of Europe' and most of the world agreed with him, especially when the Turks lost nearly all their land in Europe in the First Balkan War (see the earlier section 'Apocalypse Now: The War Starts (1914)'). Boy, were they wrong.

In 1915 the British sent an army over from India to invade Turkish-held Iraq. The Turks surrounded the invaders at Kut al-Amarah and forced them to surrender. Thousands of British and Indian prisoners starved in Turkish captivity. Not the last time invaders would get into difficulty in Iraq.

Disaster in the Dardanelles

Meanwhile, back in London, Winston Churchill, First Lord of the Admiralty, had come up with a daring plan:

✔ Send in the navy to seize the narrow Dardanelles Strait that leads from the Mediterranean into the Black Sea

✔ Take Constantinople and knock Turkey out of the war

✔ Send British and French troops into the Black Sea to aid Russia to help win the war in the east.

It was a brilliant plan – on paper. Unfortunately, the naval force sailed straight into a Turkish minefield so the Allied leaders had to rethink. Meanwhile, the Turks very sensibly poured troops into the area ready for when the Allies came back. Sure enough, the Allies landed troops on the nearby Gallipoli peninsula and the Turks pinned them down on the beaches. The Allies tried landing further round the coast, but they still couldn't crack the Turkish defences. So, after months of sitting in trenches dug into the cliffs, the Allies had to pull out, having achieved precisely nothing.

The Australia and New Zealand Army Corps (ANZAC) took part in the Gallipoli landings and suffered very heavy casualties. The Australians in particular blamed their losses on poor leadership by the British generals and the campaign started a growing sense of disillusion and resentment towards Britain, which grew steadily through the twentieth century. Peter Weir's 1981 film *Gallipoli* was an angry indictment of how British incompetence cost Australian lives. The history's a bit simplistic, but the film's good.

Arabia for the Arabs! (Not!)

Back in 1902, Ibn Saud launched a revolt among the Bedouin that eventually threw the Turks out of the eastern half of Arabia. In 1916 his rival, Sherif Hussein of Mecca, tried to organise a similar revolt in the western half, but he didn't get very far because the Turks had built a railway across the desert so they could rush their troops to wherever there was trouble. Hussein decided to link up with the Allies, hoping that they'd hand the region over to the Arabs after the war. The British and French thanked him kindly, promised him all the help they could spare, and secretly started planning to take over the region themselves.

General Allenby was leading a British army into Palestine and Syria and he could only spare one or two liaison officers to work with Sherif Hussein. However, one of them was the young T. E. Lawrence who, quite unasked, took it on himself to lead the Arabs in a daring raid over the desert to take the port of Aqaba and launch a series of spectacular attacks on the Turks' railway network. 'Lawrence of Arabia', as the press dubbed him, made great copy and did wonders for British and Arab morale. However, when the Arabs captured Damascus and tried to declare an independent Arab state, they found that running a modern city was a bit more complicated than it looked. In any case, the British had no intention of letting them do it. The British took over the city and resolved that, whoever ruled the region when the war ended, it wouldn't be the people who lived there.

The Balfour Declaration

The Jewish people had been driven out of Palestine back in Roman times and had settled all over Europe and Russia. However, anti-Semitic persecution got so bad that many thousands of European Jews emigrated to the USA. A nineteenth-century Jewish nationalist called Theodore Herzl set up a *Zionist* movement (from 'Zion', the old name for the Promised Land) to create a Jewish homeland in Palestine. The Zionist movement was very strong in the influential Jewish community in America, and since the British and French wanted America in the war, in 1917 the British Foreign Secretary, Arthur Balfour, declared that Britain would support a Jewish national home in Palestine, as long as some sort of arrangement could be reached with the Arabs who actually lived there. The Balfour Declaration certainly won the Zionists over, but it stored up serious problems for later.

The Japanese land grab

The Japanese joined in the war for one simple reason: To get land. Ideally they wanted that land in China, which is just across the water from Japan and has many more raw materials. Within days of declaring war on Germany, the Japanese attacked Germany's colony in China, Tsingtao. Never ones to miss an opportunity, the Japanese also forced the Chinese to hand over southern Manchuria and Shantung and encouraged them to overthrow their ruler, President Yuan Shih-k'ai, not that they needed much persuading (see the sidebar 'A rickety republic in China'). China came into the war in 1917 on the Allied side, mainly so that she could negotiate with her Japanese 'allies' to get her territory back.

The Japanese troops also took over the Mariana, Caroline, and Marshall Islands in the Pacific from the Germans, but they weren't the only ones to seize the opportunity to take over some prime territory from the Germans in 1914:

- ✔ **Australian** troops occupied the Solomon Islands and the German area of New Guinea.
- ✔ **New Zealand** sent troops to take Samoa from the Germans.

By the end of 1914, the German Empire in Asia and the Pacific had collapsed.

They seek him here, they seek him there – the elusive Colonel Lettow

The Germans had a lot more luck in Africa than they had in Asia (see the earlier section 'The Japanese land grab' for details). The British thought rolling up the German African Empire would be easy. They took Togo, but the Cameroons proved much more difficult. The South Africans invaded German South-West Africa, but lots of them changed sides and joined the Germans, who'd supported them in the Anglo–Boer War. In German East Africa, the local German commander, a dapper officer called Colonel Paul von Lettow-Vorbeck, gave the British a lot of trouble running a hit-and-run campaign with his small force of men. The British called in the South African general, Jan Smuts, who'd done exactly the same to them in the Anglo–Boer War, but although Smuts captured the towns he couldn't find Lettow. Lettow didn't finally surrender until twelve days after the war had ended.

Who Rules the Waves?

Before the war the British and Germans had been desperately building ever-bigger battleships. When the war came, battleships played a surprisingly small part in it, but control of the sea was still absolutely vital.

The British imposed a strict blockade of German ports, with minefields in the North Sea and surface vessels to stop any ship heading for a German port. Naval blockades were only supposed to stop actual war supplies like ammunition or spare parts, not essentials like food, but the British took no notice. The Germans knew that the effects of the British blockade would get worse with each year the war dragged on, so they were very keen on a quick victory before food shortages got really serious. In the end the blockade seriously weakened the Germans, and it was a major factor in their defeat.

The Germans tried to impose a sort of blockade of Britain. They bombarded some British ports and sent a small fleet of raiders to sink Allied ships any-where in the world that they found them. The most successful raider was the *Emden*, which attacked shipping in the Indian ocean, raided Madras and Penang, and sank a Russian cruiser and a French destroyer until it was finally sunk by the Australian navy. Meanwhile Admiral von Spee, with a small force of German warships, was attacking British bases in the Pacific. The British challenged him off Coronel, in Chile, but Spee sank two of the British ships and got away. He sailed round Cape Horn into the Atlantic, but the British trapped him off the Falkland Islands and sank his entire fleet.

Showdown at Jutland

The main German fleet stayed in harbour in Germany until 1916, when it received orders to sail into the North Sea and challenge the British. The two fleets finally met off the coast of Jutland in Denmark. When the firing started, the British discovered a serious fault in their ships – an unfortunate tendency to, er, blow up. German shells managed to penetrate the British gun turrets where the British, ignoring safety warnings, had stockpiled their own shells so they could keep up a rapid rate of fire. So a single hit from a German shell could blow up the whole ship. As a result, the Germans actually sank more ships than the British did, though when the full British fleet arrived on the scene, the Germans skedaddled. The British were very frustrated with the Battle of Jutland, but it may have been a better day for them than it seemed, because the German fleet never dared set sail again except right at the end of the war – to surrender.

U boats

The First World War saw one important new development in naval warfare: Submarines. The idea for submarines wasn't new: It came from an American, Roger Fulton, who proposed them to Napoleon and some oar-powered models had been trialled in the American Civil War (they weren't a success), but by 1914 the technical problems had been solved and the submarine, or *Unterseeboot* in German (U boat for short), was ready for war.

Surface raiders had captured merchant ships and taken their crews prisoner, but a submarine had to leave the crews to their fate. The Germans said they would sink any ship, neutral or not, which sailed to British ports. Neutral countries complained angrily, especially the USA, which sent thousands of merchant ships each year to British ports. Many American ships were sunk by German U boats, but the case which caused most anger in America was the British passenger liner *Lusitania*, which sailed from New York for England in 1915 with a large number of American passengers on board. The Germans put warnings in the New York press saying they would sink the *Lusitania*. And they did.

Isolationist America

Unlike modern America, which is so central to world events, before 1914 the US largely stuck to its policy of *isolationism* – keeping well out of international affairs. The Americans had very good reasons:

- ✔ **Immigration:** America was built on waves of immigrants fleeing persecution or poverty in Europe. They came to America to start a new life and didn't want to get dragged into the European quarrels they'd come all the way across the sea to get away from. In any case, which side should America be on? America had immigrants from both sides. Much safer to stay out.

- ✔ **America only had a small army:** The Americans hadn't fought a major war since the Civil War (1861–65) and the US army was tiny. Fighting the Sioux or the Spanish was all very well, but it was no preparation for fighting the Germans.

The strange case of the *Lusitania*

Only three years after the *Titanic* went down in 1912, the world was faced with another tragedy at sea when the British liner *Lusitania* was sunk by a German U boat off the coast of Ireland. The Germans had warned that they would consider any vessel heading into British waters a legitimate target, including the *Lusitania*, but most people thought they were bluffing, especially as many of the ship's passengers were American. The ship went down very quickly and some 1,200 people drowned, including 128 Americans. The Germans said the British had deliberately allowed American passengers to sail into a war zone; the British said it showed how inhuman the Germans were, especially when a special medallion surfaced in Germany celebrating the sinking and showing passengers buying their tickets from a figure of Death. The biggest outcry was in the US, where pressure began to grow for America to join the war against Germany. When America finally did join in (see the section 'Isolationist America'), American troops went into action shouting out 'Remember the *Lusitania!*'

Then, at the end of the century, historians looked a bit more closely at the *Lusitania*. Why on earth did the Germans sink her? Simple: The *Lusitania* was carrying arms and ammunition for the British. That meant that she was a legitimate target under the rules of war, and the Germans had every right to sink her. Whether or not the British had any right to put arms on a passenger liner, or to allow passengers to sail on an arms shipment, is quite a different matter.

✔ **America had much more pressing problems closer to home:** Specifically in Mexico, where it intervened in the free-for-all to determine who, out of a field of many, would actually be president of Mexico. Once that decision was settled, the US found itself under attack by one of the guys it hadn't backed (Pancho Villa), who'd taken up raiding towns across the US–Mexico border. (For the details, read the sidebar 'And this week's President of Mexico is . . .'.)

Ironically, although the situation with Mexico was one of the initial reasons Americans didn't have time for the war in Europe, it actually ended up by tipping the US into the First World War. In Berlin, the German Foreign Minister, Count Zimmerman, sent a telegram to the German ambassador to Mexico hinting that if Mexico supported Germany in a war with the US, the Germans would give them all the land they'd lost to America in Arizona, New Mexico, and Texas. The British intercepted the telegram, thought 'Hello: *This* is interesting' and promptly sent it to Washington. President Wilson choked on his cornflakes, and the American people united behind Wilson when he declared war on Germany in April 1917.

And this week's President of Mexico is . . .

Mexico was ruled by General Porfirio Diaz, dictator since the 1870s and with no plans to retire. In 1910 he held rigged elections and threw his opponent, Francisco Madero, into jail. Madero called on his supporters to stage a revolution, but Diaz was too strong for them. But in 1911 one of Madero's men, a bandit leader called Francisco 'Pancho' Villa, captured the town of Cuidad Juarez, up near the US border. That event triggered anti-Diaz risings all over Mexico and Diaz had to get out – fast. Francisco Madero became president, promising reforms and an end to poverty. And then the fun began:

1913: General Victoriano Huerta staged a military coup, had Madero shot, and declared himself President of Mexico, without saying a word about reforms or ending poverty. US President Woodrow Wilson refused to recognise Huerta's government, and four separate Mexican leaders staged revolts against him: **Pancho Villa** in the north, **Emiliano Zapata** in the south, **Venustiano Carranza** in the north east, and **Alvaro Obregon** in the north west. They all converged on Mexico City.

1914: The rebels trapped Huerta in Mexico City, while President Wilson sent US Marines to seize the port of Veracruz to cut off any arms shipments heading Huerta's way. Huerta resigned. End of story? Not a bit of it!

The rebel leaders all fought over who should assume power. First, Obregon declared his old chum Venustiano Carranza President (well, officially 'First Chief' but everyone knew that meant President) of Mexico. 'Oh yeah? Says who?' fumed Villa and Zapata as they saddled up and led their troops into Mexico City and sent Carranza and Obregon packing. But Carranza just phoned his very good friend President Woodrow Wilson, who immediately sent in the Marines.

1915: With US help, Obregon recaptured Mexico City and put Carranza back in charge. Villa and Zapata headed off to start a guerrilla campaign against the government. They proved very good at it.

1916: Villa launched raids over the US border and attacked Columbus, New Mexico, to punish the Americans for supporting Carranza. President Wilson sent an army under General Pershing into Mexico to capture Villa, but Villa evaded them and Pershing had to go home empty-handed. Villa became a national hero in Mexico.

The Times They Are A-Changing

The Great War proved the catalyst for long-lasting, even revolutionary, change. This was the first *total* war, in which civilians working at home were every bit as vital as soldiers at the front. The experience of war had a profound effect on people's attitudes, both towards each other and towards the leaders who had led them into the war in the first place.

On the home fronts

In the past, the men had marched off to war, the women had sighed and waved hankies and then gone home to make the beds. Not any more. Women were expected to do their bit, sometimes in traditional 'female' roles such as nursing, but also by taking over men's work so they could go off to fight. Women went into the factories to make shells and sew uniforms, they worked on farms, and kept the transport system running. Women were also recruited into the armed forces, usually in support roles, though the Russians had a female fighting unit. Most women had to go back to their domestic role when the men came home after the war, but at least they had shown what they could do. In Britain, women's war work had been so impressive that in 1918 the government finally conceded women the right to vote.

The war also brought real hardship to civilian populations. As well as the pain of losing loved ones in the fighting, civilians had to cope with ever more serious food shortages as the U boat campaign and the British blockade took their toll. The winter of 1917–18 was known in Germany as the 'Turnip Winter' because they had so little food they were reduced to gnawing on turnips. In Russia, real starvation occurred as the food chain virtually broke down. By the time the war ended in 1918, thousands of people all over Europe were facing starvation. Classic conditions for revolution.

In the colonies

Remembering that thousands of colonial troops fought in the war is important, and they suffered appalling casualties. Britain and France both enlisted colonial troops to fight in the war. Soldiers from French Africa and Indo-China were sent to France, though they were mostly assigned to fairly menial tasks; the British sent troops from India and the Caribbean into the front line in France and used Indian and African troops extensively in other theatres.

The experience of war helped to foster a sense of imperial unity against a common enemy, but the colonial peoples also thought that after all that effort they'd earned the right to more of a say in their own affairs after the war. Funnily enough, the British and French didn't see the situation that way, so the years after the war saw the start of major independence movements in Europe's overseas empires.

Russia's revolution

In February 1917 revolution broke out in Russia. The people rioted, the troops refused to obey the tsar's orders, and the whole country seemed likely to collapse. The tsar abdicated and a new provisional government took over. (You can find out more about the Russian Revolution in Chapter 4.) The

British and French were scared in case the Russians pulled out of the war, but the provisional government decided it would be better to stay in the war, knock out the Germans, and get all the credit. Bad idea. The troops had hoped the revolution would mean they could go home; when they finally did launch an attack, the Germans trounced them.

The Russians were very interested when Vladimir Ilyich Lenin told them that he and his Bolshevik Party would pull Russia out of the war and completely reorganise society on fairer lines. In October 1917, the Bolsheviks seized power in Russia and Lenin immediately started peace talks with the Germans. In March 1918, the Russians, Germans, and Austrians signed the *Treaty of Brest-Litovsk*, in which Russia gave up huge areas of territory, including Ukraine, Finland, Belorussia, Poland, Estonia, Latvia, Lithuania, and the Caucasus, and agreed to pay a huge indemnity (that's a fine to you and me). But Lenin had got what he wanted: Russia was out of the war, and he could concentrate on building the world's first communist state. Chapter 4 tells you how he did it.

No more wars?

Many people thought that one of the main causes of the war had been the way countries formed alliances and signed secret agreements behind each other's backs. US President Wilson declared that in future the nations of the world should operate by 'open agreements openly arrived at', and he proposed a League of Nations, a sort of world government, to make sure that everyone kept to this arrangement. He hoped that if countries dealt openly and honestly with each other, war would disappear. Ordinary people around the world set up their own branches of the League of Nations Union and other organisations to try to keep the political leaders on the path to peace. In the end, though, the politicians just followed their own policies – as they always do.

All Out on the Western Front: War's End

The Russian Revolution threatened to be a disaster for the Allies. America entered the war in April 1917, but the Americans would need time to recruit new troops and train them; most experts reckoned America would be ready for war by the summer of 1918. So the Germans decided to have one last go to win the war before the Americans started arriving in large numbers. In the spring of 1918 the Germans launched a massive offensive which they called *The Kaiser Battle*.

Caution: Highly inflammable ideas on board

When revolution broke out in Russia, Lenin and the Bolshevik leaders were stuck in exile in Switzerland. How to get back to Russia? The Allies wouldn't help them, and the Germans would arrest them as enemy nationals. Lenin got in touch with the German government and made a deal: If the Germans allowed Lenin and friends to cross German territory, they would immediately take Russia out of the war once they seized power. The Germans agreed, but they didn't want Lenin spreading any of his revolutionary ideas in Germany, so they imposed some strange conditions. The Bolsheviks would have to travel in a train with a single railway carriage, and no one was allowed on or off during the journey: It was to be a 'sealed' train. (Lenin couldn't stand cigarette smoke, so the Bolsheviks, who were mostly chain smokers, had to spend the journey nipping into the toilet for a fag.) But the plan worked. Lenin arrived back in Russia in April 1917 and immediately set about undermining the Russian government.

Germany's final push: The Kaiser Battle

In March 1918 the Germans launched a massive attack on the Allied trenches in France. They broke through the British lines on the Somme and headed for Paris. The Allies were thrown into confusion until the French Marshal Foch took charge and restored a bit of order. Helping the Allies even more was the fact that the Germans had advanced so far that they began to run into serious supply problems. Thanks to the British naval blockade (explained in the earlier section 'Who Rules the Waves?'), many of the German troops were badly underfed; their supply system couldn't keep up, and thousands of them went down with a deadly form of flu. Moreover, the Americans were coming over to France much faster and in greater numbers than the Germans had anticipated, and when Marshal Foch sent the Americans into action at the Battle of Chateau Thierry, they proved more than capable of beating the Germans hollow.

The British recovered from their initial shock and on 8 August 1918, 'the Black Day of the German Army' according to General Ludendorff, the British, Australians, and Canadians pushed the Germans back and took over 16,000 prisoners. The Germans were beaten and in full retreat.

After the war, the Germans simply couldn't believe that they'd lost, so they comforted themselves with the idea that they hadn't lost *really*: They'd been betrayed. They quoted a British general who said something along the lines that the Germans had in some way been 'stabbed in the back' by socialists and others in Germany who wanted to end the war quickly. Not too many years later, the Nazis went on to make full use of this idea to blame socialists and Jews for all Germany's misfortunes after the war. Modern historians, however, are under no doubt at all: Germany caught the Allies on the hop in the spring of 1918, but the Allies recovered quickly and then comprehensively and completely defeated the German army in the field. Germany wasn't stabbed in the back at all. Shot itself in the foot, more like.

The long war closes: The armistice agreement

In January 1918, President Wilson issued a set of Fourteen Points as a basis for peace. The Germans and Austrians would have to hand back the lands they had conquered, but the points also promised freedom of the seas for all nations and an end to secret alliances. They also guaranteed *national self-determination* – freedom for all peoples to govern themselves. This guarantee was very good news for the peoples of the Austro-Hungarian empire, who wanted to do just that.

By November 1918, Germany had lost the war. The Allies were ready to invade Germany; the British had conquered Palestine and Syria; the Allies had defeated Bulgaria and Turkey; the Austrians had lost to the Italians at the Battle of Vitorio Veneto; and German socialists were trying to stage a revolution in Berlin. The Germans began to look seriously at President Wilson's offer. But first the Allies made it clear that they'd only deal with Germany if the Kaiser stood down, so Germany's top military brass went in to see him and told him it was time to go. Then they got in touch with the Allies.

The Allied commander, Marshal Foch, agreed to meet the German representatives in his private railway carriage. They agreed an armistice – a ceasefire – to take effect at 11 o'clock on 11 November. In some parts of the front, things were quiet but elsewhere the shooting and killing went on right up till 11 o'clock, though it's hard to see the point.

A not very just or lasting peace: The treaties

French premier Georges Clemenceau, US president Woodrow Wilson, and British prime minister David Lloyd George were the key Allied participants at the Paris peace conference. Woodrow Wilson was the star of the show. He had drawn up a set of *Fourteen Points* which, he said, would lay the foundations for a just and lasting peace. They suggested things such as setting up free nations, allowing freedom of the seas, and keeping diplomacy open and above board. The suggestions all sounded good to the Germans and their allies so they agreed to make peace, thinking that the final treaty would be along the lines of the Fourteen Points. So did President Wilson. Boy, were they wrong.

Holding the conference in Paris was a bad start as it wasn't exactly neutral territory (okay, the food was very good) and it meant the conference was run by the bullish and deeply anti-German French premier, Georges Clemenceau. Clemenceau had no time for small nations or Wilson's Fourteen Points (or Wilson himself); in fact, Clemenceau didn't have much time for anyone except Georges Clemenceau.

Lloyd George was a wily old bird, but he was in a tricky position in Paris. He didn't think that grinding the Germans into the dust was a particularly good idea, but the people and the press back home were screaming for him to 'Hang the Kaiser', and his Liberal government needed every vote it could get. So Lloyd George had to spend his time in Paris trying to steer a middle course between Wilson's naïve optimism and Clemenceau's vindictiveness, while making sure Britain got hold of Germany's fleet and colonies, of course.

With the French premier out for revenge for all that Germany had done to France, and Lloyd George declaring to the British public that he would squeeze Germany till the pips squeaked, the odds were heavily stacked against the just and lasting peace that Wilson hoped for.

New nations for all! But not for you. Or you

Wilson arrived in Paris with two exciting big ideas: The first was *national self-determination*, which meant that each national group should have its own independent national state. This idea was fine as long as you could work out where one national group ended and the next began – which didn't prove easy. In any case, Britain and France quickly insisted that, of course, Wilson didn't mean that national groups who happened to be part of their empires should have their own states. President Wilson had to stammer out that, er, of course he had never intended any such thing. And when the Germans and Austrians asked if national self-determination meant they could join together in one big German state, the Allies said very firmly, 'No, you can't'. Already Wilson's ideas were beginning to come apart at the seams.

Wilson's second big idea was a *League of Nations*, a world government, a gathering of all the states of the world to settle disputes peacefully instead of by war. Dream on, friends. (You can read more about the League of Nations in the sidebar 'A League of Nations. Well, some of them, anyway'.)

Wilson's vision hit two main difficulties. First: The French and British had just come through four and a half years of destructive war and they weren't as ready to be nice to everybody as President Wilson seemed to be (the French made sure that everyone going to the peace conference travelled through the areas that had been destroyed in the fighting and they told the train drivers to slow down so the delegates could get a good look). Second: To the different peoples of Europe, President Wilson's talk of national self-determination sounded a good excuse for nationally determining on grabbing as much of their neighbours' lands as they could get away with.

The conference was dominated by the 'big three', Clemenceau, Wilson, and Lloyd George, who had to look particularly carefully at three main areas:

- **Central Europe:** This had been the Austro-Hungarian empire, but now the Hungarians, Czechs, Slovaks, Slovenes, Serbs, Croats, Romanians, Ruthenes, and all their friends and relations were clamouring to be given their own states. Some groups were too small to be viable, so they'd have to link up with others: Czecho-Slovakia, for example, or the Kingdom of Serbs, Croats, and Slovenes, later renamed Yugoslavia. This joining-together rule doesn't apply to the Germans and Austrians, however, and sulking about it won't get you anywhere, the others didn't start a major war, now did they?

- **Russia:** Russia didn't attend the conference as it was busy holding its own revolution (see Chapter 4), and in any case it had left the war early. However, Lenin had said that the different peoples of the Russian empire could set up their own states if they wanted and many of them, such as the Poles, the Ukrainians, the Armenians, and the Baltic peoples of Latvia, Lithuania, and Estonia, were planning to do just that.

- **The Middle East:** The old Turkish Ottoman empire had collapsed, partly as a result of the Arab Revolt that had accompanied the British advance against the Turks. The Arab delegations arrived in Paris expecting soon to be running a string of modern independent states, along the lines of what was being planned for Europe. The Allies had other ideas.

Different national delegations arrived armed with historical maps and charts to show why they had an ancient right to huge swathes of territory. The men listened and then they retired to their hotel rooms, got their maps and pencils out, and decided who should have what. This approach saved all that tedious business of actually talking to people.

Instead of setting the former German and Turkish colonies free, the Allies decided to hand them over to the new League of Nations for safe keeping. The League would then *mandate* them (that is, hand them over) to Britain and France to administer. In theory, this was so that Britain and France could prepare these territories for independence, but in the meantime these mandates were simply added to Britain and France's long lists of colonies. This meant that the Arabs had simply exchanged one colonial ruler, the Turks, for another, the British and French, and they began to wonder what the point of their revolt had been. Britain and South Africa took over the German colonies in Africa; Britain and Australia mopped up the German colonies in Asia and the Pacific. The new masters said this situation was all in the very best interests of the colonised peoples, *of course*.

Thanks to this mandate system, the British and French empires reached their greatest extent in the years after the First World War.

Everything is your fault. Sign here

Although delegations from Germany and its allies were at the Paris conference, the big three declined to meet them until the peace treaties had all been drawn up. So the first these nations knew of what was in their treaties was when they were given them to sign. As a result none of the defeated countries regarded the treaties they signed as fair or honourable, and they didn't see why they should keep to them. In time, some of the Allies came to agree with them.

The treaties were signed at various chateaux around Paris. The big one was the treaty with Germany, signed in the Hall of Mirrors at Versailles. The Germans had actually declared their own empire here after defeating the French back in 1871, so by making them sign it at Versailles the French were really rubbing their noses in it. The Treaty said:

- ✔ Germany must hand back territories it had conquered and hand over some of its territory to the new states being created. The country lost a huge section of its eastern territories to Poland.

- ✔ Germany can only have a small army of 100,000 men, no tanks, no air force, no submarines, and no big battleships.

- ✔ Germany must pay a huge financial bill known as *reparations* to cover the damage the war had caused. The French would decide how much.

- ✔ Germany must accept the *War Guilt clause*, which blamed her for starting the war in the first place.

The German delegates felt they had no choice but to sign this humiliating treaty – and they were right – but they reckoned it would cause outrage in Germany. They were right there, too.

The other defeated powers were just as unhappy with their settlements. The other treaties were:

A League of Nations. Well, some of them, anyway

Even President Wilson's most visionary idea, the League of Nations, failed to live up to expectations. He'd planned it to be a world government, but colonies weren't represented, which cut out most of Africa and Asia; Germany wasn't allowed to join because it had started the war; Russia wasn't allowed in because the Allies didn't approve of communist governments; and the United States voted against joining anyway.

Wilson had only himself to blame for the American decision. He'd been so sure that he could solve Europe's problems single-handed that he decided he didn't need any help or advice, and certainly not from his opponents. He refused to have any Republicans in his delegation and he wouldn't listen to anyone who said that joining the League of Nations would mean dragging America into more foreign wars. Voters have a way of dealing with leaders who ignore them; it's called democracy and Wilson and the Democrats learned it the hard way. Congress rejected the Treaty of Versailles and voted against the League. Wilson tried a whistle stop tour to sell his treaty directly to the American people, but this tactic didn't work and it finished him off: His health collapsed completely and he spent his last years in office as an invalid. America never did join the League and the voters turned in droves to the Republicans.

- ✔ **Treaty of St Germain** signed with Austria, which dismantled the Austro-Hungarian empire and set up a series of new national states like Yugoslavia, Czechoslovakia, and Poland.

- ✔ **Treaty of Trianon** signed with Hungary, which made them hand over large areas of land to the Czechs and Romanians.

- ✔ **Treaty of Neuilly** signed with Bulgaria, which made them hand over land to Greece, Romania, and Yugoslavia.

- ✔ **Treaty of Sèvres** signed with Turkey, which forced the Turks to hand land over to their old enemies, the Greeks.

All these treaties followed the pattern set by the Treaty of Versailles with Germany. They all handed various lands over to neighbouring countries; they all severely limited the size of their armed forces; they took away any overseas colonies; and they had *reparations* imposed on them to pay for damage caused by the war.

The peace treaties in 1919 were so unequal and so obviously unfair on the defeated countries that even critics said they would spark off another war within a generation. They were absolutely right. The Germans' resentment at the way they were treated was a major factor leading to the rise of the Nazis and, eventually, the Second World War.

Part II

The Years of the Great Dictators:

1919–45

'And the first thing they're going to do when they take power is to make sure everyone gets a good education.'

In this part . . .

After the disaster of the Great War, the world looked round desperately for security. Some people thought the brave new League of Nations would save the world; others put their trust in the economic strength of America. But the League failed and America's bubble burst. The world slid into the Great Depression.

Some turned to communism. The Russians had set up the world's first communist state, but Lenin's promises of land, bread, and freedom were soon forgotten as Stalin established his terrible dictatorship: A workers' paradise run by the secret police. Fascism proved just as bad. Mussolini and Hitler promised a future of strength and joy, but they ruled through jack-booted racist thugs. Worse: Dictatorship spread – through Europe, Asia, and South America. Was democracy doomed?

It certainly seemed so when the Second World War broke out and the Germans and Japanese swept everything before them. Hitler's power was only broken when he invaded Russia. When the war ended, the Western Allies liked to think that democracy had triumphed, in truth though they'd only won thanks to the Russians. And the Russians weren't planning on going home again. A new stand-off between democracy and dictatorship was about to begin.

One thing, though. When this period started soldiers were still riding horses. When it ended, they had nuclear weapons. The century was getting *very* dangerous.

Chapter 4

The Red Flag – Communism

Socialism was one of the most important and influential philosophies of the twentieth century, and transformed politics all over the world, from local councils to international organisations. Socialism produced revolution in Russia, drove America into panic, and encouraged nationalists to challenge the power of colonial empires. Yet this philosophy, based on equal rights and power for the people, produced some of the worst oppression and tyranny in history. This chapter explains how.

Workers of the World, Unite! Socialist Ideas

Many different movements have called themselves 'socialist'. What they have in common is that their ideas stemmed originally from those put forward by the nineteenth-century German philosopher Karl Marx. To understand why socialism had such an effect in the twentieth century, you need to understand his ideas – and to understand Marx's ideas, you need to understand how the Industrial Revolution changed people's lives, and often not for the better.

A whistle-stop tour of the political left

People sometimes get confused between the different names used for socialist groups, so here's a handy guide:

Marxist: Following the ideas of Karl Marx. Now tends only to be used for the most radical groups.

Communist: Comes from the Marxist idea that property should be held in common. It means someone who believes in Marx's ideas, though that didn't stop many communists from departing from them.

Socialist: Comes from Marx's ideas about shaping society. Originally 'socialist' and 'communist' were interchangeable, but when the movement split, 'socialists' were those who wanted to put Marx's ideas into operation but not necessarily by way of violent revolution.

Left wing (also 'on the left', 'leftist', and so on): The term comes from the French Revolution, where the more radical members of the government sat on the left side of the chamber. Their more conservative opponents sat on the opposite side – hence 'right wing'.

Social Democrat: Originally this term meant communist, but it got overtaken by 'communist' and 'socialist'. Later it came to mean very moderate left-wingers who believe in working for peaceful change through a democratic parliamentary system.

Captives of industry

The story of socialism begins with the huge changes in agriculture and industry in eighteenth-century Europe. Industrial production seemed very exciting to people at first – no, really it did – but it didn't take long before the downside became clear.

The problems started when, for reasons we still don't really know, Europe's population rocketed, leaving thousands more mouths to feed. The English worked out more efficient ways of farming, but these methods involved using fewer labourers, so people had to start moving from the country to the new and rapidly expanding industrial cities to find work.

Nineteenth-century industrial cities were dark, threatening places, with hundreds of tall factory chimneys pumping out thick black smoke. Because factories were driven by steam and steam engines don't go to bed, workers trudged to and from work at all hours of the day and night. Most bosses thought safety rails were a waste of good money, especially when cheap labour was so easy to find, so the accident rate was appalling. The workers lived in filthy hovels with no light, space, or sanitation, while the bosses lived in very elegant houses, thank you very much. You didn't have to be a socialist to see that this situation was deeply unjust. One who did was Karl Marx.

Put that pitchfork down, Pa!

Communists were mostly city folk; they never really understood the countryside. In theory, the peasants who worked the land were just as downtrodden as the workers in the factories, but in practice they took a very different line. When a group of young nineteenth-century Russian radicals went out to the countryside to preach revolution, the peasants shopped them to the police before you could say 'Ooh arr'. Peasants wanted to take over their landlords' lands, but they didn't want to share it with everyone else, least of all with a bunch of stuck-up know-it-alls from the cities. So most communists thought of peasants as useful for overthrowing the ruling class, but deadly enemies thereafter.

This situation was bad news for anyone wanting to stage a communist revolution in peasant countries like Russia, China, India, and just about all of Africa and Asia. Believe it or not, Marx actually *approved* of European colonial rule in these parts of the world; okay, he thought, imperialism was just another form of capitalism, but all those Western-built factories and railways were the raw material for communist revolution later. Marx just wasn't expecting any of these countries to turn communist any time soon.

Mr Marx's interesting ideas

Karl Marx was a German intellectual who'd picked up a useful idea at university, *dialectic* – the idea that events happen when opposing forces clash (see Chapter 1 for a few more details). Marx thought that these clashing forces were social classes, especially the middle-class bosses (known as the *bourgeoisie*) and the workers (known as the *proletariat*). The most obvious reason for the clash: The proletariat were sweating their guts out just to keep the bourgeoisie rich, so it was in their interests to kick against the system.

Marx spent most of his life in England studying how the capitalist system actually worked. His conclusion was that capitalism wouldn't collapse just because it was unfair; it would collapse because *it didn't work*. As he saw the situation, capitalism was driven by businesses expanding, ruthlessly swallowing up anyone who got in their way. In the end, Marx reckoned, so many people would be brought down by the system that the workers would rise up in revolution, take over, and share out the profits of their labour equally, thereby making life fairer, happier, and healthier. Marx called this stage of history the *dictatorship of the proletariat*, and everyone might as well get used to it, he said, because workers' revolution was inevitable.

Marxism was an international movement. Marx held that social class transcended national boundaries: Your nationality was unimportant; what mattered was that you were a worker. He believed the class struggle was the same the world over, and the inscription on his grave in London reads 'Workers of All Lands, Unite!' (Aristocrats and business people were used to moving freely among their opposite numbers in different parts of the world, so Marx was merely applying the same sort of idea to the working class.)

This religion is good stuff, man

In Marx's day the Christian churches in many parts of the world seemed to be in cahoots with the forces of capitalism. They believed that God had arranged society into separate classes and that anyone who tried to change things was defying God. Moreover, socialists attacked the rich, and most church leaders were very rich – and meant to stay that way. Marx said religion was a hypocritical way of fobbing the poor off with stories of how everything would be alright in heaven: 'the opium of the people', he called it, a sort of drug that people took each week to keep them docile and stop them agitating for change. Not surprisingly, communist regimes usually abolished religion and persecuted believers mercilessly.

Marx hated *nationalism* – the nineteenth-century idea that what defined people was their nationality. Instead, he promoted *internationalism*. He tried to set up an International Working Men's Association in London, later known as the *First International*, but international brotherhood didn't prevent it from falling apart in lots of unbrotherly arguments. Marxists had another go in 1889 with the *Second International*, which planned for revolution and sent out Have a Good Strike cards to workers around the world. The Second International ended when the Great War broke out in 1914.

What was so scary about Marxism?

To judge by much anti-socialist propaganda, Marxists didn't just want to dismantle the capitalist system and establish the dictatorship of the proletariat: They were wild, scary figures who wanted to burn your house down, dynamite the local shop, and sell your daughter into slavery.

People got so hysterical about Marxism for three main reasons:

- ✔ Marxist revolutionaries became associated with assassinations and terrorist bomb attacks (though they were far from the only people planting bombs and shooting politicians in the late nineteenth century).

- ✔ Marx's idea of putting working class people in charge meant overturning some of the most fundamental assumptions about class and the 'natural' order of society that underpinned Western society.

- ✔ Although Marx was Jewish, he and his followers explicitly rejected any belief in God.

Undermining the proper order of society and rejecting God seemed to many people to be a recipe for chaos, especially if they had any property to lose in a post-revolution free-for-all. So in many countries around the world, the middle and upper classes tended to present communists as dangerous characters, barely human, bent only on destruction, murder, and treason.

Nice tune, comrade, shame about the lyrics

Revolutionaries have always been fond of a good sing-song. The French Revolution produced the stirring *Marseillaise*, which was the international revolutionary anthem until the 1860s when the *Internationale* hit the music stores. The *Marseillaise* had a good stirring tune, which was just as well because the lyrics weren't exactly catchy:

Arise ye workers from your slumbers, Arise ye prisoners of want
For reason in revolt now thunders, And at last ends the age of cant.
Away with all your superstitions, Servile masses arise, arise!
We'll change henceforth the old tradition, And spurn the dust to win the prize.

If you couldn't sing that with a straight face, you could always sing *The Red Flag*, which went to the tune of the Christmas song *O Tannenbaum* (O Christmas Tree):

The people's flag is deepest red,
It shrouded oft our martyred dead,
And ere their limbs grew stiff and cold,
Their hearts' blood dyed its ev'ry fold.

Then raise the scarlet standard high.
Within its shade we'll live and die,
Though cowards flinch and traitors sneer,
We'll keep the red flag flying here.

Back to the drawing board: Marxists and the Great War

To any dedicated Marxist, the Great War was the long-expected opportunity for worldwide communist revolution. Unfortunately events didn't happen that way. Here's why:

- **What Marx said would happen:** Rulers call on the downtrodden masses to join the army and slaughter each other for the benefit of the idle rich, but the downtrodden masses tell rulers where they can put their war and refuse to kill their comrades on the other side.

  What actually happened: Working people eagerly joined up in their thousands and marched off to war.

- **What Marx said would happen:** Wearied by the brotherly slaughter, the workers of the industrial countries rise in revolution and establish workers' republics.

  What actually happened: Successful revolution occurred only in Russia, a huge, backward, agricultural country with only two industrial cities of any size. (See 'Early revolutions that sputtered out' later in the chapter for countries where attempts at revolution didn't go as well.)

- **What Marx said would happen:** Exhausted by the demands of war, Europe's colonial empires collapse and the capitalist system implodes.

> **What actually happened:** Britain and France emerged from the war with even bigger empires than they had had at the start and the United States emerged as the strongest economic power in the world.

Some moments of international solidarity did happen in the war. The most famous was on Christmas Day 1914, when British and German soldiers threw down their weapons and had a game of football instead. Socialists and some progressive liberals from around the world also maintained an international peace movement which campaigned for a general ceasefire, although the leaders of the countries in the war didn't take much notice.

But by the time the war finally ended in 1918, the communists had made one very important advance: They'd seized control in Russia.

The Russian Revolutions

The Russian Revolution put communism on the map and made it a world force to be reckoned with. It was lucky that this revolution happened in a big country like Russia – a communist revolution in Liechtenstein wouldn't have had anything like the same impact. Ironically, though, Russia wasn't *supposed* to have a communist revolution, at least not yet. Marx said you had to go through the capitalist stage, with a full industrial economy, before you could stage a workers' revolution. That meant revolution would break out first in countries like Britain, Germany, or the United States; Russia, which apart from Moscow and St Petersburg was almost entirely made up of peasants, was way down the list. But the Russian communists short-circuited the system, and had their revolution early. The next section explains how they did it.

Setting the stage for revolution

The tsar of Russia in 1900 was Nicholas II, a nice man, very fond of his children, but hopeless at taking firm decisions. He'd come to depend heavily on a mysterious monk called Grigori Rasputin, who was able somehow to keep the tsar's son's haemophilia in check. Rasputin was a disreputable character, always throwing wild drunken orgies and then praying to God for forgiveness before sending out the invites to the next one. When Nicholas started appointing Rasputin's friends to high political office, it looked as if Russia was in the hands of a bunch of real weirdos.

Losing to Japan

Russia in 1900 was virtually a medieval country. It had very little modern industry, its system of government hadn't changed since the Middle Ages, and neither had its method of farming. Other countries were racing ahead of Russia, but most Russians closed their eyes to the problems until 1904, when Russia went to war with Japan.

The war was about who was going to control Manchuria and Korea. The Russians thought they'd crush the Japanese easily and be back by teatime, but instead the Japanese defeated the Russian army and sank the Russian fleet. Russia was humiliated. (See Chapter 2 to see why Japan won so easily.)

A dress rehearsal for revolution

The defeat to the Japanese was a massive wake-up call to get the country in order. 1904: Lose war with Japan; 1905: revolution at home. The outcome's hardly surprising, is it?

- **Bloody Sunday:** In January 1905, a large crowd marched to the Winter Palace in St Petersburg to ask the tsar (or 'little father', as they called him. Aah.) for a proper parliament, a limit to their working day, and an amnesty for political prisoners. The tsar wasn't in, but his soldiers were. They fired straight into the crowd, killing a hundred people and leaving many more badly injured. No one called Nicholas 'little father' after that.

- **Mutiny on the *Potemkin*:** The crew of the Black Sea battleship *Potemkin* killed their officers and declared a sort of naval republic. In 1925, Soviet director Sergei Eisenstein turned it into a famous film and just about every other major director since has copied it.

- **The soviets:** Russia's workers and peasants elected their own councils (*soviets* in Russian). The most important was the St Petersburg Soviet, which set itself up as a sort of alternative government. Its leader was an up-and-coming revolutionary leader called *Leon Trotsky*.

- **The Duma:** In October 1905, Tsar Nicholas finally agreed to summon a Russian parliament or *duma*. Most of the revolutionaries reckoned this gave them what they wanted, but some wanted to hold out for more. The year ended with pro-duma revolutionaries crushing their anti-duma former comrades.

If the Russians thought they'd won a fully-functioning democracy, they were in for disappointment. The duma's powers were very limited, and Nicholas could veto anything it did in any case. He also altered the election law to keep out any awkward people who spoke their mind. His new prime minister, Peter Stolypin, had so many of the tsar's opponents hanged that people joked about the noose as 'Stolypin's necktie' (okay, it wasn't a great joke) until a revolutionary shot him in 1911.

The February Revolution

Nicholas hoped that the Great War would help the Russians forget their quarrels, but the war was going very badly for Russia and in February 1917 angry workers in Petrograd (also known as St Petersburg, but they changed the name to make it sound less German) took to the streets demanding bread and an end to the war. Nicholas's troops refused to restore order. When a ruler can't rely on his own men, their supremacy's over. Very reluctantly, Nicholas abdicated.

Although we talk about the 'Russian Revolution' of 1917, in fact two occurred (or three, if you count the 1905 Revolution – see the earlier section 'A dress rehearsal for revolution'). The first revolution occurred following the abdication of the tsar in February 1917 (see preceding section), but when things didn't improve under the new government the communists staged a second revolution in October and took control.

Russia used the old Julian calendar, which was behind the rest of the world by eleven days, so the February and October Revolutions of 1917 actually took place in March and November. Do try to keep up.

Following Nicholas's abdication, the new government was a committee drawn from the duma (see the section 'A dress rehearsal for revolution'). This committee was only a provisional government, holding things together until a proper parliament could be elected. Meanwhile, the Russians elected the soviets again, just as they had in 1905. The Petrograd Soviet sat in the same building as the Provisional Government and claimed much the same right to govern the country. But neither the Provisional Government nor the Petrograd Soviet could solve Russia's chronic problems of poverty and hunger.

The Provisional Government decided to keep Russia in the war; the soviet agreed, but said it should control the army. Each of them was hoping that, inspired with revolutionary fervour, the Russians would suddenly overcome the Germans. Dream on, friends: Russia lost. By October 1917 many Russians were deeply disillusioned with the Provisional Government and the Russian Marxists decided this might be their chance.

The October Revolution

When the tsar abdicated in 1917, Vladimir Ilyich Lenin was the leading figure in the Russian Social Democratic Party (that's the Marxists – see the earlier section, 'Workers of the World, Unite!'). Lenin was a determined, ruthless leader who knew exactly where he wanted to take Russia and would stop at nothing to do it. He'd made his name in 1903 when he brought about a split in the Communist Party between those who wanted to follow Marx's teaching, help Russia to build a capitalist system, and prepare for a communist revolution some time in the future, and those who wanted Revolution Now! Lenin wanted a very quick capitalist stage – say a weekend – before cutting straight to the revolution and the dictatorship of the proletariat. He called this new improved version of Marxist theory *Marxism-Leninism*; his opponents said it showed he wasn't a true Marxist.

In 1903 Lenin managed to swing a key vote in the Party – just – and immediately named his followers *Bolsheviks*, which means 'majority' in Russian. His opponents were known as *Mensheviks*, which means 'minority', though 'Losers!' would be a better translation – even though the Mensheviks actually outnumbered the Bolsheviks!

Following the February revolution (see the preceding section), Lenin and his pals were holed up in Zurich and had to do a secret deal with the Germans to let them cross German territory to get back to Russia. As soon as Lenin got back, he called on the Russians to overthrow the Provisional Government, but they weren't interested. Not until a crusty old tsarist general called Kornilov decided that what Russia needed was a dose of good old-fashioned discipline and got ready to march on the capital and administer it were the Bolsheviks able to show their worth. While the Provisional Government were hiding under the beds, the Bolshevik Red Guards set up defences and sent so much propaganda to Kornilov's men that they all went home. Crisis over: The Bolsheviks were the heroes of the hour. *Now*, thought Lenin, is the time to seize power.

Even after the Kornilov crisis, not all Bolsheviks wanted to seize power immediately, but Lenin was in one of his I'm-right-and-don't-you-forget-it moods (his usual mood, in fact). However, Trotsky was the man who actually planned the coup. He had been a Menshevik, but changed sides just in time. The Bolsheviks gathered their troops while the Bolshevik sailors of the warship *Aurora* trained its guns on the Provisional Government's headquarters in the riverside Winter Palace. The fighting didn't last long. The ministers of the Provisional Government were still sitting around wondering whether or not they might consider the situation under Any Other Business when the Red Guards burst into the room and placed them all under arrest.

The Great Experiment – Lenin's Russia

The first thing that happened to Russia under Lenin was that it got smaller. Finland declared itself independent in 1917, and the Poles, Estonians, Latvians, and Lithuanians soon followed suit. In 1918 Lenin and Trotsky agreed to the *Treaty of Brest-Litovsk* with the Germans, which signed over to them huge swathes of Ukraine, Poland, and the Caucasus. Following the Great War, the Allies made the Germans give the lands back.

Lenin hoped that pulling out of the Great War would leave him free to start introducing socialism into Russia. Not so fast, comrade. A host of enemies – tsarists, Social Revolutionaries, peasants, and even an army of Czech ex-prisoners of war – were gathering arms to overthrow the new Bolshevik government and the Allied powers sent troops into Russia to help them. Russia was plunged into a terrible civil war. The Bolsheviks finally emerged victorious, but then Lenin was faced with the problem of setting up a socialist system in a country already exhausted and shattered by years of war.

Chekamate: Red beats White

Lenin put Trotsky in charge of the Red Army and he proved a surprisingly good choice. He had no military experience at all but he soon learnt the secret of success in war: Make your men more afraid of you than they are of the enemy. Every unit in the Red Army had a political officer called a *commissar* attached to it, who had the authority to shoot anyone he suspected of treason or even of just being a bit dubious about the Bolsheviks – and that included the unit's commanding officer. Knowing you'd be shot if you didn't win had a remarkable effect on the Red Army's performance on the battlefield. The Reds' victory over the Whites was largely down to the ruthlessness of Trotsky and the commissars.

The Bolsheviks were equally ruthless behind the lines. Lenin set up a secret police force called the *Cheka* after its initials in Russian. Lenin decreed that peasants should send all their food to feed the cities and Cheka units were sent out to make sure they did. Anyone who hid food was to be shot. So much food was taken from the countryside during the Civil War that the peasants didn't have enough for themselves and Russia was hit by devastating famine, in which millions of them starved. The Bolsheviks covered this situation up; in any case, they didn't trust the peasants an inch, so they weren't particularly bothered that millions of them starved to death.

Reds v Whites: A Russian civil war

By the end of the Great War, Russia was sliding rapidly into civil war between the 'Red' Bolsheviks and the 'Whites' – a diverse bunch of anti-revolutionaries and non-Russians who couldn't agree on much except that whatever type of government Russia needed, it wasn't the Bolsheviks.

Each side was ruthless, especially on the peasants, who retaliated by trying to withhold food supplies to stop them being confiscated (see the sidebar 'Chekamate: Red beats White' for an explanation of this situation). For a long time it looked as if the Whites would win: They controlled most of the country and had military help from Russia's wartime allies, Britain, France, the United States, and Japan. What saved the revolution, however, was the Whites' complete inability to work together, coupled with the surprisingly effective discipline of the Red Army for which, once again, Trotsky was largely responsible. One by one the White armies collapsed until by 1921 the last of them was evacuated. The Reds had won.

Life under Lenin

The civil war and Russia's chronic economic problems forced Lenin to take some very controversial decisions:

- ✔ **War Communism:** During the civil war the Bolsheviks took over all the land and industry in the areas they controlled and forced the workers – at gunpoint, if need be – to produce exactly what the Bolshevik government told them to. This hard-line policy was known as *War Communism*, though Trotsky said it was actually just pure Marxism in action.

- ✔ **The Kronstadt Mutiny:** So many people were being killed under War Communism that the sailors at the large naval base at Kronstadt outside Petrograd called for it to stop. 'Aha!' said Trotsky, 'so you want to over-turn the revolution and return the people to tsarist slavery do you?' 'Er, no,' said the sailors, 'we just think you should stop killing people.' But Trotsky launched the Red Army against Kronstadt, crushed the revolt, and killed all the leaders. Which, the sailors thought, proved their point.

- ✔ **The New Economic Policy:** In 1921, with food supplies at rock-bottom and major food riots breaking out, Lenin announced a brand New Economic Policy (NEP) for Russia. He was going to let people set up shops and small businesses and sell things for profit, which in any other country would be called 'capitalism'. Many Bolsheviks, led by Trotsky, were appalled at this betrayal of Marxist principles; Lenin just said it was a case of 'two steps forward, one step back'. Meanwhile, groups of dodgy entrepreneurs called nepmen travelled round Russia offering bargains just for you, comrade, no, really, I'm robbing myself . . .

The arguments about War Communism and the NEP mattered because communists all round the world were looking to Russia for an example of how to implement Marx's ideas in their own countries. They were pleased to see a communist country up and running, but if it had to turn to capitalism or severe repression to survive, it would make persuading other people of the merits of communism a lot harder.

In 1922 Russia formally changed its name to the *Union of Soviet Socialist Republics*, USSR, or Soviet Union for short.

Finding a successor

In 1924 Lenin died after a series of strokes, and the Bolshevik top brass started manoeuvring to succeed him. The bookies' favourite was Lenin's right-hand man, Trotsky, but he had precious few friends among the comrades. He was too clever for their taste and they didn't like the way he attacked Lenin's New Economic Policy (see previous section). They also suspected he was planning to use the Red Army to seize power by force. Trotsky, who never really accepted that people who disagreed with him had more than one brain cell, didn't realise how his enemies were gathering until it was too late. At the 1927 General Congress of the Soviet Communist Party his enemies had him expelled from the Party and two years later he was exiled from Russia. Eventually he settled on Mexico, where he spent his time sulking and denouncing the man who had beaten him to the top: Joseph Stalin.

The Bolsheviks never took much notice of Stalin. He had been useful in the early days, dodging the tsar's secret agents, but every time he tried to talk about economics or Marxist theory it was painfully clear that he didn't really understand them. So they gave Stalin a nice, safe (okay, boring) admin job that none of the party high fliers wanted to do: General Secretary of the Party, making sure people paid their subs and deciding who would be local Party Chairman. 'Comrade Card Index', they called him. Well, never underestimate a card index, because Stalin used his position to gather huge amounts of information. Soon, thousands of Party officers owed their appointments to him, and he made sure they didn't forget it. Without anyone noticing, Stalin had built up a huge power base in the Party.

Lenin thought Stalin was too ambitious and brutal and actually wrote a testament to be read out after his death warning the Party against him, but Lenin also slated all the other Bolsheviks, so no one took much notice.

After Lenin's death, Stalin led the moves to get Trotsky thrown out of the Party, saying Trotsky had been disloyal to Lenin for attacking the NEP. But once Trotsky was out of the way, Stalin suddenly changed his tune, said it was time to sweep the NEP away and make Russia an industrial communist state. The Party delegates all clapped (he'd appointed them all, remember), the other Bolshevik leaders were left saying 'Eh? But you said . . .' Stalin wrong-footed them and by 1927 he was able to take charge of the whole country.

Stalin's Soviet Union

Turning Russia into a fully industrial society wasn't going to be easy, but Marx had always said it had to be done for any country that wanted to follow the Marxist way. Stalin managed it by a combination of central planning and ruthless enforcement.

Once in power, Stalin was paranoid that Trotsky was organising plots to murder or overthrow him from exile (see the section 'Finding a successor' to find out why Trotsky might have wanted to). For many communists, Trotsky represented the pure path of Marxism, and Stalin represented the corrupting influence of power.

Your land is our land

All agricultural land in Russia was *collectivised*, which meant that instead of belonging to individuals it belonged to the State. Villages were turned into *collective farms*, where the villages elected a leader who received orders from Moscow on what they should grow that year and how. Many villages tried to resist collectivisation, but Stalin said his opponents were *Kulaks* – rich, greedy peasants only interested in themselves. And he sent the secret police to hunt them down.

And now let's have one of you smiling with the mechanical drill

The star Soviet worker was a miner called Alexei Stakhanov, who took the country by storm in 1935 by cutting 14 times his quota of coal. He became the Soviet Union's number one pin-up, showered with flowers and medals wherever he went. 'If I can do it, comrades,' he declared, 'so can you!' His words inspired the *Stakhanovite* movement of ultra-keenies, all risking rupture to show they could work even harder and still look good for the centrespread. When the Soviet archives were finally opened in the 1980s, however, it turned out the whole stunt was a fix: Stakhanov had had the latest equipment and an army of helpers all cutting coal and putting it in his trolley.

The Soviet secret police went through many names. First they were the *Cheka*, then OGPU, and under Stalin they became the NKVD. Later generations came to know them as the KGB.

Five-year plans

Stalin set up a central planning body called *Gosplan* to turn the Soviet Union into a top-class industrial state. That meant building everything from scratch – factories, dams, canals, power stations, steelworks – before they could even think about actually producing goods. The whole population was mobilised to work on the programme, and the hardest workers became national superstars. The process was planned in a series of five-year schedules, with every factory given huge, often impossible, quotas to fulfil – usually on pain of death. By the time the Second World War broke out in 1939, the Soviet Union had a strong industrial base. Without this base, it would never have survived.

The time of terror

Stalin encouraged people to work hard by warning them that communism's enemies were just waiting for them to fail. He didn't just mean foreign enemies, though: He warned against spies and traitors in Russia itself. The NKVD had the job of hunting down traitors, and they did it by encouraging people to grass on their neighbours. No one could feel safe: Everyone feared the knock on the door in the middle of the night. Thousands of Russians, most of them entirely innocent, were sent to the GULAG, Stalin's network of slave labour concentration camps. The ambitious and ruthless leader of the NKVD was Nikolai Yezhov, so Russians referred to these terrible years in the 1930s as the *Yezhovshchina* – the time of Yezhov.

For many years, left-wing historians said the extent of the Yezhovshchina had been grossly exaggerated by right-wing writers, while the right-wingers accused the left-wingers of covering up the horrifying truth. When the Soviet archives finally opened in the 1980s, the NKVD's records seemed to suggest that the right-wingers had been right all along, but then historians suggested that the NKVD had inflated its own figures to meet its quotas. The arguments go on, but no one now denies that Stalin killed millions of his own people.

Communists outside Russia were very concerned by reports of the Yezhovshchina, but they were even more alarmed by the news that some of the senior Bolsheviks and members of the Soviet government were on trial for treason. In a series of *show trials* held in front of cameras, some of the best-known Bolshevik leaders, many of them old comrades of Lenin and heroes of the Revolution and civil war, confessed to plotting against Stalin and the Revolution and acting as spies for foreign powers. Communists all over the world were shocked. Some of them denounced the show trials as a travesty of justice (they were right – the confessions had all been extracted under torture and were entirely fabricated); others spoke up in defence of Stalin. Stalin's dictatorship split the worldwide socialist movement in bitter disagreement.

Worldwide Reds

At first, the Bolsheviks confidently expected that revolution would soon break out all over the world. In 1919 Lenin summoned a *Third Communist International* to Moscow, though he shortened its name to 'Comintern'. In 1920 the Comintern divided the international communist movement into 'Communists' who were working for worldwide revolution and 'Socialists' who weren't, though what they really meant was those who accepted Russian dominance and those who didn't. Stalin, however, said he wanted to build 'socialism in one country' and wasn't interested in spreading worldwide revolution, which he reckoned was bound to fail and would only strengthen communism's enemies.

Early revolutions that sputtered out

Although communist movements existed in most parts of the world, the Russians remained the only example of a *successful* communist revolution:

- **Germany:** The German socialist party dominated the Reichstag (the German parliament) before the Great War and the first president of the new post-war republic was a socialist, Friedrich Ebert. German communists tried to seize power in Berlin and Munich but were put down by right-wing paramilitary groups called *Freikorps*. Germany's communist leaders, Rosa Luxemburg, Karl Liebknecht, and Kurt Eisner, were all murdered.

✔ **Hungary:** In 1919 the Hungarian communist leader, Bela Kun, succeeded in setting up a Soviet republic, but the Allied powers refused to recognise it, and the peasants turned against Kun when he nationalised their land. His regime collapsed when the Czechs and Romanians invaded to grab large chunks of land, and ultra-right-winger Admiral Horthy took charge.

✔ **Austria:** Austrians in 1919 were still adjusting to losing their empire. The Austrian socialist party took control of the capital, Vienna, but the rest of Austria was staunchly Catholic and conservative and hated socialists. Each side raised private armies and by the 1930s civil war had broken out, until order was restored and Austria became a virtual fascist dictatorship. (You can find the gory details in Chapter 5.)

Attempts at communist revolution occurred in the years after the Great War in Germany, Austria, Italy, Cuba, Spain, Argentina, Mexico, Bulgaria, Indonesia, and China. The attempts all failed, but communist parties didn't give up. Many of them expected to be in power within a very short time. Because Marx had said it was *inevitable*, remember?

Changes in China

Since China had overturned its ancient monarchy back in 1911 (refer to Chapter 3), it had been in the hands of the dictator Yuan Shih-k'ai, who wanted to be emperor himself. The Chinese weren't having that, and in 1916 the country fell into bitter civil war. Much of China was controlled by local thugs known as warlords until, in 1926, they were finally defeated by China's nationalist troops, known as the *Kuomintang*, led by Chiang Kai-shek, who wanted power for himself, but didn't have everything his own way.

During this time, in 1921, Mao Tse-tung and a Kuomintang officer called Chou En-lai founded the Chinese Communist Party. The communists helped Chiang to fight the warlords, but the two groups didn't really trust each other, and in 1927, when the warlords had been defeated, Chiang suddenly attacked his communist allies mercilessly. Kuomintang troops rounded up and shot thousands of Chinese communists without any sort of trial.

Mission accomplished? Not quite:

✔ Mao Tse-tung's communists still controlled the southern province of Kiangsi, which they declared a Soviet republic, along the same lines as Russia.

In strict Marxist terms, Mao shouldn't have been founding a Soviet republic in a peasant country like China (see the earlier section 'Mr Marx's interesting ideas' to find out why not), but he believed that Marx was, er, *wrong*. Mao thought that, if you explained things to them properly, peasants could be just as revolutionary a force as the industrial workers.

✔ Western powers still controlled some of China's ports, including Hong Kong and Shanghai. Chinese students demonstrated against European colonialism on 4 May 1919, which started the *May 4 Movement* to modernise China and kick the foreigners out.

✔ The Japanese took advantage of China's weakness and invaded the province of Manchuria in 1931.

The fanatically anti-communist Chiang spent the years 1931–34 launching a series of military attacks on Mao's Soviet Republic of Kiangsi. In 1934, by burning everything in his path, Chiang finally forced the communists out of Kiangsi. But the communists didn't surrender. Instead, Mao led them on the famous *Long March* to start again in the north. (You can find out more about the Long March and the long shadow it cast in Chapter 16.)

I'm a Yankee doodle comrade

Marx had always expected that America would be one of the world's first communist states, and plenty of Americans were keen to prove him right. America had been welcoming the world's poor and downtrodden, and many immigrants packed their socialist ideas along with their toothbrush and clean socks. As America industrialised, American workers had tried to establish an effective network of labour unions. American bosses, however, were strongly opposed to the unions and often hired armed guards to break up their meetings. Americans had been horrified by pitched battles between strikers and police in Chicago in 1886 and by the violence sparked off by a Pullman railroad strike eight years later. Getting a socialist movement going in the world's most industrial country was going to be very difficult.

The main groups were:

✔ **American Federation of Labor (AFL):** The AFL dated back to the years after the Civil War and it represented skilled workers. Unskilled workers found the AFL a bit stuffy.

✔ **Industrial Workers of the World (IWW):** Known to its enemies (and, boy, did it have enemies) as the Wobblies. The IWW was much more radical than the AFL: It represented unskilled workers, immigrants, women, blacks, and anyone else who didn't fit into the American system.

✔ **Socialist Party of America (SPA):** Led by Eugene Debs, who had helped set up the IWW and was imprisoned for his part in the great Pullman railroad strike. In 1912 he stood for president and won 6 per cent of the popular vote. In 1918 he was back in jail, this time for opposing America's involvement in the First World War. The SPA and IWW despised the AFL as a bunch of spineless traitors to the workers' cause, but after the war the socialist movement split between socialists and hard-line communists.

✔ **Communist Party of America (CPA):** Founded in 1919 by radicals who thought that the SPA wasn't revolutionary enough. It never achieved the same level of support Debs and the SPA enjoyed.

While the workers were arguing amongst themselves, the rest of America was deeply suspicious of the whole socialism thing. In 1919 US Attorney General Mitchell Palmer launched a series of police raids to arrest socialists, communists, and anarchists and if possible – and it often was – to deport them back where they came from. It wasn't the last time America was to be gripped by a 'red scare'. (See Chapter 10 to read about the next one.)

Marxism in Mexico

Mexico had gone through a four-way civil war during the First World War (Chapter 3 has the details) and Venustiano Carranza, the US-backed Mexican general, came out on top. He brought in a new constitution for the country in 1917, which redistributed the land, laid down rules for education for the people, and severely limited the powers of the Church. Mexico probably had the most radical left-wing government outside Russia. The trouble was that, just like Russia, Mexico's attempts to build a secure and stable socialist state were hampered by internal conflicts and struggles for power:

✔ **1920:** General Obregon leads a revolt against his old colleague Carranza – and kills him.

✔ **1924:** Veteran radical Plutarco Calles is elected president, and he brings in more laws against the Catholic Church.

✔ **1926–28:** A Catholic rebellion against Calles's government fails.

✔ **1928:** In a presidential election, General Obregon wins. And is then assassinated by a Catholic.

✔ **1929:** Calles's Mexican Revolutionary Party takes power.

Sacco and Vanzetti

Nicola Sacco and Bartolomeo Vanzetti were two of the most tragic victims of America's 'red scare' in the 1920s. The two Italian-born Americans were accused in 1920 of the murder of two men in a bungled armed raid on a shoe factory in Massachusetts. The evidence was very flimsy but that didn't stop the trial judge from slanting the whole trial against them, mainly because of the defendants' anarchist political ideas. They were found guilty but immediately lodged appeals which took six years to hear and attracted controversy all over the world. A special commission was set up to look into the case under the President of Harvard University, which found that the judge had been heavily biased but upheld the guilty verdict. The two men went to the electric chair in 1927. To many people the event seemed a case of judicial and political murder.

All this unrest made Mexican politics very dangerous and suggested to the rest of the world that socialist states always ended up embroiled in civil war and power struggles. But despite the internal wrangling, Mexico remained a radical – and independently minded – socialist state.

Leon Trotsky thought revolutionary Mexico would be a good place to spend his years in exile from Russia. From Mexico he worked to rally socialists and communists all over the world to defend the true path of Marxism and denounce Stalin's dictatorship. But even Mexico was not beyond Stalin's reach. In 1940 one of his agents wormed his way into Trotsky's entourage, caught him working alone in his study – and drove an ice pick through his skull.

Chapter 5

Men in Black (Shirts): The Right-Wing Dictators

*T*he 1920s and 1930s saw a worrying new trend in government, first in Europe and then around the world: Right-wing militaristic dictatorship. Italy's fascist leader, Benito Mussolini, set the pattern and many rulers copied him. His most famous admirer was Germany's Adolf Hitler: The whole world felt the effects of his style of government. This chapter explains what was going on and why everyone seemed to fall for these men in uniform.

The story of the twentieth-century's love affair with dictatorship begins with the peace settlement that ended the First World War. Unlike most peace treaties, where the two sides sit down and talk things over along we'll-give-you-back-this-if-you-give-us-back-that lines, the Allies, France, Britain, and the United States, did all the talking and Germany and her allies just had to sign on the dotted line. They resented this situation. Deeply. (Chapter 3 has the details on the treaties that ended the First World War.) In fact, the first inter-war dictatorships (though, of course, they didn't *know* they were inter-war!) were set up by countries smarting at the way they were treated in the 1919 peace treaties. That didn't just mean those on the losing side – some of the *winners* were unhappy, too.

At-a-boy, Atatürk!

The first country to set up an authoritarian government in reaction to the 1919 peace settlement (refer to Chapter 3) was Turkey. Everyone had known the old Ottoman empire for its corruption and chronic inefficiency – it was even known as the 'sick man of Europe' but in 1908 a group of young army officers had seized control in Constantinople to try to restore a bit of strong government and national pride. As a result, the Turks had fought much better in the Great War than anyone, including their enemies, had expected.

The British and French had already decided to carve up the Ottoman empire in the Middle East between them back in 1916; in 1919 the Allies planned to carve up Turkey-in-Europe too. The Treaty of Sèvres handed Turkish land over to the Turks' old enemies, the Greeks, and allowed the Armenians, whom the Turks had spent the war trying to wipe off the map, to set up their own state. It also imposed reparations, though under an even more humiliating name: *Capitulations*. While the other defeated powers felt they had no choice but to accept the Allies' terms, in Turkey one man decided to tell the Allies just where they could put their humiliating treaty. His name was Mustafa Kemal (later Kemal Atatürk).

Kemal was a great believer in direct action:

- **1919:** Treaty of Sèvres gives the Turkish port of Smyrna to Greece.

- **1920:** Kemal leads a successful Turkish attack on the Greeks in Smyrna, killing as many Greeks as his men can find. Then he joins with the Bolsheviks – who'd changed their minds about allowing non-Russian peoples to pull away from Russia – in crushing the Armenians. Then he takes power in Constantinople.

- **1922:** Kemal closes down the Ottoman empire, declares Turkey a republic, and threatens the British garrison at Chanak on the Dardanelles. The Allies decide they'd better negotiate with him.

Thanks to Kemal, Turkey was the only state which, in effect, tore up its peace treaty and negotiated a new one, the *Treaty of Lausanne*. Turkey agreed to give up its claims to Arab lands and various islands in the Aegean and eastern Mediterranean, but the payoff was that the Turks got to keep Smyrna and were let off paying any capitulations to the wartime Allies. From the Turkish point of view, the treaty was a triumph.

Kemal was determined to drag Turkey, by force if need be, into the twentieth century as a secular, not an Islamic, state. He didn't actually ban Islam, but he made it very hard to practise it. He abolished the Caliphate of Constantinople, which had made the city the centre of the Muslim world, banned Islamic dress, especially the fez for men (which wasn't actually Islamic but everyone thought it was) and the veil for women, and made everyone wear Western clothes. The weekly day off moved from the traditional Muslim Friday to the Christian (and therefore Western) Sunday. Children, including girls, were to go to secular schools where they would be taught to use the Western, Latin script; in 1934 Turkish women even got the vote. If all these changes sound liberal, don't be fooled: Tough penalties were enforced for defying Kemal's liberalising policies. Turkey was now effectively a military state in civvies.

Who now remembers the Armenians?

Armenia is a region in the Caucasus that straddles Russia and Turkey. The Armenians have their own, ancient Christian Church but for many years they did not have their own state. In the 1890s the Turkish sultan, Abdul Hamid II, had ordered the wholesale massacre of Armenians and the Turks resumed their campaign in 1915, driving thousands of Armenians from their lands regardless of how many of them died. After Lenin decided that letting so many of the nationalities of the old tsarist empire, including the Armenians, set up independent, anti-communist states on Russia's borders might not be such a good idea after all, he and Kemal co-operated in crushing the briefly-independent Armenian state and the Turks resumed their campaign of ethnic cleansing. Yet, the rest of the world largely ignored what happened in Armenia and to this day the Turks furiously deny that they launched a campaign of genocide to wipe out the Armenian people, even though that's the consensus of historians. When the Nazis weren't sure if they would get away with trying to deport or intern the Jewish population of Germany, Hitler reassured them by saying, 'Who now remembers the Armenians?' He had a point.

Kemal adopted a new name for himself; henceforth he was to be known as Kemal Atatürk, which means 'Father of the Turks'. His new title started a trend for leaders of dictatorships: Mussolini was 'Il Duce' and Hitler was 'der Führer', both of which mean 'Leader'.

Present-day Turkey remains committed to the tradition of secularism, in the tradition Atatürk started, but for some Muslims, Atatürk is a controversial figure: They applaud his success in defeating the Western Allies, but they hate the steps he took against Islamic culture.

Persia and Reza Khan

The great powers were very interested in Persia (modern-day Iran), but their interest was more because of its strategic position than because of oil. Persia acted as a buffer between Russia in the north and British India and Afghanistan in the south. In 1907 the Anglo–Russian entente divided the country into three zones: A Russian zone in the north (it didn't belong to Russia but Russia was allowed to station troops there), a British zone in the south, and a neutral zone in the middle, which neither side was supposed to go into. That situation didn't mean the two sides trusted each other to keep to the terms of the deal, though, especially once the Bolsheviks had come to power in Russia. So in 1921 the British decided to take advantage of the fact that the Russians were in the throes of civil war (see Chapter 4 to find out why) and get their man in power in Tehran. They backed a coup by Reza Khan, who overturned the shah (the ruler) and took power.

Ooh, I do like a man in uniform

Mussolini liked to see himself as the heir to the great Italian nationalist leader of the nineteenth century, Giuseppe Garibaldi (find out about him in *European History For Dummies* (Wiley)). Garibaldi couldn't afford proper uniforms, so he dressed his men in red shirts: Very becoming and the blood wouldn't show. The communists had taken red as their colour, so Mussolini dressed his men in black shirts instead. Other fascist leaders followed his lead. Hitler dressed his followers in brown shirts, and the fascist movement that sprang up in Ireland wore blue shirts. The British fascists wore black jumpers with buttons along the shoulder. The idea was to get round bans on private armies by claiming these outfits weren't proper military uniforms at all, honestly, officer. No one was fooled.

Reza Khan was a sort of Persian Atatürk (see the previous section to find out what Kemal Atatürk was up to in Turkey). First Reza told the Russians to pack their bags and clear out, which they did (both sides in the civil war could do with extra troops so they had plenty of reasons for going home). In 1925 he declared himself Shah of Shahs and set up a dictatorship. As in Turkey, this was to be a Western-dressed and Western-looking dictatorship: Reza banned Islamic dress for men and women and started redrafting the country along Western lines. He drew the line at rights for women, though. In 1935 he even dropped the country's ancient name and renamed it Iran (meaning 'Aryan').

Reza was a canny operator. He owed his power to backing from the British, but he didn't let that limit him. In 1933 he started to take over the operations of the Anglo–Persian Oil Company and in the early days of the Second World War, when the Germans seemed bound to win, he started talking with Berlin. Which is why, in 1941, the British and Russians put aside their old quarrels over the region and together kicked him out.

Mussolini Muscles In

While Turkey was fretting about the settlement of a war she had lost (see the earlier section 'At-a-boy, Atatürk!'), the Italians were angry about the outcome of a war they had won. Wilson, Clemenceau, and Lloyd George, the big three at the Paris peace conference, decided Italy hadn't fought well enough to get all the territory along the Adriatic coast it claimed for itself, so they gave it to Yugoslavia. The Italians were deeply disappointed; they spoke of a 'mutilated peace' and they all cheered when an eccentric poet called Gabriele d'Annunzio did his bit to put it right by leading a military take-over of the Adriatic port of Fiume, which the Italians had decided was that year's must-have. Grabbing Fiume was all very well, though: Who would grab Italy?

The man the Italians turned to was a fire-brand journalist-turned-soldier called Benito Mussolini. Mussolini seized power in 1922 in what he liked to call, rather grandly, the *March on Rome*. In fact, Mussolini took the train to Rome (give the man a break: He marched from the station) and demanded that the king appoint him prime minister so he could restore order and put down the political violence that had erupted all over Italy. The fact that the violence was caused by his own supporters, known from their paramilitary uniforms as blackshirts, was neither here nor there. The king, who was terrified of the communists (and rather scared of Mussolini), agreed and Mussolini took power.

Socialist + nationalist = fascist

Mussolini had been a socialist, but he was a proud Italian nationalist as well, and he sought a way of tying his nationalism to his socialist principles. He got his inspiration from Italy's glory days under the ancient Romans. Mussolini took the symbol of the old Roman republic, a bundle of rods bound together to symbolise unity and strength and known as the 'fasces', and from it coined the word *fascism*.

Although we think of fascism and socialism as complete opposites, in fact the two had a lot in common. Fascism and socialism both believed that:

- All power should go to the State rather than to individuals.
- Individuals should submit their will to the will of the State.
- The State should control private enterprise, and especially heavy industry.
- The State should control education.

And, in practice, even though it went against socialist theory, both accepted that one man should control everything from the top.

Life under Mussolini

Mussolini called himself *Il Duce*, 'the Leader', and made Italians salute him in the old Roman way, with a raised right arm. He liked to present himself as a multi-talented superhero, riding horses, playing the violin, or stripping to the waist to help with the harvest (anything to show off his pecs). He reorganised Italian industry in what he called the *Corporate State*, which essentially meant the State gave all power to the bosses and told the workers to stop grumbling and get to work. Oh, and trade unions were abolished, in case you hadn't already guessed.

Mussolini's regime started another trend others would copy: Ruthless violence. His blackshirts disrupted socialist meetings and beat up political opponents, sometimes by forcing them to drink castor oil (according to the victims, if you ever get the choice, choose being beaten up). In 1922 they even went so far as to murder the socialist leader of the parliamentary opposition, Giacomo Matteotti. Mussolini's regime was successful in establishing full employment (mainly by setting the nation to work building up Italy's armed forces), and he signed an important agreement with the pope, which won many of Italy's Catholics over to his regime and set up the independent state of the Vatican City. And he really did make sure the trains ran on time, or at least the tourist trains that foreign visitors were likely to take. To many people around the world Mussolini seemed to be restoring some much-needed order to Italy, but the threat of political violence was never very far beneath the surface.

I'm the leader! And so am I! Me too! Mussolini copy cats

The fascists created a leader cult around Mussolini. His face was everywhere, and children learned to swear loyalty to Il Duce. They even learned a nice, simple slogan 'Mussolini is always right', which saved everyone the trouble of having to think things through for themselves. Perhaps unsurprisingly, other leaders were impressed and set about copying Mussolini's methods:

- ✔ **Portugal:** Portugal was suffering from serial military coups when in 1928 the finance minister, Dr Antonio Salazar, restored a bit of stability. In 1932 he took over as prime minister and he ruled as dictator until he had a stroke – in 1968!

- ✔ **Hungary:** Since the fall of Bela Kun's short-lived socialist republic (see Chapter 4) Hungary was ruled by the right-wing dictator Admiral Miklós Horthy.

- ✔ **Poland:** Marshal Józef Pilsudski seized power in a military coup in 1926 and ruled as a right-wing dictator.

- ✔ **Albania:** In 1919 Ahmed Bey Zogu seized power and ruled along fascist lines. In 1928 he declared himself King Zog I, which was *much* more memorable.

- ✔ **Yugoslavia:** King Alexander I staged a royal coup in 1929 and centred all power in his own hands. Mind you, he did so because divisions in the Yugoslav parliament had got so bad the deputies had started shooting at each other!

- ✔ **Romania:** In 1930 King Carol II seized power, overthrowing his little son King Michael. Carol set up a royal dictatorship with the support of the Romanian fascists, the Iron Guard.

> ✔ **Austria:** In 1933 Chancellor Engelbert Dollfüss, scared that the workers were going to stage some sort of revolution, closed the Austrian parliament and set up a fascist-style regime. He sent the army in to drive the socialists out of their bases in Vienna's housing estates, and he developed close links with Admiral Horthy in Hungary and Mussolini in Italy. You don't see any of that in *The Sound of Music*.

And then, of course, there's Adolf Hitler.

Hitler's Germany

To get an idea of how Germans responded to the Treaty of Versailles (see Chapter 3), you only have to visit the war memorial in Munich. The grave of the Unknown Soldier shows a Bavarian soldier lying on his tomb in full uniform and holding his rifle. He's not dead; he's asleep, and the writing on the monument says 'I shall arise'. The memorial is a sign that the Germans did not regard the Treaty of Versailles as a done deal. Already they were thinking of the Great War as Round One: Germany would arise again, ready for Round Two. And this was before anyone except his friends and his mother had heard of Hitler.

What a way to run a republic

When the war ended, armed groups of communists and anti-communists tried to seize power. The street fighting in Berlin was so dangerous that the new republican government moved out to the spa town of Weimar, where it was safer. Not such a good idea: The Germans, who reckoned – with reason – this whole democracy idea had been forced on them by the Allies, thought this relocation showed the government was running scared, and the regime was known, rather contemptuously, as the 'Weimar Republic' from then on.

Students can be fairly dismissive of the Weimar Republic and think it was bound to fail. For many years historians took the same view, but they are generally a bit kinder to it now. The Republic overcame the crises of the early 1920s, which could easily have brought it crashing down, and achieved a good level of stability for most of the decade. What brought the Weimar Republic down was the worldwide slump that started with the Wall Street Crash in 1929. No government in the world, including the United States, knew how to handle that situation.

The Weimar Republic had a balanced constitution which guaranteed everyone's civil rights and ensured political freedom for all. But first, it had some urgent problems to deal with.

Putsch attempts

Seizing power by force – using troops to overthrow the government and seize all the vital communications and services – is normally known in English by the French term *coup d'état* (literally, 'a blow of the state'). The German term for it is *putsch*, which means the same thing, but for events in Germany historians usually use the German term.

In 1919 the German communists tried to take power in Berlin and Munich (see Chapter 4 to find out a bit more about the German communists). That attempt failed when right-wing ex-army groups known as *Freikorps* took the law into their own hands and shot the communist leaders. Next, some of those self-same right-wing ex-army groups tried to take power in Berlin and the real army seemed ready to stand by and let them do it. That attempt also failed when the socialists called a general strike that paralysed the capital and forced the putsch leaders to give in. Not until the end of 1920 could the actual elected leaders of the Republic finally come out from behind the sofa, dust themselves down, and start governing.

Economic meltdown

Any war costs money, and the Great War cost a great deal. The German government was deeply in debt to all those it had borrowed from during the war. And the Treaty of Versailles' insistence that Germany should pay reparations made this bad situation ten times worse. Much of what Germany produced in terms of coal or steel or manufactured goods, as well as a significant part of her annual budget, had to be shipped straight off to France and Belgium. In 1923 the German economy took a downturn and the government asked the French if they could suspend reparation payments until things picked up. 'Definitely not!' said the French, and when the Germans suspended the payments anyway, the French and Belgian armies marched into Germany, occupied the industrial Ruhr region, and insisted on overseeing the flow of reparations themselves. Result: The Germans called a general strike, production came to a halt, the French troops got angry, and ugly incidents occurred in which some German civilians were killed. Meanwhile, the German mark had collapsed. Really collapsed.

With nothing being produced in the Ruhr, the whole basis for Germany's financial system disappeared, and the German mark began to lose its value rapidly. The Germans responded by printing more banknotes, which simply meant they became worthless. Prices went through the roof and became silly: A cup of coffee cost a billion marks, and you'd be well advised to pay when you got it because the price would have gone up by the time you'd drunk it. Less funny was seeing your life savings becoming worthless or having all the people who owed you money coming round to hand over worthless notes with grins all over their faces.

Stresemann to the rescue!

Germany wasn't rescued by Hitler, but by a man who's largely forgotten nowadays, though he was a big figure in his day: Gustav Stresemann. Stresemann was a no-nonsense German nationalist, who, like many Germans, dreamed of a stronger – and much larger – Germany, but he was a practical man and he knew he had to sort out Germany's problems first. In his few months as prime minister in 1923, he simply called in all the useless bank-notes circulating in Germany and burned them. He told the workers in the Ruhr to get back to work, and he assured the French and Belgians that the reparation payments would resume. Then he issued a new, solid, sensible currency called the Rentenmark, which means 'mark-with-profits' and sounded very reassuring. Immediately the economy started turning again.

Stresemann also negotiated a deal with the American financier Charles Dawes for a schedule of reparation payments, so Germany knew exactly how much she had to pay each year, instead of having to pay extra every time the French decided they were a bit short. In 1926 Stresemann negotiated the *Locarno Treaties*, signed at a nice lakeside retreat in Switzerland, which were a sort of renegotiation of the Treaty of Versailles, on fairer terms this time, which agreed Germany's western borders, left the eastern borders to be set-tled some other time, and got Germany admitted to the League of Nations. People often say that Hitler tore up the Treaty of Versailles, but Stresemann started the process.

In 1929 Stresemann went back to the thorny reparations question and did a deal with the American financier Owen D. Young for a massive reduction (75 per cent) in the reparations bill, with a schedule of ever-smaller payments, not to France and Belgium but into an international bank, with a definitive end-date of 1988.

Stresemann managed to get Germany floating again but he did it by negotiat-ing deals with the Americans. In effect, the German economy in the 1920s was based entirely on American loans. This situation was fine as long as the American economy remained strong; if it ever collapsed, Germany was in deep trouble.

If you enjoy historical speculation you can have fun wondering how things might have been different if Stresemann had carried on. You can certainly argue that he was doing so well that Germans didn't see any need for extrem-ist parties such as the Nazis and the communists. Unfortunately, in 1929 two things happened which changed their minds: The Wall Street Crash brought the American economy hurtling down, and Gustav Stresemann died.

Race and 'Science'

Hitler's regime is notorious for its racism. The Nazis believed in a strict hierarchy of races and Jews, Gypsies, and the Slavic peoples came at the bottom. They liked to claim their thinking was purely scientific, derived from Darwin's ideas about natural selection in the animal and plant worlds. They drew particular pleasure from the rambling writings of an English racist, Houston Stewart Chamberlain, and Nazi professors churned out one pseudo-scientific 'racial science' volume after another. Children were even taught 'race theory' at school.

Racism wasn't some peculiarity of the Germans; until Hitler came to power the most anti-Semitic countries were probably Poland, France, and Russia. Some fascist regimes were as racist as the Nazis, but not all. In particular, the Italian fascists and Admiral Horthy's regime in Hungary weren't particularly interested in Nazi racial theory until the Germans forced them to start applying the same racial laws as in Germany. After the Second World War and the creation of the state of Israel, anti-Semitism spread to the Arab world, though it had more to do with religion than with discredited pseudo-science.

Hitler comes to power

In 1923, just after the inflation, Adolf Hitler made his first attempt to seize power. He'd joined a small political party which felt that Germany was going to the dogs and the communists were to blame. Hitler gave the party a make-over, changed its name to the National Socialist German Workers' Party ('Nazi' for short), and in November 1923 he tried to lead it to power by armed force. He attempted to take the government of Bavaria hostage in a beer hall in Munich but, on this occasion at any rate, Hitler proved incapable of organising a putsch in a beer cellar; he and his gang were rounded up and sent to prison. However, the judge was clearly sympathetic to the Nazis and they were kept in very comfy surroundings. Hitler used the time to dictate his deadly dull book *Mein Kampf* (*My Struggle*).

Hitler's first real chance for power came with the worldwide slump that followed the Wall Street Crash of 1929 (see Chapter 8 to find out about this event). As unemployment soared and the government seemed powerless to get the economy going again, Germans lost confidence in the mainstream parties and turned to the extremists. Enough right-wingers with money were scared of the communists to lend their support to Hitler and the Nazis started winning votes in large numbers. In January 1933, after a bit of political wheeler-dealing, Hitler was appointed Chancellor of Germany.

Doing away with democracy

In 1933 the Reichstag, the German parliament building, was set on fire. The Nazis claimed the fire was a communist plot to seize power and started rounding their opponents up and sending them off to detention centres, or concentration camps, as they were called. The first one, at Dachau on the outskirts of Munich, opened only two months after Hitler became chancellor. Parliament, meeting in its temporary quarters in the Berlin Opera House, passed a law saying that the government could pass whatever laws it liked without having to pass them through parliament, and when old President Hindenburg died in 1934 Hitler didn't bother electing a new president; he just rolled the post together with the chancellorship and created a single ruler whom everyone had to obey: The Führer.

The Nazis set up a number of organisations to run different sections of German life: The Hitler Youth and the League of German Maidens for young people, Nazi organisations for lawyers, teachers, and doctors, and a labour corps for workers (no trade unions were allowed, of course – far too social-ist). The Nazis even laid down 'proper' rules for how artists and sculptors should work. The Olympic Games held in Berlin in 1936 provided a wonderful showcase for all this nazification of German society. Famously, the black American athlete, Jesse Owens, spoilt Hitler's show by winning a string of gold medals (which, according to Nazi racial theory, shouldn't have been pos-sible), but don't underestimate the effect of the staging of the games: It made the Nazi regime look strong, organised, and efficient to the rest of the world.

Underlying the Nazis' efficiency, however, was a network of terror. The secret police, the 'gestapo', used informers to make people too scared to act, or even speak, against the regime; anyone who did ended up in a concentration camp. Rules against Germany's Jews got steadily tougher: They lost their jobs, found it harder to get educated, and were even excluded from public parks and telephone boxes. In November 1938 the government organised a 'spontaneous' attack on Jewish property throughout Germany; so many shop windows were smashed that it became known as 'Reichskristallnacht', the Reich's Night of Broken Glass. Not only the glass suffered that night: Thousands of Jews were murdered as well.

If understanding why people put up with dictatorship is difficult, look at the benefits it could bring. As long as you weren't Jewish or a communist or oth-erwise fell foul of the government, life could be great in fascist Italy or Nazi Germany. The government provided work and cheap, even free, holidays, and it gave the people a sense of pride in their nation. Most people thought that a bit of curtailing of their civil liberties was a small price to pay for a higher standard of living. And these smartly dressed, efficient, and active regimes looked so much better than the rather shabby, inefficient, and weak-willed democracies.

For most Germans, Hitler's trump card was that he intended to tear up the hated Treaty of Versailles: He would build up Germany's armed forces and start taking back the territory the Treaty had taken away. Then he would take over land in the east as German *Lebensraum*, 'living space', an area where Germany could expand and Germans could move to settle, like in the American West. Chapter 9 looks at how he did it.

Go ahead, priest, make my day

The long years of Spanish rule had left South America overwhelmingly Catholic. However, the Catholic Church had become closely associated with the power of the State and of the rich landowners, so many of the poorer people were cynical about the Church and about religion in general. Revolutionary movements in South America – and the region had plenty of them – therefore tended to be fiercely anti-clerical, that is, they saw priests and nuns as the enemy, and were quite prepared to kill them, often very brutally.

Jackboots in South America

The countries of South America were very proud of having gained their independence from Spain in the nineteenth century. However, they were new countries, heavily dependent on outside help. For most of the nineteenth century and well into the twentieth, most of them turned to Britain for investment and trade, and even for population: Large numbers of Irish and Welsh settlers headed for Argentina and Chile. The South Americans were also very wary of the growing power of their northern neighbour, the United States.

- **Argentina, 1916:** Radical Party of Hipolito Irigoyen wins the election by promising all kinds of reforms. Radical Party forgets these promises once it has been in power for a bit and gets used to chauffeur-driven cars and state dinners. A military coup in 1930 puts the landowners back in charge, with an oppressive right-wing regime – until the next coup, thirteen years later.

- **Brazil:** Population going up fast; price of coffee coming down, also fast. Result: Trouble. Military coup in 1930 brings Getulio Vargas to power and he stays there until 1945.

- **Venezuela:** Juan Gomez, 'the tyrant of the Andes', runs the country as a brutal dictatorship since seizing power in 1908. He stays in power largely because the economy is doing well since the discovery of oil in 1913.

To add to the region's problems, war broke out in 1932 between Bolivia and Paraguay over a border dispute. The League of Nations tried to sort the conflict out, but neither side took any notice. Finally, in 1935, the United States stepped in. It was not to be the last such border dispute, nor the last border war.

Big in Japan

For westerners, the Japanese were always the big exception in their view of Asia. They saw most Asian peoples as backward and needing to be ruled by Europeans, but they recognised that the Japanese were different. Japan had been single-mindedly westernising itself since the 1860s and had shown in its war with Russia (1904–5) and in the First World War that it was perfectly capable of taking on Western powers and defeating them. Japan's treatment at the Paris peace conference (see Chapter 3), however, suggests that westerners didn't really view them as racial equals.

The Japanese didn't see why, if Western powers could have empires, they shouldn't too. In fact, by the 1930s the Japanese were increasingly sure that they didn't just *want* an empire: They *needed* one. The population of Japan was soaring and the Japanese were beginning to feel very crowded in their small islands. Even worse, the economy went into recession in the 1920s and into nosedive in the 1930s. In the Great Depression (you can find out more about this in Chapter 8) no one was trading with anyone much, and they certainly didn't want Japanese silk. Then, just when the Japanese didn't need it, the paddy fields produced a bumper crop of rice, which sounds good but actually meant that rice farmers were ruined because the price slumped. So by the 1930s Japan was experiencing the same sort of economic crisis that had helped bring Hitler to power in Germany. The answer seemed to lie in a Japanese version of – you've guessed it – fascism.

The divine emperor is all-powerful and will do as he's told

Japan never got its own Mussolini or Hitler because it already had its emperor, Hirohito, a mild-mannered man who enjoyed marine biology and treasured his Mickey Mouse watch, which he'd picked up on a trip to America. The Japanese owed their emperor unquestioning obedience and nothing could happen in terms of policy without his say so, yet at the same time they made sure he had virtually no power at all. He presided over cabinet meetings and clearly followed the arguments carefully, but he had to agree with every decision that was taken, even if he didn't. The emperor couldn't stop anyone who wanted to twist Japanese politics for their own ends. By the 1930s, the Japanese army wanted to do just that.

Asia for the (Japanese) Asians!

The Japanese liked to claim they were fighting on behalf of all Asians, but in reality they were trying to extend their own borders. When they crushed the Russians in the Russo–Japanese War of 1905, riots broke out in the streets because the Japanese were so disappointed they hadn't ended up with more land, and they were similarly disappointed with their share of the 1919 peace settlement at the end of the Great War. They had been looking forward to taking over large sections of China, but all they got were some of the areas the Germans had controlled. They put forward a proposal to uphold racial equality, but everyone knew it was just an excuse to try to grab more land in China, so they didn't get it.

Japan's young army officers decided to act. Nationalists had already assassinated two – yes, two! – prime ministers, in 1921 and again in 1932, and in 1936 these Mussolini-admiring officers tried to stage a coup and seize power. The emperor stood firm and had the ringleaders executed, but the lesson wasn't lost on the army generals, who thought these young officers may have been a bit hot-headed, but they had the right idea. Under the Japanese constitution no government could meet without a Minister of War chosen by the army (not by the prime minister, note) so all the army had to do was say 'Right, the Minister of War is resigning' and the government collapsed. That situation meant that by the 1930s Japan was effectively controlled by the army, and the army was increasingly inspired by the examples of Hitler and Mussolini. Japan didn't have a fascist leader as such, but it was a fascist state.

Chapter 6

The Twenties: The Decade that Roared

*T*he 1920s have become famous as a period of wild parties and jazz. The decade was certainly dominated by America and its culture, which is why this chapter mainly looks at this period through the eyes of the United States. During the 1920s many aspects of modern Western life, such as driving a car, going to the cinema, or buying things on credit, first really took hold. The 1920s look a lot more 'modern' to our eyes than do the 1910s: The fashions were closer to ours, at least to our formal wear, and the music was beginning to sound more funky. But not everyone went partying and those who did were living on borrowed time. If the 1920s were a party, the world was going to wake up to one big hangover when the decade was out.

Lest We Forget: Dancing in the Shadow of the Great War

However much people let their hair down in the twenties, no one forgot the terrible war they'd just come through, especially in Europe. The rituals of remembrance that we are used to today were first devised in this decade. The British, for example, decided to select at random an unidentifiable soldier to be buried in Westminster Abbey, alongside the nation's great statesmen and heroes, with full military honours and in the presence of the king, as the 'Unknown Soldier' representing all those who had fallen in the war. (He was unidentifiable, of course, because no identifying marks had survived, so completely had his body been mangled.)

Other countries buried their own Unknown Soldiers; France buried hers beneath the Arc de Triomphe in Paris. The battlefields of the war were turned into huge cemeteries, often very peaceful and beautiful; the British ones had words by Rudyard Kipling carved into a sort of altar and were designed by Sir Edwin Lutyens, the foremost architect of the day. Around the world, the 11 November, the date of the armistice in 1918 when the fighting stopped, became a time of solemn remembrance, and ordinary people subscribed out of their own pockets for war memorials inscribed with the names of everyone from their town or village who had gone off to the war and never came back.

The American historian Paul Fussell wrote a study of the way people remembered the Great War. He pointed out that on the one hand these memorials showed that people had been shocked by the horror of the war, but on the other hand the language and imagery they used showed they were trying to dress it up in more heroic terms. So soldiers were never 'shot in the head' or 'blown up', let alone 'gassed' or 'bayoneted', which is what really happened to them: They 'fell' or were 'sacrificed' or were just 'dead'. You should visit some of these memorials if you can, but bear his words in mind.

Your Mother Wouldn't Like It: Sex, Lies, and Reel to Reel Film

You can't really understand what was going on in the twenties until you remember how close they were to the nineteenth century. People were either trying hard to cling on to the certainties of society before 1914 or they were kicking furiously against them. To young people, at least in advanced countries, this was a new era, a time to blow away the cobwebs, try something new, and have fun. To many older people, the young appeared to have lost any sense of moral values. Mind you, older people usually think that about the young. So do the younger people – when they get older.

In the past, people had filled their free time by making their own entertainment. The 1920s was the first point in history when people could turn to mass media for ready-made entertainment. This was the age of radio and motion pictures.

Radio ga-ga

Radio had been developed before the war, thanks largely to the Italian engineer Guglielmo Marconi, as a means of sending messages across long distances. At first it was just used by special wireless operators sending messages to ships or telegraph offices, but after the war it developed rapidly thanks to the 'radiogram', a radio receiver you could set up in your own home. Anyone could now 'listen-in', though the earliest sets came with headphones, which made you look very odd if the music set you tapping and swaying to the beat, though no odder, I suppose, than people do nowadays when they dance to their iPods. Soon sets came with built-in loudspeakers so people could sit at home and listen together. We're not talking about a radio in every room, mind: Radio (or 'wireless' as it was called; note how that term has come round again!) was something you switched on solemnly, almost as a family ritual, and sat quietly and listened to together after supper.

In those early days radio output was mostly dance music, but broadcasters were experimenting with other types of programmes, including regular news bulletins and drama. Outside broadcasting enabled listeners around the world to hear commentary on events as if they were there: Very good news for sports fans. The British King George V used radio to send a personal message to the whole empire each Christmas; other world leaders also learned how to make use of radio, but they specialised in political propaganda rather than Christmas greetings.

Radio remained the major source of information and entertainment for people around the world until it was eclipsed by television well after the Second World War. This technology has proved very adaptable, thanks to in-car systems, portable transistors, and personal stereos, and local radio is often an important part of the life of a community. Fears that film and television would kill off radio have, thankfully, proved unfounded.

Hooray for Hollywood!

When early moviegoers first saw film of a train approaching at speed, apparently they all screamed and leapt out of the way. This story may well be true: Even today's highly technologically-aware cinema audiences can be taken in and scream in terror at what they see coming towards them on the screen.

Film historians argue endlessly over exactly who deserves the credit for creating the first moving pictures (the leading contenders are the Englishman Edward Friese-Green and the French brothers Auguste and Louis Lumière) but what's not in doubt is that by the First World War cinema was already well established.

In the United States, filmmakers had quickly discovered the potential of the American West for making action movies, often using real ex-cowboys. In British India, filmmakers offered to make films for the government (in return for government funding, of course) to show the benefits of British rule and counter the claims of the Indian nationalist movement, and in 1900 an enterprising bunch of filmmakers shot exciting action footage of the Boer War. Okay, it was filmed on the hills around Manchester with actors, but hey. A few years later filmmakers put together a mixture of real and staged footage (some doubt still remains about certain sections) to produce a startlingly vivid film of the Battle of the Somme. It was shown both to audiences in Britain and to soldiers at the front. One of them, who saw the film in a makeshift cinema just behind the front line, wrote that it was so realistic that the only thing missing was the sound of the guns. But the incessant shelling in the background more than made up for that.

The Bolsheviks, great believers in new technology, were quick to learn to use cinema for propaganda. Special 'agitprop' units went into the Russian countryside, setting up their projectors and screens inside tents and inviting the local peasantry in for a glimpse of the future through crude animations with a simple communist message. We're not talking *Toy Story* standards here, but remember how breathtakingly new this all was to people at the time.

The development of cinema isn't just a topic for film buffs: It played a crucial part in creating a new world culture. Thousands more people could see a film than could ever see a live performance; what's more, they all saw exactly the same film, with no local variations. Films became a sort of social and international bonding process, drawing people from all classes and in all countries together in a common cultural experience. So the fact that the image that people around the world were seeing was often an American one is important. You might be laughing at Laurel and Hardy, but you couldn't help noticing that the nice suburban house they were busy wrecking had good quality furniture and all the latest gadgets. Very interesting to people who had neither.

A star system is born

D. W. Griffith, the great director, took over a small village in California with the rather pretty name of Hollywood to shoot his films in. Griffith was astonishingly prolific: Between 1908 and 1913, he shot some 450 films. These were short films, of course: In those days, you got five or six such 'shorts' for your money before the main feature. Griffith then experimented with longer films, including his controversial 1914 masterpiece *Birth of a Nation*, a hymn to national unity set in the American Civil War, which had a strong plot line and epic battle scenes. Unfortunately the film also had the appallingly racist premise that American blacks were an untrustworthy and murderous bunch, intent on kidnapping white women for their own nefarious ends, and that the nation's only hope lay with the Ku Klux Klan. Inevitably, the new medium threw up big stars but it also made big bucks for the studios: MGM, Columbia, Paramount, and Universal were all up and running in the twenties. Many stars felt restricted by the studios' demands and in 1919 Griffith joined up with three of them, the comic Charlie Chaplin, the dashing hero Douglas Fairbanks, Jr. and the beautiful Mary Pickford (byline: 'The world's sweetheart') to found United Artists, a new company that would actually be run by the stars themselves. The company lasted; the ideal didn't.

I can do angry, I can do sad. I don't do subtle

The earliest films had no sound: A generation of pianists grew up who could improvise appropriate music to fit whatever was happening on screen. The actors in these early movies had mostly come from the stage, where melodrama called for *big* movements and gestures; this style suited the movies just fine.

Silent movies were surprisingly versatile:

- **Slapstick comedy:** The ideal genre for silent cinema. The producer Mack Sennett, who created the hapless Keystone Kops, was the king, though some of the most highly polished comedies came from Buster Keaton and Harold Lloyd, whose high-rise stunts can still leave your palms sweating.

  Charlie Chaplin made his name in silent comedy with his 'little tramp' character, who stood for all the put-upon 'little people' of the world, though to my mind he always looked a tad too well dressed to be entirely convincing as a tramp.

- **Romance:** The comedy was often a curtain-raiser to the big romantic picture. Rudolf Valentino set female hearts a-flutter with his manly chest bared in *The Thief of Baghdad* and *The Sheikh*, while men gazed adoringly at Greta Garbo or Mary Pickford.

- **Historical epics:** Lack of dialogue was no hindrance to mounting epic dramas with massive sets and thousands of extras. D. W. Griffith's *Intolerance*, which was meant to be his 'Oops. Sorry' for *Birth of a Nation*, was so expensive it bankrupted the studio – not the last time an epic turkey would do that. Epics came with a built-in moral: In *Ben Hur*, whose chariot race had people leaping onto their neighbours' popcorn, it was Christianity; in Sergei Eisenstein's Russian Revolution epics, *October* and *Battleship Potemkin*, it was the superiority of the communist system and the dangers of leaving baby buggies on flights of steps.

- **Science fiction:** The German director Fritz Lang created a terrifying vision of the future as an oppressive dystopia (that's a utopia gone badly wrong) in his 1926 film *Metropolis*, which showed people reduced to unthinking drudges and barely-human slaves. His vision proved eerily prescient of what happened to people a few years later in the concentration camps and the gulags.

- **Horror:** Audiences could enjoy some seriously creepy moments in the classic German horror flicks *The Cabinet of Dr Cagliari* (1920) and what is still one of the scariest vampire films ever made, *Nosferatu* (1922).

The first 'talkies' appeared in 1927 and Al Jolson burst into 'Mammy' in the middle of *The Jazz Singer*. Another notable talkie of that year was a rather scary British film called *The Lodger*, loosely based on the Jack the Ripper murders and directed by a young Englishman called Alfred Hitchcock. I wonder what happened to him?

Thanks to the cinema America and its capitalist values, rather than Russia and its communist ones, became most people's image of how a better society ought to look. But although America seemed rich and powerful, it also kept its distance: It brought in immigration controls and reduced its overseas commitments, although it did retain a presence in world affairs. So for people around the world, America seemed like a far-away wizard, who could solve all their problems if he only knew about them, rather like the one in *The Wizard of Oz*. And like the Wizard of Oz, what you saw of twenties America in the movies didn't necessarily match up to the reality.

We're the young generation

In 1921, Roscoe 'Fatty' Arbuckle, one of Hollywood's biggest comedy stars, found himself in the headlines for all the wrong reasons when a young actress was found dead after a sex, drugs, and booze-fuelled party at his house. This event was just the latest scandal for news reporters only too happy to retail the seamier side of Hollywood life and for church-going Americans denouncing the sinfulness of the movies all the way to the news stand. But America's parents weren't just worried about what was going on behind the scenes; they were increasingly worried about what was going on in the back row.

Young Americans in the 1920s had three big advantages their parents hadn't had:

- **Cash to spend:** Thanks to America's booming economy and near full employment.
- **The cinema:** Which meant going out for the evening rather than staying in under your parents' gaze.
- **A car:** Which meant you had somewhere private however you decided to spend the evening.

Particularly worrying was the behaviour of young women. They adopted the 'flapper' look, with hair cut short in a bob, like a boy's, and slimline dresses only just below the knee, which revealed a lot more than a glimpse of stocking. They smoked – in public, too – they rode motorbikes, and they spoke in slang (if this is all too much for you, look away for a paragraph or two). They danced the Charleston, which shocked the older generation not only because it involved shaking your legs and body in wild abandon, but also because – shock, horror – it was derived from black music. American parents suspected their daughters (often rightly) of reading *Married Love*, the best-seller from the British gynaecologist Marie Stopes, who had established the world's first birth control clinic and who encouraged women to take more control of their own bodies. To traditionally-raised Americans, the 1920s seemed to add up to a whirlwind of debauchery and promiscuity. Where would it all end?

I don't like it: It must be foreign

Americans in the twenties were increasingly disturbed by some of the more radical new ideas coming out of Europe. They already knew they didn't like the sound of socialism and communism (see Chapter 4 to see why). Two court cases reinforced their suspicions of foreign ideas:

✔ **Criminal trial of Leopold and Loeb (1924):** Two college students from extremely wealthy families, well educated and with every advantage in life, were arrested for the brutal and apparently senseless murder of a fourteen-year-old boy. They made no attempt to deny it; they'd killed him, they said, to demonstrate their innate superiority, though they weren't quite superior enough to do it without getting caught. Their defence attorney, the celebrated Clarence Darrow, was able to argue – successfully – that they'd been heavily influenced by the philosophy of the German thinker Friedrich Nietzsche, whose writings were in fashion at the time. Nietzsche held that certain people are naturally superior, in intellect and general worth to society; no surprise that Leopold and Loeb, who spent the trial sniggering at everyone and looking very pleased with themselves, had lapped this idea up (and also no surprise that the Nazis used Nietzsche to justify their racial theories). Darrow managed to save his clients from the electric chair, but to most Americans the case seemed to show how fancy foreign ideas could corrupt all-American boys. Better to have as little to do with the rest of the world as possible.

✔ **The Scopes monkey trial (1925):** In the unlikely setting of small-town Tennessee, a high school biology teacher called John Scopes found himself in deep trouble for teaching his pupils about Charles Darwin's theories of evolution and natural selection. The Bible-believing school board was outraged that a high school teacher could so challenge the literal truth of the Book of Genesis and took Scopes to court in what became known around the world as the 'monkey trial'. In heat that was so sweltering the judge moved the sitting out of doors, the court listened to arguments not about what went on in a high school classroom but about the very existence of God and the authority of the Bible. Traditional God-fearing Americans were dismayed when Scopes's defence lawyer, Clarence Darrow (the same man who defended the murderers Leopold and Loeb; Darrow enjoyed difficult cases!) pointed out illogicalities and contradictions in the Bible. Scopes still lost his job, but the case had challenged the religious basis for American life that went back to the days of the Pilgrim Fathers.

Increasingly Americans didn't like the look of European culture either, which seemed to be either Sigmund Freud telling them that repressing sexual desire is bad for you and that all boys want to sleep with their mothers ('At least wait until I've finished cooking dinner, son') or Picasso painting portraits and landscapes that seemed to be made up of boxes. Even worse were the 'Dada' poets, who just put words in a hat and took them out at random. And these guys got *published*.

By the 1920s many Americans were more than ever convinced that foreigners just meant trouble. Attitudes hardened towards immigrants and many Americans were delighted when the government introduced tough immigration controls in 1921 and 1924. We've had quite enough of your poor and huddled masses, thank you.

The Noble Experiment: Prohibition

Soon revivalist preachers such as Aimee Semple McPherson were carrying the message to America to stand up for morality and decency and denouncing the rising tide of moral filth that threatened to engulf the country. And in 1919 America's moral majority did indeed score a remarkable success. It completely banned the sale, production, and consumption of alcohol, even at home, between consenting adults. They called this idea *prohibition*.

One important point must be stressed about prohibition: Alcohol and drunkenness constituted a genuine and massive problem in the United States. Picture the saloons in westerns: Swing doors leading into a large room with men playing poker, women in their undies with feather boas round their necks, a honky-tonk piano in the background, and a shiny long bar for sliding bottles of whisky along. Wrong. Outside of big hotels, most saloons were small, not much bigger than a couple of sheds, and they were there for one purpose and one purpose only: For people to spend money and get drunk. Fights certainly broke out, but they were shorter and nastier than in the movies: Real chairs and bottles don't smash harmlessly over people's heads. But the people who suffered most were the families of the men who went drinking: They depended on the wages their menfolk were busy drinking away. The problem wasn't confined to the West: Excessive drinking blighted the whole country.

A huge anti-saloon movement grew in the nineteenth century, led by the churches. Women took a leading role and so did employers: To them, a drunk worker was a bad worker. The idea was to close down the bars and saloons, though not to outlaw a social glass of sherry at home. However, as individual states began to outlaw alcohol, the prohibition movement gradually grew in strength – beer was mostly German, so during the war you could accuse beer drinkers of helping the enemy – and the brewers and distillers found they were having to fight vigorously to stay in business. So a couple of senators hit on what seemed a good idea to show up the absurdity of the extreme anti-alcohol brigade: Propose a law to make *any* consumption of alcohol illegal. Ho ho, they thought, everyone will see what a stupid idea prohibition is.

Congress didn't see the joke and passed it. Oops. By the 18th Amendment to the US Constitution, buying, selling, making, or drinking alcohol was made illegal. They called this amendment 'the noble experiment'.

Dying – for a drink

Before we bring in all those gangsters and g-men (gangster slang for FBI agents) you see in the movies (Hollywood wasn't slow to see the potential for making money out of prohibition), you need to realise one important point: In many parts of the country, especially in rural areas, prohibition worked. People supported it, they didn't try to get round the law, and cases of drunkenness slumped. These areas stayed proudly 'dry' throughout the period prohibition was in force and often stayed so after it ended. But in other areas, especially in the cities, prohibition quickly became a law and order nightmare.

Many people simply made their own alcohol, or tried to. They set up stills deep in the woods to make 'bootleg' liquor (so called because some people smuggled it in specially widened boots) out of potatoes or anything else they could get their hands on. The trouble was, you never knew quite what they had used – and, often, neither did the distillers. Some people died in terrible agony after drinking 'liquor' masquerading under fancy names such as Moonshine or Mountain Dew. Some poor saps even turned to industrial alcohol, which is poison. What thirsty Americans really wanted was proper alcohol, genuine beer or spirits, and anyone who could get it for them was going to make a fortune. At which point, some very shady gentlemen stepped forward who were only too happy to oblige.

Mobsters, Inc.

Criminal gangs had existed in America long before prohibition, as anyone who's seen the film *Gangs of New York* will know. They tended to be based in particular immigrant communities and they maintained a strong sense of their separate identities: You got Irish gangs, Sicilian gangs, Calabrian gangs, Russian Jewish gangs, and so on. They usually kept to their own particular areas of operation, but prohibition gave them an unprecedented opportunity to expand.

First, the gangs had to get hold of the liquor. They did a certain amount of their own distilling or brewing but for the most part they imported it illicitly, usually from Canada. That's why Chicago, just a nice boat ride down Lake Michigan from Canada, was such an important centre for gangland activity. Just selling the stuff under the counter was a bit boring: Much better to set up a secret nightclub, called a 'speakeasy', where people could drink and have a good time too. With musicians, bartenders, waiters, dancers, cleaners all to be hired, not to mention someone to keep an eye out for the cops, speakeasies became very big business. Rival gangs soon moved into each other's territory and horrified Americans began to read regularly of drive-by shootings, bombings, and assassinations. If the authorities seemed unable to do anything about it, the reason was simple: The gangs had bought, blackmailed, threatened, and bribed so many police officers and local politicians that they could do more or less as they liked – and they did.

Some gangster leaders became celebrities. Al 'Scarface' Capone was the most famous, the ruthless Sicilian mafia boss who for most of the decade virtually controlled Chicago. Even after the St Valentine's Day Massacre of 1929, when Capone's men, some of them wearing police uniforms, murdered seven members of a rival gang in a garage, the FBI couldn't gather enough evidence to convict him of murder or extortion. Finally it was left to the Treasury Department to nail him for tax evasion (criminals tend not to pay tax on their illegal earnings) and even then they had to do a last-minute switch of courts because Capone's men had infiltrated the jury.

By the end of the decade it was clear that the good intentions behind prohibition had gone disastrously wrong. When the Depression set in, the Democrats, who recognised a vote-winner when they saw one, included repeal of prohibition in their electoral programme and in December 1933 Congress finally passed the 21st Amendment to the Constitution, repealing Federal prohibition and leaving individual states free to prohibit or allow the sale of alcohol as they pleased.

So You Thought Slavery Had Been Abolished, Did You?

The twenties were a very bad time for America's black community. In the South, blacks were already kept in dire poverty with special laws and tests to prevent them from voting. Now they faced a sudden revival in the Ku Klux Klan. The Klan had originally been formed after the Civil War, to terrorise the former slaves, but it had died away. Saying exactly why the Klan revived is difficult: It was probably a reaction against immigration and socialist ideas. The revived Klan attacked Jews and Catholics, but saved its particular efforts for attacking black communities, burning homes and churches, and lynching any black person who was accused of cheeking or harming a white person, especially if it involved any sexual contact.

Often these lynchings were carried out quite openly (the Klan even sold souvenir postcards): Klan members knew that the local courts would never convict them – and they were right.

The situation was no better in the North. Many black Americans had moved to the northern states in search of work, and they soon found that racial attitudes could be just as hostile there. The Chicago race riots of 1919 were sparked off by a black man straying onto the whites-only part of the beach.

Black music was popular in the twenties, and black jazz musicians played at all the best clubs and dance halls, but this only helped to underline most white people's image of their black fellow-citizens: Good at providing background music for other people's enjoyment. This attitude would take a long time to change.

You Need Wheels

Before the Great War cars were luxury items, built by highly skilled craftsmen and only affordable for the rich. Henry Ford – one of the most important Americans of the decade, and the century – had broken down the process of building a car into a sequence of separate tasks; instead of hiring craftsmen, he used large numbers of unskilled workers who stayed put while the car came to them along a conveyor belt. Ford's contributions are important for two reasons:

- ✔ **Providing motorised transport that ordinary people could afford** revolutionised American life and attitudes more than anyone could have predicted.
- ✔ **Ford's methods of mass production** turned American industry upside down, gave the American economy a massive lead over the rest of the world, and even inspired foreign leaders such as Mussolini and Stalin.

Ford had gone into production before the Great War, but in the twenties his business increased enormously. In 1919, 6 million cars were on the road in America; by 1929, that number had risen to 29 million.

You can have any colour you want, so long as it's black

Ford's methods meant employing many more workers, but he reckoned this would be more than covered by much bigger sales. He was right. He kept prices right down by keeping to one or two designs (you could buy the famous Model T, or 'Tin Lizzie', in the popular open-top version or as a small family saloon) and one colour: A dazzling display of black. It sold very well.

You can have any opinion you want, so long as it's mine

Ford had a very simple way of attracting the large number of workers he needed: He paid them well. Ford workers earned $5 a day, about twice what other workers earned, the hours were reasonable, and employees could join a profit-sharing scheme. The flip side was that Ford didn't allow any disagreements and certainly no trade unions. He employed a private police force to seek out anyone trying to set up a union and anyone who did was sacked.

Ford was a true visionary who transformed American society. But he also helped create the idea that, as long as business was profitable and gave its workers a share in its material benefits, their civil rights didn't really matter. Unsurprisingly, Ford's methods appealed strongly to Joseph Stalin, who sent special representatives over to America to study them closely. You can find out more about Stalin and about America's attempts to get a trade union system going in Chapter 4.

Let's get this country on the road

Even Henry Ford cannot have anticipated quite how much his invention would change America. To start with, his production methods stimulated a massive demand for supplies of:

- ✔ **Steel:** The demand for steel (no posh wooden chassis in Ford's vehicles) meant massive expansion for the US steel industry.

- ✔ **Rubber:** Rubber tyres meant a great boost for the Malayan rubber trade.

- ✔ **Oil:** Oil wells were being dug in Texas and Oklahoma, though large oil deposits were also turning up in various parts of the Middle East.

- ✔ **Black paint:** Of course.

A lot of domestic production and international trade had gone into Ford's cars before the first car went onto the production line.

After people had bought their cars (how they afforded them is explained in the later section 'The Boom Town rats'), they needed somewhere to fill up. All those blacksmiths and farriers and wheelwrights who were suddenly out of business quickly retrained and set themselves up as garage mechanics and petrol stations. Travellers needed somewhere to stay along the road, so chains of motels sprang up, not all of which were kept by strange young men rather too fond of their mothers. Publishers and booksellers got in on the act with new guidebooks and road maps. Small fishing communities suddenly became popular seaside holiday destinations, where you could join thousands of others, all owning identical cars, and all sit on the same beach. *Fun!*

Not all of the money being produced in America stayed in the country. A lot of it was invested abroad. As Europe recovered from the effects of the Great War, many American investors saw their chance to sink money into European rebuilding schemes and rake in a huge profit. Sometimes they lent far more money to European towns or businesses, especially in Germany, than the Europeans could ever hope realistically to pay back. This situation meant that Europe's own recovery in the 1920s depended very heavily on the strength of America's economy.

Money, Money, Money

America in the twenties became the financial capital of the world. Its whole life seemed to revolve around business and money-making. The new symbol of America was no longer the humble log cabin but the skyscraper, buildings taller than the world had ever seen and built not for people to live in but for firms to do business in.

Farmers and workers didn't do so well in the twenties, but America's political leaders were more interested in helping the big bosses of American business to get even bigger.

The West Wing

America's position of financial dominance carried with it serious responsibilities. It was down to America's leaders how well the country would fulfil them.

Warren Harding

Republican leader Warren Harding won the 1920 presidential election. He realised that Woodrow Wilson had made the Democrats unpopular by taking such an active role in foreign policy and that Wilson's League of Nations idea looked likely to tie America down to foreign involvement for the foreseeable future. Okay, said Harding, the Great War was an emergency, but it's over now: Time to get back to 'normalcy'. It was a simple message and it worked.

Harding was one of the nicest men to sit in the Oval Office, though nice guys don't always make the best presidents. Harding certainly didn't. He didn't seem to be very aware of what was going on, even under his very nose. Mind you, having an affair may have diverted his attention; allegedly, he and his lady friend once had to hide in a cupboard in the White House. Perhaps more important, Harding didn't seem to be aware of the corruption in his administration, even though accusations were being made against it. He surrounded himself with friends from his native Ohio, including his old pal Albert Fall, whom he made Secretary of the Interior. Then he took the management of the US naval oil reserves at Teapot Dome, Wyoming, away from the Navy

Secretary and gave it to Fall. Who then leased out the running of the depot and pocketed the profits. When this corruption was finally revealed, Fall went to prison and Harding – who had died in 1923 – just looked very naive.

'Silent Cal' Coolidge

Harding's vice president was Calvin Coolidge. Coolidge got the news that he was the new president while he was staying overnight with his father, who was a district judge. Dad got down the family Bible and administered the oath of office to his son there in the kitchen, by the light of a kerosene lamp, both of them in their dressing gowns. It was the sort of homely scene Americans loved. It was also about the only memorable thing Coolidge did as president.

Coolidge was a man of few words and fewer actions. One story tells how a woman told him she'd made a bet that she could make him say three words together. 'You lose,' said 'Silent' Cal. Keeping quiet wouldn't have mattered so much if Coolidge had been more active, but he genuinely believed that the president's job was to keep government and Congress out of the way of business and let the economy govern itself. 'The business of America,' he once said, 'is Business,' which, at six words, was something of a record for a Coolidge sentence.

Historians disagree about Coolidge. Some say that his approach to the economy was about right, and that governments should maintain a hands-off approach. That's certainly the classical school of economic thought, which underwent a big revival in the 1980s. Others point to the terrible economic collapse which followed so soon after Coolidge stood down from office and point out that he can hardly escape his share of the blame. If he had taken more steps to provide safeguards, they say, especially for ordinary savers and investors, the Crash, when it came, wouldn't have had quite the catastrophic consequences it did.

Herbert Hoover

Herbert Hoover didn't have long in office before the Wall Street Crash brought the American economy down on his head (see the later section 'Crash!' for more on these events). He was a highly competent administrator and had done tremendous work organising relief provision for refugees in Europe after the First World War. Hoover had a good grasp of economics and he was much more flexible and imaginative than Coolidge: He didn't like government interfering in the economy but he was prepared to get the government involved in organising and leading private companies' efforts to deal with a crisis. But Hoover had a rather lordly view of the importance of his office and wasn't good at appearing open or approachable to ordinary people. When the Crash came, Hoover's efforts were actually very good, and most historians reckon that if his advice had been followed much of the trouble could have been avoided. But it's probably too late to rescue Hoover's reputation in history as the man who couldn't cope.

Down on their luck on the farm

America's farmers were definitely not sharing in the general prosperity. Their problems had started during the Great War, when the Europeans had found themselves badly short of grain. The Americans planted and harvested huge quantities of corn for export to Europe, which was fine until the war ended. Suddenly the European demand for American grain slumped, for three reasons:

- ✔ European farmers could start growing grain again
- ✔ American tariffs were deterring Europeans from trading with the US anyway
- ✔ Europeans started importing grain from Canada, Argentina, and Australia

But American farmers still had huge areas of land under cultivation for grain and they kept growing more and more of it. That situation just meant that prices fell: Good news for consumers but disastrous for farmers.

To make the situation worse, many farmers had borrowed heavily to buy extra land to cultivate during the war, which sent them even deeper into debt. They had no choice but to keep growing grain, in the hope that the price would rise. But the more they grew, the less likely that outcome was.

The plight of America's farmers should have been a warning that all was not as well as it looked with the American economy. But America was much more concerned with its growing, happening cities and was increasingly turning its back on its historic roots in the West.

The Boom Town rats

History is full of examples of spectacular investment crashes. Somehow no one ever seems to learn that a booming economy cannot boom forever and the more rapidly it grows, the more dramatically it will collapse.

Never-never land

America's economic boom depended entirely on credit. Banks lent people the money to buy the furniture and clothes and cars that people around the world saw in the movies. People talked airily of buying 'on the never-never', thinking that payment day would never actually come. Easy credit provided a huge market for American goods, but it also meant that thousands of Americans were actually deeply in debt. If the credit ever dried up, they were in equally deep trouble.

Bonanza!

Shareholding came naturally to a people used to living on credit. The idea was that you bought some shares in a company and then sat back while the company's production (not that you bothered yourself much about that) drove the value of your shares steadily upwards. Anyone could join in. Businessmen found themselves rubbing shoulders on Wall Street with shop-keepers or lift boys: Everyone wanted to buy shares while they were still fetching good prices. Many of these smaller investors had to borrow money known as 'margin' to enable them to buy shares, so they were in debt twice over. Never mind: They'd pay it off easily with their profits.

Here comes the snake oil

Most of the companies people were investing in were perfectly reputable 'blue chip' concerns, but soon characters appeared offering glittering terms to investors in bogus projects. Everyone likes the idea of owning land, so the dodgy dealers invited investors to put money into what appeared to be big, exciting new building projects, complete with plans and maps and artists' impressions. In fact most of these parcels of land didn't exist or else were in the middle of the Florida swamps. One scam claimed to be a new housing development near an entirely fictitious American city! But no one read the small print, never mind looked in an atlas: They handed over their money, got their share certificates, and rang home with the good news while the company agents looked for the next mug.

Crash!

Pinpointing what started the loss of confidence is difficult, but suddenly, in late October 1929, everyone stopped buying and wanted to sell. Prices began to wobble, and then, as people lost confidence, tumbled. When the scams (see the preceding section) came into the open, investment collapsed. No one was buying any shares, even in the blue chip companies, and on 24 October the whole stock market crashed. 'Wall Street,' declared one newspaper, 'lays an egg.'

For people who had invested their personal fortune in companies, the crash was a disaster: They were ruined and many of them committed suicide by jumping from hotel windows. The smaller investors had also lost everything they invested, and they were faced with the little problem of paying back all the money they'd borrowed to buy the shares in the first place. But that's just what happened to the shareholders: Why did the Wall Street Crash bring the whole American economy grinding to a halt?

President Herbert Hoover insisted that the crisis was not as bad as it seemed because America's basic economy was sound – that is, American factories were still producing and selling. Strictly speaking he was right, but that fact was irrelevant because America didn't *act* as if its economy was sound:

- **Run on the banks:** Everyone rushed at the same time to withdraw their money from the banks and the banks, which had themselves invested their customers' money, went bust. This ruined anyone with money in the bank, even if they'd never touched the stock market.

- **Investors and creditors call in their loans:** Anyone who'd lent money to anyone else now demanded it back immediately. These demands didn't just hit shareholders: Other countries were also affected, especially Germany, which had received big American loans (refer to Chapter 4). Now they were faced with crippling demands for repayment.

- **Protective tariff:** Congress passed a heavy tariff on foreign goods coming into the US, so as to guarantee the market to American producers and help them recover. Unfortunately, this kept cheap foreign goods out, and Europe and Japan immediately placed their own tariffs on American goods. America could no longer export, so companies began to go out of business, resulting in massive unemployment.

- **Hunger:** With international trade at a standstill, American agriculture completely collapsed. Farmers were still overproducing but couldn't afford to sell at such low prices, so they had to destroy much of the food they produced. With no State social security, America's millions of unemployed had no money for food and had to queue up at outdoor soup kitchens.

President Hoover put his faith in the 'rugged individualism' that had conquered the West and would, he hoped, see America through the crisis. He looked to business to exercise voluntary codes to provide work and help for the unemployed. Business didn't do so. The decade ended with America and the world falling ever deeper into economic meltdown. Prospects for the new decade looked very bleak.

Chapter 7

I'm the King of the World! Europe's Empires

In This Chapter

▶ Touring the empires of Europe

▶ Understanding how Europeans controlled their colonial holdings

▶ Fighting for independence from colonial rule

*E*urope's worldwide empires were at their strongest in the years before the First World War, but to people at the time it seemed that they became even more powerful after the war was over. In the 1920s and 1930s Europeans could travel the world going from one colony to another, feeling like lords of the earth. They could see no reason why this way of life shouldn't go on for ever. But the Asian and African peoples they ruled had very different ideas. The days of the great European empires were rapidly running out.

The White Man's World

By the 1920s, Europeans held colonies in the following parts of the world:

✔ **Britain:** India; Burma; Malaya; Singapore; huge areas of southern, eastern, and western Africa; islands in the Caribbean, the Pacific, the Mediterranean, the Indian Ocean, and the South Atlantic; Honduras; Hong Kong; Australia; Canada; New Zealand. Also League of Nations mandates in Palestine, Transjordan, Arabia, and Iraq.

✔ **France:** Western and northern Africa including Senegal and Algeria; islands in the Pacific and the Caribbean; Indochina; Guyana. Also League of Nations mandates in Syria and Lebanon.

✔ **Portugal:** Angola, Mozambique, and Goa.

✔ **Netherlands:** Indonesia.

✔ **Belgium:** Congo.

✔ **Italy:** Tripoli (Libya).

The European empires were all based on the idea that white people being in charge of non-whites was the natural order. The European colonialists often downplayed this idea and tried to pretend that imperial rule was based on ideas of common identity, but this didn't fool many of the colonised people. In some colonies, such as Australia and South Africa, the original inhabitants had virtually no rights in their own land. The Europeans thought their empires were part of the natural order of things, but the twentieth century presented them with a problem. How could Europeans say they stood for democracy, freedom, and the rule of the majority when they were clearly not applying these principles in their colonies?

The First World War had a profound effect on Europe's empires. It brought down four empires – those of Germany, Austria-Hungary, Russia, and Turkey – and prompted some serious rethinking in the empires that survived, both by the rulers and the ruled.

Empire of the trenches: The colonies in the Great War

It's easy to overlook the fact that European colonies played a vital role in the First World War and that troops from Africa and India were fighting on the western front. After the war, many people from Europe's colonies assumed that they'd receive some sort of self-government in recognition of all that they had done to help their imperial masters. They assumed wrongly.

Colonial troops fought on all the major fronts in the First World War:

- **African and West Indian troops:** The French brought colonial troops over to France from North Africa to fight the Germans. The British used African troops against the Germans in Africa itself and West Indians as auxiliaries on the western front.

- **Indian troops:** Indian troops fought for Britain on most fronts: Indian battalions fought in France, where they badly scared the Germans, in Africa, and against the Turks in the Middle East.

- **Chinese troops:** The British used Chinese troops as labour battalions on the western front, where they suffered high casualty rates.

- **Australians, Canadians, and New Zealanders:** They fought alongside the British on all fronts in the war, particularly the disastrous Gallipoli and Somme campaigns.

The peace settlement of 1919 (refer to Chapter 3) was meant to be based on the idea of treating countries equally, but that looked pretty hollow to the people in Europe's overseas colonies.

- ✔ **Only the 'white' colonies were represented at the peace conference:** Australia, Canada, Newfoundland, South Africa, and New Zealand all had official representatives in Paris; other colonies had to be content with the French and British representatives speaking for them.

- ✔ **Only white colonies got national self-determination:** President Wilson's great idea for spreading global peace by allowing nations to set up their own independent states (refer to Chapter 3) somehow didn't apply if those nations were ruled from overseas by Europeans. This meant that the Poles and Czechs apparently deserved their freedom, but the Indians and Africans didn't.

- ✔ **Only white colonies were allowed to join the League of Nations:** To join the League you had to be self-governing. That meant that 'white' colonies, who had their own elected governments, could join but colonies who were ruled directly by an imperial power like Britain, France, Portugal, or the Netherlands couldn't.

Just to make things even more unequal, the League of Nations took over the former colonies of the old German and Ottoman empires and then *mandated* them – handed them over – to the British and French to rule. In theory, the British and French were supposed to prepare these mandated territories for independence, but in practice they treated them as colonies. That's why the British and French empires actually emerged from the Great War a lot bigger than they were when they went in.

Dominions: All grown up, ready for independence . . . and white

The British made a distinction between 'white' colonies – that is, colonies where white settlers were a majority – and the rest of their empire. Australia, Canada, Newfoundland, New Zealand, and South Africa were often referred to as 'dominions' rather than 'colonies', and before the First World War they enjoyed a degree of self-government. Self-government, of course, meant the white population ruling themselves: The Maoris, Aborigines, and black Africans didn't get much of a look-in. In 1926 these dominions (which included Malta from 1928, another safely 'white' colony) were given full control of their own affairs and the whole situation was topped off in 1931 by the *Statute of Westminster*, which gave the dominions complete independence in all matters, including foreign and defence policy, but kept the link to the British crown.

The tragedy of the child migrants

One of the saddest stories of the inter-war empires is of the fate of the children sent from Britain to Australia. The Australian government had a policy of only allowing white people in as immigrants; Britain wanted to get rid of some of its orphans and illegitimate children: Shipping them off to Australia seemed the perfect solution. Some children found good homes, but many ended up being treated as cheap labour. Many suffered abuse at the hands of unscrupulous foster parents or in church-run children's homes. Even worse was the deceit involved in sending them away: Their mothers were often tricked into letting them go and the children were often told that their mothers had died. Not until many years later, when the child migrants had grown up and started to look into their own stories, did the shameful truth finally become known.

Dominion status was a recognition that a colony had 'grown up' and no longer needed to be ruled from Europe. But granting this status to some countries raised the question of when other colonies, in Asia or Africa, might also be judged to have 'grown up' and to be ready to govern themselves. If the empires weren't based on racial ideas, and the Europeans always denied that they were, then, logically, at some point all the colonies would qualify for dominion status and these mighty European empires would become redundant. The Europeans took a long time to accept this point of view.

Life, colonial style

Europeans who went out to the colonies could live like kings. They thought themselves superior to every 'native', even the highest ranking. They lived in nice bungalows or villas, often built in the styles they were used to from home. Even today you can see houses and churches in Africa and Asia which look as if they've come from an English or French village. They had armies of servants to look after their needs, operating the fans and bringing them nice cool drinks. It's no wonder that they found it hard to adapt when they went home and found they had to carry their own bags and clear up their own mess.

Moving in

Wherever possible the Europeans encouraged their own people to emigrate – that's how Australia and New Zealand ended up so 'white' – but people would only go if the climate suited them. Nice, easy climates like Kenya or South Africa were fine; hot, sticky, and disease-ridden areas like central Africa took a bit more persuasion. The Italians seized Libya in 1911, but not many Italians fancied living in the desert, so Mussolini had to force 30,000 of them to move there whether they wanted to or not.

Did we really teach them those ideas?

Ironically, the ideas that would finally bring the Europeans' empires down had been developed in Europe itself. As European education spread in the colonies, many of the best students at colonial schools travelled to Europe to finish their studies at university in England or France. They learned two new ideas in particular: Socialism and nationalism. As socialists, they rejected the way in which the Europeans were exploiting the colonies for their own economic advantage: Lenin called imperialism 'the highest form of capitalism'. European nationalists had developed the idea that every nation had a right to be free and to have its own national state, especially if that meant overthrowing foreign rule. This idea appealed very strongly to overseas students whose own nations were under European rule. Funny, that.

What a way to run an empire

The British ran their vast empire with a tiny number of administrators and large numbers of native officials. Wherever possible they operated *indirect rule*, through the native kings or chiefs. In India, the Europeans worked closely with the Indian princes; in Nigeria, they operated through local tribal chiefs, though doing so worked better in some areas than in others.

The missionary position

Christian missionaries often saw the colonies as an opportunity to spread the gospel. Many of them set up mission stations with services and Bible classes and often a school or a hospital as well. Many colonised people got their education through missionary schools and some went on to college and university, often in Europe. The idea was that they could then serve in the civil service and help run their countries on behalf of the Europeans, though, needless to say, natives were only allowed onto the lower levels of the administration. However, many nationalist leaders used the education they received in mission schools to read radical texts and develop ideas about democracy and national independence – and about how to get them.

Although the settler peoples usually attended church, they were nervous about the idea of the native peoples joining them there. Christianity teaches awkward ideas like equality in the sight of God and loving your neighbour as yourself, which didn't sit very easily with thrashing your servant if the champagne wasn't quite chilled. Settlers were often suspicious of missionaries – and the feeling was mutual.

We are one big, happy family: Empires united?

The Europeans tried to foster a sense of unity in their empires. Children in French colonies learned French history at school, just as if they were in

France. The French empire also tried to tie its people to France by offering them full French citizenship, though the qualifications for citizenship were often so difficult that very few Africans or Asians actually got it. The British introduced their own home-grown sports, especially rugby and cricket, to try to develop a sense of everyone-in-the-empire-together.

Technology played an important part in holding empires together and creating a sense of imperial unity. In 1924 a wireless link was established between Britain and Australia, and in 1930, only three years after Charles Lindbergh became the first man to fly solo across the Atlantic, the British aviator Amy Johnson flew all the way from Britain to Australia. Soon airlines were establishing regular flights from Europe to the colonies. As technology shrank distances, so it cemented empires together. In theory.

'Buy empire'

During the years of economic depression in the 1930s, the British and French tried to make use of their empires to climb out of the economic mess. They encouraged trade within their empires and urged people to 'buy empire'. This tactic wasn't enough to resolve the economic crisis; nor could it stop the growing tide of nationalist criticism that all empires were having to face.

Ireland lights the fuse

The first colony to throw off its European masters in the twentieth century was itself in Europe: Ireland. The English had conquered Ireland back in the Middle Ages, and although Ireland had been a part of the United Kingdom since 1801, to Irish nationalists the country was essentially a British colony. The question of Irish independence was complicated by the fact that the Protestants of Ulster were determined to stay within the UK but Irish nationalists thought they could soon be won over (or ignored). Uprisings had occurred before, but at Easter 1916, at the height of the Great War, the nationalists struck and set in motion a chain of events that would lead to the separation of much of Ireland from the UK:

✔ **Easter Rising in Dublin, 1916:** Irish nationalists stage a coup but fail. The British defeat the rising but then alienate Irish public opinion by executing many of the prisoners.

✔ **Irish parliament established, 1919:** Irish nationalist *Sinn Fein* MPs set up an Irish parliament, *Dail Eireann*. Nationalist leader (and half-American) Eamon de Valera escapes from prison in England and is elected Dail president. The Irish Republican Army under Michael Collins leads a guerrilla war against British security forces.

✔ **'The Troubles' 1920–1:** Bitter and bloody guerrilla warfare between Collins's IRA and the British army. In the worst incidents, the IRA assassinate twelve British secret agents, and in retaliation British troops open fire at the crowd at Croke Park football ground. The British deploy a paramilitary force, the 'Black and Tans', against the IRA. After a failed attack on the Dublin Customs House, the IRA is forced to negotiate with the British.

✔ **Anglo–Irish Treaty, 1921–2:** Collins negotiates a deal with the British which sets up an Irish Free State within the British empire but without the Protestant counties of Ulster, which remain part of the UK. Irish anger at these concessions erupts into civil war, in which Collins himself is assassinated.

Many nationalists elsewhere in the world took enormous encouragement from the Irish success in throwing off British control. The Irish example seemed to show that guerrilla tactics could force even the most powerful nation to talk with insurgents and even to grant their demands. It also showed that the authorities might be able to retaliate with heavy force, but doing so would be bound to lose them public support, both at home and abroad. These were lessons that many governments, including the British, would often forget.

The Natives Are Restless

The British and French may have felt pleased with themselves when they took over the former German and Turkish colonies as League of Nations mandates (see Chapter 3) but many of these territories merely presented their new rulers with serious problems to solve. In the years between the wars, nationalist groups became active in European colonies all around the world, demanding the right to rule themselves. Some of them worked through peaceful means; most of them didn't.

Middle Eastern promise

The Middle East had been part of the Turkish Ottoman empire, but the Turks had been driven out by the British, helped by an Arab nationalist revolt led by Prince Feisal. The Arabs thought they'd been fighting so they could rule themselves; the British and French had other ideas. Both wanted to take over land in the Middle East. Both had their eyes on Palestine and Syria, but in the end they decided to divide the region between them rather than fight over it.

The Europeans wanted the Middle East for a mixture of strategic and sentimental reasons: It lay on the route between Europe and its rich colonies in the Far East and it was the scene of events from the Bible and the Crusades. The British had their eye on Iraq's oil fields, but it wasn't until after Britain and France had carved the region up that they discovered just how much oil they were sitting on top of.

Dodgy dealings in Damascus and Iraq as the consolation prize

The Arabs had driven the Turks out of Syria and ensconced Prince Feisal in Damascus as king of Syria pending the Peace Conference in Paris. This situation was awkward, though, because the French wanted Syria for themselves. Feisal went to Paris to plead his case: The French rather grumpily gave him a tour of the battlefields and the *Légion d'Honneur*, France's highest award, before doing a deal with the British to take his kingdom off him. Feisal tried to resist the French take-over but the French proved too strong for him. As a final insult, the French general who turfed Feisal out of Damascus was the same man who'd presented him with his *Légion d'Honneur*. No wonder the Arabs regarded the whole 1919 settlement of the Middle East as a piece of European trickery and hypocrisy.

After what happened over Syria (see previous section) you could hardly have blamed Prince Feisal if he'd decided to go home and sulk but instead he took up a British offer to become king of their new mandate in Mesopotamia, which they were renaming Iraq. Feisal proved a canny ruler: He kept on good terms with the British, who used bomber aircraft to defeat Kurdish rebels trying to set up their own state in the hills. In 1930 he got the British to agree to end the mandate and go home as long as Iraq remained a British ally; two years later they did just that. With extensive oil fields being discovered in his kingdom, Feisal was now one of the most important figures in an increasingly important region of the world. And yah boo sucks to the French.

While Britain, France, and Feisal were working out the future of Syria and Iraq, big things were happening in the rest of the region:

- ✔ **San Remo Agreement between Britain and France (1920):** Britain gets the mandate for Palestine; France gets Syria and the newly-created Lebanon. Arabs launch attacks on British troops in Palestine.

- ✔ **Transjordan Mandate (1921):** Britain hives off Transjordan from Palestine and makes it a separate mandate, under Prince Abdullah Ibn Hussein, brother of King Feisal of Iraq. Abdullah and Feisal are both of the Hashemite house, which claims direct descent from the Prophet Muhammed.

- ✔ **Coup in Arabia (1924):** The Hashemites' old rival, Ibn Saud, stages a coup and takes control of Arabia, which is later renamed 'Saudi Arabia'.

- ✔ **Saudi Arabian attacks (1928):** Saudi Arabia launches raids against the British mandate in Iraq and the British protectorate of Kuwait. The Saudis are driven back by the RAF and bands of Iraqi tribesmen.

If the British thought Iraq and Transjordan were problematic, Palestine was to prove even worse.

Your land is my land: Palestine

Palestine is the 'promised land' of the Bible where the Israelites settled after Moses brought them out of Egypt (have a look in the Book of Exodus if you're a bit hazy on the details). However, the Jews had been thrown out of Palestine, or 'Judaea' as it was called, by the Roman emperor Titus in what is known as the 'Jewish diaspora' (diaspora means dispersal over a wide area). From the first century to the twentieth, Jewish communities had settled and sometimes prospered in different parts of the world, but each year at Passover they would say, 'Next year in Jerusalem' – they were dreaming of home.

Until the nineteenth century Jewish people could only dream of going back to Palestine, but in 1896 a Jewish journalist called Theodor Herzl, fed up with European anti-Semitism, called for the establishment of a Jewish national state in Palestine. The idea caught on among Jewish communities around the world: It was known as *Zionism* (from 'Zion' the ancient name for Jerusalem).

However, the Arab people who had actually lived in Palestine since the days of the Roman emperor Titus also regarded it as home and they didn't look kindly on the idea of lots of Jewish settlers coming to stay. Before 1914 none of this mattered very much because the whole place belonged to the Turks, but when the British decided to drive the Turks out, London had to start thinking seriously about who would get the land after the war.

In 1917 the British foreign secretary, Arthur Balfour, wrote to the banker, Lord Rothschild, to say that Britain would support the idea of a Jewish homeland in Palestine, as long as the rights of the Arab Palestinians were fully respected. This *Balfour Declaration* was a bit vague on details – especially how you could respect the rights of people if you were moving them to make way for new people – and it meant that when Britain got the Palestine mandate in 1920, the British had to:

✔ Allow Jewish people to settle in Palestine, but not too many

✔ Take some of the Palestinians' land off them, but not too much

✔ Stop Palestinians attacking Jewish settlers

✔ Stop Jewish settlers attacking Palestinians

✔ Get used to both sides hating them

The British tried to work with both sides, but as clashes between Jews and Arabs became progressively more violent, the British found they'd created an impossible situation. In 1929 they declared martial law and in 1930 they imposed strict limits on Jewish immigration, but that made the Zionists more angry, especially once the Nazis started persecuting Jews in Europe. The British hadn't found a solution by the time the Second World War broke out in 1939, but were wishing the Palestine mandate had gone to someone else.

Morocco bound

Some of the fiercest resistance to European colonial rule was in Morocco. The French and Spanish had long been angling to take the kingdom over, and in the fuss that followed the German Kaiser's interference in Morocco back in 1905 (see Chapter 3) the two countries agreed to divide the country between them. The Moroccans put up a fight, but by 1912 Morocco was officially divided into a French and a Spanish protectorate. End of story? Not quite.

The French and Spanish had reckoned without a Moroccan journalist-turned-judge called Abd al-Krim. Al-Krim organised a resistance army which in 1921 wiped out an entire Spanish garrison of 2,000 men at Mellila and declared a new 'Republic of the Rif'. The Spanish had to call on French help to fight al-Krim, and in 1926 a joint Franco–Spanish force under the French war hero Marshal Pétain finally forced al-Krim to surrender.

The Moroccans kept up their resistance to French and Spanish rule, though they didn't make any real progress until after France had itself been occupied by Germany in the Second World War. However, one Spanish officer posted to Morocco was able to make his mark: General Francisco Franco raised an army in Morocco that crossed over to Spain, set off civil war, and eventually put Franco in supreme power until his death in 1975.

Walk like an Egyptian

Egypt became a British protectorate (which means 'not strictly a colony but it is really') in 1914. The British had long wanted to control Egypt because it lay directly on the route to India; it became doubly important once the Suez Canal had opened in 1869. The canal was owned by a private company in which the British government was the major shareholder. On the other hand, the Egyptians didn't appreciate being ruled – er, protected – by the British. So in 1919, a delegation of Egyptian nationalists led by Saghlul Sa'd asked the British if, now they'd won the war, Egypt could have its independence, please? The British told them to get lost. Saghlul took that as a no, and the next few years were rather eventful ones:

- ✔ **1920:** Egyptians stage anti-British riots.
- ✔ **1921:** British send more troops to Egypt.
- ✔ **1922:** British grant Egypt sort-of independence as a constitutional monarchy, though the British still keep their troops there, still guard (and own) the Suez Canal, and can veto anything the Egyptian government does.

Saghlul set up his own political party called Wafd ('delegation') after the original delegation that went to see the British. Although Wafd remained anti-British, it quickly discovered that it hated King Faud of Egypt more: Wafd even turned to the British for help against the king. This meant the British could play their old divide-and-rule tactic to keep their hold on the country.

Get out of Africa!

The most active nationalist movements in Africa grew up among the white population of South Africa and Rhodesia. Like other nationalists they resented colonial rule, but their agenda was significantly different.

Britain and France both gained land in Africa after the First World War: France got Togo and Senegal, Britain got Tanganyika (modern-day Tanzania), and South Africa got South West Africa (modern-day Namibia). Both countries thought they had a 'mission' to rule the 'dark continent'. Moreover, getting Tanganyika fulfilled the British dream of owning land in an unbroken line from the north of Africa to the south.

Southern Africa was different from the rest of Africa as it had a substantial white settler population, some of whom were descended from European settlers who'd arrived in the seventeenth century. The two main groups were:

- **Afrikaaners:** Descended from the seventeenth-century Dutch and speaking a form of Dutch called Afrikaans. Afrikaaners loathed the black Africans and had no time for the wishy-washy liberal attitudes of the British. They'd given the British a bloody nose in the Anglo–Boer War (see Chapter 1) and don't you forget it.

- **British:** More recent settlers than the Afrikaaners, whom they didn't like much. Keen to maintain the link with Britain and uneasy with the tough racial laws the Afrikaaners were so keen to introduce.

British South Africa was divided into three main areas:

- **The Union of South Africa** set up in 1910 out of the old British colonies and Boer republics that had fought in the Anglo–Boer War. The prime minister was the strongly pro-British Afrikaaner Jan Christiaan Smuts. Smuts was opposed, however, by the growing Nationalist Party led by J. B. M. Hertzog.

- **Southern Rhodesia (modern-day Zimbabwe)** originally set up by the British South Africa Company, but in 1923 the British government took it over and set the area up as a self-governing dominion. Unlike South Africa, with its substantial white population, the whites in Southern Rhodesia made up barely 5 per cent of the population. They therefore tended to be in favour of anything that would keep the black population under strict control. In 1933 they elected the United Party, which set about doing just that.

- **Northern Rhodesia (modern-day Zambia).** In 1924 the British government took this region over from the British South Africa Company but ruled it from London as a crown colony, rather than allowing it to govern itself, like its southern neighbours. The reason is probably obvious: Not nearly enough white settlers lived there and Europeans simply could not conceive of Africans ruling themselves.

In 1924 Hertzog's Afrikaaner nationalists won the elections in South Africa and started bringing in laws to limit the freedom of movement of black South Africans and to cut South Africa's ties with Britain. The king wasn't allowed to grant titles to South Africans and they even removed his head from the stamps. The national anthem changed from 'God save the King' to 'God save South Africa' – from its black population, presumably.

Not all white South Africans were happy with this anti-British policy (though they didn't have any problems with the limits on black South Africans) and in 1933 Hertzog was forced to enter into a coalition with Smuts. Extreme Afrikaaner nationalists – and white supremacists – set up a new Nationalist Party under Dr D. F. Malan. The Nationalist Party sympathised strongly with the Nazis and thought South Africa fought on the wrong side when war came.

Malan's Nationalist Party was responsible for the apartheid system to keep the black population out of public life and to keep them under white control. Apartheid would not collapse until 1993. Chapter 19 tells you how.

Rage against the Raj

South Africa's racial policies (see previous section) also provided the starting point for the nationalist movement in India. Large numbers of Indians lived in South Africa (the British 'exported' vast numbers of Indians to work in different parts of their empire) where they were classified as 'coloured' rather than 'black', but they still had to carry special passes to allow them to move about the country or get a job. A London-trained Indian lawyer, with a taste for the finer things in life, led the protest movement that eventually lifted these restrictions: Mohandas K. Gandhi.

Don't hit back

Gandhi was a devout Hindu, but he had deep respect for other faiths: He incorporated elements of Islam and Christianity into his philosophy and prayers. After his success in South Africa he returned to India, where he found inspiration in the simple world of the Indian peasants. Gandhi believed it would be pointless for India to throw off British rule if it simply meant that rich Indians took the place of rich Britishers; India had to rediscover its soul and embrace a simpler, less sophisticated way of life. To show he meant what he said, Gandhi set up communes known as *ashrams* where people lived and worked on equal terms, rejecting the deeply-ingrained Indian concept of separate castes. Gandhi took up spinning cotton on a simple spinning wheel and insisted that his followers wear Indian homespun cloth, instead of cloth imported from Britain.

Gandhi developed a philosophy for fighting the British. Instead of pitched battles in the streets, he said Indians should stage protests and allow the

British to attack without hitting back: Doing so would show the British for the bullies they were. This philosophy of non-violence was known as *satyagraha*; to many of his followers, this idea seemed like madness. Would it work?

Massacre at Amritsar

One event changed everything in India. On 13 April 1919, with rioting sweeping through Punjab province (by no means did all Indians follow Gandhi's line of non-violence), British General Reginald Dyer decided to use shock tactics to restore order. He ordered his men to open fire on an unarmed crowd of Sikhs holding an illegal meeting in an enclosure in the Sikh holy city of Amritsar: 379 people were killed and some 1,200 wounded. This act certainly had a shock effect: Even moderate Indian nationalists were appalled and decided that the British would have to go. Some of the British supported what Dyer had done and even raised a fund to support him when he was forced to retire from the army; but the official inquiry into the massacre, and most public opinion in Britain, came down firmly against him.

The Amritsar massacre made it difficult to claim that British rule was for India's good. If that sort of violence was needed to keep order, what was the point of the British staying on? Following the massacre, several events occurred:

- **Government of India Act (1919):** sets up an elected parliament for India, though the British viceroy can still do more or less as he likes. Indians in the provinces are now allowed to control education and health but the British keep the big things, like justice and the police, in their own hands.

- **Gandhi calls on Indians to boycott foreign cloth (1921):** Doing so hits the British cotton industry significantly. Gandhi also tells Indians to have nothing to do with a tour of India by the Prince of Wales. This act hits British pride significantly.

- **Gandhi thrown into jail (1922):** Meanwhile riots are spreading, both against the British and between Muslims and Hindus.

- **British introduce a tax on salt (1923):** Indian nationalists launch a campaign of civil disobedience, refusing to obey British laws. Many of them join Gandhi in prison.

- **Gandhi released from prison and goes on hunger strike until the Muslim–Hindu violence stops (1924):** It does.

- **Gandhi launches a 240-mile march to the sea to gather salt in defiance of the British (1930):** This gathers enormous support and international publicity.

- **British hold talks with Indian leaders in London (1930):** Gandhi goes, and even meets the king. The talks fail.

> ✔ **Gandhi and other nationalist leaders arrested and thrown in jail (1932):** Again.
>
> ✔ **British hand provincial government in India over to Indians (1935):** Was this a crack in the wall? It certainly looked that way.

I say, can't you nationalist chaps let a man get some peace?

If unrest in Iraq, Syria, Egypt, Palestine, Morocco, Africa, and India wasn't enough, the Europeans were having to face nationalist revolts in almost every other corner of their empires, too:

✔ **Burma (1920):** Buddhist students lead opposition to British rule. Students stage anti-British strikes in 1920, 1936, and 1938. Burmese nationalists go on to help the Japanese during the Second World War.

✔ **Kenya (1920):** Established as a British colony. The Kikuyu people, especially the young, protest against European settlers taking over the fertile 'white highlands'.

✔ **Philippines (1924):** US President Coolidge dashes hopes of nationalists by saying the Philippines won't be getting their independence any time soon.

✔ **Java (1926):** Rebellion breaks out against Dutch rule.

✔ **Hong Kong (1927):** Anti-foreigner protests and a boycott of trade with Britain.

✔ **Indochina (1930–1):** Nationalist risings against French colonial rule, especially in Vietnam. The rebels are brutally suppressed.

✔ **Cyprus (1931):** Greek Cypriots riot in protest against British rule and in favour of *Enosis* – union with Greece. Turkish Cypriots don't join in.

✔ **Nigeria (1936):** Missionary-educated young people found the Nigerian Youth Movement to campaign for independence.

✔ **Jamaica (1938):** Nationalist leader Norman Manley founds the People's National Party to campaign against British rule.

Chapter 8

Depression and Aggression

. . . .

In This Chapter

▶ Finding out about the Depression and the New Deal in America

▶ Watching fascists and communists fighting in the Spanish Civil War

▶ Examining the causes of the Second World War

. . . .

*A*ccording to one writer, the 1930s was a 'low, deceitful decade'. Certainly, a good case can be made for calling it the most troubled and disturbing of the century. Worldwide economic collapse made the 1930s bad enough, but these years also saw a wave of aggression by expansionist dictatorships which the League of Nations and the Great Powers seemed powerless to halt. This chapter takes you through the folly, weakness, betrayal, and despair of the century's worst decade.

The World Stops Working

The Depression was the twentieth century's economic equivalent of the Black Death. It swept across whole continents, devastated people's lives, and no one seemed to know how to stop it.

The Depression began with the Wall Street Crash in October 1929 (refer to Chapter 6), which is hugely significant because during the twenties America had become the economic centre of the world. Not only was America producing and exporting more than any other country, but thanks to its overseas investments, American money virtually kept the industrialised world afloat. And since the Europeans ruled most of the rest of the world, American investments were essentially underwriting Europe's empires, too. So when American money suddenly dried up, every other country in the world was hit – hard.

American dream, American nightmare

America in the 1930s was only a generation removed from the last of the pioneers who'd gone out West, built their own log cabins, and tilled the soil without asking for help or handouts from anybody. 'Rugged individualism' they called this spirit; if you found yourself looking down the barrel of a shotgun held by a gentleman telling you to 'Git offa mah lee-and' you knew you'd met a rugged individualist.

Rugged individualism was fine and dandy for building character and making films but it left people without many resources for when things went badly wrong. (Of course, no one thought that things *could* go wrong in America: That was the whole point.) Moreover, the wealth was concentrated in a few of America's cities; most Americans were still very poor. They were about to get even poorer, because the Wall Street Crash and the trade collapse that followed it (see Chapter 6 for more on what had gone wrong on Wall Street) forced so many businesses to close that workers couldn't get work anywhere. By 1933 some 13 million Americans were unemployed. People found themselves in a bizarre, impossible situation: Out of work in the land of opportunity and with no prospect of ever having a job again.

Black Americans were in the worst position of all. Employers didn't take them on if they could avoid it, and got rid of them as soon as they could: 'Last to be hired, first to be fired', as people said at the time.

Better think again, Mr Hoover

US President Herbert Hoover had the job of dealing with the crisis. He'd made a name for himself for the efficient way he organised relief (soup kitchens, tents, medical help, and so on) for refugees in Europe after the war, so he should've been at home sorting out similar problems in America. But Hoover was convinced that the situation in America was different, and he refused to use the techniques of State relief that had worked so well in Europe ten years earlier.

Governments dealing with an economic crisis have a choice between two courses of action:

- ✔ *Plan A:* **Play it low-key and let the economy get on its own feet with as little government aid as possible.** Just doling out government money or providing temporary jobs on big construction schemes is no good because once people have spent the money and built their roads they'll be out of work and poor again. Key idea: Keep calm!

- ✔ *Plan B:* **Get active and use government money to spend your way out of the crisis.** Set up poor relief schemes to deal with the immediate problems and then set up big public works schemes to get people back to work and gradually stimulate private industry as well. Key idea: Spend! Spend! Spend!

All this, and Martians too!

Just how traumatic the Depression was is difficult for us to appreciate. Looking back, people said it was worse than the Second World War, because at least you knew the war would end one day; no one could see any reason why the Depression shouldn't go on forever. In 1922 the German philosopher Oswald Spengler wrote a best-seller called *The Decline of the West*, which argued that all civilisations go through a lifecycle of youthful vigour in the early years, followed by tiredness and a tendency to make mistakes in middle age, and ending in senility, slippers, and final collapse. He reckoned Western civilisation was at the rug-over-the-knees stage; the Depression suggested he could be right.

'The end of civilisation as we know it' became a popular theme in books and films in the 1930s, especially in the new science fiction genre. Real life added to everyone's fears: The decade saw the development of new bombing aircraft, which were soon in action destroying cities in China, Abyssinia, and Spain. The terrifying newsreel images of people running in terror from murderous bombing attacks all added to the general sense that Western civilisation was heading to hell in a handcart. In 1938 the young producer Orson Welles threw America into a panic with his scarily realistic radio version of H. G. Wells's *War of the Worlds* about a Martian invasion of America. We tend to laugh at the poor saps nowadays, but don't: If you'd gone through the Depression years, you wouldn't have found the idea that your whole world was going to end in a cataclysmic disaster all that far-fetched.

President Hoover preferred Plan A. He thought that Americans would have to find it within themselves to pull themselves out of the Depression, like those rugged individualists of the old West. Americans reduced to standing in line for soup on the streets of Manhattan got rather tired of hearing about those characters.

When unemployed people could no longer pay the rent and had to live in shanty towns made of scrap metal and old boxes, they called them 'Hoovervilles' in honour of the man they blamed for what had happened to them. President Hoover certainly never really understood why America couldn't just pull itself together, but he didn't just sit back and do nothing. Unfortunately, though, his ideas didn't work:

- ✔ **Voluntarism:** Hoover didn't want to interfere in industry, telling bosses what wages they should or shouldn't be paying their workforce. He thought he could rely on them to keep to a voluntary code of conduct. No dice: The bosses carried on paying their workers peanuts. Big business was badly out of favour in the 1930s and Hoover didn't do himself any favours by lining up with it.

✔ **Government help:** Hoover did set up a few public works schemes. He also cut taxes and provided people with easy credit from the Federal Reserves, so they could begin to get on their feet again. But he didn't like using government money in this way, so he kept his schemes to a small scale. Result: The benefit was small scale too.

✔ **Help for farmers:** Hoover tried to help farmers by buying up food and cotton at something more like a fair price, but that tactic just encouraged them to grow more and more, expecting the government to buy it all. But doing so wasn't Hoover's way, so the farmers ended up with huge surpluses, which then had to be destroyed. To most Americans the sight of milk churns being emptied down the drain or cotton plants being ploughed back into the ground just seemed crazy.

✔ **Cuts in State spending:** Hoover cut taxes but he also cut back on State and local spending. Result: Less help for the poor. Philadelphia actually ran out of money for poor relief entirely. Hoover thought poor relief should be left to private charities but they couldn't cope with the huge numbers who turned to them when the State soup kitchens and hostels closed. Result: More people begging on the street and more people in the Hoovervilles.

✔ **The Smoot–Hawley Tariff:** Not all historians agree on this point, but most see Hoover's support for the high tariffs on foreign goods brought in by Senators Smoot and Hawley in 1930 as one of the main reasons why the stock market crash became a worldwide depression. The idea was to protect American producers from foreign competition, but the other countries retaliated by bringing in their own tariffs. Result: International trade virtually collapsed and unemployment soared throughout the industrialised world.

Just when you thought it couldn't get any worse

Two developments made Hoover's last two years in office even worse. In 1931 America experienced a flood of bank closures. So many people rushed to withdraw their savings that many banks folded. Between 1929 and 1931 five thousand American banks closed and the government did nothing to help.

1932 saw a horrifying clash with America's ex-soldiers. The government had promised them a bonus in a few years' time, but they thought, 'Why not pay us now, when we need the cash?' So they marched to Washington and set up a makeshift camp at Anacostia Flats, within sight of the Capitol building, to demand their money. When they refused to move, Hoover sent the army in to clear them out. A brutal and shameful scene took place: American soldiers, under one Douglas MacArthur, attacked the defenceless men and set fire to their shelters. America seemed to have turned on itself and was eating its own heart out.

Sing your troubles away

You can get a good idea of the changing moods in 1930s America by listening to the songs that people hummed along to. In the darkest days of the Depression, Bing Crosby recorded a powerful and mournful ballad called *Buddy, can you spare a dime?*, which tells of a man who used to have a job and people's respect, lost everything, and is now reduced to begging. In 1932 Franklin Roosevelt unleashed his jaunty, optimistic campaign song on America: *Happy days are here again!* You get the message. At the end of the decade many Americans found their dreams of better times beautifully captured by Judy Garland's wistful ballad *Somewhere over the rainbow.*

America's New Deal

In the 1932 presidential election, Hoover was standing but everyone's eyes were on his Democratic opponent, Franklin D. Roosevelt. Roosevelt seemed to embody the idea that America could get on its feet again: He'd been struck down by polio and couldn't stand or walk without help, but he hadn't let his disability stop him pursuing his career. His can-do attitude won him the election.

Roosevelt had an unusually talented team around him, which included his energetic First Lady (and cousin) Eleanor. Eleanor became almost as big a star as her husband, travelling round America to support his programmes and appealing especially to America's women. Roosevelt consulted with a panel of economic experts who became known as the Brain Trust: He would use good ideas from anyone if doing so could help get America working again.

War on fear

Roosevelt used his inauguration address to declare that he was claiming the same emergency powers as he would exercise in time of war. He realised that the first thing he had to do was to convince the Americans that they *could* beat the Depression, so he crammed his first hundred days in office with a bewildering stream of announcements of new initiatives and programmes and agencies: At long last things were happening. 'The only thing we have to fear,' Roosevelt announced, 'is Fear itself' and he made them a promise: Americans deserved a better deal, a new deal, and he would give it to them.

One of Roosevelt's first acts was to end Prohibition. America breathed a sigh of relief and no doubt raised a few glasses too. Good start.

Next Roosevelt dealt with the banks. Using his emergency powers he closed all of them, stopped them getting rid of their gold and silver, and then brought in strict banking regulations. Only the safest ones were allowed to reopen.

Time for a chat

'I'd like to talk to you tonight about banks.' Roosevelt began the first of his famous 'fireside chat' radio talks with that line, explaining his policies in plain, ordinary language that everyone could understand. His talks made Roosevelt seem friendly and approachable. Thousands of Americans wrote letters to him telling him their problems and thanking him for all he was doing to solve them. He was able to use the radio to develop a strong personal bond with the American people – a technique that later presidents would copy.

Roosevelt decided that what the American economy needed was higher prices. That idea might sound odd – who likes price increases? – but producers need to sell at a reasonable price or they go bust, and if producers go bust, then shops have nothing to sell and workers have no wages to spend anyway. So higher prices were the key to getting the American economy going again. But how to get them? Roosevelt did a bit of manipulating the money supply and devaluing the dollar, but he couldn't duck the main event: To stop America's farmers and manufacturers from producing so much. Roosevelt needed to get America back to work by persuading America to work *less*. Tricky.

Down, down, down goes our production; up, up, up go our prices!

Roosevelt needed to cut production and raise prices both in industry and in agriculture. He soon found that different experts disagreed – loudly – about what he should do to limit industrial production, so he put them all together in a room, locked the door, and wouldn't let them out till they'd agreed on a plan. They did and Roosevelt put their ideas into one of his most important New Deal laws: The *National Industrial Recovery Act* (*NIRA*). The NIRA set up two new agencies:

- **The Public Works Administration (PWA):** Its brief: Build big. It provided work for thousands of construction workers, building schools, hospitals, roads, subways, warships – anything as long as it was big and needed a lot of workers.

- **The National Recovery Administration (NRA):** Its brief: Get American industry back to work. The NRA drew up a series of codes laying down rules about how much each firm would agree to produce and how much the workers would be paid. The codes also said that workers had the right to join a union. If you kept to your code, you got the big NRA blue eagle badge to display on your wall. The badge was that season's absolute must-have.

The NRA soon hit problems. The bosses didn't like government telling them how much to pay their workers and they resented having to work with the unions. Big firms started to ignore the NRA codes. In 1934 many workers

came out on strike and some of the strike meetings were broken up
by troops.

The NRA didn't just annoy big business. Some liberals and democrats were
worried that Roosevelt was setting up a *centrally planned economy* resem-
bling those Mussolini and Stalin had introduced in Europe (see Chapters 4
and 5 to find out about the European examples). They thought that, for all his
popularity and good intentions, Roosevelt was beginning to turn America into
a dictatorship. And shoppers complained about having to pay higher prices.
You can't please some people.

In 1935 the Supreme Court looked into the NIRA and declared the whole act
unconstitutional. The Court said that it was against the constitution for the
federal government to start interfering in how a business conducts itself and
treats its workers. This wasn't the only time the Supreme Court intervened
to disrupt the New Deal (see the section 'New Deal, new danger' below).
Afterwards, Congress passed the *Wagner Act*, named after Senator Robert
Wagner who introduced it, which brought in strong federal government
protection for labour unions.

Trouble on the land

America's farmers were in a desperate plight. As prices Depressioned, many
of them could not pay their rents and their farms were repossessed. Farmers
banded together to fight back: They even attacked the courtrooms where
cases were being heard and one judge was dragged out and nearly lynched.

Roosevelt decided that America's farmers need three changes:

- ✔ **Higher prices for the goods they produced:** The *Agricultural Adjustment
  Agency (AAA)* provided compensation for farmers who agreed to cut
  down on their own production and farming incomes went up significantly. However, the idea also meant destroying cotton plantations and
  on one occasion slaughtering thousands of young pigs to cut down on
  agricultural production.

- ✔ **To buy their own farms:** Doing so would stop the repossessions, but the
  farmers would need help raising the money. The government came up
  with a scheme to lend them money at easy rates of interest. To repay it,
  though, they would need to up their income, along the lines laid down
  by the AAA.

- ✔ **To improve land cultivation:** Many farmers had overworked their land
  disastrously, mainly to grow grain during the war. They needed help and
  advice on how to farm effectively without taking all the goodness out
  of the soil.

One of the most successful land reclamation schemes was in the badly
eroded lands of the Tennessee Valley. The Tennessee Valley Authority (TVA –
Roosevelt loved initials!) helped farmers replant their lands and it also
oversaw the construction of a huge network of hydroelectric dams.

Heat and dust

Towards the end of the 1930s disaster hit the farmers of the Midwest. The rains failed, which produced a drought. Worse than that, though, the topsoil turned to dust and high winds blew enormous dust clouds over a vast area of some 25,000 square miles. This area became known as the Dust Bowl. Houses were buried in dust and the people had to pack up and get out. Long lines of refugees called Okies (a lot of them came from Oklahoma) headed west for the sunny lands of California, but California didn't prove very welcoming. John Steinbeck's novel *The Grapes of Wrath* provides a very good picture of these events.

The Dust Bowl added to the misery of the Depression years for America's farmers, but important lessons were learnt. They planted long lines of trees to break the high winds and dug huge reservoirs to provide more moisture in the air. Above all, they learned to give the land time to rest after it had been ploughed and harvested. The Midwest still suffers occasional droughts, but it hasn't had another Dust Bowl.

And still Roosevelt hadn't finished:

- ✔ **Civilian Conservation Corps (CCC):** Forest conservation for young men. You earn a wage and get to work outdoors: What more do you want?

- ✔ **Work for artists, actors, and writers:** The Works Progress Administration (WPA) commissioned work from a wide range of professions, especially in writing and the arts. Even from historians, I'm glad to say.

- ✔ **Strict regulation of the stock market:** Since that was where the trouble had all started.

- ✔ **Social Security:** At long last America got a proper system to provide for the poor, the sick, and the unemployed. This was one of the most important of all the acts of the New Deal.

New Deal, new danger

Not everyone liked the New Deal by any means. The Republicans didn't approve of the government effectively trying to spend its way out of the Depression. Many of them objected to the way Roosevelt was taking more and more power into his own hands, especially when he won the 1936 election as well.

One of Roosevelt's bitterest critics was a fiery Catholic priest called Father Coughlin, the 'Radio Priest'. Coughlin was a fanatical admirer of fascist regimes in Europe; he denounced Roosevelt as a communist. Many people from Roosevelt's own aristocratic background saw Roosevelt as a traitor who'd turned against his own class.

Roosevelt's most important source of opposition, however, was the Supreme Court. Roosevelt's opponents challenged the legality of some of the New Deal laws and the Supreme Court kept ruling against the president. Roosevelt was furious: He said the Court was made up of a lot of conservative old Republican fuddy-duddies. He decided to hit back.

Roosevelt introduced a law to force Supreme Court judges aged over 70 who had served for ten years or more to retire. This move would virtually empty the court and he could appoint some democrat justices. Bad move. 'Aha!' said all his opponents, 'he's trying to silence the Supreme Court and subvert the Constitution. Told you so.' Even Democrats thought he'd gone too far this time. Congress defeated his bill. But maybe the Court had taken his point: It stopped ruling against him and Roosevelt was able to bring in the rest of the New Deal in peace and quiet. And then all the old judges died anyway, so he could appoint some democrats after all.

The worldwide Depression

The economic collapse in America (see the previous sections) had an immediate impact on the rest of the world. The Europeans had borrowed nearly $3,000 million from the USA by 1929 on top of the money America had lent during the war. When the Americans started calling in their loans, European economies collapsed.

Sorry – there's no demand for it

As the Americans brought in high tariffs and world trade virtually ceased (see the earlier section 'Better think again, Mr Hoover' to find out why this happened), European countries tried to protect their own producers by bringing in tariffs and providing government subsidies. Doing so was no good: Subsidy or no subsidy, empty order books meant no work. By 1933 unemployment levels in Europe were at frightening levels: Over 20 per cent in Britain and Belgium, and nearly a third of the workforce in Norway and Denmark. However, the worst figures by far (a whopping 44 per cent) were in Germany.

The Europeans were very conscious that high unemployment could cause serious social trouble. They feared that the unemployed would turn to extremist political groups. Experience in Germany suggested that they were right.

Just like in America, the problem was that prices were too low. Low prices meant that producers couldn't afford to stay in business, so their workers were laid off, and with no wages in their pockets people couldn't afford to buy consumer goods. That situation meant goods had to come down in price if they were to sell at all, which in turn meant that producers lost money – and so on. A vicious circle operated.

Sorry, guys: You're in this too

The collapse of manufacturing industries in Europe and America had huge knock-on effects.

- ✔ **Chile:** The country's copper and nitrates mines had to close, throwing thousands out of work.

- ✔ **Malaya:** No one buying cars = no need for tyres = collapse of Malaya's rubber industry, devastating the entire country.

- ✔ **Japan:** Ninety per cent of its silk exports ended up as stockings for American women. When Americans stopped spending on luxuries, the Japanese silk industry collapsed, throwing thousands of people out of work.

- ✔ **China:** The country depended heavily on its exports of iron ore and coal. But with manufacturing closing down around the world, China's export trade dried up.

Only a few staple commodities needed to fall in price for whole countries to be devastated. When wheat, tea, and rice prices all Depressioned, South America and Asia were hit, as well as Australia, New Zealand, Canada, and Egypt. Farmers tried desperately to make a living by growing more and more crops, but this tactic just pushed prices down even further. In some parts of the world, farmers gave up trying to sell in the market place altogether and just went back to subsistence farming. Brazilian farmers used their coffee crops for fuel. But industrial workers didn't have that option. Many of them went hungry and staged special hunger marches to make the world sit up and listen. Not many did.

On the dole

The Depression forced many countries to review their systems of social security – or, in most cases, to start thinking it might be a good idea to have one. The most advanced system of State benefits for the elderly or the unemployed had been set up in Britain before the First World War, but even that system struggled to keep up with the demands of the Slump. People had always thought that if you were out of work it was somehow your fault – the unemployed were often referred to as 'the Idle', which tells you a lot about how they were regarded – but the Depression showed that disaster could happen to anyone, no matter how hard-working or thrifty they might be. The Scandinavian countries in particular learned from the terrible years of unemployment to set up comprehensive systems of State benefits that, by the 1970s, had become the model for the rest of the world to follow.

Going to extremes

The economic crisis was almost inevitably going to lead to extremist politics. Some people thought the crisis showed that the communists were right: Capitalism was collapsing around them. Others preferred the fascist way out. (You can find out more about the appeal of communism in Chapter 4 and about fascism in Chapter 5.)

Tired of the Depression? Try a Soviet planned economy instead!

The Soviet Union was the one country that seemed to escape the Depression. That situation was partly because it was cut out of the world's trading and financial networks, but mainly because, while the rest of the world was out of work, the Russians were busy building up their own industry and agriculture through Stalin's centrally-controlled Five-Year Plans (explained in Chapter 4). Many Western VIPs visited the Soviet Union to see what was happening, and the sight of thousands of smiling Russians building dams and factories and getting their entries in for the Tractor of the Year competition proved too much for some of them. 'I have seen the Future!' exclaimed the American journalist Lincoln Steffens 'and it works!'

What these visitors didn't see (and usually didn't want to see) was the cruelty and corruption behind the Plans. Managers were given impossible quotas to fulfil and had to bribe their way out if they weren't to be shot for failing to meet their targets. Huge areas of Russia were devastated by famine, because Stalin's secret police had confiscated all the food. And some of the biggest prestige projects of the Five-Year Plans, like Moscow's shiny new underground system, had been built by slave labour from Soviet prison camps.

In Germany, the Nazis were able to blame the Depression on the hated Treaty of Versailles (outlined in Chapter 3). If it hadn't been for the reparations payments the treaty imposed, Germany wouldn't have needed so much American investment in the first place. The Treaty even created a huge banking crisis in 1931. The Austrians wanted a customs union with Germany, but the French, who were virtually running the Austrian economy, said it went against the Treaty of Versailles and forbade it. To teach the Austrians a lesson, the French stood by when the main Austrian bank, the Credit Anstalt, collapsed. Bad move. This action sparked a run on the banks across the continent, which brought the whole of Europe's financial system crashing down.

Hitler had a simple solution to Germany's unemployment crisis: Massive rearmament.

We're on the Road to Warfare

After the carnage of the Great War people in all countries were determined that never again should the world embark on such a destructive course of events. They trusted in the League of Nations to maintain world peace through *collective security*. This collective security meant that all countries would act together to stop any aggressor; no one would dare defy the united wishes of the rest of the world, would they? Yup, I'm afraid they would.

Tomorrow . . . the world!

Three countries had plans to expand at the expense of their neighbours:

- ✔ **Italy:** Mussolini had visions of himself as a new Roman emperor. He taught Italians to call the Mediterranean 'Mare nostrum' (= 'Our sea – Keep out!'). He also wanted to avenge Italy's humiliating defeat in Abyssinia in 1896 and found a new Italian empire in Africa.

- ✔ **Japan:** The Japanese felt hemmed in on their crowded islands and wanted to expand in order to get hold of vital raw materials such as coal, iron ore, and oil. They had their eyes on their vast, vulnerable neighbour – China.

- ✔ **Germany:** Hitler had laid out his vision for Germany's future in his book *Mein Kampf*. He thought Germany needed 'living space' in Russia and the east. He wanted to bring all the ethnic Germans living in other countries, like Austria, France, Poland, and Czechoslovakia, into Germany (not by getting them to emigrate; by taking their countries over), and he wanted to tear up the restrictions imposed on Germany by the Treaty of Versailles. Apart from those issues, he often pointed out, he had no further territorial demands in Europe.

Who could stop these aggressive nations from attacking their neighbours? These were the possibilities:

- ✔ **The USA:** The States was too busy with the New Deal (see the earlier section) to start getting involved in international disputes and it wasn't in the League of Nations anyway. Americans were *isolationist* and proud of it.

- ✔ **The USSR:** Stalin had turned his back on spreading world revolution and declared it was time to build 'socialism in one country' (see Chapter 4 to see how he set about doing it). In any case, Stalin was busy having thousands of Russians, including top Party officials and all the leaders of the Red Army, shot as traitors. The USSR couldn't have helped much even if other countries had asked it to, and, since Stalin wasn't trusted anyway, until 1939 no one did.

- ✔ **The League of Nations:** The League was meant to maintain peace, but it had some serious weaknesses. First, it needed every member state to agree before it could take any steps. Second, it could only impose economic sanctions on any country that broke its rules. Thirdly, it could only impose sanctions on a state that was a member; so, if a state didn't like the League's decision, all it had to do was leave. Easy!

- ✔ **Britain and France:** These two powerful countries were the major powers within the League and in theory gave it the power it needed to enforce its will. In practice, however, the French didn't want to take action without Britain, and the British didn't want to take military action. Result: No action at all.

It's raining death

People around the world in the 1930s were terrified that the next war would take the form of a sudden, terrifying attack from the air. By the 1930s bombing aircraft had got bigger and more powerful than anyone had imagined; 'The bomber will always get through' declared British Prime Minister Stanley Baldwin, gloomily. The film of H. G. Wells's *Things to Come* showed a sky full of evil-looking bombers wiping out London in a single, mass attack. Mussolini liked that idea: He boasted that he would create an air force so huge that it would blot out the sun.

During the Second World War people in Europe learned to run to the shelters when the air raid sirens sounded and to carry their gas masks in case the enemy dropped gas bombs. The Italians had used gas bombs in Abyssinia. The Germans invented the *Stuka* dive bomber, which could dive straight down at terrifying speed with a screaming siren attached to its motor to drive the people on the ground mad with fear. With everyone so scared of megadeath from the skies, you can easily see why so many people were relieved when the big crises of the 1930s resolved themselves without starting a war, even if it meant handing a bit more territory over to the Germans. Many people thought ceding territory was a price worth paying for peace.

The French were still smarting from the humiliation they'd suffered when they'd invaded the Ruhr to enforce reparations payments on Germany in 1923 and found that no one supported them (see Chapter 5 for details). Rather than go through that experience again, they built a line of defensive fortresses known as the *Maginot Line* along their border with Germany and sat behind it, waiting on events.

You say Manchuria and I say Manchukuo

A good case can be made for saying that the Second World War started when the Japanese invaded the autonomous Chinese province of Manchuria in 1931. The Japanese had long had their eyes on Manchuria, but they needed an excuse before they could launch an invasion. In 1931 they had an idea. Japan ran the main railway through Manchuria, so in September 1931 Japanese agents blew it up at the junction at Mukden and then said the Chinese did it! 'Blow up our railway, would you?' said the Japanese government to an understandably nonplussed Chinese government, and immediately sent troops into Manchuria to, er, restore order. They restored order so well that they took the province over, renamed it Manchukuo (it sounded more Japanese), set up a puppet government under the ex-emperor of China, Pu-Yi, and set about stripping 'Manchukuo' of its resources and shipping it all back to Japan.

As a fully paid-up member, China appealed to the League for help. Result:

- ✔ League of Nations sends Lord Lytton, an elderly British statesman, off to Manchuria to report back on what's going on.
- ✔ Lord Lytton reports that the situation's all rather confusing. It was very naughty of the Japanese to invade, but as ownership of Manchuria seems unclear, perhaps they should set it up as a separate state and sort it all out over a nice cup of tea.
- ✔ Japan leaves the League.

That was easy: Now let's get the rest

Getting hold of Manchuria had proved so easy that in 1937 the Japanese came back for more. They staged another of their 'They attacked my railway!' incidents, this time at the Marco Polo Bridge in Beijing, and then launched a full-scale invasion of China itself. They attacked Shanghai and Nankin with terrifying force; many historians allege that Japanese troops in Nankin carried out a programme of mass rape. But although the Japanese quickly seized control of the towns, they couldn't control the Chinese countryside. The Chinese nationalists and communists (see Chapters 4 and 5 to find out more about them) sank their differences and joined together in a highly effective guerrilla war of resistance. The Japanese found themselves getting bogged down fighting an insurgency they just couldn't defeat.

Mussolini muscles in

Mussolini liked to present an image of himself as the heir to the heroes of Italian history, completing and improving on their achievements. In 1929 he completed the unification of Italy by reaching a deal with the pope by which the Vatican finally accepted the Italian state in return for keeping its own independence. Next he wanted to complete the work of the men who'd built Italy's empire in Africa. The Italians had conquered Tripoli and part of Somaliland, but Mussolini had his eyes on Abyssinia.

Abyssinia in the 1930s was a decidedly odd mixture of the modern and the medieval. It was an ancient Christian kingdom ruled by an emperor and a class of feudal lords known as *Ras*. Abyssinian soldiers wore chain mail and carried swords and shields, like medieval knights, but they had still defeated the Italians at the Battle of Adowa in 1896. In 1930 Ras Tafari was crowned Emperor Haile Selassie I (his name meant 'Power of the Trinity' but he was also known as 'The Lion of Judah'). Haile Selassie began the long process of dragging Abyssinia into the twentieth century, abolishing slavery, and, sensible chap, buying a few modern weapons.

Excuse me, do you know you're trespassing – aagh!

In 1935 Italian troops marched sixty miles into Abyssinian territory and had a shoot-out at the Wal-Wal oasis in the Ogaden desert with a detachment of Abyssinian troops. True to form, the Italians tried to claim that the event had happened inside their territory, even though their own maps proved them wrong. Whatever: Mussolini declared himself shocked – *shocked* – at this sneak Abyssinian attack and ordered a full-scale invasion.

With all their modern weaponry the Italians should have been able to deal with Abyssinia in the time it took to cook the pasta, but in fact six months passed before the Italian leader Marshal Badoglio led his men into Addis Ababa. The Italians declared they were bringing Western civilisation to the country, and just to prove it, they sprayed the capital with poison gas.

World reaction

The importance of the Abyssinian war wasn't so much about who would win, but how the rest of the world reacted. The course of events:

- **Help yourself, Duce!** The French foreign minister, Pierre Laval, is quite happy for Mussolini to take as much of Abyssinia as he wants. The British foreign secretary, Sir Samuel Hoare, agrees with him. The *Hoare–Laval Pact* was a disgraceful secret deal to carve Abyssinia up without even telling the emperor. The pact created a huge stink when it was leaked and both men were forced to resign.

- **Haile Selassie appeals to the League of Nations:** He makes a very dignified appeal, while the Italian delegates jeer and whistle at him.

- **The League imposes special sanctions on Italy:** They are special because they don't hurt. The British and French still think Mussolini will help them against Hitler, so they don't want to alienate him. So they impose sanctions on lots of things that don't matter but don't stop him importing oil or using the Suez Canal, which do matter.

- **Italy leaves the League and immediately cosies up to Hitler:** And after all that *trouble*.

Winning against Abyssinia's elite cavalry and rapid reaction spear carriers gave Mussolini the notion that he was some sort of military genius. He was badly mistaken in this impression.

Civil war in Spain

Spain in the 1930s was deeply divided between right and left, with not much room for anyone in the middle. The government was a left-wing 'Popular Front' coalition ranging from liberal types who thought something really ought to be done for the poor through to out-and-out anarchists. In 1936

General Francisco Franco crossed over to Spain from Morocco with his men and declared war on the government. Some of the Spanish regions promptly took the opportunity to declare themselves independent. The country fell apart in savage civil war.

For fascists and communists around the world, the Spanish Civil War was the chance they'd been waiting for to take a crack at their enemies. Men and women from all backgrounds travelled to Spain to join in the fighting on one side or the other. Stalin sent money; Hitler and Mussolini sent men. The German Condor legion used the war to perfect its bombing techniques; its most notorious deed was an attack on the crowded Basque market town of Guernica. The Popular Front fell apart and the different groups within it started fighting each other; in 1939 Franco and his men finally captured the last strongholds at Toledo, Barcelona, and Madrid and took control.

Many Spanish republicans fled to France, where the French interned them in concentration camps. In 1940 they handed them over to the Germans, who were delighted to meet their old enemies again and promptly sent them on to their own concentration camps.

Springtime for Hitler

In the 1930s everything in Hitler's foreign policy plans seemed to go right. As soon as he was in power he pulled Germany out of the League of Nations. He did have a go at taking over Austria in 1934 but Mussolini, who at that stage controlled Austria and was decidedly unimpressed with Hitler, rushed troops to the border and stopped him. Hitler went back to rearming in secret. The Treaty of Versailles (see Chapter 3) put a cap on the size of the German army and banned the German air force, which is why the German police and fire services suddenly got thousands of new recruits all learning how to march and carry out a flanking manoeuvre and hundreds of young men enrolled in flying clubs. Hitler finally came clean about Germany's rearmament in 1936.

Hitler also set his plans into operation in 1936:

- **Hitler sends troops to the Rhineland:** This action is in direct defiance of the Treaty of Versailles. Will the French throw him out? Not without British backing they won't, and the British say he's only going into his own back yard, bless him. Large 'Phew!' heard in Berlin.

- **Germany and Italy sign the Rome–Berlin Axis Pact:** Not a military alliance yet but Mussolini has finally come out as a Hitler fan.

- **Germany and Japan sign the Anticomintern Pact:** No one was exactly surprised to learn that they were opposed to the Comintern (the Communist International, a Moscow-based body to spread communist revolution), but the pact was also a military commitment to resist the spread of communism. Italy joined the following year.

In 1938, Hitler did a couple of other interesting things:

- ✔ **The *Anschluss* whereby Germany takes over Austria:** Britain sighs 'Well, what can we do?' and the French follow this firm British lead. And do nothing.

- ✔ **Hitler demands the German 'Sudetenland' area of Czechoslovakia:** The British and French decide that this time they must do *something*. They must at least talk to Hitler before giving in.

To appease or not to appease? That is the question

The British and French policy of appeasement can seem very difficult to understand today. Latching onto Winston Churchill's warnings about German rearmament and tearing your hair out and saying 'Why couldn't they *see*?' is easy from this distance. Well, keep your hair in: Appeasement wasn't as stupid, or even as dishonourable, as it might sound. Consider the following issues:

- ✔ France was so deeply divided between right-wing and left-wing that the French feared that if they went to war with Germany, the country would fall into civil war like Spain. So the French let the British do the talking.

- ✔ The British did not have anything like enough men to fight a full-scale war with Germany. In any case, the British were more directly concerned about the Italian threat in the Mediterranean and the Japanese threat to their colonies in the Far East.

- ✔ Like it or not, Hitler's demands did not sound unreasonable to anyone who thought the Treaty of Versailles had been too harsh – which nearly everyone in Britain did.

- ✔ Rearming would take time, especially since public opinion in Britain and France was strongly against it.

In the light of these considerations, the only practical course to follow was to keep Hitler talking and avoid war for as long as possible, even if it meant handing over large areas of (other people's) land. I'm not saying appeasement was right (the British and French badly misjudged Hitler's personality and objectives, and abandoning allies to save your own skin is never a great way to win friends). The British and French could have tried manoeuvring or bluffing rather than simply appeasing Hitler, but it can't be denied that appeasement seemed to many people at the time the only *realistic* policy.

So, in September 1938, British Prime Minister Neville Chamberlain met Hitler to discuss how best to hand over the Sudetenland and whether he'd like it gift wrapped. A war crisis ensued when Hitler demanded the whole area immediately, before they'd worked out the borders or what to do about the non-Germans living there or sent the invites out for the invasion party or *anything*. Chamberlain met with Hitler, Mussolini, and Daladier, the French prime minister, at Munich and they agreed on exactly how much Czech territory to hand over to Germany. The Czech prime minister wasn't even invited.

When enough isn't enough

The British and French had intended that appeasement would conciliate and deter Hitler. It did neither.

- ✔ **November 1938:** 'Kristallnacht', the 'night of broken glass': Nazis launch a night of attacks on Germany's Jewish community, smashing shop windows, rounding Jews up for concentration camps, or just murdering them. This event makes leaders more wary of making any more concessions to Hitler.

- ✔ **January 1939:** Germans take over the rest of Czechoslovakia. No special conference this time: They just march in. Public mood in Britain and France turns away from pacifism and towards war.

- ✔ **August 1939:** Germany starts demanding land from Poland. British and French pledge to support the Poles; though, looking at a map, it's hard to see how. Perhaps we ought to have a word with the Russians, they say. Too late.

- ✔ **23 August 1939:** Nazi Germany and the Soviet Union sign the *Nazi–Soviet Pact*, swearing eternal friendship and pledging to carve up Poland between them. The Devil rings up to say it's very chilly in hell for the time of year.

All these events led up to 1 September 1939, when the Germans invaded Poland (like the Japanese in China and the Italians in Abyssinia – see the sections earlier in this chapter – the Germans attacked one of their own border posts and then claimed the Poles had attacked *them*). The British and French told the Germans to clear out of Poland, or else. On 3 September Britain and France declared war on Germany. The thirties were over; the Second World War had begun.

Chapter 9

The War of the World

The Second World War was a global disaster. No war in history has killed so many people in so many different parts of the world. And not just soldiers: Civilians died in their millions, by bombing and by systematic mass murder. When the war began, armies were still sending men into battle on horseback; when it ended, men were sent out to drop the atomic bomb. The Second World War was the central, defining event of the twentieth century. The world still hasn't fully recovered.

A New Strategy: Blitzkrieg

During the long years of the Depression (see Chapter 8) military strategists had been reflecting on the Great War. They decided that the next conflict was to be a war of *movement* and the key was to have plenty of tanks and aircraft. A French officer, one Charles de Gaulle, wrote a book about How to Make Best Use of Your Tank but it was a German general, Heinz Guderian, who wrote the book *Achtung! Panzer!* (Attention! Tank!), which outlined a whole new approach to warfare: 'Lightning war' – *Blitzkrieg*.

Blitzkrieg was based on the idea of winning victory very fast. Here's how:

1. **Attack without warning:** Don't tell your enemy you're coming by declaring war: That approach is, like, *sooo* last century.

2. **Deploy overwhelming force:** Throw in everything you've got. Shock and awe, my friends, shock and awe.

3. **Send in the dive-bombers:** Bomb your enemy's airfields while their planes are still lined up neatly outside their hangars. Don't let a single enemy plane take off, not even a paper one. Now you control the skies.

4. **Dive bomb the columns of refugees:** Doing so spreads panic and clogs up the roads, so your enemy can't get troops forward. Forget ethics: This is *total* war.

5. **Send in the tanks:** Lots of them, moving very fast. They'll need to be light and able to swamp even the heaviest enemy tanks.

6. **Send in the infantry:** The enemy will be too dazed from the planes and tanks to put up much of a fight, so you won't have any trouble.

7. **Grab your enemy's capital:** Great for morale. Mission accomplished. And make sure you stage a *big* victory parade.

The German High Command liked Guderian's ideas and decided to put them into action. Starting with Poland.

Whirlwind War

The Second World War had two main phases. From 1939 to 1942 everything moved bewilderingly fast: Whole countries fell to the Germans and Japanese, sometimes in a matter of days. From 1942 until 1945 events moved at a much more agonising pace, as the Allies gradually regained the initiative and pushed their enemies back.

Germany, Italy, Japan and their allies, Bulgaria, Romania, Hungary, and Finland are usually referred to as the 'Axis' powers, because of the 1936 'Axis Pact' between Germany and Italy. Their opponents, Britain and its commonwealth, France, the USSR, and the US are usually known simply as 'the Allies'.

Poland pole-axed

The German invasion of Poland followed Guderian's book (see preceding section) to the letter: The German Air Force (*Luftwaffe*) destroyed the Polish Air Force while it was still on the ground, Poland's elite cavalry, who could do a lot of damage to infantry, found themselves charging against tanks, and Poland's roads were soon full of terrified, dive-bombed refugees. Warsaw was the only fly in Germany's ointment, which proved tougher than the Germans had anticipated. But then the Russians invaded Poland from the east, as per the terms of the Nazi–Soviet Pact (see Chapter 8 for more on this) and the Poles had to surrender.

Germany and the USSR annexed huge areas of Poland. The country was reduced to a rump in the centre called the General Government and ruled by a singularly unsavoury Nazi, Hans Frank. Thousands of Poles were forced to work in German labour camps. Even more sinister: Frank forced Poland's huge Jewish community into small, cramped ghettos in each city. They soon found out why.

The Nazis believed in a strict hierarchy of races, with Aryans like themselves at the top and Slavs like the Russians and Poles at the bottom. In consequence the Germans had no qualms about treating Poles as slaves – or murdering them.

Even the Nazis were shocked when in 1943 they dug up the corpses of thousands of Polish officers in Katyn forest, in what had been the Soviet zone of Poland. The Russians had rounded the men up and shot them: Stalin wanted to eliminate anyone who might resist a Soviet takeover of the country after the war. The Russians tried to blame the Germans until 1990, when Mikhail Gorbachev's government finally acknowledged the Russians' crime.

War in the west

After Poland fell to the Germans (see previous section) Britain and France sat around waiting for something to happen. Someone called this period a 'phony war'; someone else called it *Sitzkrieg*. Whatever: This waiting period ended suddenly in April 1940, when the Germans unleashed Blitzkrieg in Norway and Denmark. They were after Scandinavia's important mineral reserves but Hitler was also angry because the Norwegians had allowed a British ship into their waters, where it raided the German ship *Altmark* and rescued some 300 British prisoners. The French and British rushed troops to Norway and recaptured the town of Narvik, before they were forced to withdraw. Beaten.

The disaster in Norway brought down the British government. Neville Chamberlain resigned and Winston Churchill became prime minister. The very next day the Germans invaded Belgium and Holland. German bombers launched a devastating raid on the Dutch port of Rotterdam. Then German *panzers* (tanks) tore through the Ardennes forest into France itself.

Abandon front!

The German attack on France caught the French and British by surprise. They were busy guarding the Belgian frontier, so the Germans came up behind them and cut them off.

The French had built a formidable defence system, the Maginot Line, but ran out of money before they covered the Ardennes. 'Never mind,' they consoled themselves, 'tanks can't get through a forest.' Which was odd, since the Ardennes had plenty of pretty forest roads, just right for a drive in the country. Or for German tanks.

In response to the German assault, the French appointed a new commander, Marshal Philippe Pétain, who'd stopped the Germans in the First World War, but even he couldn't stop them this time. The British and most of the French army were trapped in the port of Dunkirk. The Royal Navy organised a rescue, using hundreds of ships and small craft, even pleasure boats, to get the men off the beaches and back to England. Meanwhile the Germans marched into Paris and France surrendered. France had fallen in a matter of weeks.

Game over? No chance!

Once France had fallen, everyone assumed the war was over. The British didn't have anything left to fight with and stopping a Blitzkrieg with your bare hands was hardly possible. But to everyone's amazement, Winston Churchill announced that the war was still on. 'We shall fight on the beaches,' he growled, 'and in the hills. We shall *never* surrender.' Brave words, but many people, including members of his own Cabinet, thought Churchill had gone mad. What was Britain going to fight *with*?

Churchill knew that Britain wasn't as weak or as alone as people thought:

- **Britain still controlled the sea:** The Royal Navy could sink any German invasion fleet. Much of the German navy had been sunk in the Norwegian campaign.

- **Britain had a sophisticated network of air defences:** The British used radar to detect incoming planes and direct the Royal Air Force's fast, effective fighter planes to intercept them.

- **Britain's empire and commonwealth were at war with Germany, too:** Large numbers of Canadian troops were stationed in Britain, and many pilots from commonwealth countries, as well as from European countries the Germans had occupied, were in the RAF. Churchill had plans to carry the war on from Canada if Britain did fall to the Germans.

Battle over Britain

The Germans had expected a nice post-conquest holiday; now they had to cobble together an invasion plan for Britain using small boats and barges: *Operation Sealion*. Just one problem: What if the RAF bombed them? 'Leave that to me,' said Hermann Goering, head of the German *Luftwaffe*, 'I'll wipe out the RAF while they're on the ground drinking their tea.' Radar, the British early warning system, got the RAF into the air in time and told them where to find the enemy, but the Germans bombed the RAF airfields so the planes had nowhere to land. Churchill called this campaign the 'Battle of Britain' and the RAF came very close to losing it. Then the Germans made their big mistake. They stopped attacking airfields and started bombing London: The *Blitz*.

The Blitz started when a German bomber got lost and bombed London by mistake, so the RAF bombed Berlin back. Hitler was so incensed, he told Goering to bomb London back to the stone age. The Blitz was terrifying: It destroyed thousands of homes and factories, but also gave the RAF time to recover. In September 1940 the RAF finally defeated the Luftwaffe in a massive showdown battle over the south of England. The Germans lost so many planes that Hitler filed Operation Sealion in the bin. 'So I can't invade Britain,' he thought, 'but the British can't harm me either. Time to start planning the real business: Invading Russia.' *Bad* mistake.

The Battle of the Atlantic

If you can't break in, starve them out. Germany tried this tactic with Britain after Hitler cancelled plans to invade it (see previous section). He couldn't use Germany's battleships: The British cornered the *Graf Spee* in Montevideo and the captain had to scuttle her; the *Bismarck* was sunk at sea after an epic chase, and the *Tirpitz* was sunk at anchor in a Norwegian fjord by British midget submarines. But Germany's huge fleet of U boats (*unterseeboot* – underseaboat, meaning submarine) could sink the merchant ships Britain depended on for food and supplies.

The British tried sailing in protected convoys, but the U boats still sank hundreds of them. US President Roosevelt did what he could to help Britain, even though the United States was neutral. Under his *lend-lease* scheme, America 'lent' Britain pretty much anything she needed to carry on the fight (even though Roosevelt knew the British wouldn't be able to pay for the goods), which meant even more ships crossing the Atlantic for the U boats to hunt down. Churchill called this life-or-death struggle at sea 'the Battle of the Atlantic': The prospect of losing it was truly scary.

Eventually the Allies developed long-range aircraft which could detect the U boats, even when they were far out at sea, and attack them. The Germans developed the *schnorkel*, which enabled a U boat to stay under water for long periods so that aircraft couldn't find it, but by then the war was nearly over.

Mussolini in a mess

Mussolini wanted to prove that anything Adolf could do, he could do better. In April 1939 he'd conquered the not-exactly-mighty state of Albania (and then found himself having to deal with a very effective Albanian communist resistance movement) and in 1940, just when the French had virtually collapsed (see the earlier section 'Abandon front!'), he dramatically sent his troops in to invade the French Riviera, occupy Nice, and confiscate the pedalos. He ordered massive celebrations in Rome when Italian troops from Libya advanced over the border into British-run Egypt, but the British, with their African and commonwealth troops, counter-attacked, conquered Abyssinia, restored the emperor (see Chapter 8 to find out what the Italians were doing in Abyssinia) and started driving the Italians out of Libya as well.

Meanwhile Mussolini, one of history's best examples of a man in denial, decided for his next trick to launch a stunningly successful invasion of Greece. And it was stunningly successful – for the Greeks. They defeated the Italians and chased them out of the country. At which point Hitler looked up from his maps of Russia and told his generals to drop everything and get their men down to Greece pronto.

The German intervention turned the tables on the British. The Germans tore through Yugoslavia and into Greece, where they drove the British out and captured Crete in a daring, though very costly, airborne attack. Hitler sent a special 'Afrika Korps' to North Africa under General Erwin Rommel, who immediately pushed the British out of Libya, took, lost, and retook the port of Tobruk, and invaded Egypt.

Even though invading the Balkans and North Africa went well at first, this tactic proved disastrous for Germany in the end. The Yugoslavs launched a successful guerrilla resistance movement, first a royalist one and then a communist one led by Josip Broz (codename: Tito), which kept large numbers of German troops pinned down. Above all, the Balkans campaign delayed the German invasion of Russia – with disastrous results.

Operation Barbarossa

Hitler was born to invade Russia. Everything he'd ever believed in, *lebensraum* (living space) in the east, anti-communism, anti-Semitism, an Aryan 'master race', and 'subhuman' Slavs, pointed to the idea that Germany should invade Russia, clear it of communists, Jews, and most of its population, and move German settlers in like homesteaders in the American West. Other great rulers had invaded Russia in the past (and you can find out about them in *European History For Dummies* (Wiley)) and had all come to grief, but Hitler thought this time would be different. He told his generals to prepare for the Mother of all Blitzkriegs. Codename: Operation Barbarossa.

The original Barbarossa ('Red Beard') had been a medieval German emperor, a mighty figure in his day, but he went on crusade, fell off his horse, and drowned in a river. Which, for the Germans' 'crusade' against communist Russia, was a bad omen.

Kick in the USSR

The Germans attacked on 22 June 1941 and caught the Russians by surprise. The British and Americans had warned Stalin the attack was coming but he refused to believe it. The Germans tore through the Russian defences and took thousands of prisoners. City after city fell to the Germans, and they pushed on towards Leningrad and Moscow. Stalin ordered the Russians to burn all the crops and dismantle factory equipment and move it east, across the Urals. Then the Russians set their factories up anywhere they could find, even in the open air, to start producing tanks and planes so they could fight back.

The Germans had marked Russia down for sinister special treatment. As the army advanced *einsatzgruppen* – special units – moved in to round up whole villages and kill them. They were clearing the land ready for Hitler's dream of *lebensraum* for the German people (see Chapter 5 for more on this). The Russians fought back fiercely and the Russian campaign became a life and death struggle between two peoples who hated each other bitterly and utterly rejected what the other stood for.

USSR kicks back

The Germans had hoped to reach Moscow and Leningrad before the Russian winter set in, but didn't make it. They cut Leningrad off and tried to starve it into surrender. Thousands of Leningraders died in a siege that lasted from 1941 to 1944, falling dead in the street from starvation with their relatives often too weak to bury them. The people of Leningrad were reduced to eating paste from their wallpaper. But the Germans could never break through the city's defences and eventually the Russians were able to get supplies through.Thanks to having to invade Greece and the Balkans (see the earlier section 'Mussolini in a mess') the Germans had invaded later in the year than they'd planned, which meant they hadn't reached Moscow by the time the Russian winter set in. First snow, then a thaw which turned everything to deep mud, and then the real, deep, freezing snow. The Germans had been so confident they'd reach Moscow easily they hadn't bothered about heavy winter equipment. So when the Russians, who knew how to dress properly for their own climate, launched a devastating counter-attack in front of Moscow, the Germans were sent reeling back. German propaganda films had to launch appeals for winter woollies for the lads.

You Are Free to Do Whatever We Tell You: Occupation

At first the Germans treated various parts of Europe differently according to what they thought of the people there. The Nazis felt contempt for Poles and Czechs, so their countries were cut up, with a part annexed to Germany and the rest ruled directly by a German governor or *Gauleiter*. In contrast, the Nazis thought that the Scandinavians and the Dutch were racially similar to them, so tried to govern them more lightly. They put Vidkun Quisling in charge in Norway, thinking (wrongly) that the Norwegians would appreciate a local man; 'Quisling' came to mean 'collaborator' or 'traitor'. The Germans soon found they had to impose harsh, direct rule on these so-called 'kindred' countries.

The Germans regarded the French with a mixture of respect for their great history and culture and contempt that they had lost so quickly. France was cut into three sections. Alsace and Lorraine were annexed to Germany, the whole of northern and southwestern France, including Paris and the whole of the Channel and Atlantic coastline, was occupied by the Germans, and the centre and south of France was a supposedly 'independent' state with its own government based at the spa town of Vichy and led by Marshal Pétain. The French authorities in the occupied zone and in 'Vichy France' collaborated fully with the Germans, even rounding up Jews and resistance fighters for transportation to the concentration camps.

Not all Nazis were Germans: Collaborators and sympathisers

Plenty of people across Europe came forward to help the Nazis. Many were just as anti-Semitic and anti-communist as the Nazis and volunteered to go to Germany to work in the German war effort. Vicious Nazi militia units were set up in France, Croatia, and the Baltic states to round up Jews and resistance fighters, and even to help run concentration camps. Pro-Nazi volunteers from occupied countries formed their own units of the *Waffen-SS* (armed SS), the army wing of Hitler's dreaded elite security corps.

Not all Germans were Nazis: Resistance fighters

Resistance groups fought back in any way they could, blowing up railway lines or important installations, or shooting individual German soldiers. Even Germany had resistance movements, such as the White Rose group, who distributed anti-Nazi leaflets among their fellow students at Munich University. The Nazis countered resistance with savage punishments and reprisals. The White Rose students were guillotined; elsewhere, for every act carried out by the resistance, the Germans rounded up groups of innocent people and shot them. When Czech resistance fighters flown in from England assassinated Reinhardt Heydrich, the SS 'Protector' of Bohemia-Moravia (that is, what was left of Czechoslovakia), the Germans chose a Czech village at random called Lidice, and murdered its entire population.

Genocide

The Nazis' crime against Europe's Jewish population was so appalling that it helped create a new term: 'Genocide' – the murder of an entire people. The Germans had been forcing Jewish people in every country they conquered to wear a yellow star on their clothing and sometimes to live in special ghettos so they could be easily identified and located. In 1942 the Nazis decided on the 'Final Solution' to what they called the 'Jewish Question'. Rather than shipping the entire Jewish population of Europe off to Madagascar or even

Palestine, both of which they had considered, they decided to kill them. Those who could do useful work were to be kept alive for a time; others, including the elderly, the sick, the children and most of the women, were to be murdered in gas chambers and their bodies burned in industrial death camps. The best-known was Auschwitz-Birkenau, which was a vast complex including a labour camp and even a prisoner of war (POW) camp, as well as the extermination camp. More typical was Treblinka, which only needed a couple of huts for the guards because everyone who arrived there was to be gassed.

Most historians agree that something like six million Jewish people were murdered in the Nazi death camps. The Nazis also rounded up and murdered Roma (gypsies), homosexuals, Jehovah's Witnesses (because they refused to make the Nazi salute), as well as political opponents and resistance fighters. Many major German firms had contracts with the concentration camps and prisoners marched through villages and towns on their way to and from work. The Nazis did what they could to keep the details of the extermination camps secret, but reports leaked out, and everyone in occupied Europe knew that Jews were sent east and never came back.

War Around the World

For its first two years the Second World War was essentially a European conflict, even the fighting in Africa. In 1941, however, the Japanese attacked the Allies and the war became truly global.

The rise of the Rising Sun

Japan had allied itself to Germany and Italy in the 1930s (see Chapter 8 to discover why). The Japanese were desperate to expand, partly to cater for their growing population and partly to acquire raw materials. The question was: Should they head north into China or south into the Pacific? At first the 'head north' brigade won: The Japanese invaded Manchuria in 1931 and the rest of China in 1937. But conquering China wasn't the pushover the Japanese had been expecting; they took the Chinese cities, but the Chinese, especially the communists, kept up a very effective resistance in the countryside. To make things worse, in 1939, when the Japanese pushed into Mongolia, near the Soviet border, the Russians sent an army under Marshal Zhukhov to push them back. The two sides fought a battle at Nomanhan and the Japanese lost. As the cost of the long war in China rose, the Japanese government started looking again at those maps of the Pacific.

Bombing

No aspect of the war provoked as much controversy as bombing. The Germans used heavy bombers to attack British cities. At first they aimed at industrial cities such as Manchester or Birmingham in order to disrupt war production. Bombing was also meant to destroy civilian morale: The beautiful centre of Coventry, including its medieval cathedral, was completely destroyed. Bombing did produce enormous suffering and hardship, but it also made people more determined to fight on and not to give in. The Germans reacted in the same way when the British, and later the Americans, started bombing their cities even more heavily than the Germans had bombed Britain. Bombing was carefully planned to create the maximum chaos: Incendiary bombs set buildings on fire and high explosives blew them apart, allowing the air in to fan the flames. Second and third waves of bombers arrived in time to hit the rescue operation after the first wave. The biggest raids of the war, on cities such as Hamburg and Dresden, created terrible firestorms – heat so intense it sucked the oxygen out of the air and created vacuums, which led to burning hot tornados. The Germans accused the Allied bombers of war crimes; the Allies replied that the Germans had started it and, anyway, bombing was necessary to win the war. More recently, historians have questioned how much damage the bombing really did to industrial production on either side. The arguments go on to this day.

This may sound crazy, but let's attack Pearl Harbor

Attacking in the Pacific was a very high risk strategy. South East Asia had huge reserves of oil and rubber as well as industrial production, but they all belonged to the Europeans who ruled the area. But the French and Dutch had been conquered by the Germans and were in no state to resist, and the British were fighting for their life in Europe, North Africa, and the Atlantic. No, the country the Japanese had to fear was the United States.

The US regarded the Pacific as its own special area. The Americans had taken over some Pacific islands as colonies and had even made Hawaii part of America itself. Roosevelt had warned the Japanese to keep out of the Pacific and he imposed a crippling oil embargo to force them to withdraw from China. By 1941 the Japanese situation was getting desperate: They had to launch an attack now or never. The Imperial Japanese Navy then hit on the idea of attacking the US Pacific fleet at Pearl Harbor, Hawaii.

The Japanese weren't fools. They knew they could never win a war with the US. Their thinking went like this:

- ✔ **We must have oil.** The European colonies in South East Asia have got it. They're weak, we're strong – let's take it.

- ✔ **Wait a minute, the Americans will intervene to stop us.** They are stronger than us and we cannot hope to beat them.

- ✔ **Hang on, we might force them to accept a compromise peace which leaves us with most of what we want.** But we'll only achieve that peace if (a) we're in a commanding position and (b) the Americans have suffered badly and need a breather.

- ✔ **Therefore, if we conquer lots of European colonies in South East Asia very fast and destroy the American Pacific Fleet, we might be in with a chance.** You'll find the fleet at anchor in Pearl Harbor. Keep them guessing and don't let them know what's in the wind.

The Japanese ambassador in Washington was actually on his way to meet the US Secretary of State to talk peace terms when the first Japanese planes swooped down on the US fleet on 7 December 1941, a day, Roosevelt stated, that would live in infamy. And so it has.

The Japanese destroyed 19 American ships, nearly 200 aircraft, and killed over 2,000 men at Pearl Harbor, nearly half of them on the USS *Arizona*. The American people were stunned. But the damage wasn't as great as it could have been because the US Pacific Fleet aircraft carriers weren't at Pearl Harbor that day. In a long-range war that would hinge on air power, that detail was crucial. Japanese Admiral Yamamoto, who'd planned the Pearl Harbor attack, said he thought all the Japanese had done was to waken a sleeping giant who would take terrible revenge on them. He was right.

Asian Blitzkrieg

As their planes attacked Pearl Harbor, the Japanese launched a series of devastating attacks across South East Asia and the Pacific. They captured the Dutch East Indies, French Indochina, and British Hong Kong. Churchill sent two warships, the *Prince of Wales* and the *Repulse*, as a 'vague menace' to warn the Japanese not to get ideas about attacking the naval base at Singapore. So Japanese aircraft sank both ships (the Brits hadn't thought to provide any air cover, which made any menace they posed very vague indeed) and invaded Malaya and Burma. Singapore fell with hardly a struggle when the Japanese captured the city's water supply. In Burma, the British and their Australian, New Zealand, and Indian troops had to retreat over 900 miles to reach India before the monsoon. They made it – just – and the Japanese took Burma. Meanwhile they were capturing islands across the Pacific, including the Philippines, where they trapped the American garrison in the Bataan peninsula and forced them to surrender. 'I shall return,' vowed the US commander, General Douglas MacArthur, but he couldn't save his men from the nightmare ahead of them.

Did Roosevelt know?

Conspiracy theorists love the idea that Roosevelt knew in advance about the attack on Pearl Harbor and let it happen, so he could take a united American people into war. That Washington knew more about the Japanese threat to Pearl Harbor than they told Admiral Kimmel and General Short, the commanders in Hawaii, is certainly true. Short thought he had to guard against sabotage, so he bunched all his fighter planes together where guards could keep an eye on them: Perfect for the Japanese to destroy them all on the ground. That Washington did its best to put all the blame for the disaster on Kimmel and Short and covered up its own failures is also true. But the evidence points to a mixture of complacency and jaw-dropping incompetence at the Washington end, rather than a deliberate plot to sacrifice the entire Pacific fleet.

Prisoners in the east

The Japanese regarded surrender as shameful: A soldier who hadn't fought to the death didn't deserve to be called a soldier. They force-marched thousands of American prisoners in the Philippines in a death march to prison camps, beat, tortured, and murdered Allied POWs and worked them to death as slaves, especially building the notorious Burma railway. By the time the war ended, many Allied prisoners of war were in the same state of starvation and disease as the inmates of German concentration camps.

Strange liberators

The Japanese circulated propaganda claiming they were fighting to liberate the peoples of Asia from foreign colonial rule. They weren't fighting for a Japanese empire, they said, but to set up a *Greater East Asia Co-Prosperity Sphere*. In fact this liberation turned out to mean ruthless Japanese exploitation of every area they took for Japanese purposes, and just to terrify their Asian brothers and sisters into doing as they were told, the Japanese army engaged in the systematic rape and murder of civilians.

The people of Malaya, Burma, and Thailand who helped the Allies fight back against the Japanese weren't doing it so the Europeans could simply take over again once the war was over. Japanese claims to be liberators may have been so much bunkum, but the war in the east *did* spell the end of Europe's age of empire. (Chapter 11 tells you how these empires finally fell).

Turning the Tables

For most of 1942 the situation for the Allies was pretty desperate. But by the end of the year they'd won important victories on all fronts:

- **The Coral Sea and Midway:** Two major naval battles between the Americans and the Japanese fought by planes from the two sides' aircraft carriers. At the Coral Sea on 9 May each side lost an aircraft carrier, but the Japanese fleet was badly damaged and had to turn back. At Midway Island a month later, American planes sank four Japanese carriers.

- **Operation Cartwheel:** The Americans launched their campaign to retake Japanese-held islands in the Pacific, beginning in August with Guadalcanal in the Solomons. The Japanese fought back very fiercely but the Americans won. From now on the Japanese were in retreat.

- **Stalingrad:** The Germans launched a huge offensive in southern Russia and took Stalingrad – Hitler only really wanted it because of its name. The Russians fought back and trapped the Germans. The fighting was so intense the two sides fought in the rubble, and as Hitler refused to allow Field Marshal von Paulus to be sensible and retreat, the whole German army in Stalingrad surrendered. It was a massive German defeat.

- **El Alamein and Operation Torch:** Rommel invaded Egypt to seize the Suez Canal but the new British commander, Montgomery, counter-attacked at El Alamein and drove him back. Then American troops landed in Algeria and tried to trap Rommel from behind. The American campaign went badly wrong to begin with, but eventually, in 1943, Rommel was forced to withdraw from North Africa altogether.

1943: Slogging away on all fronts

We can see now that 1942 was the turning point; at the time no one could see an end to the war. In 1943 the Allies stepped up their bombing raids on Germany, even breaching two German dams and devastating Hamburg, but the Germans didn't surrender. German U boats sank over fifty ships in two British Atlantic convoys. The Japanese were fighting the Australians in New Guinea and the Americans in the Solomon Islands. The British launched a big offensive in Burma and then got pushed back again. Specially-trained British jungle fighters known as *chindits* (from the *chinthe* – a half-lion-half-dragon beast seen in Burmese temples) landed deep behind Japanese lines in Burma, but so few of them came back it wasn't clear that the attack had been worth the cost.

The two biggest developments in 1943 were:

- **The Battle of Kursk:** A huge tank battle in Russia which finally broke the strength of the Germans.

- **Italy falls:** The Allies landed in Sicily and the Italian mainland. 'At last!' say the Italians, as they overthrow Mussolini and lock him up. Hold on: The Germans moved in, rescued Mussolini, and stopped the Allies in their tracks. The Allies did make progress in Italy but it was so hard and slow you'd hardly notice.

1944: Second front now!

In 1942 and 1943 the Russians were still doing most of the fighting and Stalin demanded to know when the British and Americans would land in France and open up a second front against the Germans. The British and Canadians had tried landing at Dieppe on the French coast in 1942 but it was a disaster. Still, some people in Britain demanded a 'Second Front Now!' and suspected the Allied governments were deliberately holding back to weaken the Russians. In fact invading France was difficult and complex, but eventually, on *D-Day*, 6 June 1944, American, British, and Canadian troops landed in Normandy and began the slow business of liberating western Europe from German rule.

The Germans fought back fiercely but once the Allies had broken through they were able to drive the Germans out of France, liberate Paris, and push into Belgium. The Western Allies attempted a daring airborne attack in Holland, but the British landing at Arnhem were slaughtered by a German SS-panzer division. Liberating western Europe was a long, slow haul as the Western Allies advanced into Germany from the west while the Russians crossed into Poland and German-occupied eastern Europe.

As the Allied troops advanced, they began to uncover the awful truth of what the Germans had been doing in Europe. The Russians found Auschwitz and the other death camps in Poland; the Americans liberated Dachau and the British Bergen-Belsen. The Germans had forced their prisoners to walk hundreds of miles on death marches away from the Russians to camps in the west, so the Allies found scenes of indescribable squalor and misery. The Allies determined to make the Nazis pay for these crimes against humanity.

1945: Endgame in Europe

By April 1945 even Hitler knew it was all over. The Russians were in Berlin and had raised the Red Flag over the Reichstag. Russian troops had met up with the Americans deep in southern Germany. Still refusing to believe that he might in some way have been responsible for the disaster that was happening to Germany (he preferred to blame the German people for not living up to his own high standards, if you please), Hitler married his girlfriend, Eva Braun, and then they both killed themselves. A few days later the German government surrendered.

As Germany began to collapse, Stalin, Roosevelt, and Churchill met at the Russian Black Sea resort of Yalta and agreed to divide Europe between them, with a communist zone in the east and a non-communist zone in the west. 'You will allow people to hold free elections, won't you?' said Roosevelt to Stalin. 'But of course,' said Stalin. Well, Roosevelt believed him. By the time the leaders next met, at Potsdam outside Berlin, Roosevelt was dead, and Harry S. Truman was president. Truman wasn't as star-struck by Stalin as

Roosevelt had been, and protested vigorously when it was clear Stalin was going to impose a communist government on the Poles whether they liked it or not. When they talked about how to defeat Japan, Truman let slip ever-so-casually that the Americans had a powerful secret weapon that would change everything. Stalin wasn't too worried: He'd already heard all about this weapon from his agents in America. The Japanese hadn't, though.

Endgame in Japan: Hiroshima

Fighting for each Pacific island was costing huge numbers of American lives. Taking Okinawa, the last island before Japan itself, cost the Americans nearly 50,000 casualties. The Japanese were launching devastating *kamikaze* (suicide) bombing missions, flying aircraft full of fuel straight into American ships. The Americans blanched at the idea of how many men would be killed invading Japan itself. Also, by then the Allies had found out how the Japanese had been maltreating prisoners, so no one had much sympathy for them. The Russians had agreed to declare war on Japan and were hoping for large areas of Asia. All of these considerations weighed with Truman as he took one of the most controversial decisions in history: To drop the atomic bomb.

On 6 August 1945 the crew of the *Enola Gay* dropped a single atom bomb on the Japanese city of Hiroshima. That bomb destroyed the entire city. People were burnt to cinders where they stood, and thousands died in the months – and years – that followed from the effects of radiation. Still the Japanese did not surrender, so three days later the Americans dropped a second bomb, on the city of Nagasaki. Finally, on 14 August the Japanese government surrendered and the Second World War was over.

End of Round One. Stand by for Round Two

The end of the Second World War led almost immediately to a period of even *more* dangerous conflict and tension. The Nazis had always predicted that the Western Allies would soon fall out with the Russians and events after 1945 quickly proved them right. Both sides kept their troops in Europe, and the Allied positions across Germany at the end of the Second World War soon became the front line in the Cold War that followed.

Weapons of mass destruction

The Germans had perfected deadly Vengeance Weapons, which they launched against Britain as the Allies advanced in 1944. The V1 was a flying bomb with its own engine which could, with a bit of luck, be shot down, though enough of them hit their targets to cause massive damage. But you couldn't shoot down a V2 rocket: It exploded without any warning at all. The attacks only stopped when the Allies captured the launching grounds. The Allies knew a good idea when they saw one, so the Americans were delighted when the German engineer responsible for the rockets, Wernher von Braun, came over and offered to work for them. Meanwhile, American scientists working for the secret Manhattan Project were completing the world's first atomic bomb. It wasn't long after the war before scientists thought: 'What if you took one of these rockets and attached an atomic bomb to it?' The Second World War was the origin of the post-war arms race.

Part III
The Divided World: 1945–89

'Oh, no — we've got the Marcoses
staying with us.'

In this part . . .

These were the years of unity; they were the years of division. Television, sport, and music helped bring the whole world together and build bridges between peoples and nations. But these were also the Cold War years, when people had to live knowing that the world could end at the press of a button.

Communist East and Capitalist West squared up to each other on every continent of the globe. War broke out for real in Korea, Vietnam, and Afghanistan, and the world came within a whisker of nuclear war in 1962 over Cuba. The Cold War even extended into space.

The rest of the world knew no peace either. The European empires collapsed, all too often in bloodshed and carnage. The United Nations set up a Jewish homeland in the Middle East and the whole region exploded in bloody conflict that remains unresolved to this day. The Arab states found they could use their control of the world's oil supplies as a very powerful weapon.

And then, suddenly, the Cold War ended. The Russians and Americans started talking and 1989 witnessed popular revolutions *against* communist regimes. With the Cold War over, the whole world wanted to buy Western goods and buy into Western culture. The nuclear weapons were dismantled. Surely now life had to get better?

Chapter 10

You're Cold as Ice! The Cold War

. . . .

In This Chapter

▶ Dividing Europe into eastern and western blocs

▶ Discovering how the Cold War brought the whole world to the brink of destruction

▶ Seeing how the Cold War ended

. . . .

From the 1940s to the 1980s the world was cut in two in a frightening stand-off between the Soviet Union and the United States that often threatened, but never quite managed, to tip over into full-scale war. Each side suspected the other of planning to invade or subvert it, and sent spies to find out what the other side was up to. The whole world was caught up in this frosty atmosphere of East–West suspicion and distrust: People called it the 'Cold War'.

Things Can Only Get Better! (Can't They?)

After the Second World War, people all round the world were determined that this time lessons would be learnt and war would never be resorted to again. The tired old League of Nations was to be given a decent funeral and replaced with a new, improved, body with attitude: The *United Nations*. (If you're not sure why the League of Nations was so tired, see Chapter 8.)

Churchill and Roosevelt mooted the idea of the United Nations when they met in 1941 and drafted the *Atlantic Charter*, saying they wanted to establish certain basic freedoms after the war. In 1944 representatives from the different Allied nations, including China, came together at Dumbarton Oaks, in Washington DC, to plan how such an organisation might work, and on 26 June 1945, representatives of fifty-one nations met in San Francisco and signed the Charter of the United Nations Organisation. Here's how it worked:

✔ **A *Security Council* to keep world peace:** The place for the big decisions: The Security Council can impose sanctions and order military action, unlike the poor old League of Nations. Five permanent members: The USA, USSR, China, Britain, and France, each with the power of veto. Non-permanent members (originally two, nowadays ten) are elected for two years by the General Assembly.

✔ **A *General Assembly* to represent the world:** Every member state has one vote. Simple majority needed for most decisions but big issues require two-thirds. The General Assembly has limited powers and is mostly a place for airing opinions.

✔ **Special *UN agencies*:** UNICEF (United Nations Children's Fund) looks after children's welfare, UNESCO (United Nations Educational, Scientific and Cultural Organisation) encourages the spread of education, the World Health Organisation (WHO) co-ordinates medical research, and the Economic and Social Council deals with population growth and human rights. Many of these agencies had been inherited from the League of Nations, which goes to show that the League did have a few good ideas worth keeping!

✔ **Other:** The United Nations also runs an International Court of Justice to decide legal disputes and an International Monetary Fund to lend money to countries in financial difficulties.

No one had thought about what would happen if the wartime Allies, with their permanent seats on the Security Council and their right of veto, ever fell out with each other. That's why, for all its prestige and all the hopes that surrounded it, the UN could do nothing to stop the Cold War.

When Two Tribes Go to War: A Bit of Background

Any quarrel the size of the Cold War has causes that go back a long way. To explain why the Cold War happened, you have to go back to the early years of the century.

World revolution? No thanks!

When revolution broke out in Russia in 1917 (Chapter 4 tells you how) most Americans were horrified at the idea of world revolution pulling down the capitalist free enterprise system they believed in, but some Americans welcomed the news. The labour unions liked the sound of it and American communists, like the journalist John Reed and the anarchist Emma Goldman, openly supported the Bolsheviks. They had their work cut out defending their views, though. Bosses employed private armies to break up union meetings and beat up any communists they found there. Attorney General Mitchell Palmer launched a series of raids to find America's communists and either locked them up or deported them.

John Reed wrote a gripping account of the Russian Revolution called *Ten Days That Shook the World* which made him a hero in Russia. The 1981 film *Reds*, starring Warren Beatty and Diane Keaton, tells Reed's story. It's a good film, but at over three hours long, best take your sandwiches.

When the American economy collapsed after the Wall Street Crash (Chapter 8 has the details), many communists thought America's revolution would happen at any minute. Not a chance: The authorities stamped on even the least hint of communist activity during the Depression.

Then President Franklin Roosevelt's New Deal (see Chapter 8) set America's right-wing communist-finders' noses twitching. 'Big building projects?' they said. 'All paid for by the State? Sounds familiar. That's just what Stalin's doing in Russia. I knew it: Roosevelt's a red!' True, if you just looked at newsreel of people building dams or factories, the New Deal did look a bit like Stalin's Five-Year Plans (see Chapter 4); the small-but-vital difference was that Stalin was using unpaid slave labour whereas the New Deal was using America's unemployed – and paying them, too. Even so, a hard core of American Republicans remained convinced that Roosevelt was in the pocket of the communists. When Roosevelt started co-operating with Stalin during the war and US government posters appeared praising 'Uncle Joe' and saying what a grand country the Soviet Union was, you could hear Roosevelt's critics muttering 'Told you so' into their morning newspapers.

Historians are still divided over Roosevelt's New Deal. No one seriously suggests that he was trying to set up a communist dictatorship, but some historians do say he was encouraging socialist ideas and methods. Many people at the time viewed the economic disaster of the Depression as the failure of capitalism, and looking for alternative ways of doing things in this atmosphere must have seemed justified to Roosevelt. Many people felt, though, that he allowed this to blind him to the true nature of Stalin's regime.

Many Republicans in the 1940s and 1950s believed that the New Deal had been a communist plot to undermine American free enterprise and they suspected anyone associated with it of being a communist 'fellow traveller' (that is, someone who sympathises with communism but has never actually joined the Communist Party). They also reckoned that if you'd been 'prematurely' anti-Nazi in the 1930s – that is, before America officially came into the war with Germany in 1941 – it was a sign that you were a communist sympathiser.

Whoa there, Winston! Leave Berlin to Joe

As the war closed, Churchill wanted Roosevelt to tell Eisenhower, the Allied Supreme Commander, to race forward to Berlin to stop the Russians getting it. But Roosevelt thought Churchill was scaremongering and Eisenhower reckoned that charging ahead without clearing the land on either side was far too risky. So the Western Allies stuck to their slow-but-sure advance along a wide front while the Russians charged forwards and took Berlin. And then took over eastern and central Europe, just as Churchill had said they would.

A whole new world!

By 1945 everyone agreed that the world could not afford such a destructive war ever again. The post-war world was to be new, exciting, and happy, with peace and plenty for everyone. All they had to do was make it happen.

Tough talking at the table: Yalta and Potsdam

During the war the Allied leaders held summit meetings to decide on strategy and to start planning for after the war. The most important summits were:

- **Yalta, a very nice holiday resort on the Black Sea, February 1945:** Stalin, Roosevelt, and Churchill discussed plans for Germany and Poland. They rejected US Treasury Secretary Henry Morgenthau's plan to dismantle German industry and send the country back to the Middle Ages and decided instead to divide Germany into four zones, Russian, American, British, and French. (The French were insisting on being equal with the Big Three and giving them a zone in Germany seemed a good way to keep them quiet.) The Russians promised to declare war on Japan three months after Germany surrendered and to set up democratic governments in all the countries they liberated. No, really.

- **Potsdam, the old imperial palace of the Kaisers outside Berlin, July–August 1945:** Roosevelt had died and Churchill lost the British General Election, so the Big Three were now US President Harry S. Truman, British Prime Minister Clement Attlee, and Stalin. They agreed to extract reparations from their German zones and redrew the borders of Poland and Czechoslovakia so that millions of Germans would have to leave their homes. Stalin wrecked the happy atmosphere by putting a communist government in charge in Poland and refusing to allow the pre-war Polish government to come back from exile in London. Truman and Attlee could do little but grumble, but Truman did at least let Stalin into the deadly secret that the US had the atom bomb and was prepared to use it. If he thought Stalin would be scared, he was disappointed. Stalin didn't seem surprised to hear the news at all. Fishy.

Nuremberg – the court of history

Churchill wanted to have the Nazi leaders shot, but the Allies decided instead to hold a proper trial in Nuremberg, scene of the big Nazi rallies. The prosecutors and judges were drawn from Britain, France, the USA, and USSR. Reconciling these different countries' legal systems wasn't easy: Britain and America based their systems on English Common Law, the French system was based on Roman principles, while the Soviet idea of a trial was to introduce the accused formally to his firing squad. Inevitably, many people have argued that the Nuremberg trial was 'victors'

justice' but most commentators agree that the Nazis got a fair trial: By no means all of them were sentenced to death and three were acquitted. The Nuremberg Trial was almost the last time the Allies worked together harmoniously; by the time the courts had worked their way down to the concentration camp guards who actually carried out the mass killings, the Allies were barely speaking to each other. The Americans decided to halt the trials in case they needed some of the accused to help fight the Russians.

The Allies had agreed to divide Germany into four zones, a Russian one in the east and the British, American, and French zones in the west. They also agreed to divide Berlin into four sectors in the same way, even though it was deep in the heart of the Russian zone. This decision was partly because of Berlin's symbolic importance but mainly because it meant the Western Allies could keep an eye on what the Russians were up to. As Stalin realised full well.

Small weapon – mass destruction

By 1945 the United States was the only country in the world that knew how to construct nuclear weapons and to use them successfully. This situation gave America a massive advantage over every other nation. But for how long?

President Truman's decision to drop the atomic bomb on Hiroshima was one of the most controversial of the Second World War. To this day, people argue furiously over whether or not it was justified and about Truman's motives. Some historians argue that it was necessary to end the war; others say that Truman wanted to demonstrate American strength to the Russians, to warn them not to get any ideas.

Money can't buy me love – though it's worth a try, General Marshall

The United States emerged from the war with the strongest economy in the world. The Americans could have turned their backs on Europe as they'd done in 1918, but with the Russians occupying eastern and central Europe, doing so simply wasn't an option. No, America was going to have to keep troops in Europe and make friends with western Europeans. The trouble was that Europe was shattered – literally: Buildings and railways had been bombed to pieces, the shops had no food in them, and millions of refugees were trying to get home – or to find a new home, if they didn't fancy living under Soviet rule in the old one. The Americans were worried that this poverty and misery would make people turn to communism. And then US Secretary of State George C. Marshall came up with a cunning plan.

The *Marshall Plan* offered American money, expert advice, food, machinery, and raw materials to any European state that signed up to it. These goodies were all free: No catch. 'Yeah,' thought Stalin, 'right.'

Although the Marshall Plan didn't contain any clause saying 'If you sign up for this, you agree to become an American ally', the idea behind the Plan was that countries who received American aid would be friendly to America, if only out of gratitude. You can't get a free lunch in this world, my friends, and the same goes for international aid handouts.

Western European countries signed up for Marshall Aid eagerly, but Stalin reckoned the Marshall Plan was an American ploy to turn Europe into a set of capitalist puppet states, so he turned the offer down and told all the other east European governments to do the same.

You could see the contrast between those who took Marshall Aid and those who didn't most starkly in Berlin. The western half of the city became a little island of capitalist wealth in the communist east. 'Hmm,' thought many Germans, 'in the capitalist West they get toilet paper while we have to use old copies of *Pravda*. Work that one out.' Increasing numbers of Germans slipped over into West Berlin or into the western zones of Germany to do just that.

Iron curtain and Truman Doctrine

By the spring of 1946 Truman was deeply worried about the way Soviet policy was going. Stalin broke his agreement to withdraw Soviet troops from Iran and only finally did so because Truman took a tough line with him. Truman invited Winston Churchill, no longer prime minister but still a world figure, to come to Fulton, Missouri, to accept an honorary degree and to make a speech about East–West relations. Churchill declared that the Soviet Union was isolating its half of Europe from almost any contact with the West: It was, he said, as if an 'iron curtain' had descended, cutting Europe in two. Good phrase: It stuck.

President Truman soon had a chance to show that the confrontation with the Soviet Union wasn't just words. The chance came in Greece.

Russia planning world takeover, stop

George F. Kennan was an experienced diplomat at the American embassy in Moscow. He was very concerned about Stalin's intentions for the post-war world, and frustrated that no one in Washington seemed to think they had anything to worry about. So in 1946 he put his concerns into a long telegram to the State Department, outlining how the Russians had always felt themselves under siege from their enemies and how the drive to expand was built deep into the Russian psyche and the communist soul. At 8,000 words, the missive was more an essay than a telegram but it worked: Truman's government began to take a much tougher line towards the Soviets. Mind you, you didn't want to be there when the embassy finance department got the telegram bill.

Like other wartime resistance movements, the Greek resistance was dominated by communist groups who expected to take the country over after the war. But the Allies agreed at Yalta that Greece should be in the non-communist zone – Churchill had insisted on it – so the British sent troops to help the Greek government fight the communists. By March 1946 Britain was running out of cash and its troops wanted to go home, so London asked Washington for help. Truman immediately went to Congress and announced a new policy: The United States would send military and economic help to Greece, or any other country, anywhere in the world, which was resisting a communist takeover. He called this policy the *Truman Doctrine*. Greece was its first big success.

Slicing salami, or how to take over a country without anyone noticing

Stalin had promised the Western Allies that he would hold free elections in eastern Europe. How could he hold free elections and still produce a set of communist governments? The trick was to start slicing little segments of democracy away gradually, like slicing salami, as the Hungarian communist leader Matyas Rakosi put it. Here's how the tactic worked:

✔ *Stage 1. Form a coalition government with your political enemies.* Remember to smile at them nicely. Make sure you hold the ministries which control the police, the intelligence services, and the armed forces. (If your coalition partners prove difficult about this, throw a tantrum and threaten to resign. Doing so usually brings them round.)

✔ *Stage 2. Use your control of the police, intelligence services, and armed forces to arrest or threaten your political opponents.* (Hint: Either accuse them of something heinous or say you're taking them into custody for their own protection. Someone will believe you.)

✔ *Stage 3. Sack any civil servants and other State employees who seem able to think for themselves.* Replace them with Communist Party members who luckily just happen to be between jobs at the moment.

✔ *Stage 4. Hold an election.* Make sure all the voters are thoroughly intimidated and that the only candidates are communists. (If some aren't, go back to Stage 2.) You should aim for a 95 per cent vote for the Communist Party. Don't get cocky and go any higher or people might think you've rigged things. Silly, I know, but people do get these ideas.

Thanks to salami tactics, the countries of central and eastern Europe fell to communist rule one by one. In 1947 the Russians set up the *Cominform*, an international organisation to make sure all these different communist governments did as they were told. Only two countries didn't quite fit into Stalin's salami tactics pattern:

✔ **Czechoslovakia:** The Czechs dared to hold a democratic election and the communists lost. The Czechs wanted Marshall Aid, even though Stalin told them they didn't need Western toilet paper when the woods were full of twigs. In 1948 Stalin authorised a military coup to get rid of this dangerously independent Czech government. All non-communists in the police and government were arrested and a new election was held, this time with all-communist candidates. Guess what? They won.

✔ **Yugoslavia:** Yugoslavia was the only European country that liberated itself during the war without the help of Allied troops. The Yugoslav resistance was led by Josip Broz, codename: 'Tito', which sounds a lot better, you've got to admit. Tito was a proud Yugoslav nationalist and he didn't like taking orders from Moscow. Tito told Stalin to stop trying to dictate Yugoslavia's agricultural policy and, while he was at it, to call off his spies. Stalin raged and threw Yugoslavia out of the Cominform. 'And he'll get no economic aid off me!' he added. Stalin confidently expected that Tito's regime would collapse within weeks; instead Tito simply opened up economic links with the West.

Tito's actions showed that it was possible to be a communist state without cutting yourself off from the rest of the world. He'd also shown that communists didn't have to do as Moscow told them: A dangerous message.

Berlin's blockade

Stalin hated the way the Western Allies were still based in West Berlin, deep in the heart of the Russian zone of Germany, watching and listening to what the Russians were up to. Worse than that, ordinary Germans could see how much better life was in the West every time they popped over to West Berlin to do some shopping. Many Germans went over to West Berlin and didn't come back. West Berlin had become an escape route out of the Russian sector and Stalin was determined to close it. But how? Attacking West Berlin would mean war with the Western Allies and he didn't feel ready for that. Then he had an idea: Starve them out.

In June 1948 the Russians suddenly announced that they were cutting all access to West Berlin. Road and rail links from the western zones of Germany were closed and no one was allowed in or out. Stalin hoped that the Western Allies would abandon West Berlin. No chance. The Western Allies decided to keep the city supplied with everything it needed to live – food, fuel, medical supplies – by air. They launched the massive *Berlin Airlift*, with hundreds of planes landing in the city every day. One plane landed every three minutes and the schedule was so tight that if you missed the runway you had to go all the way back to base and start again. Stalin couldn't shoot any of the planes down because doing so would start a war. Eventually, on 12 May 1949 after eleven months of blockade, he admitted defeat and opened up the land links to West Berlin.

Where did THAT come from? The USSR goes nuclear

Stalin had a much nastier surprise for the East up his sleeve than blockading Berlin. In 1949 Western scientists monitoring the Soviet Union recorded high levels of radiation deep in Russia. They could only think of one possible explanation: The Russians had exploded an atomic bomb.

No one knew how the Russians had got hold of the formula for making an atom bomb, but the Americans didn't wait to find out. They went all-out to build the much more powerful hydrogen bomb and in 1952 they tested it on a harmless little Pacific island called Eniwetok Atoll. The bomb worked. Americans could relax: They were still ahead of the Russians. Phew.

The next year the Russians exploded a hydrogen bomb too. Eek.

With all this posturing and provocation, you can easily see how two war-time allies eventually found themselves on different sides of the ideological battle-field. It was a strange war, with relations so icily suspicious that it became known as the 'Cold War'. Luckily the Cold War never actually turned hot, though no one could discount the possibility of that happening, as the events of the following decades demonstrated only too graphically.

Spies 'R' Us!

Both sides in the Cold War were obsessed with the fear of spies and traitors. Just to make the paranoia complete, these fears weren't entirely unfounded:

- **1948 Alger Hiss on trial:** Hiss was a high-up official in the US State Department. He was brought before the House of Representatives Committee on Un-American Activities (whatever those might be) and found guilty of passing secrets to the Soviet Union.

  For many years historians assumed that Hiss was innocent, if only because the prosecution case was flawed and depended on information passed on illegally by the FBI. However, more recent evidence suggests that Hiss, who made no secret of his communist sympathies, had indeed passed on secrets and lied about it under oath.

- **1950 Klaus Fuchs caught:** Fuchs was a German-born British scientist. He was a communist and had fled to Britain from the Nazis. In 1950 he was found guilty of passing atomic secrets to the Soviet Union.

- **1951 Julius and Ethel Rosenberg:** An American husband-and-wife team, both of them staunch communists, they were found guilty of passing on the atomic secrets that enabled the Russians to perfect their atom bomb. They both died a horrible death in the electric chair.

- **1951 Guy Burgess and Donald MacLean:** One of the most dramatic spy stories of the Cold War. These two British diplomats fled to Moscow when they got a tip-off that they were about to be arrested for passing intelligence secrets to the Russians. But who'd tipped them off?

- **1963 Harold 'Kim' Philby:** Another high-ranking British diplomat and devoted communist agent, Philby was exposed as the 'third man' who'd tipped off Burgess and MacLean. Like them, he managed to escape to Moscow.

Why were all these people passing secrets to the Russians? They weren't spying just because they believed in the communist system as a better alternative to the capitalist system: They also believed that only one country having nuclear weapons was dangerous and that if they evened the playing field and helped the Soviet Union catch up with America, the world would be safer. You won't be surprised to hear that not many people in the West agreed with this view.

See? I've Got Friends! Cold War Alliances

The Berlin Airlift (see the earlier section 'Berlin's blockade') convinced the Western Allies that they needed to start acting together to defend themselves against the Soviet Union. In May 1949 they joined the western zones of Germany together into a new independent state, the *Federal Republic of Germany* or 'West Germany' for short. They couldn't use Berlin as a capital in case it got cut off again, so instead they used Bonn, a quiet little town where nothing much had happened since Beethoven was born there. The first Chancellor of this new West Germany was Konrad Adenauer, a veteran anti-Nazi whose policy was to get close to the United States and stay there.

Not to be outdone, the Russians announced that their zone of Germany was also going to be a new state, the *German Democratic Republic*, known to its friends as East Germany. Capital: Berlin. Well, okay, the eastern half of Berlin. Its Chancellor was Walter Ulbricht, a communist who'd got out of Nazi Germany and spent the war in Russia. The Russians reckoned he was just the man to turn East Germany into a Soviet puppet state.

Settling the division of Germany was just the first step: Next, both sides had to organise their friends into fully-fledged military alliances.

NATO to the rescue!

With both sides starting to talk tough, the United States decided it was time to organise its allies into something more than a bunch of states who just sat round shaking their heads about how awful Stalin was. In 1949 eleven Western countries – the USA, Canada, Britain, France, Belgium, the Netherlands, Portugal, Iceland, Denmark, Norway, and Italy – signed up to the *North Atlantic Treaty Organisation* or 'NATO', saying they would all help if one of them was attacked by an unfriendly power. In 1952 Greece and Turkey joined, though the Americans had to stop them going to war with each other over who should get Cyprus. And in 1954, in a great symbolic *coup*, West Germany joined. Less than ten years after the end of the war, Germany, or at least its western half, was allied to her wartime enemies against the Russians. This state of affairs was just what the Nazis had always said would happen!

The French didn't like other people commanding their armed forces, so in 1966 they pulled their troops out of NATO but, rather paradoxically, said they were staying in the alliance. Er, *right*. What really annoyed the Americans, though, was that they had to move NATO headquarters from Paris to a very boring office block in Brussels. They've never quite forgiven the French.

Two can play at that game, capitalists!

The Russians were never going to let the Americans get away with forming NATO, especially once they'd brought the Germans in. In 1955 Moscow announced the East European Mutual Assistance Treaty, though it was always known, after the place where it was signed, by the more catchy name of the *Warsaw Pact*. It worked as follows:

Are you now, or have you ever been, a liar, a bully, and a cheat?

In 1950 US Senator Joseph McCarthy of Wisconsin launched a bizarre campaign to 'uncover' communists in American public life. He accused the State Department of harbouring fifty-seven card-carrying communists and some two hundred communist sympathisers. When the Senate asked for a bit of proof, McCarthy just started throwing more and more accusations around, which wasn't hard, since his idea of showing communist sympathies amounted to using the same coffee machine as a Red. But many Americans thought 'their Joe' might be onto something. McCarthy used his position as chairman of the Senate's Permanent Investigations Subcommittee to bully and intimidate writers, actors, scientists, and government officials into confessing they had been communists and to name others who had been too. He even accused Robert Oppenheimer, the physicist who had led the Manhattan Project to develop the atom bomb, because he'd had a change of heart about working on the hydrogen bomb. Not until 1954, when McCarthy turned on the US army and his hysterical antics were shown on television, did Americans finally realise he was a fraud. By then he had done a lot of damage to America's reputation as a home of tolerance and free speech.

✔ **Members:** Albania, Bulgaria, Czechoslovakia, East Germany, Hungary, Poland, Romania, and the Soviet Union.

✔ **Rules:** 1. Do as Moscow says. 2. Do not question Moscow's orders. 3. Make sure everyone else is obeying Rule 1.

✔ **Penalties for not obeying Rule 1:** The other Warsaw Pact countries attack you. In a spirit of friendly comradeship, of course.

Western countries weren't the only ones that were jittery about spies. Stalin had long feared that his enemies were out to get him. In 1953 he 'discovered' a 'plot' by a group of doctors to kill the head of the Leningrad Communist Party, Andrei Zhdanov. 'Good,' thought Stalin, who hated the city, 'now I can shoot lots of people in Leningrad for helping the Doctors' Plot.' Even better: Most of the doctors were Jewish so Stalin, who was deeply anti-semitic, could have lots of Jews arrested too. The purge was well under way when Stalin died of a stroke in March 1953. He could possibly have survived a bit longer, but he didn't trust anyone well enough to have a doctor to hand. Serve him right.

The Cold War Goes Global

At first the Cold War was concentrated around the stand-off in Europe, but in the 1950s other parts of the world began to come centre-stage.

Red flag in China

China had been gripped by civil war between Mao Zedong's communists and Chiang Kai-shek's nationalist Kuomintang since the 1930s (Chapter 5 has the details). The two sides agreed to work together against the Japanese but as soon as the Japanese had been defeated they resumed fighting. US Secretary of State George C. Marshall offered to mediate but Chiang wouldn't deign to speak to Mao, not even through the Americans. The Kuomintang had such a reputation for incompetence and corruption that huge numbers, even whole army divisions, changed sides and went over to the communists. In the spring of 1949 Mao crossed the Yangtze river and invaded the Kuomintang-held south. Chiang fled to the island of Formosa (modern-day Taiwan) while in Beijing, Mao announced the People's Republic of China.

Chiang Kai-shek's haven on Formosa soon became the centre of an international confrontation. The United States had invested a lot in the Kuomintang and simply would not accept that China was now a communist state. The US declared that the Kuomintang on Formosa was the only legitimate government of China. This declaration mattered, because the legitimate government of China had the right to a permanent seat on the UN Security Council, complete with veto. So the Americans sent troops to Formosa and told Mao to keep his grubby paws off.

The Russians protested against the Americans for not allowing the People's Republic of China to be represented at the UN and boycotted meetings of the Security Council. Bad move: Boycotting meant the Russians weren't there when the UN decided to stop another Asian communist takeover: Korea.

War in Korea

The Russians and Japanese had fought over Korea back in 1904 (see Chapter 2). The Japanese had conquered the country and exploited it ruthlessly, enslaving the Koreans and trying hard to destroy Korea's culture, language, and identity. Two Korean independence movements started, one in exile led by Syngman Rhee and a Russian-backed communist guerrilla movement in Korea itself led by Kim Il Sung. In 1945 the Russians rushed troops into the northern half of Korea and put Kim in charge; the Americans had to make do with the southern half, which they gave to Syngman Rhee. Kim and Rhee both claimed the whole of Korea and in 1950 Kim got permission from Stalin to launch a full-scale invasion of the South. The South Koreans appealed to the Americans for help, the Americans took their case to the United Nations and the UN voted to send military aid to South Korea, though this could only be done because the Soviets were boycotting the Security Council because the UN wouldn't recognise communist China.

The UN forces were commanded by US General Douglas MacArthur. At first, everything went well. MacArthur halted the North Korean advance by landing troops at Inchon behind North Korean lines and forcing them to retreat. Why not press on into the North? he thought. Unfortunately, Truman had given MacArthur strict orders not to invade North Korea. What had begun well started to go bad:

- ✔ **MacArthur invades North Korea:** President Truman is furious; MacArthur becomes a national hero. Truman can guess what's coming.

- ✔ **China invades North Korea and forces the UN forces back:** 'Serves you right,' thinks Mao, 'for not letting me into the UN.' MacArthur starts talking about dropping an atom bomb on Beijing, so Truman sacks him before he can spark off World War III. Or – as Truman strongly suspects he plans to do – take over the White House.

- ✔ **New UN commander Matthew Ridgeway pushes the Chinese back:** The two sides stop fighting and the border between North and South Korea is settled at the 38th parallel – where it had been in the first place.

The two Koreas settled into uneasy co-existence after the war. South Korea blossomed into a vibrant capitalist economy; North Korea remained an enclosed, poverty-stricken, and secretive Stalinist state under Kim Il Sung and later under his son, Kim Jong Il. Neither side trusted the other, but they both dreamed of the day when they would reunite their country.

New Leaders – No Change

Stalin finally died in 1953 and the rest of the Soviet politburo (the Soviet governing committee) breathed a sigh of relief. They set up a collective leadership, sharing power between them and reassuring the world that the bad old days were over. In 1955 the joint Russian leaders Nikolai Bulganin and Nikita Khrushchev travelled to Geneva for a summit meeting with US President Eisenhower and the British and French prime ministers. East–West relations appeared to be on the mend. (See Chapter 16 for more on the messy political manoeuvring that followed Stalin's death.)

Did he really say Stalin was a murderous tyrant?

At the twentieth Communist Party Congress in 1956 Nikita Khrushchev got up, cleared all the press out of the room, and made a remarkable speech, denouncing Stalin for his tyranny and wholesale murder. He wasn't telling the delegates anything they didn't know but no one dared say these things in public, even though Stalin had been dead for three years. *That's* how scared they'd been of him!

MiGs in Space

The Cold War was the first conflict in history to be fought out in space. Science fiction films in the fifties were all about freedom-loving earthlings fighting off evil invaders from outer space (geddit?) while the Americans and Russians were racing to be the first into space for real. The Americans were pretty sure they were leading until, in 1957, the Russians launched *Sputnik*, the world's first communications satellite. The Americans were still hyperventilating when the Russians launched Sputnik 2, with a little dog called Laika onboard who could wave her tail down to the panicking Americans. Then in 1961 the Russians got the first man into space, a fighter pilot called Yuri Gagarin who orbited the earth and reported back that God couldn't exist or he'd have bumped into him. The Americans managed to get astronaut John Glenn up to do three orbits and in 1963 John F. Kennedy reassured his fellow Americans by announcing that the United States would send a man to the moon and bring him safely home again by the end of the decade. In theory the 'space race' was about stretching the boundaries of human knowledge and endeavour; in reality it was all about gaining the maximum political and military advantage.

News of Khrushchev's 'secret speech' (so-called because he'd had no press present) soon leaked out. Did this mean a new, more friendly Soviet Union?

Hungarian tragedy

The Hungarian communist leader, Imre Nagy (pronounced 'Nodge'), thought that Khrushchev's secret speech was a green light to start introducing a few changes, for example certain basic rights like freedom of speech, that had got rather overlooked in the Stalin years. Nagy also allowed farmers to indulge in a bit of free enterprise and even allowed non-communist parties to stand for election. When he announced that he was taking Hungary out of the Warsaw Pact, Khrushchev threw off his Mr Nice Guy mask and ordered his tanks into Hungary. The Hungarian people fought back with every weapon they could find, but they needed help. The West was sympathetic but was too taken up with the Suez crisis (Chapter 11 has the shameful details). Khrushchev crushed the Hungarians and put the hard-line dictator Janos Kadar in charge. And he had poor Imre Nagy shot.

Another brick in the (Berlin) Wall

During the night of 19–20 August 1961 teams of bricklayers watched by East German border guards began building a wall across the centre of Berlin. The East German government had finally worked out how to stop people slipping over to the bright lights and job opportunities of the West.

The Berlin Wall featured machine gun posts and a death strip, where anyone even approaching the wall would be shot. Even so, many East Germans risked their lives trying any means they could to climb, fly, tunnel, or trick their way past the Wall and into the West. President Kennedy flew in to reassure West Berliners that the West wouldn't abandon them, but he couldn't actually do anything about the situation without sparking off a war. And that meant nuclear war.

Are there missiles on Cuba?

In 1962 the Cold War – and the world – seemed to come within a hair's breadth of nuclear destruction when the Soviet Union placed missiles on the Caribbean island of Cuba. The corrupt and oppressive – but pro-American – Cuban government was overthrown in 1959 by guerrillas led by Fidel Castro (Chapter 13 has more on this). Castro wasn't particularly communist but when President Kennedy backed a botched invasion to get rid of him, Castro understandably decided to make friends with the Russians. He was delighted when Khrushchev decided to station a number of Soviet nuclear missiles on Cuba, capable of reaching the United States.

When American spy planes reported seeing missile bases on Cuba, Kennedy ordered a naval blockade of the island. The Soviet Union angrily denied everything until the Americans produced their aerial photographs in the Security Council. 'Oh *those* missile bases,' said the Russians, 'Tell you what, we'll move ours if you move your missiles in Turkey.' Kennedy refused to budge; meanwhile, the Russian ships carrying the missiles themselves were getting closer to the US blockade. Nuclear war really did seem imminent, in mere hours, when the Russians suddenly backed down: Their ships turned back and they dismantled the missile sites. Kennedy became a national hero; Khrushchev was forced to resign. A few months later, the Americans very quietly dismantled their own missile sites in Turkey.

Historians disagree about Kennedy's role in the Cuban missile crisis. Some historians have praised Kennedy for his firmness, but others have said he took far too great a risk and should have been prepared to use the missiles in Turkey to reach a deal with the Russians. On the other hand, he certainly got what he wanted. Just don't think about what would have happened if he'd failed.

Easy like Sunday morning – not

After Cuba both East and West tried to calm things down. The buzz word in the 1970s was *détente*, which is French for 'chill out': Difficult when you don't trust the other side farther than you can spit. The two sides negotiated a series of Strategic Arms Limitation Treaties (SALT), but these just meant 'We'll only build a few thousand missiles if you only build a few thousand'. And in the 1980s both sides tore up the SALT agreements and started arming to the teeth. Here's why:

- ✔ **1968, Czechoslovakia:** Czech communist leader Alexander Dubcek tries to reform the communist system, releasing political prisoners, ending press censorship, and allowing free elections. The Warsaw Pact is horrified, invades Czechoslovakia and, despite worldwide protests, crushes Dubcek's government. Soviet leader Leonic Brezhnev announces the *Brezhnev Doctrine*, saying that the Soviet Union reserves the right to intervene in any communist country that seems to be off-message. 'He ain't kidding' say the Czechs.

- ✔ **1979, Afghanistan:** The Soviet Union invades to support an Afghan communist coup. The Americans boycott the 1980 Moscow Olympics in protest; more to the point, the Afghans keep up a deadly guerrilla campaign against the Russians. Note to Western leaders: (a) the Soviet Union hasn't changed, and (b) don't invade Afghanistan.

- ✔ **1981, Poland:** The dockers' trade union *Solidarity*, led by Lech Walesa and based at the Lenin shipyards in Gdansk, gathers enormous support for its demands for freedom of speech and free trade unions. In December 1981 the hardline Polish government bans Solidarity and imposes martial law.

Relations were so bad that in 1983, when NATO organised a military exercise codenamed Operation Able Archer, playing out an invasion of Russia, the Russians genuinely thought it was for real and got ready for all-out nuclear war. The crisis blew over when the NATO exercise ended, but it was the closest the world had come to nuclear war since the Cuban Missile Crisis.

Ending the Cold War

In 1980 America elected the screen actor Ronald Reagan as president. Reagan denounced the Soviet Union as an 'evil empire' and started positioning Pershing and Cruise nuclear missiles on the territory of America's NATO allies. The Russians did the same with their SS-20 missiles. In 1983 Reagan increased the stakes still further with the *Strategic Defence Initiative* (SDI), better known as 'Star Wars': The US would launch killer satellites into space that could shoot down Soviet missiles while they were still in the air. The Russians protested loudly at this unacceptable Yankee capitalist barbarism and urgently asked their scientists if they could do the same. Not, they learned, without the Soviet Union going bankrupt.

Peace, man

Big protests against nuclear weapons started with marches to the atomic research centre at Aldermaston in England in the 1950s and by the 1980s they were a worldwide movement. The Campaign for Nuclear Disarmament (CND) called on governments to disarm unilaterally – that is, to get rid of your own weapons before your enemy gets rid of his. Opponents of the peace movement accused it of being naïve or even of helping the Soviet Union; the peace campaigners said they were the only ones with any sanity.

In 1985 Mikhail Gorbachev became leader of the Soviet Union. He realised that the Russians would never sort out their own internal troubles while they were still trying to match the Americans missile for missile. Gorbachev met Reagan and the two men, who got on surprisingly well, agreed to start dismantling – yes, *dismantling* – their nuclear weapons. By 1988 the Cold War was effectively over.

Chapter 16 gives you more information about the changes within the Soviet Union in the run-up to the Cold War coming to an end. Turn to Chapter 18 to read about the backlash against communism that flared up in eastern Europe in the wake of these events.

Chapter 11

Don't Let the Sun Go Down on Me: The End of Empires

After the Second World War, the Europeans reverted to their role of ruling their mighty empires, but this proved to be more difficult in some places than they expected (Chapter 7 has the details on Europe's empires). Within a few years, they were packing up their pith helmets, hauling down their flags, and heading home. What had happened to the Age of Empire? This chapter explains.

All of the events in this chapter were happening while the Cold War was getting under way (Chapter 10 outlines the Cold War). The Americans and the Russians were on the lookout for any sign that these new states might join their side in their great stand-off. Since the colonial powers were all western Europeans, the Americans were scared that the new states might turn to the Soviet Union along my-enemy's-enemy-is-my-friend lines. This possibility had not escaped the Russians' notice either.

Sunset for the British Empire

Although the British liked to talk as if their empire would go on forever (that old 'Empire on which the sun never sets' idea), the signs of wobble were visible even before the Second World War. Nationalist movements in Asia and Africa were demanding independence, and the Brits were having to resort to force to keep them quiet. Two other countries – the United States and Japan – also wanted the Brits to clear out of the empire business, but for very different reasons.

The masters humbled

Imperialism was always heavily based on *image*: The Europeans were the masters and the colonised people were their servants. Criticising European rule seemed pointless if you thought that Europeans were somehow naturally superior to other people. That's why the sight of European troops surrendering to the Japanese – an Asian people – in Hong Kong and Singapore during the Second World War had such an impact. Suddenly, the European masters didn't seem so big any more, and once that sort of image has been broken, it can never be entirely mended. Even worse, though, was the way the Japanese treated their prisoners. They starved, beat, and tortured them and used them as slave labour. To Asians, the sight of white Europeans in loin cloths working as coolies for the Japanese was an eye-opener. The image didn't necessarily make them pro-Japanese, but it did show that the Europeans weren't some sort of super-race: They were ordinary human beings like anyone else. No empire can survive long when people know that about their masters.

The Americans liked to think of themselves as a colonised people who'd freed themselves from an evil empire back in the eighteenth century (actually, they'd been the ones colonising the natives' lands, but let it pass). President Franklin Roosevelt in particular disliked empires and didn't want Churchill or anyone else imagining that the Second World War was being fought so the Europeans could get them back again. In 1941 he and Churchill drew up the *Atlantic Charter*, which said the war was about establishing the freedom of people everywhere. Churchill hoped that this freedom would only apply to the European countries the Germans had conquered; but Roosevelt was serious: he wanted the war to see an end to Europe's age of empire.

The Japanese were great believers in empires; unfortunately they wanted them all to be ruled from Japan. However, they pretended that they wanted to drive the Europeans out so that Asian peoples could rule themselves, and some Asian nationalists, like the Indian nationalist leader Subhas Chandra Bose, did come over and join the Japanese side in the war (see the sidebar 'The cosy myth of Chandra Bose' for more on this particular Japanese ally). The Japanese even called the areas they conquered the *Greater East Asian Co-Prosperity Sphere* to make it sound like an Asian free trade area, instead of the zone of ruthless Japanese exploitation it actually was.

Perhaps the most significant sign that Europe's days of empire were numbered wasn't guerrilla activity by nationalist groups but the British General Election of 1945. To the stunned amazement of the rest of the world, the British turfed Winston Churchill out of 10 Downing Street and elected the Labour Party instead. Churchill was an old imperialist – as a young man he had fought for Queen Victoria in India and Africa – and he was determined to keep the British empire going. The Labour Party also wanted to keep the empire and they tried to make it more economically viable, though their schemes mostly didn't work. But they were committed to making one enormously important and symbolic concession: They were going to grant independence to Britain's biggest, most populous, and most important overseas possession: India.

India's night of freedom

Ever since the British ordered troops to fire on an unarmed crowd at Amritsar in 1919, the Indian nationalist movement had been growing stronger (see Chapter 7 to discover more about what the nationalists were doing before the war). Although the British hadn't granted India independence – and hadn't said they would, either – they had started allowing Indians to sit on provincial governments and even on the Viceroy's Council. And, of course, they had negotiated at the top level with the leaders of the Indian National Congress. That sooner or later the British would pack up and go home seemed obvious.

When the war broke out, Gandhi launched a new campaign calling on the British to 'Quit India!' Congress organised marches and rallies and the British, who were incensed that Congress was taking advantage of the war in this way, rounded up the Congress leaders and locked them up. In 1943 Lord Wavell became Viceroy of India. Wavell didn't think locking people up was any way to settle India's future, so he released the Congress leaders and took them into his own Council. But Wavell still needed to know if the British government was planning to hold on to India or pull out. He couldn't get any sort of decision out of Churchill but he did get one from Attlee, though it wasn't quite what he wanted to hear: Attlee sacked Wavell and appointed Lord Mountbatten instead. Mountbatten got the job of bringing Britain's long rule in India to an end.

The tragedy of partition

Mountbatten's brief was to pull Britain out of India by the summer of 1948. That deadline didn't leave much time to work out the most thorny problem: What to do about India's Muslims.

Gandhi and Congress had simply campaigned for independence, but the more likely it looked that the British would go, the more worried India's Muslims became. The leader of the Muslim League, Muhammed Ali Jinnah, said that Muslims didn't want to become a minority group within a huge Hindu state; he demanded a separate Muslim state, to be called Pakistan. This situation made the arrangements for granting India its independence very difficult:

 ✔ **Muslims lived in towns and villages all over India.** How could they be separated into two separate states? Plus the two areas where Muslims were in a majority were in north-west and north-east India, over a thousand miles apart. And thousands of Hindus lived in both areas too.

The cosy myth of Chandra Bose

Subhas Chandra Bose was a prominent member of the India National Congress, and even became its president until Gandhi outmanoeuvred him and got him thrown out. Bose hated the British (and he didn't much like Gandhi either), and in 1941 he headed to Berlin to team up with Hitler and his Japanese allies. He recruited disillusioned Indian soldiers in Japanese prisoner of war camps into a new Indian National Army (INA), which operated alongside the Japanese army, though it was so disorganised and ill-disciplined the Japanese very wisely kept it to menial and support roles. The INA joined in the failed Japanese attack on British India in 1944 and the following year Chandra Bose was killed in an air crash. End of story, you might think.

Wrong. Modern India much prefers Chandra Bose to Gandhi as a national hero. Chandra Bose statues and Chandra Bose Streets appear all over India and Indian children learn how he escaped from British arrest, led the INA to victory, and will return one day to lead India again. The awkward truth is that he wasn't actually under arrest when he slipped off to Germany, and he led the INA to defeat, but who wants the history to spoil their national myths?

- ✔ **The Congress leaders didn't accept the case for a separate Muslim state.** They thought Jinnah was just stirring up trouble. For his part, Jinnah refused to compromise and insisted on getting Pakistan. That Mountbatten didn't like Jinnah much and found getting on with the Hindu leaders, Gandhi and Jawaharlal Nehru, much easier didn't help.

- ✔ **Hindus and Muslims were staging violent riots, killing thousands.** Some six thousand people were killed in three days of Hindu–Muslim violence in the 'Great Calcutta Killings' of 1946. The politicians were going to have to sort out their differences fast before even more people were killed.

Gandhi was so upset by the idea of dividing India into Hindu and Muslim states that he pulled out of the negotiations. Reluctantly, Nehru persuaded Congress to accept partition. Mountbatten had come up with a cock-eyed scheme for dividing India into a huge federation of separate states which managed to anger everyone, but once it was clear that partition couldn't be avoided, he too accepted the idea. He also suddenly announced that Britain would be pulling out not in 1948 but in a few months' time – in August 1947. The British Raj would have to be dismantled in double-quick time.

Historians still argue about why Mountbatten brought the date of Indian independence forward, and their work isn't made any easier by the fact that Mountbatten himself was such an unreliable witness, always maintaining that he knew exactly what he was doing and everyone else was wrong. He liked to claim that he made the decision on the spur of the moment, in answer to a question from a reporter (though if that response is true, it's nothing to be proud of). In fact, at the time, bringing the date forward wasn't seen as that big a deal: The Indian leaders thought that if the British were going they might as well go quickly, and no one wanted some sort of interim period between the British going and the Indians taking over. Some people blame Mountbatten for the carnage that followed, though passions were so inflamed in India in 1947 that putting the blame on one man doesn't really make sense.

After the decision of partition was settled and the pull-out date moved forward, the most urgent issue to work out was where the border would run between India and Pakistan. A British lawyer called Sir Cyril Radcliffe, who'd never been to India before, was given this task of defining the border. Inevitably, both sides claimed he'd given the other too much. Two Indian states, Bengal and Punjab, had to be partitioned between the new countries. Some *two million* people who found themselves living on the 'wrong' side of the border were going to have to pack up, leave their homes, and start a new life in the other state, and they resented it bitterly.

Stand-off in Kashmir

One particularly thorny problem was the beautiful mountain kingdom of Jammu and Kashmir, on the border of India and Pakistan. The people were mostly Muslim and wanted to join Pakistan, but their ruler, Hari Singh, was a Hindu. He tried to sit on the fence, not joining either state, but that just inflamed the situation. Mountbatten persuaded him to agree to join India and Indian troops immediately moved in to occupy the country, but Pakistan protested that Hari Singh had signed under duress and that the Indians were occupying the country illegally. The dispute continues to this day, and on a number of occasions has brought the two countries to the brink of war.

Partition – and massacre

On 15 August 1947, Britain ended two hundred years of rule and handed power over to the two new independent states, India and Pakistan. 'At the stroke of the midnight hour,' said Nehru, the first prime minister of independent India, 'when the world sleeps, India will awake to life and freedom.' Almost immediately, however, the killings started again.

Faced with having to uproot themselves and move sometimes hundreds of miles from their homes, communities in Punjab and Bengal which had lived together for centuries suddenly turned on each other. Hindus and Sikhs slaughtered Muslims, Muslims slaughtered Hindus and Sikhs. Columns of refugees attacked each other and in the worst cases armed gangs attacked trains carrying refugees, systematically slaughtering anyone of the 'wrong' group. Some 200,000 people were slaughtered that year in Punjab alone.

The final irony

In January 1948 one Hindu group decided to take revenge by killing the man they thought had betrayed India by allowing it to be partitioned. A young man walked up to Gandhi as he was on his way in to prayers and shot him. It was a cruel fate for a man who'd always spoken against violence, and even more so since he was the one nationalist leader who *couldn't* accept partition. But then, fanatical young men with guns tend not to think too carefully before pulling the trigger.

Palestine pull-out

Palestine was an even more thorny problem than India (see previous section). The area had been part of the Turkish empire until the British drove the Turks out during the First World War (see Chapter 3). After the war much of the region was taken over by the League of Nations and divided into separate *mandates* which were entrusted to Britain and France. Palestine went to Britain (see Chapters 3 and 7 for more about the wheeling and dealing over the Middle East). The Palestinians weren't particularly keen to be ruled by the British, but they were even less keen when boatloads of Jewish refugees started arriving, claiming Palestine was their promised land from the Bible. The British had tried to limit the number of Jewish immigrants and had also tried to keep the two groups apart, but each side turned to violence and was prepared to shoot at any British troops who came between them.

The legacy of the Second World War

As the Nazis began rounding up Europe's Jews into ghettos, more and more Jewish people applied desperately for permission to settle in Palestine, but the British maintained strict immigration controls. When the war ended, however, big questions began to be asked about Britain's policy in Palestine:

- ✔ **What should be done with the people liberated from concentration camps?** Images from camps like Bergen-Belsen and Auschwitz shocked the world and created a huge wave of sympathy for Jewish people.

- ✔ **Where can Jewish people go if they can't go back home?** When Jewish people returned home from the concentration camps, especially in Poland and Russia, they often found their neighbours were still hostile to them. Some survivors were murdered.

The new Labour Foreign Secretary, Ernest Bevin, was a tough old trade unionist. He didn't take kindly to being hassled or bullied. Bevin's problem was that the louder Jewish people demanded the right to settle in Palestine, the louder the Palestinians complained that they were being swamped by these incomers and that their land was being taken off them. In 1946 Bevin tried to contain the situation by announcing a complete halt to all Jewish immigration into Palestine, and when US President Truman appealed to the British to rescind the decision, the British told him to mind his own business.

Jewish terrorism

Bevin's tough stance meant that Jewish groups simply turned to terrorism. Three main Jewish groups carried on the armed struggle against the British:

- **Irgun Zvai Leumi,** or 'Irgun' for short. Led by Gideon Paglin and Menachem Begin. Irgun claimed responsibility for over 200 acts of terrorism against British and Arab targets.

  Menachem Begin later went into politics and in 1977 became prime minister of Israel, where he took a very tough line against Palestinian terrorism. Perhaps you need to be a former terrorist yourself to know how best to fight terrorism.

- **The Stern Gang,** named after its founder, Avraham Stern. Rivals of Irgun and just as ruthless.

- **Haganah,** a Jewish army-in-waiting, with ranks and military organisation. Irgun and the Stern Gang hated it, and Haganah spent as much time fighting them as it spent fighting the British.

The political voice of the Jewish people was the Jewish Agency, led by David Ben-Gurion. The Council put pressure on the British to lift the ban on immigration while at the same time calling on Irgun and the Stern Gang to stop their attacks. This call was not heeded:

- **July 1946: Irgun blows up the King David Hotel in Jerusalem, home to British military headquarters.** This huge attack, which killed 91 people, badly damaged their cause in the eyes of world public opinion.

- **March 1947: Britain imposes martial law.** In response, the Stern Gang blows up a British barracks outside Tel Aviv.

- **July 1947: Jewish terrorists kidnap, torture, and hang two British army sergeants.** This event merely hardens British public attitudes towards the Jewish groups.

- **July 1947: Pitched battle scenes at Haganah's ship, *Exodus*.** The ship was carrying 5,000 Jewish immigrants from Europe. The British raided the ship and in the fighting that followed, three immigrants were killed. The rest were taken to Cyprus and interned.

Israel – a new state

The British were fed up with the Palestine mandate and desperate to pass the problem to someone else. In 1947 they handed the mandate back to the United Nations, which had taken over from the old League of Nations, and went home. The UN decided that Palestine would have to be partitioned, with a Palestinian state and a new Jewish state, to be called Israel, to be launched the following year. All happy now? Not a bit of it.

The Arabs were incensed that the Jewish immigrants were not just going to stay, but were going to get a huge area of land for their own state. As far as the Arabs were concerned, that land was Palestinian and that was how it should stay. Moreover, by 1948 the Arabs had their own independent states (see the section 'Suez – Two Empires Humiliated ') and felt more than strong enough to take on some flimsy new state made up of refugees from Europe.

So when David Ben-Gurion formally declared the State of Israel with its Star of David flag in May 1948, everyone watched to see how the Arabs would react. Easy: They attacked.

- **Arab forces from Palestine, Egypt, Transjordan, Syria, Lebanon, Saudi Arabia, and Iraq attack Israel.** And on its independence day, too.

- **Arab forces push into the south and east of Palestine and into the Old City area of Jerusalem.** But then the Israeli army – which is what Haganah had become – stop them.

- **The United Nations gets both sides to agree to a truce and sends Swedish Count Bernadotte to make sure they keep to it.** The Stern Gang assassinate Count Bernadotte.

- **Israel forces the Arabs back on all fronts.** The Israelis take over more land and declare West Jerusalem (the new part but without the historic Old City) their capital city.

Lack of effective planning and coordination, poor logistics and supplies, and competing ambitions of the different Arab nations all contributed to the outcome. The Arabs had to go home and lick their wounds.

Thousands of Arabs packed their bags and cleared out during the events of 1947–8. They took refuge in camps set up hurriedly in neighbouring Arab states, like Jordan and Lebanon. They dreamed of one day returning to their homes in Palestine. These Palestinian refugee camps became major centres of resistance to the Israelis.

Pirates of the Caribbean – go home!

Britain was also busy granting independence to its Caribbean possessions.

- **Jamaica:** Serious rioting had broken out against British rule in 1938, but Jamaicans, like the people of Britain's other Caribbean colonies, had rallied to the 'Mother Country's' side during the war. In 1944 Jamaicans got the vote and in 1953 Britain granted Jamaica self-government.

- **Antigua:** Antiguans got the vote in 1951 and finally won full independence in 1967.

- **Trinidad and Tobago:** Won their independence in 1962.

- **Barbados:** Became independent in 1966.

The Caribbean states set up a short-lived West Indies Federation, but then changed their minds and decided to join the *British Commonwealth*, which was rapidly replacing the old British empire. Some states, like Bermuda, remained tied to Britain and British law still applied. In particular, the Privy Council in London remained the final court of appeal for legal cases in many of Britain's former Caribbean colonies. This situation caused tension when Britain abolished the death penalty in 1964 because many Caribbean states resented the way a group of foreign judges sitting in London commuted death sentences passed in Caribbean courts to life imprisonment.

The new Caribbean states were often extremely poor, and despite independence many of their citizens decided to look for work abroad. British firms such as London Transport were advertising for people to work for them, usually doing low-paid jobs. Still, such employment was better than nothing and many West Indians had happy memories of being well received in Britain during the war. The first big group of Caribbean immigrants arrived in 1948 on the SS *Empire Windrush*. They found that many white Britons were hostile and suspicious of these new immigrants with their different skin colour.

One of the most important legacies of the Europeans' empires has been the ethnic mix in modern Western societies and the racial and religious tensions they have so often had to deal with. People tended to emigrate to the country which had been their colonial ruler, so Indians, West Indians, Pakistanis, and Hong Kong Chinese went to live in Britain, Algerians and Vietnamese settled in France, Indonesians in the Netherlands, and so on. In the 1960s and 1970s this emigration often produced serious racial tension and violence, especially as extreme racist political groups sprung up in European countries. Only as new generations grew up during the 1980s and 1990s did the different ethnic cultures begin to assimilate more, though by then religious issues between Muslim and Western cultures were becoming more problematic.

Don't forget Africa

The British did not intend simply to abandon their empire. They had no plans to hand Hong Kong over to China, Gibraltar to Spain, or the Falkland Islands to Argentina, even though all three countries claimed them. The British were also hoping that they would be able to stay in their colonies in Africa at least for another generation. The British were only too aware that they'd done little to develop their African colonies' education systems or economies, so they wanted to invest more money in Africa before they started granting the Africans independence. Unfortunately, these investment schemes didn't work: One scheme to plant thousands of tons of groundnuts (that's peanuts to you and me) in East Africa proved a costly failure: No one had bothered to check whether or not groundnuts were really suited to East African conditions (they're not, in case you think you spy a money-winner).

Meanwhile, the British had counted without a big growth in African nationalism. Many Africans had studied in England and had been attracted to the idea of *pan-Africanism*, the idea that all Africans should be brothers and sisters and should set up a sort of united African state or federation of states. One of the most important of these leaders was Kwame Nkrumah, who came from the area of West Africa the British called the Gold Coast. Nkrumah formed the

Convention People's Party which campaigned for the British to clear out, and in 1957 they finally decided to go. The new state was to be called *Ghana*, and it was the first time Europeans had granted full independence to a 'black' (that is, south of the Sahara) African state.

One of the guests at Ghana's independence celebrations was another black man making a name for himself as a fighter for freedom. Dr Martin Luther King was travelling the world after winning his famous fight against racial segregation on America's buses. He took tremendous encouragement from the sight of black people throwing off white power and setting up their own government. (See Chapter 15 for more about Martin Luther King.)

Elsewhere in British Africa things were turning very nasty. A vicious war broke out in Kenya where a nationalist group called the Mau Mau was fighting both against the British and against its African tribal rivals. The violence lasted until 1960, by which time the British had virtually decided the time had come to get out of Africa entirely. Chapter 12 takes a closer look at events in Africa.

Malaya

The people of Malaya had fought alongside the British against the Japanese and they expected Britain to give them independence in return. Matters were complicated by the fact that Chinese settlers had set up a communist movement to force the British out and take over the country. The British didn't want Malaya to become communist (and they valued Malaya's natural resources, too) and the Malays didn't want the Chinese running the place, so together they fought a long campaign against the Chinese guerrillas. The British made use of helicopters and special jungle warfare training, so that by 1957 the country was secure enough to gain its independence. In 1963 it was expanded further to form the modern state of Malaysia.

Some people contrasted the British success in Malaya with the failure of the Americans in Vietnam. But although they were both fighting communists in the jungle, the similarities between the two wars stopped there. The Brits had recent experience in jungle warfare during the Second World War and – crucially – had the local population on their side; this was not the case in Vietnam. See Chapters 14 and 15 for more about the impact of Vietnam.

Taking French Leave

Like the British empire, the other European empires were also drawing to a close, and some of them didn't like it one bit. The French in particular found adjusting to the new situation so soon after their traumatic experiences during the Second World War very difficult.

What exactly *is* the Commonwealth?

The Europeans were keen to retain links with their former colonies and the Commonwealth (originally termed the 'British Commonwealth', but the British bit was dropped in case it sounded too imperialistic) was Britain's attempt. To join you usually had to have been a British colony, though in recent years some former French and Belgian colonies have applied to join. For many leaders of Commonwealth countries a spell in a British jail seemed to be a necessary qualification too. At first the British seem to have hoped that the Commonwealth would be a sort of third superpower balancing the Americans and the Russians, but that situation was never going to happen: The Commonwealth wasn't anything like politically or economically powerful enough and its members had too many differences between them. The Commonwealth did, however, act as a trading area, though Britain had to drop out of that when it joined the European Common Market in 1973. The Commonwealth set itself up to act as a guardian of human rights: It expelled South Africa and imposed sanctions on it in protest against the apartheid system. Unfortunately, many other Commonwealth countries were just as oppressive as South Africa. On the other hand, as a friendly group of nations who all have historic links with Britain, and therefore with each other, the Commonwealth somehow still seems to work.

Zut alors! Does anyone know which side we're on?

Events in Europe during the Second World War effectively broke Europe's empires in the east. When the Germans conquered Holland, for example, the Dutch East Indies could expect no help from home when the Japanese attacked them, as they did in 1941. The situation was more complicated for the French colonies because they had a government at home but it was collaborating with the Germans and fighting the Allies (see Chapter 9 for more about the situation in wartime France). Did this position mean that French colonies were at war with the Allies too? In 1940 the British decided to take no chances and destroyed the French fleet at Oran in Algeria to stop it joining the Germans. This provoked massive anti-English outrage in France, which delighted the Germans and more than made up for not getting the ships.

One man who tried to persuade the French colonies to change sides and fight the Germans (or to stay on the same side, depending on which way you looked at it) was General Charles de Gaulle. De Gaulle had held a junior position in the French cabinet just before France fell. When he escaped to London in 1940, he used that position as the basis for saying that he and his Free French movement were the true government of France, but no one listened to him, not even the Allies. So he decided to find some French territory that would accept his authority.

De Gaulle hit on French West Africa, modern-day Senegal, where the local people had been demonstrating in support of him and against the Vichy regime in France. In September 1940 de Gaulle arrived off Dakar, the capital, with a combined British and Free French force. But instead of welcoming him, the French troops in Dakar opened fire and de Gaulle was forced to retreat. Two years later, the Americans landed in French North Africa. They too hoped the French would help them, but again the French opened fire, though this time they couldn't turn the invaders back. Meanwhile, over in French Indo-China, the Japanese were demanding that the French allow them to take over, and the French were giving in without firing a shot.

De Gaulle had more luck in Syria. The pro-Vichy colonial government tried to hold out, but in 1941 the British and Free French invaded and took the colony over. De Gaulle now had his political base on French territory.

All these twists and turns made moving back into their colonies at the end of the war very difficult for the French. The people of Indo-China, for example, felt the French had betrayed them by handing them over to the Japanese. France had managed to fight on the losing side not once but twice – against the Germans in 1940 and against the Allies later; the only people who emerged with any credit from the war were the French resistance fighters. This situation was all very encouraging for anyone thinking of resisting French colonial rule after the war.

At first, the French seemed to be getting into the spirit of setting their colonies free. Back in 1926 they had formed Lebanon out of Syrian land and in 1944 they made it independent. Two years later they did the same for Syria. But the French had no intention of pulling out of their two most prestigious possessions – Indo-China and Algeria.

Indo-China: The rocky road to Dien Bien Phu

The French colony of Indo-China was made up of Annam and Tonkin in the north and Cochin-China, based around Saigon, in the south (these are all within modern-day Vietnam), as well as the ancient kingdoms of Cambodia and Laos. The French settlers had lived a very comfortable life while most of the population worked in the fields, but Indo-China had a nationalist move-ment that staged a major uprising against the French in 1930 and kept up a campaign of bombings and raids. Two of its members were a history teacher called Vo Nguyen Giap and a former primary schoolteacher (and one-time washer-upper in a London hotel!) called Nguyen Tat Than, better known by his codename 'He Who Enlightens' – Ho Chi Minh.

Ho and Giap both became members of the Communist Party. Like many people in Indo-China, they felt angry when the French meekly handed the whole area over to the Japanese in 1941 (see the preceding section to find out why the French did this) and they seized the chance to start up an anti-Japanese resistance movement. They called this movement the 'League for Vietnamese Independence', or *Viet Minh* for short.

A land divided

The Viet Minh kept up a strong resistance against the Japanese and in 1945 it declared a Vietnamese Republic under Ho Chi Minh. The victorious Allies had other ideas. The Potsdam Conference divided Vietnam in two: The Chinese were to occupy the north, which suited Ho since the Chinese recognised his republic, and the British were to occupy the south, which didn't suit him at all as the British didn't. The British soon handed over to the French who were determined to hold on to the south, come what may. They even offered to let Ho have the north, Cambodia and Laos, but he said he wanted all of Vietnam, north and south. So in 1946 the French launched a bombing raid on the north and sparked the war.

What did the Americans think?

The Americans weren't involved in the fighting but they were following events in Indo-China very carefully. Although they didn't like empires, they wanted the French to win, because they thought if they didn't the whole of Indo-China would fall to the communists. When China became communist in 1949, the Americans were even more anxious for a French victory.

The Korean War and the war in Indo-China (they were happening at the same time) were the first wars that saw extensive use of an exciting piece of new technology – the helicopter. Helicopters could drop troops just where they were needed and didn't need big airstrips. Plus, you didn't need to risk life and limb in a parachute jump. Helicopters could also ferry the wounded away from the battle zone straight to medical bases far behind the front. Helicopters certainly changed the way wars could be fought but, as the French and Americans both found, they couldn't win wars on their own. (You can find out more about helicopters in Chapter 22.)

The final battle – for the moment at any rate

The French were trying to conquer North Vietnam and sent some of their ablest generals to do it, but they proved no match for the Viet Minh. General Giap was able to use his experience against the Japanese to keep up the pressure on the French. By 1954 he had the French surrounded in a hill-top fortress at Dien Bien Phu. The French held out desperately, but in the end they had to surrender. The French government decided to sue for peace.

The two sides worked out a peace deal in Geneva but no one was entirely happy with it. The French agreed to pull out and go home and the Viet Minh were left in charge of North Vietnam. But the country was still to be divided, this time between two independent states, North Vietnam (capital: Hanoi) and South Vietnam (capital: Saigon). Ho Chi Minh still claimed the whole of Vietnam, however, and he started looking for opportunities to destabilise the government in Saigon. South Vietnam would need some strong friends and it found them in America. (See Chapters 14 and 15 for more about what happened next in Vietnam.)

Algérie Française?

The French had conquered Algeria, just across the Mediterranean from France's southern coast, back in the nineteenth century and it had become almost as important to them as India was to the British. Thousands of French people settled there, where they were known as 'pieds noirs' (black feet) from the black boots the original soldiers wore. So attached did the French feel that in 1882 they incorporated Algeria as part of France (though the Arab population didn't enjoy the same rights as ordinary French people) rather than keep it as a colony. To many French people, losing Algeria resembled losing a limb or a vital organ. Algerians, on the whole, did not share this view.

Blood for blood

Algeria's war for independence began with a terrible outburst of violence in the town of Sétif on VE (Victory in Europe) Day, 9 May 1945. What was meant to be a victory parade for the end of the war in Europe turned into a march by Algerian nationalists telling the French to go home. Someone fired a shot and the marchers pulled out guns and knives, killing every European they could find. The killings went on for five days, in the towns and outlying farms. In total, 103 Europeans were killed and many of their bodies were mutilated. That outcome was bad enough, but it was nothing compared with the reprisals the French took.

French armed forces toured the area, shooting people as they went; the French air force dive bombed Arab villages; French settlers lynched Arabs in prison and any others they could find. Inevitably, people argue over the exact figures, but some 6,000 people at least were killed.

For many Algerians, especially Algerian army units coming home after the war, the massacres of 1945 killed their faith in the French and turned them into fierce nationalists.

The Algerian nationalist movement was the FLN (*Front pour la Libération Nationale*), led by Ahmed Ben Bella. After the 1945 killings the FLN was wary of challenging the French, but in 1955 it came back on the scene:

- ✔ **1955:** FLN systematically massacre French settlers at Philippeville. In reprisal, French troops massacre Arabs. Algeria is engulfed in violence.

- ✔ **1956:** FLN launches terrorist attacks in cafes and milk bars across Algiers. Crack French paratroopers arrive under General Massu. They use torture.

Third world – third way?

By the mid-1950s more and more new countries were emerging after getting rid of their colonial rulers. One of them, President Sukarno of Indonesia, thought these countries might usefully act together. Sukarno had played a leading role in Indonesian nationalist movements against the Dutch before the war. In 1941 the Japanese invaded Indonesia, but instead of simply saying 'Right, lads, new enemy!' as so many other nationalist leaders had done, Sukarno played a rather more clever game, helping the nationalists but also working closely with the Japanese. He managed to manoeuvre himself into a position where he could declare Indonesia independent in 1945, at the end of the war. The Dutch fought hard to defeat him, but in 1949 they had to withdraw. For this victory over the European colonialists Sukarno became an Asian hero.

In 1955 President Sukarno had the idea of getting all the new states just emerging from colonial rule to meet together. He invited them all to a big conference at Bandung in Indonesia where they could work out common ground and form a powerful new third force in world politics. The idea was that these countries, which people were beginning to talk of as the *third world*, should form a huge *non-aligned* movement, not linked to either side in the Cold War, and would tell these superpowers and their lackeys where they could get off. (Ideas about what the first two worlds were differed according to whom you spoke to. They were either the two sides in the Cold War or else 'Old World' Europe and 'New World' America.)

Twenty-nine countries came to Bandung, mostly from Africa and Asia (delegates also came from Cyprus and from the American Civil Rights movement). They had fun comparing their experiences in different colonial prison regimes over the canapés, but when they got down to business, problems soon emerged. For one thing, claiming the movement was non-aligned when communist China was represented was a bit difficult, and claiming it was unified when its two biggest members, China and India, were rapidly falling out with each other (Chapter 14 will explain why) was even harder.

The conference members agreed that colonialism should go and called on the Europeans to clear out of their remaining colonies, but once you'd said that you'd said everything. These countries simply didn't have enough in common with each other, except that they'd all been ruled by white Europeans. Each country had its own ideas about what it wanted to do now they'd gone. Some of these countries did try to revive the Bandung idea at later conferences, but none of these had the impact of the original one, and even that didn't have much impact in the long term.

✓ **1957:** FLN calls general strike in Algiers, but paratroops break it up. Paratroops defeat FLN and take control of Algiers.

✓ **1958:** Controversy over Algeria brings down the French government.

General de Gaulle's hour of triumph

Both sides in Algeria wanted General de Gaulle to take over in France. Each side thought he supported them. Under the terms of France's new constitution, de Gaulle became president in 1958 with much greater powers than his predecessors. He soon crossed over to Algeria to find out exactly what was happening. The Muslims welcomed him, but so did the settlers, especially when he addressed a huge crowd of them with the words 'Je vous ai compris!' (I have understood you!). De Gaulle had understood all right: He'd understood that it was impossible for France to hold onto Algeria and as soon as he got back to Paris he opened negotiations with the FLN.

The settlers' revenge: The OAS

The settlers were furious with de Gaulle and thought he'd betrayed them. They were right: He had. Four army commanders in Algiers decided to stage a coup, seize control in Algeria, and then cross over to France to overturn de Gaulle, but the president appeared on television to appeal to the French to remain calm and he poured scorn on the rebel generals. The coup collapsed and the generals were arrested. All except one: General Raoul Salan.

Two pieces of technology came into their own in the Algerian war. One was television, which de Gaulle used very effectively to speak to ordinary French and Algerians and establish his own authority. The other was the transistor radio. During the confused days of the generals' coup, people tuned into their radios on the street, standing round listening to find out the latest news. For the first time people could keep up with major events as they happened.

Salan hit back at de Gaulle by setting up a terrorist organisation, the *Organisation de l'Armée Secrète* (OAS) to assassinate Arabs, French liberals, and de Gaulle. (This is the group featured in the film *The Day of the Jackal*.) They missed de Gaulle, but they killed plenty of others: Over 500 in February 1962 alone. Even the pieds noirs turned against the OAS, however, when one of its bombs caught a little girl of four by mistake and blinded her. In 1962 General Salan was arrested and the OAS folded.

In 1962 France finally recognised Algeria as an independent state under the FLN leader, Ben Bella. Three years later Ben Bella was overthrown in a coup.

Suez – Two Empires Humiliated

The British and French liked to think they were still great powers in the world and that, even when they'd hauled down their flags and gone home, somehow they still controlled what happened in their former colonies. The Suez affair finally showed them that those days were over.

Egypt – an independent-ish country

The British and French were interested in Egypt mainly because of the Suez Canal. It was one of the world's most important waterways, and it belonged to the private Suez Canal Company, which had its headquarters in Paris and whose principal shareholders were the British and French governments. The

British, who had conquered Egypt back in the 1880s, set Egypt up as an independent kingdom in 1922, but they kept troops in the canal zone and they maintained their influence in Cairo. Egypt was an important British base in the Second World War and the scene of the Battle of El Alamein, Britain's favourite wartime victory over the Germans.

In 1936 King Farouk came to the throne. He was a fat, corrupt playboy, who lived for pleasure and didn't care who knew it. In 1952 officers of the Egyptian army staged a military coup and got rid of him. Colonel Gamal Abdel Nasser then took over and became head of state in 1954.

Nasser realised that Egypt was a poor country with few natural resources beyond the all-important River Nile. He drew up plans to build a massive hydro-electric dam on the Nile at Aswan, and planned to borrow the money from the Americans. But when Nasser negotiated a deal with the communist government of Czechoslovakia (and everyone knew this was really a front for the Soviet Union), the Americans pulled out (the Czech deal made the Americans wonder whether Nasser was *quite* as pro-Western as he claimed). So Nasser looked round for another source of revenue. His eyes fell on the Suez Canal.

Take your hands off my canal!

The Suez Canal made money from the tolls ships paid to go through it; controlling such an important waterway also made the British and French feel they were still world powers. Nasser had already approached the British in 1953 about the troops they had stationed in the canal zone and suggested that perhaps they might go home. 'My men will look after the canal for you, honest,' he reassured the British. They pulled their troops out and shortly afterwards Nasser seized the canal.

Nasser's action caused a storm of controversy in Britain and France. The British prime minister, Anthony Eden, was determined not to take losing the canal lying down. He compared Nasser's regime to 'fascist governments' and said the situation was just like the 1930s all over again and if he wasn't stopped a third world war would break out and the world would end and then they'd be sorry. Even the British queen thought Eden should go and lie down, but many British people were strongly behind him. And then the French received a very interesting call. From Israel.

I have a cunning plan . . .

The Israelis had been looking for a chance to hit at Egypt, their number one enemy ever since the 1948 war (see the earlier section 'Israel – a new state'). In secret, they proposed a plan to the British and French:

- ✔ **Israel attacks the Egyptians.** Don't worry about the pretext – we'll think of something.

- ✔ **Britain and France call for a ceasefire.** Don't worry – the Egyptians won't agree to one.

- ✔ **Britain and France send troops in to 'protect' the Suez Canal.** Don't worry – we'll make sure we don't harm it.

- ✔ **Britain and France keep their troops there to protect the Suez Canal.** Don't worry – no one will suspect a thing.

Enactment of the plan was agreed for October 1956. At first the plan seemed to work. Fighting started between the Israelis and Egyptians and the British and French threw up their hands in horror at this outbreak of fisticuffs before airlifting in thousands of their own troops to take control of the canal. The fighting was going their way on the ground too. But then the politicians weighed in.

The Russians denounced the Anglo–French invasion, which was only to be expected. What the British and French hadn't expected was that the Americans would turn against them. President Eisenhower, no great admirer of European imperialism at the best of times, was outraged that they should have started such a major action without consulting the US; he thought they were entirely in the wrong anyway. Eisenhower turned the screws on the Europeans: He put pressure on the pound sterling, causing it to lose value like water running through a sieve, and said he'd only stop if they pulled their troops out. So the British and French pulled their troops out.

The Suez affair was a disaster for the Europeans. It managed to make them look simultaneously aggressive and weak, and when news of the secret deal with the Israelis eventually came out, it made them look untrustworthy and devious too. The whole affair revealed how low the European powers had fallen and how completely they now depended on the Americans.

Eden, who had genuinely been ill during the crisis, resigned. Nasser became an Arab hero and immediately turned to the Soviet Union for financial help for the Aswan Dam. Oh, and he kept hold of the canal, too.

Chapter 12

Africa's Wind of Change

. . . .

In This Chapter

▶ Finding out about African nationalism

▶ Seeing how the colonial powers withdrew

▶ Learning about apartheid in South Africa

. . . .

*E*lderly Africans in the 1960s must have felt as if they were watching history repeat itself in reverse. When they were very young, the Europeans barged their way into Africa and took over nearly the whole continent. So unedifying was the process it was known as the 'Scramble for Africa'. In the 1960s, the Europeans seemed to be scrambling all over again, but this time to get out – fast. Unfortunately, all too often they left conflict and misery behind them. This chapter looks at how the Africans gained their independence from the Europeans – and at just how far reality lived up to their dreams.

Be Off, and Never Darken My Continent Again!

Back in the nineteenth century the Europeans referred to Africa as 'the dark continent'. They meant that it was a vast and rather scary Unknown Land (unknown to Europeans, that is; the Africans knew it quite well). Westerners still often look at Africa and its history in a patronising way: First they see it as a backward continent with everyone living in mud huts and fighting with spears, then the Europeans take over and modernise it, and when the Europeans have gone, the Africans take charge and the place falls apart with military coups every other day and women and children starving to death.

Now, no one's going to deny that Africa has an image problem. Many westerners' image of 'Africa' is a starving child staring out from a charity disaster appeal poster. African countries have suffered from endemic corruption and civil war, and some African leaders have been odious. But other continents have produced their own wars, dictators, and famines, too. Africa had a long way to catch up with the rest of the modernised world and it made a lot of big mistakes along the way, but it also saw huge advances in nation-building, education, medicine, and economic development. The continent produced some of the century's most respected figures, like Julius Nyerere of Tanzania or the anti-apartheid leaders, Bishop Desmond Tutu and Nelson Mandela. Twentieth-century Africa needs to be taken seriously.

I use the word 'tribe' quite a lot in this chapter, but it needs qualifying. Don't think mud huts and drums – at least, don't think *just* mud huts and drums (and don't scorn these either, until you've had to construct a shelter or a musical instrument out of whatever you've had to hand). Tribes are sophisticated societies, with their own culture and traditions, their own political hierarchies (not just a chief, but a whole network of princes and nobles), legal systems, communications networks, and military forces. The Asante of west Africa produced intricately crafted treasures in gold. But westerners tended to use the word 'tribe' to denigrate other peoples, to suggest that they weren't as advanced as Western 'nations' – and to use that as an excuse for grabbing their lands. Westerners insisted that 'tribes' were backward and refused to accept any evidence to the contrary. For many years the whites of southern Africa flatly denied that Africans could possibly have built the famous stone walls of ancient Zimbabwe because that would have meant that these 'tribes' had in fact been an advanced civilisation, and white South Africa couldn't accept that. Avoiding the word 'tribe' in talking about African history is difficult, but when you see 'tribe' think 'people'.

White on black: European colonies in Africa

In 1896, at the Battle of Adowa, the Ethiopians sent the Italians packing, and maintained their independence from European rule. Liberia, on the west coast of Africa, was also independent, but in the first half of the twentieth century the rest of the African continent was ruled by Europeans:

- ✔ **Britain** controlled a huge area from Egypt to South Africa. Britain also controlled areas in west Africa such as Nigeria, the Gold Coast, Gambia, and Sierra Leone. White Europeans had settled in Kenya and in southern Africa and were very happy to be in charge, thank you very much.

- ✔ **France** ruled a huge area of north and west Africa. Large numbers of French settlers were living a very comfortable life in Algeria.

- ✔ **Portugal** took over Angola and Mozambique back in the sixteenth century. As the British and French started pulling out of their colonies, the Portuguese were all the more determined to hang on to theirs.

- ✔ **Belgium** had taken over a huge area of central Africa along the river Congo. In the nineteenth century King Leopold II had claimed the Congo as his personal property and had allowed his agents to exploit the Congolese ruthlessly. The Belgian government bought the Congo off the crown back in

1908. Like the Portuguese, the Belgians weren't planning on handing over power to the Africans any time soon.

✔ **Italy** held Libya and part of Somaliland.

✔ **Germany** held Togo, Cameroon, South West Africa, and Tanganyika (modern-day Tanzania) until these territories were taken away from her at the end of the First World War. South Africa took South West Africa, Togo and the Cameroons were partitioned between Britain and France, and Britain got Tanganyika.

Moving toward independence

The Second World War completely changed the Europeans' position in Africa. Firstly, the war revealed all of them to be weak. This situation made them all the more determined not to show any weakness in Africa after the war. The war also encouraged three important new developments:

✔ **Education:** Only a tiny proportion of Africans went to school. The ones that did usually went to mission schools, where they learned that all men are equal in the sight of God. Curiously, their white rulers didn't seem to apply this idea to their black neighbours. Africans also learned their colonial rulers' language and culture so they could work in their administration when they left school. Some even went on to university. Many of these Western-educated Africans went on to lead the nationalist movements fighting for independence.

✔ **Nationalism:** When Africans went to college in Europe or America they encountered the Western idea of *nationalism*, which said that nations should rule themselves and shouldn't be under foreign rule. Very interesting. They also encountered socialist ideas, which said that rich people exploit the poor and that the exploited poor should seize power. No one was more exploited than the downtrodden workers in Europe's colonies. Very, *very* interesting.

✔ **Pan Africanism:** Pan Africanism was the idea that the Africans should set up one vast pan-African state (the word 'pan' means 'across all'). They should then join together in a vast anti-European crusade and drive the white people out.

The idea of a single African state didn't take hold for very long, but the idea that all Africans should show solidarity did.

Tribes or nations?

African nationalists had one important question to answer before they got out the banners: Did they want to keep the national borders the Europeans had imposed or go back to the old tribal boundaries? Tribal identity was very strong – it still is – but the nationalists couldn't ignore the fact that some important things had changed since the Europeans arrived:

Role models

Africans had a number of important outside figures they could look to for inspiration. Two key people were

- **Marcus Garvey (1887–1940):** Garvey was a flamboyant character, always dressing up in European-style military uniform, complete with cocked hat. He was born in Jamaica but spent most of his life in the United States, where he campaigned for equal civil rights for black people. Garvey thought that white America was so deeply prejudiced that black Americans would be better off moving back to Africa and he collected a lot of money to finance his 'Republic of Africa', until it turned out he'd been pocketing it, which rather ruined his image. Garvey had spread the idea that black people all over the world should join together in the fight against racial prejudice; just don't give him your savings.

- **Gandhi (1869–1948):** Gandhi's successful fight against British rule in India (see Chapter 11) was a huge inspiration to nationalists across the world. He'd actually launched his first campaign in South Africa, where he fought successfully against new racial laws brought in against South Africa's Indian population (or 'coloureds', as the race-obsessed South Africans called them), so African nationalists followed his career with interest.

- The borders between different colonies often ran across old tribal boundaries and included different peoples with very little in common with each other.

- Some colonies contained rival religious groups, especially Christians and Muslims.

- The peoples in different colonies spoke their own languages plus the language of their colonial rulers, so some Africans spoke Portuguese, some spoke French, and some spoke English.

These factors meant that most nationalists decided that working with the borders the Europeans had drawn would probably be best. This solution was probably the most practical, but it made for serious tribal problems once the new states had won their independence.

Now or never?

Planning to take over a country is pointless if you're not going to be able to rule it properly. A country needs a government, a legal system, a police force, armed forces, a health service, an education system, banks, some sort of economy to bring in a bit of cash – and you can't ask your fairy godmother for them. The Africans desperately needed large numbers of people educated and trained to a high enough level to run all these things once the Europeans had gone home. Ideally, they ought to have some experience as well. The trouble was that most African countries had very few people of this sort, and didn't have many schools and hospitals for them to run anyway. When Malawi became independent in 1964, it had only two secondary schools in the whole country. So even the most enthusiastic nationalists had to check whether their country was really ready for self-government or whether it mightn't be better to hold off for a few years and get a bit more experience under the colonial regime before placing a bomb under the governor general.

Recognising some inconvenient truths

The Europeans had long thought that Africans were less advanced than other peoples and hadn't bothered investing in them. Most of colonial Africa was still given over to hunting or farming. After the Second World War the Europeans realised that building their African colonies up a bit and maybe introducing a bit of industry, mainly mining some of Africa's rich seams of minerals, might be a good idea. But even the most die-hard European colonialist couldn't hide for-ever from some rather inconvenient truths:

- ✔ Most African colonies had nationalist movements demanding self-rule.

- ✔ The United States was hostile to European empires and thought the longer the Europeans held out, the more likely it was that the Africans would turn to the Russians for help.

- ✔ Big multinational companies wanted to invest in Africa and thought they would get many more openings with poor, independent states than with the European colonialists.

- ✔ The 1956 Suez affair held the European imperialists up to international condemnation and ridicule (see Chapter 11 for the details).

- ✔ The more the nationalists demanded independence, the more European troops would be needed to keep them quiet, and the Europeans simply couldn't afford it.

Don't worry, chaps, I have a cunning plan

By the 1950s European governments – and especially European businesses – were beginning to look again at the issue of independence for Africa. They began to think that granting colonies their independence and then moving in on them to win contracts to build up their infrastructure might actually be better. Ultimately, the new independent African states would actually be just as dependent on the former colonial powers as they had been when they were colonies. Sneaky, eh?

This tactic of turning a nominally independent state into a virtual colony, dependent on a Western country or company, became known as *neo-colonialism*. Neo-colonialism wasn't confined to Europeans: Many American firms were accused of establishing neo-colonial rule in Africa.

I say, don't forget we live here too

What to do about the large white settler communities in different parts of Africa was one of the most difficult problems. Some of these communities were quite small, but others were large, especially in southern Africa and

Algeria. Some of these people would no doubt want to go home to Europe if the Africans gained independence, but most would probably want to stay. The trouble was, they didn't just want to stay: They wanted to keep their hold on power. Africa's whites would try various ways to maintain that hold.

You'd better go now

The great scramble out of Africa began with Libya and Ghana, but in the 1960s it quickly spread across the rest of the continent.

Libya liberated

Libya was the first African country to become independent after the Second World War. It had been one of Italy's colonies, but the British conquered it and handed it over to the United Nations, who decided to grant it independence. In 1951 it became the United Kingdom of Libya under King Idris. No one took much notice until oil fields were discovered in the 1960s, when suddenly the Western powers realised that King Idris had always been their best friend. Not all Libyans, however, liked the way the Americans and their allies were gaining influence in the country.

In 1969 King Idris was overthrown in a military coup led by Colonel Muammer el-Gadaffi. Gadaffi set up a radical revolutionary regime and started providing money, arms, and training facilities to terrorist groups from all parts of the world, as long as they were anti-Western. Gadaffi softened over the years, eventually repenting of his terrorist ways, and was still in power in Libya as the century drew to its close.

One old Gold Coast equals one new Ghana

Kwame Nkrumah set up the Convention People's Party (CPP) in the British colony of the Gold Coast in 1949 to call for independence. Some of the CPP's marches turned violent and, inevitably, the British threw Nkrumah in jail. But when the CPP won the 1951 elections by a convincing margin, the British had

Where did all these Indians come from?

Various parts of British Africa had substantial Indian populations. They had come to Africa in the nineteenth century to work in the colonial administration. They cost less than European staff and were more used to working in the heat. By the 1960s countries such as Kenya, Uganda, and South Africa had large Asian populations, usually doing well in business. They tended not to mix with the Africans, partly for racial reasons and partly because they had brought their own Hindu religion with them. Some Africans resented this large Asian presence and both Kenya and Uganda threw them out as a way of uniting African opinion behind the government.

to let Nkrumah out: After all, he'd just been appointed a minister in the new government. The following year he became prime minister and in 1957 Britain finally granted the Gold Coast (new name: Ghana) independence.

Ghana was important because it was the first African country to *win* its independence. Once the British had allowed the Ghanaians to elect an African government, it would only be a matter of time before the other Europeans were forced to do the same.

Unfortunately, Ghana's experience of democratic rule didn't last long. Nkrumah had hoped to start building up a big pan-African state with Guinea and Mali, but they lost interest and the plan collapsed. Instead, he set about turning Ghana into a one-party socialist dictatorship and locking up or deporting anyone who dared criticise him. These actions just made his opponents more determined to get rid of him, which they did in 1966 while he was on a state visit to China. Ghana fell into a descending spiral of civil war and tribal conflict, with endless military coups, until in 1979 Flight Lieutenant Jerry Rawlings took charge, had all his rivals executed, and set about building up Ghana's wrecked economy and re-establishing democracy.

Rawlings got help from the World Bank and the International Monetary Fund and the economy began to recover. Rebuilding democracy proved more tricky, mainly because Rawlings was running a one-party state. Whenever he held democratic elections the people voted for his opponents, which wasn't the idea at all. So Rawlings felt he just had to bribe the electors by massive government spending that Ghana could ill afford, and he even staged a coup to *keep* himself in power as the, er, democratic ruler of Ghana. Not until 2000 did Ghana finally hold properly democratic elections. Rawlings lost.

Hit the road, Jacques!

France had two main areas of Africa: Algeria and Morocco in the north and a huge area over the Sahara and through west Africa down as far as the Congo. Most French people expected to take control of their colonies again after the war ended but one man had rather different ideas: General Charles de Gaulle.

De Gaulle had no reason to love the settlers of French Africa, who had fought against his Free French forces during the war (see Chapter 11 to find out why). He wanted France to regain her strength and importance and he thought that hanging on to overseas colonies was not the best way to do it. In 1944, even before the war was over, de Gaulle went to Brazzaville in the French Congo and announced that France's African colonies would be getting some democracy at long last once the war was over. Sure enough, they got proper elected councils and more seats in the French parliament.

De Gaulle was only in power for a few months after the war. After that, he spent much of the time sulking at home in his village of Colombey-les-deux-Eglises because the French hadn't given the presidency the strong powers he had hoped for. So he wasn't in power when the French empire began coming apart at the seams. In 1954 the Viet Minh defeated the French at Dien Bien Phu (in Indo-China) and France had to withdraw. In 1956 France had to withdraw from Egypt in international disgrace, and the Algerian crisis in 1957 brought down the French government. (You can read about these events in Chapter 11.) Spotting his chance, de Gaulle grabbed a quick cup of coffee and headed for Paris to become president of France. He had plans for Africa.

But I'd like us still to be friends

Nationalists in French West Africa didn't just want a few more seats in the French parliament: They wanted to rule themselves. Their leading figure was Dr Felix Houphouët-Boigny of the Ivory Coast, though the French managed to draw some of his claws by inviting him to join the French cabinet. Clever. Once de Gaulle was in power, though, he went further and offered France's west African colonies a choice:

- **Option 1:** Independence immediately, whether they were ready for it or not (most of them weren't, as de Gaulle well knew).

- **Option 2:** Semi-independence within a sort of French commonwealth called the French Community. France would still run foreign policy, defence, and the economy. So not very independent then.

All of the colonies voted for Option 2 except Guinea. So in 1958 the French cleared everything out of Guinea, administration, police, even the typewriters, and headed back to France, half expecting the locals to call them back before they'd got to the airport. So Guinea became independent and the rest of French West Africa thought to itself, 'Hmm, maybe we were a bit hasty'. Between 1958 and 1961 *all* of France's colonies in west Africa changed their minds, left the French Community, and declared independence.

De Gaulle had intended that the French Community would merge all France's former colonies into two big federations, one in north Africa and one in the west. But when the colonies opted for independence they became fourteen separate states. Some were very small, such as Upper Volta, Gabon, or Benin. Others, like Mali and Niger, were larger but mostly desert. As they were all very poor, the French calculated that independence would provide openings for aid and trade agreements with France – and they were right.

Gone with the wind of change

In 1960 the wily British prime minister Harold Macmillan set off on a long tour of Africa. With France pulling out of its colonies, Macmillan wanted to gauge the strength of nationalism in the rest of Africa. The final stop on the tour was South Africa, where he was due to address the South African parliament in Capetown. He had a surprise up his sleeve.

Macmillan told the South African MPs – all of them white, of course – that he had been struck by the strength of the nationalist feelings he had encountered on his tour. In a phrase that became famous he declared that a 'wind of change' was blowing through Africa, a change towards democracy and Africans ruling themselves. White South Africa had better get used to it.

The South African prime minister, Dr Verwoerd, managed to stammer out a 'Thank you, Mr Macmillan for that most interesting address' speech, though he looked like he was chewing a wasp, and he added that it was the whites who had brought civilisation and medicine and education and engineering to Africa – in other words, everything the apartheid system stopped black Africans having access to (see the section 'The struggle in the south' later in this chapter to find out more about apartheid).

The fact that it was the British prime minister issuing this warning to South Africa was enormously significant. Macmillan meant that Britain would do nothing to help Africa's white population resist the rise of African nationalism. The whites were on their own.

Free at Last! Well, Sort Of . . .

Most of Africa finally won its independence in the 1960s. The Europeans withdrew, some with good grace, others more unwillingly, and the new African nations unfurled their flags, learned their national anthems, and took their seats at the United Nations. Many of them discovered important reserves of minerals and even oil: For the first time in its history Africa was going to have a significant industrial economy. Things could only get better.

But gaining independence wasn't the whole story. The old tribal rivalries hadn't gone away: In fact, independence seemed to make them even worse. Some areas were industrialising, but most of the continent still lived and farmed the same way it had for centuries. This situation meant that many of these new states soon featured among the world's poorest nations. Not entirely unconnected with that fact, many of the regimes running the new states proved just as oppressive and corrupt as governments anywhere else in the world. Many African states thus had to turn to other countries for aid and support, and international help never comes free. These new independent states were soon almost as much under the control of the outside world as they had been in colonial days.

The Congo: How not to start a state

The Congo was one of few places with no nationalist movement in the 1950s, mainly because the dreaded Belgian colonial police force, the *Force Publique*, arrested anyone caught suggesting that life under Belgian rule wasn't just what the doctor ordered. But even the Force Publique couldn't keep the Congo isolated from international opinion forever, and by the end of the 1950s a Congolese nationalist party was growing fast, led by a charismatic young leader called Patrice Lumumba.

Belgium had finally made an economic success of the Congo: It was a leading producer of metals, minerals, and diamonds, Congolese farming had improved, and the general standard of living was much better. Even so, in 1959 major riots broke out when Congolese nationalists held independence demonstrations. As a result, in 1960 the Belgians held a big conference in Brussels and announced that they were pulling out of the Congo in a few months' time. On 30 June 1960 the Congo became independent, with Joseph Kasavubu as president and Patrice Lumumba as prime minister. The transition was so quick that something was bound to go wrong.

The trouble started when the Force Publique suddenly mutinied. Then the wealthy province of Katanga, home to Congo's important copper industry, declared itself independent. The international copper companies reckoned an independent Katanga would be easier for them to control than a single Congo, especially as Lumumba proved unpredictable, so they sent money to the Katangan leader, Moise Tshombe, which he spent hiring foreign mercenaries. Lumumba appealed to the United Nations for help, and UN troops arrived to stop Katangan secession and restore order. Then things got complicated:

- In addition to asking the UN for help, Lumumba also approaches the Russians, so the Americans decide that Lumumba is a dangerous Red and has to go.

- President Joseph Kasavubu, encouraged by the Americans, sacks Lumumba. Lumumba refuses to be sacked and sacks President Kasavubu instead. President Kasavubu says he *isn't* sacked and arrests Lumumba , but Lumumba arrests him back and no returns. Finally Lumumba arrests the Public Prosecutor, so President Kasavubu can't arrest him any more.

- Americans secretly back a military coup by Colonel Mobutu, who sacks President Kasavubu and arrests Lumumba. For real. And Mobutu hands Lumumba over to Moise Tshombe in Katanga so Lumumba's men can't rescue him.

- Lumumba's men take out their frustration by attacking Europeans, spurring Belgium to send in troops. Congo now has a five-way war between Lumumba's men, Mobutu's men, Tshombe's men, the UN troops, and the Belgians.

- Lumumba escapes and flees to UN lines for protection; then he decides to leave the UN lines. Bad idea: The Katangans catch and kill him.

Rumble in the jungle

For a time in the 1970s Zaire became quite the fashionable place for the jet set. Richard Burton and Elizabeth Taylor got married there (again) and in 1974 the world heavyweight boxing championship was held in Kinshasa between Muhammed Ali and the world champion George Foreman. The fight attracted massive coverage and the press billed it as 'the Rumble in the Jungle'. Ali won (again). Foreman hung up his gloves and started a new career preaching and selling kitchen appliances instead. I suppose, given its recent history, Zaire was really quite an appropriate place to watch two men of African descent battering each other to a pulp.

On top of all this chaos, the UN Secretary General, Dag Hammarskjöld, was killed in an air crash while trying to bring peace. Now, instead of keeping the warring sides apart, the UN forces found themselves dragged into the war, fighting against Katanga until the UN pulled them out in 1962. Meanwhile President Mobutu established a firm military grip on the country. Mobutu tried to cut the Congo's historic links with Belgium: He renamed streets and cities (Leopoldville became Kinshasa) and even told citizens to drop their French names and take African ones. He renamed the country Zaire.

Behind all this establishment of power, though, Zaire was still heavily dependent on Belgian economic aid. The Katangans didn't give up either: For another twenty years they launched regular raids into Zaire from neighbouring countries until they finally admitted defeat in 1983. By then President Mobutu had turned Zaire into a one-party state.

Portugal won't go quietly

The Portuguese were the first Europeans to land in sub-Saharan Africa and they did their level best to make sure they were the last to leave. Portugal was ruled by a military dictatorship under Dr Antonio Salazar who had no intention of granting freedom to the Africans. Or the Portuguese.

Portugal ruled two African countries, Angola in the west and Mozambique in the east. Legally they weren't even colonies: They were part of Portugal itself. The Angolans rose up in 1961, but Salazar crushed them mercilessly. Not until he died in 1968 could Angola and Mozambique even think about pushing off Portuguese rule.

Mozambique's nationalist movement was *Frelimo* (Front for the Liberation of Mozambique). Angola had three rival groups, who all hated each other:

✓ **MPLA (Movimento Popular de Libertaçao de Angola):** Formed in 1956. Backed by the USSR and Cuba. Wanted a socialist state along Marxist–Leninist lines.

✔ **FNLA (Frente Nacional de Libertaçao de Angola):** Formed in 1962. Backed by the USA and Congo. Wanted not to have a socialist state along Marxist–Leninist lines.

✔ **UNITA (União Nacional par a Independência Total de Angola):** Formed in 1966. Backed by the USA, South Africa, and Portugal. Wanted a pro-Western anti-communist Angola. Unita was for anyone who thought the FNLA were a bunch of liberal wimps.

The wars in Angola and Mozambique soon degenerated into a bloodbath. Neither side could win, until in 1974 a group of left-wing generals in Lisbon decided enough was enough, overthrew the Portuguese government, seized power, and announced that Portugal would withdraw from both territories. In Mozambique, Frelimo simply took over, but in Angola the rival groups could now start the *real* fight for power. Against each other.

In 1975 the Portuguese left and the war started. The MPLA in the north and Unita in the south gradually crushed the FNLA in the middle. With extra troops sent by Cuba, the MPLA then drove Unita back, but with Western and South African help, the Unita leaders carried on a guerrilla campaign from bases in Zambia and Zaire. The war lasted for several years before a truce could be negotatiated and then several more years passed before the nation finally was at peace. A quick rundown:

✔ **UN brokers a truce (1988):** Angola, South Africa, and Cuba agree that the Cubans and South Africans should go home.

✔ **Peace agreement (1991):** MPLA and Unita agree to stop fighting and hold elections.

✔ **Elections (1992):** MPLA wins. Unita says the election wasn't fair, and fighting starts again.

✔ **More elections (1994):** MPLA and Unita agree to stop fighting (again) and hold fresh elections. Unita refuses to give up any of its land to the MPLA.

✔ **Civil war breaks out again (1998):** Thousands are killed, some three million become refugees.

✔ **Peace (2002):** Unita leader Jonas Savimbi is killed in the fighting. The two sides finally sign a peace agreement.

Tragedy in the horn of Africa

Ethiopia, Sudan, and Somalia make up the land called the horn of Africa, because of its shape on the map. This area proved the scene of some of independent Africa's worst tragedies.

Ethiopia

Ethiopia is home to one of the oldest Christian churches in the world. The country was run as a sort of feudal monarchy until the Italians invaded in 1935 and forced the emperor, Haile Selassie, into exile in London. He stayed there until the British cleared the Italians out of Ethiopia during the Second World War and put him back on the throne.

Haile Selassie became known as 'the Lion of Judah' for his strong leadership, but by the 1960s he was falling behind the times: He ran an autocratic regime and only made very limited moves towards democracy. Radical students started to demand a Marxist republic in Ethiopia.

Ethiopia also had territorial disputes with Sudan and Somalia and a serious problem with the Muslim region of Eritrea, which had only been annexed in 1963 and now wanted to pull away. To make matters a lot worse, 1973 brought terrible draught and famine. In 1974 a group of army officers decided the time was ripe to get rid of the emperor and pull the country into the twentieth century. They staged a coup and drove Haile Selassie back into exile. The new president, Mengistu, declared that Ethiopia was henceforth a peace-loving socialist people's republic. Then he declared war on Eritrea.

The long war in Eritrea was a humanitarian catastrophe. The conflict dragged on because the Eritreans got help from Somalia while the Ethiopians got help from the Russians and Cubans. Just to make things more complex, the province of Tigré, which was part of Eritrea, also declared independence. President Mengistu didn't let a little thing like a civil war get in the way of restructuring the country: He pressed ahead with a programme of nationalising the land, limiting the amount allocated to each family, which caused maximum chaos just in time for an appalling drought that struck the country in 1984. Result: A devastating famine that shocked the entire world.

The war and the famine in Ethiopia dragged on through the 1980s. When the Soviet Union collapsed after 1989, so did Russian help for the Ethiopian government. Eritrea and Tigré saw their chance and launched a big attack into Ethiopia itself. In 1991 the Tigreans took the Ethiopian capital, Addis Ababa, and put their leader, Meles Zenawi, in charge. Meles immediately announced that he was introducing free elections and that provinces that wanted to pull out and set up on their own could do so. Eritrea took the hint and declared independence. This division didn't quite end the fighting – the two countries had another war over territory in 1998–2000 – but Meles seemed to be restoring a bit of stability by the time the century drew to its close.

Lowdown on Sudan and Somalia

Sudan and Somalia went through depressingly similar cycles of civil war and famine in the last decades of the twentieth century.

Dreadlock holiday

'Haile Selassie' ('Might of the Trinity') was the name the emperor took when he succeeded to the throne, rather as popes choose a new name when they're elected; his actual name was Ras (Prince) Tafari. In the 1970s and 1980s young Jamaicans and African-Americans looking for an inspiring African figure adopted Haile Selassie, as the exiled emperor of an ancient African Christian kingdom, and their Christian-with-back-to-my-African-roots religion was named 'Rastafarianism' after Ras Tafari. You could usually tell 'Rastas' by their dreadlocks, their fondness for reggae, and by a curiously sweet smell which seemed to emanate from the self-rolled cigarettes many of them were to be seen smoking.

Sudan

Africa's largest country became independent in 1956, but has seen years of internal strife since then.

- **Warring groups:** Christians in the south versus Muslims in the rest of Sudan.

- **Fighting about:** Christian south wanted to break away, until it got devolved government in 1972. Thereafter conflict between the south and the government over attempts to introduce Islamic Shariah Law.

- **Rest of the world interested?** Once oil was discovered there in the 1970s the rest of the world was very interested indeed. In 1998 the Americans launched a missile attack on a Sudanese chemical plant. They said it was making weapons and accused Sudan of acting as a base for Islamic terrorism.

- **Who came off worst?** The ordinary people. Thanks to the war, famine struck in 2001.

Somalia

In 1960 Somalia became an independent state, but the years since have been amongst the most turbulent seen by any African country.

- **Warring groups:** Marxist government backed by the USSR; Islamic fundamentalists; local warlords.

- **Fighting about:** Somalia attacked Ethiopia in 1977 to get territory but the USSR supported the Ethiopians (who were Marxists too, so perhaps the Russians tossed a coin). Fundamentalists wanted to establish an Islamic state, regions wanted to pull away, and warlords just liked killing people.

- **Rest of the world interested?** The USA and the UN sent troops into Somalia in 1992 to restore peace, but their losses were so heavy they pulled out (see the film *Black Hawk Down*). Mission: Impossible.

- **Who came off worst?** The ordinary people. Thanks to the war, famine struck in 2001.

Band Aid

Famine was nothing new to Africa, nor even to Ethiopia, but a BBC news report in 1984 showing desperate people, including small children, dying from starvation, somehow touched a nerve in the West. Bob Geldof of the Boomtown Rats phoned round other singers to form a one-off group called Band Aid which released the single 'Do They Know It's Christmas?' to raise money for famine relief in Ethiopia. He followed it up with a huge rock concert called Live Aid at Wembley Stadium in London in front of Prince Charles and Princess Diana, with headline acts from around the world. Live Aid raised a lot of money, and Bob Geldof made sure it was spent properly.

The end of British Africa

After Harold Macmillan's 'wind of change' speech in Capetown (see the earlier section 'Gone with the wind of change'), the British Colonial Secretary, Iain Macleod, decided to get the African colonies ready for independence as soon as possible. Some historians have criticised Macleod for rushing things, but at the time he was greatly respected by African nationalists, even though things didn't always go according to plan.

Nigeria

The British made Nigeria independent in 1960, but the different regions didn't trust each other (they were of different tribes and different religions). The British set up a federal system so the regions could run their own affairs. But:

- **Military coup by the east (1966):** Officers of the Ibo tribe in the east seize control, tear up the federal constitution, and set up a centralised state. With the Ibo in charge.

- **Military coup by the north (1966):** Officers of the northern region mutiny and assassinate the Ibo president, General Ironsi. The northern leader Yakuba Gowon takes charge.

- **The east pulls out (1967):** The Ibo declare the eastern region, the more prosperous part of Nigeria, the independent state of *Biafra* and tell General Gowon to put that in his pipe and smoke it.

- **Civil war (1967–70):** General Gowon leads his troops to crush the Biafrans. The civil war is bitter and tragic. Some *one million* people die of starvation and disease, many of them children, until Biafra surrenders.

After the war, Gowon tried hard to heal the country's divisions. Nigeria was becoming an important oil producing country: In 1971 it joined OPEC (the Organisation of Petroleum Exporting Countries), which proved a mixed blessing for General Gowon, because while he was away at an OPEC meeting in 1975 he was overthrown in a military coup. This was the first of many coups in the

1970s and 1980s. By the 1990s the Nigerian regime was promising a return to democratic government. Unfortunately, anyone who pointed out that it hadn't happened yet was arrested and in some cases, like the Nigerian writer Ken Saro-Wiwa, put to death.

Of course we always called it Keenya

The Brits took to the mild climate and rolling hills of Kenya – or 'Keen-ya', as they pronounced it – like a duck to water. It reminded them of home: They even talked of 'white highlands'. Three ethnic groups lived in British Kenya:

- **The British:** Owned the land and lived (very well) in 'happy valley' – one long round of golf, cocktails, and adultery.

- **The Asians:** Large numbers of Indians had settled in Kenya to work in the administration or to set up as shopkeepers and tradespeople.

- **The Africans:** The (vast) majority of the country's population with (by far) the least share of its wealth.

The Kikuyu tribe wanted their tribal lands back from the British who had settled on them. They tried negotiating, but in 1952 a militant group called Mau Mau began to use force. The British responded with savage repression and encouraged other tribes to attack Kikuyu villages. Both sides carried out appalling atrocities, sometimes massacring whole villages. The British kept Mau Mau suspects in camps where they were tortured and starved. All rule of law appeared to have collapsed in Kenya.

Historians still argue over exactly how many people died during the Mau Mau campaign: Some say about 12,000, others say it was twice that figure. About 1,000 were hanged by the British. What everyone agrees on is that only a very small number of European settlers were killed, even though those were the deaths that got most of the news coverage.

By 1960 the Mau Mau had been put down and the British were willing to talk about independence. Two political parties appeared, KANU (Kenya National African Union) for the Kikuyu and KADU (Kenya African Democratic Union) for everyone else. KANU won the election, and Jomo Kenyatta, a Kikuyu, left jail to become president of an independent Kenya. The settlers of happy valley packed their golf clubs and cocktail shakers and headed home.

The Kenyans resented the country's prosperous Asian population. The government started restricting their freedom of action, making it impossible for them to earn a living. Most got out and headed for Britain, where controversy about immigration was raging, so their welcome was about as warm as the British weather.

Tanzania and Uganda

The nationalists in Tanganyika, as it was called, were led by Julius Nyerere. He won the 1960 election and led his country to independence in 1961. In 1964

Tanganyika joined with the island of Zanzibar to form Tanzania. Nyerere proved one of Africa's most respected politicians, and he made Tanzania an oasis of stability in a continent where that was in short supply.

A very different story was happening in next-door Uganda, which became independent in 1962. The Kingdom of Buganda tried to go its own way, but in 1964 President Milton Obote took away the kingdom's right to govern itself, which soon made it behave. In 1971 General Idi Amin staged a coup and took power. Amin was a brutal dictator, as his people soon discovered. In 1972 he expelled Uganda's Asian community and forced them to flee to Britain. Some 400,000 people died during Amin's reign of terror. However, he made the mistake of attacking his neighbours; in 1979 Tanzania sent troops into Uganda who toppled Amin and put Milton Obote back in charge.

Idi Amin was an appalling tyrant and murderer: He had opponents beheaded and kept the heads in his fridge. He was also a big, flamboyant character who liked to dress up in a kilt and claim to be Head of the Commonwealth. You can get a sense of his personality in the film *The Last King of Scotland*. Milton Obote was just as ruthless a dictator, and may have killed even more people than Amin, but he didn't dress up or make wild threats against other countries, so the world hardly noticed.

The struggle in the south

British southern Africa had four states: Nyasaland, Northern Rhodesia, Southern Rhodesia, and the Union of South Africa. The first two had relatively small white settler communities; the other two had many more Europeans. The British tried proposing a single federation of Nyasaland and the two Rhodesias, but the black Africans realised (correctly) that this idea was a ploy to give the whites control even in the states where they were a small minority. The British tried locking the nationalist leaders up but when that didn't stop the opposition to federation they finally gave in and in 1964 set up three separate states. Nyasaland became *Malawi* under Dr Hastings Banda and Northern Rhodesia became *Zambia* under Kenneth Kaunda. Southern Rhodesia became a self-governing colony just called 'Rhodesia' with a right-wing, white supremacist government led by Ian Smith.

Smith was keen for Rhodesia to be independent too but the British insisted they would agree to it on the basis of black majority rule (or 'democracy' as this idea's also called). The white Rhodesians weren't having that situation – never in a thousand years, as Smith once famously put it – so in 1965 they declared UDI, their *Unilateral Declaration of Independence*. Though it sounded very like the Americans declaring independence from Britain back in 1776, the UDI sprang from much less noble motives.

All talks between Smith and the British failed and the African nations were pressing London to send in troops. The UN imposed sanctions on Rhodesia while the African nations helped the nationalist guerrilla movements. By 1979 white Rhodesia could not continue. Smith hoped to hand over to the moderate nationalists led by Bishop Abel Muzorewa, but the 1979 Lancaster House agreement insisted that the UDI should end and the British should resume power and organise free elections. So in 1980 colonial rule briefly *returned* to Africa, and the Rhodesians elected the left-wing Robert Mugabe as president of the new state of *Zimbabwe*.

South Africa's painful walk to freedom

Racial tensions were even worse in South Africa, which had a much larger white population. Since the right-wing Afrikaaner National Party won the elections in 1948, South Africa had operated a policy of *apartheid*, strict segregation of blacks, coloureds, and whites, even for public toilets and park benches, with all the best facilities, jobs, schools, and houses reserved for the whites. The regime operated strict censorship and didn't hesitate to arrest anyone who dared criticise it. Suspiciously large numbers of those arrested by the South African police never emerged alive.

Opposition to apartheid was led by the *African National Congress* (ANC), many of whose leaders, including Nelson Mandela, were imprisoned in 1964. Mandela remained in prison until 1990 despite a worldwide campaign for his release. Even worse, the police opened fire on unarmed demonstrators at Sharpeville in 1960 and on schoolchildren protesting at their inadequate education in Soweto township in 1976.

The UN imposed wide-ranging sanctions on South Africa to pressurise the government into abandoning apartheid. Peaceful protests in South Africa were led by religious leaders such as Archbishop Desmond Tutu; at the same time the ANC carried out armed raids with help from neighbouring states. In the 1980s the South African government began, reluctantly and with great trepidation, to relax some of the 'petty' apartheid laws, until finally in 1990 President F. W. de Klerk released Nelson Mandela and dismantled the whole apartheid system. South Africa experienced a free election for the first time in its history and the president it elected was Nelson Mandela.

South Africa had taken over South West Africa from the Germans as a League of Nations mandate after the First World War and had held on to it ever since. It extended the apartheid laws into South West Africa and took no notice when the UN withdrew the mandate and told South Africa to hand the country over. SWAPO (South West Africa People's Organisation) kept up a guerrilla campaign with Cuban help until South Africa finally gave in and gave independence to *Namibia* in 1990. The last African nation was finally free.

Chapter 13

Going Bananas: Latin America

*L*atin America experienced a very difficult time in the twentieth century. For much of the period these countries were ruled by military dictators and dominated by the economic might of the United States. All too often, the gap between rich and poor grew so large that many workers were reduced to living in shanty towns on the outskirts of the big cities. The native peoples of South America were often even worse off, as their homelands were bulldozed to make way for the expanding cities. Some countries managed to establish democratic rule for a time, but for the most part Latin America fell victim to brutal dictatorships and an endless cycle of military coups.

Latin America and Its Colonial Past

Geographically 'Latin America' means the continent of South America, Central America, which includes Mexico and Panama, and the Caribbean islands. This area is called 'Latin America' because the Spanish and Portuguese ruled it and their languages, which are derived from Latin, are still spoken there.

Ethnically Latin America, especially Brazil, is very mixed. Most of the people are a mixture of Spanish or Portuguese and native blood, but the region has also assimilated large numbers of people from Africa, Europe, and Asia. The black people of Latin America are mostly the descendants of slaves brought over by force during the slave trade. During the nineteenth century large numbers of Irish and Welsh settled in the region; more recently immigrants have arrived from Asia, especially Japan.

Yet you can't really understand Latin America today unless you've got a grasp of its colonial heritage. The people never forget that in ancient times their ancestors produced great civilisations, like the empires of the Incas, the Maya, and the Aztecs, which were destroyed by the Spanish *conquistadores* back in the sixteenth century while the Portuguese muscled in on Brazil. The Spanish and Portuguese held onto their Latin American possessions through the seventeenth and eighteenth centuries even though their own countries were rapidly losing their old power and influence: In fact, holding on to Latin America so fiercely was their way of trying to retain a bit of their old power and influence. (If you're intrigued by all this, you'll find the whole story in *European History For Dummies* (Wiley)).

Four main ethnic groups lived in colonial Latin America:

✔ Spanish and Portuguese people born in Europe

✔ Spanish and Portuguese people born in Latin America, known as Creoles. Creoles often intermarried with native people

✔ Natives, or 'Indians' as they were mistakenly known

✔ Africans brought over by force to work as slaves

Colonial Latin America had a governing class of great landowners – typically either European or Creole – who owned vast estates and had hundreds of natives and slaves to work on them. The powerful Catholic Church supported the governing classes and told all Catholics to do the same. So when ordinary people turned against their governments, which they did in due time (see the later section 'Throwing Off the Foreigners'), they usually turned against the Church as well.

Oh, Columbus!

Each year countries throughout the Americas mark 12 October as Columbus Day, the day the famous explorer first landed in the New World. Originally a day of celebration, nowadays Columbus is regarded more as a villain than a hero. His landing had a disastrous impact on the native peoples of America – if they weren't massacred or didn't die of European diseases, they got worked to death as slave labourers – and people in Latin America are gradually turning this date into a day of protest against what they see as Columbus's legacy: Poverty and oppression throughout the Americas. Statues of Columbus have been toppled and streets named after him have had their names changed.

Throwing Off the Foreigners

The Caribbean island of Haiti was the first Latin American country to eject its colonial rulers. In the 1790s the African slaves rose up, threw their French rulers out, and declared a 'black republic' along the lines of equality and fraternity the French Revolution was proclaiming to the world. Other countries in the region weren't very keen on the idea of slave risings, mainly because they owned slaves themselves and didn't want them getting ideas. But that doesn't mean other Latin American countries didn't want to do a little revolting themselves. The Creoles in particular were keen to take control from the Spanish but they didn't want slaves joining in and fighting for their own freedom.

The Creole leaders who fought for independence in South America in the nineteenth century are still regarded as national heroes, but they were often just as brutal and oppressive as the Spanish rulers they helped to get rid of. They had no intention of spreading freedom to the slaves or native peoples of Latin America. All too often the military figures who ruled South America in the twentieth century thought along exactly the same lines.

South America: The years of revolution

South America got its chance to throw its rulers out partly because of ideas of liberty and equality inspired by the French Revolution (details in *European History For Dummies* by Sean Lang) but mainly because in 1808 Napoleon invaded Spain and Portugal and forced their rulers to flee. Far away in South America, the Creoles saw this event as their chance to strike.

Big in Brazil

Probably the easiest handover of power was in Brazil, which was ruled by Portugal. With Napoleon's armies close on their tails, the Portuguese royal family fled to Brazil in 1808 and set up their court in Rio de Janeiro. They liked it so much they decided to make Brazil a kingdom in its own right. Rio became the capital of Brazil and the capital-in-exile of Portugal. Even after Napoleon finally fell in 1815, the Portuguese royal family stayed in Brazil until, in 1820, the Portuguese government got fed up with this arrangement – well, it was odd, you must admit – and tried to turn Brazil into a colony again. The king thought perhaps he'd been away too long and hurried back to Lisbon to take charge, while his son Dom Pedro simply declared Brazil an independent empire, with himself as Emperor Pedro I. Brazil remained an empire until a military coup in 1889 overturned the emperor and set up a republic.

The bloody end of Spanish South America

While the Napoleonic wars were raging in Europe, the Creoles of Spanish South America fought a fierce campaign to drive the Spanish out while simultaneously checking over their shoulder in case the slaves or the natives were staging their own revolts against their Creole masters. The campaign was led by a number of military rulers known as *caudillos* ('strongmen'), such as José de San Martin in Argentina, Simon Bolivar in Venezuela, and Bernardo O'Higgins in Chile.

This very bloody war didn't end until 1824 when Simon Bolivar became president of the brand new federation of *Gran Colombia*, which covered the old Spanish colonies. However, even Bolivar couldn't stop the different states of Gran Colombia quarrelling over territory. He tried to restore order by declaring himself Dictator of Gran Colombia in 1828 but it didn't make any difference. Bolivar died in 1830 and so, in effect, did Gran Colombia. In its place emerged the separate states of South America that we know today.

Independent South America was a very good place to be if you had a huge estate and believed in Power for the Rich. Unfortunately, South America was very poor and needed a big injection of foreign money, which at that time usually meant British money. The South American republics depended so heavily on Britain that they had effectively left the Spanish empire and joined the British one.

The heroes of South American independence were generals who led their people to military victory in war and then set up military dictatorships at home, like the ruthless General Rosas of Argentina. They had elected parliaments but the elections were rigged so that power still rested with the military. Staging a military coup was thus the only way to change government. This pattern continued right the way through the twentieth century.

Equally bloody revolution in Mexico

Mexico threw off Spanish rule in 1821. Independent Mexico was split between conservatives such as President Antonio de Santa Anna, who wanted a strong centralised empire, and radicals such as the fiercely anti-clerical Benito Juarez, who took power in 1861. That event prompted the French emperor Napoleon III to invade Mexico and install an Austrian prince, Maximilian, as emperor, but the Mexicans fought a fierce guerrilla war against the French and beat them at the Battle of Puebla on 5 May 1862 – Cinco de Mayo – still an important national festival in Mexico. The French scarpered; Maximilian stayed and the Mexicans shot him. Mexico became a republic again and in 1876 the radical José Porfirio Diaz was elected president. He stayed in office until he was finally overthrown in the Mexican Revolution of 1911.

Good Neighbour is Watching You: US Influence in Latin America

Latin America could never afford to ignore its mighty neighbour to the north, the United States. The (north) Americans regarded Latin America as 'Uncle Sam's back yard', which was another way of saying that they wanted to control it. The famous Monroe Doctrine warned the Europeans to keep their paws off the American continent or face war with the United States. As British power declined, the United States increasingly moved into the region as the main investor in Latin America. US investment meant, in effect, US control. The official term was a 'Good Neighbour' policy: The sort of neighbour who tells you what to buy when you go to the shops. This involvement had other effects, too.

Have a banana?

One of the results of having their economies completely dominated first by the British and then by the United States was that the Latin American states had to produce goods for export to satisfy these foreign markets. Many of them became heavily dependent on only one or two crops such as coffee, cocoa, or bananas. Whoever controlled these key trades effectively controlled the country; small, corrupt, and unstable Latin American states soon became known as 'banana republics'.

(South) America for the (North) Americans!

The British had been quite prepared to use force to protect their interests in Latin America. In the 1890s they sent troops into Chile, Brazil, and Nicaragua to stop governments threatening to nationalise private business. 'Hmm, why didn't we think of that?' thought Washington, so when Britain and Venezuela squared up to each other in a boundary dispute in 1895, the United States announced it was standing shoulder to shoulder with Venezuela and the Brits had better give way or it would be war. Very sensibly, the Brits backed off. From then on it was the US who called the shots in Latin America.

- ✔ **1898–1902: US pushes Spain out of Cuba** and takes over. US also gets Puerto Rico in the party bag at the end.

- ✔ **1903: US helps Panama win independence from Colombia** and gets a 99-year lease on the Panama Canal zone. Which wasn't the reason for helping the Panamanians at all – how could you possibly think that?

- **1904: President Theodore Roosevelt issues his *Corollary* to the Monroe Doctrine** saying the US is a 'civilised nation' so it can do what it likes in the savage Caribbean. All in the interests of international law and order, you understand.

- **1912: US takes over Nicaragua.** Just to protect US interests.

- **1914: US invades Mexico.** Aim: To bring down the Mexican government. Result: Mexicans unite against the US. Oops.

- **1915: US takes over Haiti.** Just to protect US interests.

- **1916: US General Pershing invades Mexico** to catch rebel leader Pancho Villa but can't find him.

- **1916: US takes over the Dominican Republic.** Just to protect US interests.

- **1917: Puerto Ricans become US citizens.** Which is very handy because they can now be drafted to fight in a world war.

- **1926: US takes over Nicaragua.** Again. Just to protect US interests. Again.

Life in Latin America: The Middle Years

At the start of the twentieth century Latin America had two major problems:

- **Neo-colonialism:** That means economic dependency on another country to such an extent that you might as well be one of its colonies. The obvious 'neo-colonial' power in the early years of the century was the US (refer to the preceding section, 'Good Neighbour is Watching You: US Influence in Latin America').

- **Latifundismo:** That means domination of the country's economy and society by the landowning classes on large estates. Many Latin American countries had very powerful (and small) ruling classes.

Latin American nationalists who wanted their countries to be truly free would therefore have to stand up both to the US and to the conservative, and usually pro-American, latifundismo within their own countries. Dealing with these two wasn't going to be easy.

Down Mexico way

Mexico had always been one of the more radical countries in the region. In 1911 the Mexicans staged a revolution and overthrew President Porfirio Diaz, who'd been in power since 1876 and was becoming increasingly autocratic in his old age. The revolution was followed by a rather complex multi-party power struggle – revolutions often are – but the key moment came in 1917 when Mexico unveiled its new revolutionary constitution. It said:

- All land to be nationalised, and the villages can take over land from the big private estates (*haciendas*)
- Full rights and social benefits for all workers
- No more church schools – all education to be run by the State

Radicals all over Latin America asked Santa to send them a Mexican constitution for Christmas – it seemed the perfect model for running a modern republican state. Unfortunately, the Mexican government didn't seem in a hurry to implement the new constitution. President Carranza gave women legal rights but he didn't implement the more radical parts of the constitution. He certainly didn't want the peasants taking land from the big estates.

In 1920 Carranza was overthrown and murdered in a coup. Cue chaos and civil war:

- **1920: Moderate President Obregon takes office.** Concentrates on reconciliation and reconstruction. These cannot be achieved, he decides, by implementing the more radical bits of the constitution. So he doesn't.
- **1924: Not quite so moderate President Plutarco Calles takes office.** He allows a little bit of land distribution but not so as you'd notice. He also closes all Catholic primary schools. Result:
- **1925–9: War between President Calles and the Catholic Church.** Church suspends all church services in protest at closure of Catholic schools. Catholic guerrilla group the *Cristeros* intimidate and murder state schoolteachers and kill former President Obregon. In his fight with the Church, President Calles becomes increasingly autocratic.
- **1929: Wall Street Crash.** American investment in Mexico slumps. Mexico's National Revolutionary Party calls for radical change. You know, like actually implementing Mexico's constitution.
- **1933: National Revolutionary Party** wins the election. New President Lazaro Cardenas redistributes land and starts a major industrialisation drive.
- **1938: President Cardenas nationalises oil companies.** Which is a very patriotic step but Mexicans are getting tired of Cardenas.
- **1939: Right-wing President Camacho elected.** He undoes all the changes Cardenas introduced, suppresses freedom of speech, and starts arresting trade unionists.

Mexico had seemed to show how you could follow a successful radical policy in Latin America, but the dream had gone sour. By the 1940s and 1950s Mexico's government was as authoritarian, oppressive, and corrupt as any other in Latin America.

Argentina – the Peron years

Argentina had started the century as Latin American State Most Likely To Succeed. Thanks to the invention of the refrigerated ship, Argentina had found a huge overseas market for its beef exports and it looked forward to a new century of prosperity and plenty. Well, the cattle ranchers did.

Like much of Latin America, Argentina was heavily dominated by Britain. Much of Argentina's industry was supported by British investment and British influences could be seen throughout Argentine society, especially at the upper end. The Argentine upper classes enjoyed taking tea on the lawn while watching polo and reading *Country Life*.

But underneath this happy façade Argentina was changing.

- ✔ **Industrialisation:** Under radical president Yrigoyen (1916–22) Argentina industrialises rapidly. This produces a large urban working class who are very open to radical ideas. Industrialisation also produces a middle class who look conservative, especially when they go into politics or the army, but aren't.

- ✔ **Inequality:** As long as Argentina's wealth depends on exporting beef, power lies in the hands of the big landowners. A huge gulf opens up between them and Argentina's poor.

- ✔ **Investment:** Argentina has a large balance of payments deficit, which means it is importing more than it exports. This situation makes the country heavily dependent on foreign investment and loans. These foreign investors can, and do, intervene in Argentina's internal affairs.

When countries industrialise rapidly they don't usually have much time to think about feeding or housing their workers properly, and Argentina was no exception. In 1916 the shipping workers came out on strike demanding better pay and conditions. The British didn't want their lucrative trade with Argentina jeopardised, so they put pressure on Buenos Aires to put the strike down, by force if necessary. So the government sent troops in to crush the strike – it wouldn't be the last time.

- ✔ **1919: 'Tragic week':** Government sends troops against strikers and Jews.

- ✔ **1922–8: Trouble in the shops:** Under President Alvear prices go up and wages go down.

- ✔ **1930: Crisis:** The Depression hits Argentina. General José Uriburu seizes power in a military coup.

Uriburu tried to show that all you need do to pull a country out of international economic meltdown is to arrest a few lefties and pinkoes. His brutal purges of opponents may have made him feel better but they did nothing for Argentina's economy, which was in freefall. With the world putting up trade barriers and no one buying Argentine beef, the country was more in debt to foreign investors than ever.

Enter Juan Peron

In 1943 a group of army officers overthrew General Uriburu and took power, promising a big industrialisation drive, full rights for women, and work for all, as long as the workers didn't join any of those pesky trade unions. The workers, who had every intention of joining those pesky trade unions, decided that these soldier boys weren't quite the saviours they'd thought and both sides lined up for confrontation. The situation was looking very ugly when in 1946 the Minister of Labour, the only truly popular character in the government, stepped forward and put himself up for election. He won and became president of Argentina. His name was General Juan Peron.

Peron was one of those middle-class professional soldiers with radical ideas. He appealed directly to the workers – the *descamisados* ('shirtless ones', because they couldn't afford clean shirts) – to Argentina's ethnic minorities, and especially to women. And to one woman in particular.

Evita!

You've seen the film, you've got the CD, now meet the woman. Eva Duarte (or Evita – 'little Eva' – as the public called her) was an ambitious young actress who captivated the then-Colonel Juan Peron. She certainly proved surprisingly good for him: She was glamorous, popular with the crowds, in short a major political asset. Women were playing an increasingly important part in radical Argentine politics and Eva appealed very strongly to them: She got them the vote, the right to divorce, and in 1947 she even started up a Peronist Feminist Party.

The powerful Argentine military, however, thought her a jumped-up little gold-digger and blocked Peron's proposal that she become vice president. Her Eva Peron Foundation to give money to charitable causes was wildly popular until people began asking awkward questions. Some people complained of being forced to contribute; others just pointed out that the money would have been better spent on trying to eradicate poverty itself, instead of handing out sweets and shoes. What the public didn't know was that Eva had cancer: She finally died, with her husband next to her, on 26 July 1952. Argentines really did weep in the streets at the news and 'Evita' instantly became a sort of saint, whose memory was always invoked whenever times got hard. In that sense, Evita was probably more significant after her death, as a symbol of Argentina's glory days under Peron, than she was when she was alive. So maybe the musical got it right: Argentina didn't need to cry for her.

It takes two to tango!

The tango is one of Argentina's most important cultural gifts to the world and it even played a part in Argentine politics. Peron was one of many who feared that Argentina was going down the pan because its men had lost their macho image and the tango, with the man throwing the woman around like a sack of old potatoes, seemed just the thing to instil a bit of manliness back in the Argentine breast.

Aficionados (ardent followers) will point out that tango exists in different forms and that most people get to see the rather tame version designed for tourists. Tango developed out of Spanish flamenco but got rid of all the stamping and clamping roses in the teeth. It was meant to be a dance you could do between the tables in a crowded nightclub – that's why tango dancers appear to walk in a straight line. The idea is that the man is a *gaucho* (cowboy) getting off his horse, striding into the saloon (a bit saddlesore, hence the bent legs), and sweeping a girl off her feet. Being a practical chap, he keeps a hand open behind his back for someone to pay him, and he holds the girl in the crook of his arm so she doesn't get too close to his sweaty armpits. How thoughtful.

We must be due for a military coup by now

Peron was a radical leader: He nationalised foreign companies operating in Argentina and brought in a proper system of social security. But after Eva died, Peron's fortunes began to crumble. Argentina's economy had done well during the Second World War, but by the 1950s the United States and the Europeans were offering serious competition again. Argentina began to go into the red and Peron had to turn to those old get-me-out-of-economic-trouble cards: Foreign investment and borrowing more than you can afford. As the situation worsened his rule became harsher: Critics were arrested and tortured and he attacked the Church, which is always a risky policy in Latin America. Worse: He alienated the army. In 1955 the army launched a coup and sent him into exile.

But after Peron things didn't get better: The economy was still weak, unemployment was up and so were prices. Argentina's answer to any economic problem was 'If in doubt, stage a military coup': Between 1930 and 1973 Argentina had *thirty* military coups. By 1973 civil war seemed around the corner, with students and workers rioting against the military government. Juan Peron came out of retirement and was elected president, but not even he could restore order. He died in 1974 and handed over power to his third wife, Isabelita, but in 1976 she was overthrown in yet another military coup. This coup brought a military junta (council) to power that would plunge Argentina into its darkest period yet.

Argentina's years of terror

Argentina's military rulers from 1976 to 1982 ruled the country through terror. During what became known as the 'dirty war' waged against Argentina's people, some 30,000 people simply 'disappeared' into torture cells set up in small police stations and disused schools up and down the country. These weren't all left-wing activists either: To be classed as an enemy of the regime you only needed someone with a grudge to denounce you. Men and women were taken, and any children were handed over to other parents to be brought up as their own.

In 1977 four brave women staged a demonstration in the Plaza de Mayo in Buenos Aires demanding to know news of their children and they were soon joined by a group of grandmothers who had given up trying to get news of their own children but thought they might have a chance of tracing their grandchildren. Every week an ominously silent – and ever larger – group of mothers and grandmothers would gather in the Plaza de Mayo with posters and photos of the Disappeared, making sure the world knew what was going on.

Democracy, good; nearly bankrupt, bad

Ironically, it was military action which finally brought the military government down. In 1982 the junta, led by General Leopold Galtieri, tried that classic tactic for uniting an angry country: Launch a foreign war. He ordered the invasion of the Falkland Islands, British-owned and settled but long claimed by Argentina, where they are known as the Malvinas. At first the public went wild with joy but when the British fought back and retook the islands, public joy turned to anger. All the pent-up fury about years of military oppression burst out: The military junta fell and for the first time in years Argentina elected a democratic government.

In 1989 Argentina elected Carlos Menem as president. Menem was a charismatic figure and he managed to reduce the power of the military, but he couldn't cut government spending and by 1999 Argentina was virtually bankrupt. Inflation went crazy and money became worthless. The country was in political and economic turmoil as the new century dawned.

Meanwhile, back with the neighbours . . .

Latin America was badly hit by the worldwide slump of the 1930s. Both the export market and foreign investment collapsed. Many Latin American countries needed strong leadership through the economic crisis; all too often army officers thought that this was a job for SuperDictator and his sidekick, Tortureman.

- **Chile:** Has a military coup in 1927.

- **Nicaragua:** Engages in a guerrilla war against occupying American troops that lasts from 1927 to 1933.

- **El Salvador:** Brutally suppresses a peasant rising in 1932.

   ✔ **Brazil:** Experiences a military coup in 1930.

   ✔ **Uruguay:** Experiences a military coup in 1933.

   ✔ **Nicaragua:** Sees the assassination of the guerrilla leader Sandino in 1934. In 1937 General Somoza sets up a family dictatorship.

Most dramatic was a territorial dispute between Bolivia and Paraguay over the Gran Chaco region. Landlocked Bolivia wanted it, mainly because this region would give the country access to the Atlantic. The fighting was extremely bloody, and an economic disaster for Bolivia (it lost). Under the peace terms, Paraguay got some Bolivian land and Bolivia got a narrow passage to the sea as a consolation prize.

A second world war? No thanks!

Latin America's military governments had a lot in common with fascist regimes in Europe (see Chapter 5 for more on these regimes). But when the Second World War started, Latin America stayed neutral and took advantage of the fighting to muscle in on the Europeans' trading markets. President Vargas of Brazil wanted US investment to build up his country's iron and steel industry and suggested ever so carefully that if the Americans didn't help, he just might have to turn to the Germans for the money instead; suddenly the Americans were fumbling for their cheque books.

After the war many Nazis fleeing from the Allies made their way to South America, where some of them, like Klaus Barbie, the infamous Gestapo chief in Lyon who made his way to Bolivia, advised the military regimes there on how to operate a secret police force and rule a country by terror, though most of the regimes had it down to a fine art already.

The Cold War Years and Beyond

After the war, the United States faced a dilemma in Latin America. On the one hand, the US was the world's leading democracy, devoted to the ideals of freedom and liberty. On the other hand, it was fighting the Cold War against the Soviet Union and could not afford to give its enemy a toehold on the American continent. The military regimes in Latin America were so brutally oppressive that the region's jungles and mountains were full of left-wing guerrilla movements who looked to the Russians for help. So the US had to hold its nose and support Latin America's repressive military governments. The Americans did sometimes suggest that their protégés might do something about their people's chronic poverty, but not many took much notice. They reckoned the US would back them whatever they did and by and large they were right.

Guatemala – don't fight the fruit

Before the Second World War, Guatemala's economy depended almost entirely on exporting fruit through the US-owned United Fruit Company, which effectively controlled the country. In 1944 the Guatemalans elected a progressive government committed to dealing with the country's appalling poverty, and in 1951 President Jacobo Arbenz announced that the government would take over all unused land so it could be put into agricultural production.

Unfortunately, a lot of that land belonged to the United Fruit Company, which got on the phone to Washington DC and by an extraordinary coincidence in 1954, the US government backed a military coup that toppled President Arbenz. The new government scrapped Arbenz's land programme and gave the United Fruit Company its land back. It also sent death squads out into the countryside to massacre whole villages and force the native people into exile. When Archbishop Casariggo protested, he was kidnapped by right-wing vigilantes. By the 1990s the country was torn apart by civil war.

The Guatemalan coup of 1956 had one important consequence. A wealthy young Argentine visiting the country was so disgusted by the American action that he decided to devote his life to anti-American communist revolution. His name was Ernesto 'Che' Guevara.

Great poster, Che

Alongside General Kitchener, Che Guevara can claim to be pictured on one of the twentieth century's most famous posters. His black-on-red photo, showing him all rough and unshaven and wearing a beret, was for years the must-have for every student bedsit wall. In fact Che, who came from a very well-heeled family in Argentina, usually dressed rather smartly but who wants that on their wall? As a young man he toured South America on a motorbike and saw for himself how the poor could be exploited by ruthless landowners or factory bosses (as shown in the film *The Motorcycle Diaries*), but it was the US-backed coup in Guatemala in 1954 that finally turned him into a professional revolutionary and instilled his hatred for the United States. He joined in with Castro's guerrillas and helped plan the campaign that toppled General Batista in Cuba. He served in Castro's government, trying to plan Cuba's industry along independent socialist lines, but was itching to get back to the jungle, so in 1965 he resigned and went off to lead the communist guerrillas trying to bring down the military government of Bolivia. Unfortunately the military government of Bolivia proved too strong for him and in 1967 he was killed fighting against its US-trained troops.

Che Guevara was an important symbol of revolution, but apart from helping Castro his influence on events was, frankly, fairly limited.

Cuba

Cuba in the 1950s was virtually an extension of the United States. Under the terms of the Platt Amendment, the US had the right to intervene in Cuba's internal affairs whenever it wanted to, which was often, and it kept a large naval base at Guantanamo Bay in case it ever came in useful. Cuba's economy served America's needs and Americans got used to hopping over to Havana for a fun weekend. Cuba's middle classes did very well out of this close relationship with the US; unfortunately, little of the money trickled down to the poor.

General Batista, who seized power in 1952, wanted to run Cuba along fascist lines, but in 1956 one of his leading opponents, Fidel Castro, started a guerrilla resistance movement. Batista's regime was so oppressive and corrupt that many Cubans supported the rebels and by 1958 even Batista's army was giving up on him. At New Year 1959, the rebels entered Havana and Batista had to flee into exile. Fidel Castro was the new ruler of Cuba.

Because we know that Castro became a great enemy of the United States, it's easy to assume that he was always an out-and-out communist. He certainly became a communist later, but the evidence suggests that he wasn't anything of the sort when he took power. Castro was a *nationalist* and just wanted Cuba to govern its own affairs. He didn't trust the Americans, but he was prepared to work with them. The Americans didn't trust Castro overmuch either, but they were prepared to work with him. For now.

You're playing with the big boys now, Mr Castro

In 1960, a year after Castro seized power, John F. Kennedy was elected president of the United States. Kennedy knew that many world leaders viewed him as young and inexperienced. Or, to put it another way, a push-over. His opposite number in Moscow was Soviet leader Nikita Khrushchev, a tough old Bolshevik who thought he could make mincemeat of Kennedy. Both of them looked to Cuba as the place to play out their particular brand of he-man diplomacy.

Bay of Pigs invasion, 1961

Anti-Castro Cubans in exile in the US were plotting to bring down Castro's government. President Kennedy allowed the CIA to help them with weapons and transport but he wouldn't allow US troops to get involved. This decision was a recipe for disaster:

- ✔ **What was meant to happen:** Anti-Castro Cubans land at the Bay of Pigs on the south coast of Cuba, overcome the border guards, and are greeted as liberators by happy crowds dancing all night in the streets. Fidel Castro is put on trial and shot for being left wing and growing a beard.

- ✔ **What actually happened:** Cuban border guards shot the invaders to pieces and President Kennedy refused to send help. Kennedy looked a fool and Castro grew his beard even longer.

Only after the Bay of Pigs did Castro announce that he'd taken up Marxism-Leninism. That doesn't mean he wouldn't have done so anyway, but it does show that any chance of co-operation with his powerful neighbour had completely disappeared. The attack also helped unite Cubans behind Castro: He had always said the Americans would attack and he'd been proved right.

Cuban missile crisis, 1962

In 1962 the Soviet Union planned to station nuclear missiles on Cuba which would be able to reach most of the mainland United States. When US spy planes reported what was going on, President Kennedy ordered an immediate blockade of Cuba. Moscow threatened war if the Americans bombed or invaded the island and as Soviet ships carrying the missiles approached the US blockade, nuclear war seemed frighteningly close. Only a last-minute climbdown by the Russians saved the world from destruction. (You can find out more about the Cuban missile crisis in Chapter 10.)

Castro played a crucial role in the crisis. He was very keen for the Russians to put missiles on Cuba as a way of warning the Americans off any thought of invading and overthrowing him and he never forgave Moscow for backing down in the face of American threats.

Castro's Cuba

Castro had a good eye for image. He presented himself as a Robin Hood-type figure, protecting the poor from the Big Bad Rich and cultivated the 'professional revolutionary' look, chomping a big Cuban cigar and wearing jungle fatigues even in the office. Cuba gained a reputation for exporting revolution, especially in Africa, where Cuban soldiers fought alongside Marxist groups in the 1970s (you can find out more in Chapter 12). Castro oversaw big advances in education and healthcare in Cuba. Getting the economy right proved more tricky.

At first Castro and his Industries Minister, Che Guevara, tried to set Cuba up as an autonomous socialist economy, but an American boycott made this impossible without Soviet help. So in the 1970s Castro tied Cuba into the increasingly stagnant Soviet economic bloc. When the Soviet Union collapsed in 1991, Castro had to open the country up to Western investment and tourism or go under. The US still tried to maintain an international boycott of Cuba, especially after Cuba shot down two American aircraft in 1996, but the rest of the world increasingly began to open up economic links with the Castro regime. What no one could predict was whether Cuba could remain a hard-line communist state if it was operating as part of the global economy.

Okay, how about exploding socks?

From the moment Castro overthrew Batista, the Americans came up with a catalogue of amazing ways of getting rid of their Least Favourite Foreign Ruler. First they tried snipers. No joy. So they turned to the Mafia but even they couldn't penetrate Castro's security. So the CIA really put its thinking caps on. They sent Castro boxes of poisoned cigars and when he didn't smoke those, they sent him exploding ones instead. They tried poisoning his shoes when he was in New York to address the United Nations, sticking him with a poisoned syringe disguised as a pen, and they even sent him poisoned handkerchiefs, which was very silly as everyone knows that a good proletarian revolutionary uses his sleeve – why else would he wear green all the time? They tried sending a woman to seduce him with poison pills hidden in her cold cream, but the pills melted and even she drew the line at smearing cold cream on his lips. Castro guessed what was going on and offered to shoot himself to save her the trouble! 'Right!' said the CIA, 'bring in the exploding molluscs!' The idea was to plant them on the sea bed ready for when he went scuba diving. That's if the specially poisoned scuba diving suit hadn't done for him first. It's been calculated that the CIA came up with *638* different plots to assassinate Castro and at the time of writing (2007) not one of them has worked.

Chile

Chile had a proud history of leading South America's fight for freedom from the Spanish. Since independence, however, Chile had been dominated by wealthy landowners living very comfortably on their *haciendas*. As Chile industrialised, it developed a working class who looked to radical left-wing groups to speak for them. President Alessandri tried to take some of the radicals into his government in 1920 but the upper classes weren't having that and they used their control of the Senate to stop him. The situation was deadlocked until the army took the usual Latin American step of launching a military coup.

Chile's military government was good at locking up its critics but it had no idea how to cope with the economic crisis the country faced during the Depression. The Chileans tried electing radical governments and they tried electing right-wing governments until finally in 1970 they became the first country in the world to elect an out-and-out Marxist government. It was headed by Salvador Allende.

Allende nationalised the country's copper mines and all foreign-owned industry, took land away from the rich, gave the workers a pay rise, and kept prices down. The trouble was, he didn't have the means to pay for all these developments and as the nation sank into economic crisis, the people took to the streets. By 1973 the country had a serious problem of law and order and Allende's enemies, both in Chile and in Washington, decided to make their move. On 11 September 1973, with covert American backing, army units under General Augusto Pinochet overthrew and killed President Allende. Pinochet promptly set up a brutal and repressive military regime.

Pinochet brought foreign investment into Chile and brought inflation under control. On the other hand, plenty of people still lived in dire poverty and anyone who tried to speak for them was soon in trouble: Pinochet's regime was notorious for torturing its opponents.

Historians and commentators have very different versions of what happened in Chile in the 1970s. Some argue that Allende was leading Chile to economic collapse and that General Pinochet restored the economy and saved the country from chaos. Others argue that economic recovery was no excuse for the whole-sale murder, torture, and repression of the Pinochet regime.

By 1988 Pinochet bowed to intense international pressure and handed power over to a civilian government, which gradually restored some basic freedoms to the Chilean people. In 1998 Pinochet was arrested in London on charges of torture, but he argued successfully that he was too ill to stand trial and the British government sent him back to Chile, where he made a miraculous recovery by the time the plane touched down. After furious debate, the socialist government of Ricardo Escobar decided to grant him immunity from prosecution.

Peru

Like so many Latin American countries, independent Peru was dominated by a small number of very wealthy families. However, when Peru discovered it was sitting on a large oil supply, it developed the same sort of middle and working classes as other industrial states. Industrial classes usually challenge the landed classes for power and Peru was no exception. The native peoples of Peru were also being increasingly marginalised. In 1924 Haya de la Torre formed a radical party called the American Popular Revolutionary Alliance to speak for Peru's workers and downtrodden, but it took until 1962 for him to get elected president and then he was prevented from taking office by the army.

Peru was developing rapidly as an oil-producing nation but despite extensive American investment the country was deeply in debt, especially when oil prices slumped in the 1980s. The economy collapsed, production fell, unemployment soared, and the whole country seemed to be going backwards. Alberto Fujimori, from Peru's Japanese immigrant community, finally installed a bit of discipline. Fujimori became president in 1990 and brought in a tough regime of economic cuts and constitutional changes to give more power to the presidency. He took firm action against the drug barons and against the ruthless communist terrorist group 'the Shining Path'. However Fujimori's brand of discipline meant giving the secret police a free hand to terrorise the people. His regime was deeply corrupt and when he won the 2000 elections with a suspiciously huge majority, his government found itself accused of massive vote-rigging. Fujimori fled to Japan while the Peruvian former United Nations Secretary-General Javier Perez de Cuellar stepped in to oversee new elections.

Contra-versy: Nicaragua and El Salvador

The United States was particularly concerned to keep control of Central America with the vital Panama Canal. Not everyone in the region saw eye to eye with this policy.

Nicaragua

The United States had twice sent troops into Nicaragua, in 1912 and in 1926, because it didn't like the country's government. In 1937 the ruthless General Somoza seized power. Somoza hated communists, so the US could rest easy: Nicaragua was in safe right-wing hands as long as he or anyone in his family entourage was in charge, which they were until 1979.

The main opposition to the Somoza family came from a guerrilla group called the Sandinista National Liberation Front, named after Cesar Sandino, the guerrilla leader executed on Somoza's orders in 1934. The Sandinistas finally forced the Somoza regime to collapse in 1979. At first the US was prepared to work with the Sandinistas but that changed when Ronald Reagan was elected US president in 1980. He decided that the Sandinistas were the spawns of Satan and must be destroyed at all costs, so his administration sent money and arms to the 'Contras', a group of former Samoza officers who had started a guerrilla resistance group against the Sandinista government. The Reagan administration even financed his military aid programme by a secret and highly illegal deal to sell arms to the government of Iran.

With Washington funding its enemies, the Sandinista government turned for help to Cuba and the Soviet Union; unfortunately, doing so didn't help with the economic crisis the country was going through in the 1980s. However, ultimately the Sandinistas fell to something much less spectacular than US-backed rebels: President Daniel Ortega simply lost the 1990 election to his right-wing opponents. For a while civil war seemed imminent, but Ortega accepted a plan put forward by President Arias of Costa Rica (see the next section) and stepped down. The US lifted its sanctions and the Contras laid down their arms. Nicaraguan politics in the 1990s were a confusing picture of splits and faction fighting. The Sandinistas won the local elections of 2000, though, and they remain an important force in Nicaraguan politics.

El Salvador

El Salvador was a coffee republic where power, land, and pretty much all the nation's wealth lay in the hands of a small group of fourteen powerful coffee planter families. They maintained their control through ruthless repression: The peasant uprising in 1931 was savagely crushed by the military. By the 1970s, however, opposition to the planters was growing fast, much of it voiced by the Catholic Church, which protested against the blatant exploitation of the country's poor.

In 1980 government agents murdered the Archbishop of El Salvador, Oscar Romero, in his own cathedral. This assassination shocked the world and prompted the different opposition groups to join together in a united front against the government. By 1981 the country was torn apart by a civil war that lasted for ten years. The US, fearful of a communist victory, supported the government.

The man who brought peace to El Salvador was Oscar Arias, president of Costa Rica, one of the very few Latin American countries to remain more or less stable through the twentieth century. In 1987 Arias negotiated the basis for peace in Nicaragua and El Salvador. His recipe:

- ✔ **Free and fair elections** (and everyone to abide by the result).
- ✔ **Superpowers keep out.** Let the people choose their own government.

In 1992 El Salvador accepted a peace plan along the lines Arias had laid down. The opposition groups gave up the armed struggle and took up the much more vicious game of parliamentary politics.

Liberation Theology

In the 1980s the Catholic Church in Latin America started speaking up forcefully on behalf of the region's poor. It wasn't just telling people to put a peso in the collecting box: The Church was voicing full-blooded criticism of government terror tactics. A Peruvian priest called Gustavo Gutierrez provided the inspiration for this change in emphasis; he wrote a book called *Theology of Liberation* which argued that Christianity was about justice or it was about nothing. He pointed out that the poor are only poor in the first place because the rich are rich. Other priests took up Gutierrez's message and a whole brand of preaching developed called 'Liberation Theology', led by priests such as Leonardo Boff, Jon Sobrino, and Oscar Romero, the Archbishop of El Salvador murdered by a government hit squad.

Not surprisingly, the governments of Latin America had very little time for Liberation Theology; perhaps more surprisingly, neither had the Vatican. Pope John Paul II had no time for military dictators (he'd been in Poland when the Nazis invaded) but he hated communism even more. He was afraid that Liberation Theology would help communist governments to come to power in Latin America and that Liberation Theologians were letting their concern for justice for the poor get in the way of preaching the gospel to them. He even summoned Leonardo Boff to Rome for a severe reprimand. By the 1990s Liberation Theology had largely died away, but this did not stop priests from speaking out in defence of the poor or dispossessed.

We all like the idea of the good man who saves the day so giving President Arias all the credit for bringing peace to Nicaragua and El Salvador is tempting. He certainly thoroughly deserved the Nobel Peace Prize he was awarded for his work. But historians would have to point out that his plan probably wouldn't have worked were it not that by 1992 the Soviet Union had collapsed and could no longer help left-wing guerrilla groups in Latin America. So he had good timing as well as good sense.

And elsewhere . . .

Other states in Latin America have had their share of economic ups and downs and military coups. Here's a quick tour of some of the highs and lows:

Venezuela did very well from oil until prices slumped in the 1980s and the country fell into debt. Venezuelans rioted against President Perez's economy measures and attempted a very bloody coup. They also accused him (rightly) of corruption. In 1999 Hugo Chavez became president on an anti-corruption ticket, but he soon proved just as bad, taking more power for himself and censoring the press. None of these developments helped Venezuela's poor.

Brazil's response to the Great Depression was to set up a military government under President Vargas, which modernised the economy until the next coup in 1945. The new government borrowed so heavily that the country was up to its ears in debt and corruption. The new state-of-the-art capital city, Brasilia, proved a costly failure, so everyone headed back to Rio de Janeiro. The police response to the country's chronic poverty and high crime rate was to send death squads out to murder people. Meanwhile the native people of the Amazon rainforest were being systematically wiped out by police action and by the government's policy of deforestation.

Er, it's only a game, guys

Latin America took to football with tremendous passion and the region has produced some of the game's legendary players. Best known is the Brazilian footballer Edson Arantes do Nascimento, better known as Pele. Pele's almost magical control of the ball led Brazil to victory in the 1970 World Cup. Diego Maradona did the same for Argentina in the 1986 tournament, though his goal against England, four years after the Falklands War, was almost certainly a case of hand-ball, as even he seemed to admit. The storm over that incident was nothing compared to the 1969 World Cup qualifying match between El Salvador and Honduras: The two countries actually went to war over it. Even more somberly, Latin America's most brutal military regimes sometimes used football stadiums to hold and torture political prisoners. Football symbolises the best and the worst of Latin America's history.

Paraguay was ruled for more than thirty years by a ruthless dictatorship led by General Alfredo Stroessner until he was overturned in a coup in 1989. The democratic government that followed was rocked by allegations of corruption, threats of a coup, and in 1999 the assassination of the vice-president.

Uruguay had a military dictatorship, which, by the 1970s, had made the country 'the torture chamber of Latin America'. In 1984 huge public protests forced the government to reintroduce democracy, though the new government soon had to deal with a crippling economic crisis.

Mexico struck oil in the 1970s but the country's poor didn't see much of the profits. Mexican students protested against the status quo by listening to Status Quo and other rock bands – very loudly. Meanwhile a native Mexican guerrilla force, the Zapatistas, took on the government troops and did win some autonomy for themselves. In 2000 the opposition leader Vicente Fox was elected and started to hold inquiries into previous governments' record of murder and torture.

Bolivia overthrew its military regime in 1952, but the left-wing regime that followed was overthrown in a military coup in 1964. This was the US-backed military government that proved too strong for Che Guevara (see the sidebar 'Great poster, Che' to find out more). Different generals deposed each other but Bolivia remained under military rule until 1982. The civilian government pledged to eradicate the drugs trade even if it meant economic ruin for the country. They did and it did.

Colombia was torn by ten years of civil war in the 1940s and 1950s until left and right agreed to try sharing power. By then drugs barons had taken advantage of the chaos to terrorise farmers into growing coca and make Colombia one enormous cocaine factory. It was also the world homicide capital. As the century drew to its close, not even full-scale military assault could break the power of the drugs cartels.

Grenada overthrew and murdered President Maurice Bishop in 1983. US President Reagan, fearing that Grenada would become another Cuba, ordered an invasion of the island. Grenada returned to democratic government and exporting bananas.

Haiti was ruled by a brutal father-and-son team: François Duvalier, known as 'Papa Doc', and his son Jean-Claude, or 'Baby Doc'. They claimed to have supernatural voodoo powers; they certainly had a terrifying secret police force known as 'Tonton Macoute' after the bogeyman in children's stories. In 1986 'people power' finally overthrew Baby Doc but Haiti's troubles weren't over: The military seized power in 1988 and 1991 and three years later US President Clinton ordered the invasion of Haiti to restore the legally elected president, Bertrand Aristide. In 2000 Aristide's election victory with a not-very-credible 90 per cent brought accusations of industrial-scale vote-rigging. The twentieth century had done little to solve Haiti's problems.

Panama became a major centre of international trade and finance under General Torrijos in the 1970s but he died in a plane crash in 1981, leaving the way open for the ambitious and erratic head of the National Guard, General Noriega. Noriega was up to his neck in the international drugs trade, and after he seized power in 1989 he started threatening the US. In response, the Americans invaded Panama, forced Noriega out of hiding in the Vatican embassy (they blasted the building with heavy rock music, which did the trick!), and whisked him off to face trial; he got 40 years for drug dealing. Ten years on, in 1999, the US finally handed Panama control of its own canal.

The fundamental things apply

Despite all the military coups and fights for freedom, Latin America's biggest problems weren't political at all. A series of natural disasters devastated the region: 23,000 people were killed in Colombia in 1985 when the Nevado del Ruiz volcano erupted, and an earthquake the same year devastated Mexico City. In 1998 Hurricane Mitch hit Nicaragua; the following year heavy rains caused disastrous floods and mudslides in Venezuela; two years later Bolivia had the same, and El Salvador suffered a major earthquake.

By the 1990s world opinion was increasingly worried about changes in the climate. The earth seemed to be building up greenhouse gases that eroded the earth's protection from the sun and much of the blame seemed to lie with Brazil's policy of cutting down the Amazon rainforest. Brazil hosted the 1992 Earth Summit in Rio, which called on everyone to limit their greenhouse gas emissions but didn't seem to make much difference.

You can find out more on the environmental debate in Chapter 20.

Chapter 14

Asian Tigers

This chapter looks at the independent states of Asia after the Europeans had pulled down their flags and sailed home. It deals with India, Pakistan, Indonesia, Malaysia, and the states of south-east Asia like Vietnam and Thailand. It also covers Australia and New Zealand, which might surprise you, though in fact the continent of Australasia is essentially an extension of Asia. One rather big Asian country – China – isn't dealt with in detail here. Communist China was such an important power that it gets separate treatment in Chapter 16.

Before the Second World War, Asia was dominated by the Western powers. By the end of the century, the 'Asian tiger' economies dominated the world. How did the continent make this amazing change? And just how far did the people of Asia share in the new wealth their leaders enjoyed? Asia changed in the twentieth century more than any other part of the world, but change and prosperity sometimes came at a terrible price.

A Quick Rundown of Key Events in Asia

Like the rest of the world, Asia started the second half of the century recovering from the devastating effects of the Second World War and adjusting to the Cold War. Some Asian countries tried to set up a 'non-aligned' movement free of either American or Soviet influence, but keeping Asia free from Cold War conflict proved to be an impossible task. By the last decades of the century, some Asian countries had established themselves as economic powerhouses, but all too often economic prosperity came at the price of human rights.

The terrible price of the Second World War

The Second World War was a disaster for Asia. In fact, strictly speaking, the Second World War *began* in Asia, when the Japanese invaded the Chinese province of Manchuria in 1931 and the rest of China six years later. The Chinese kept up a fierce resistance movement which meant the Japanese were bogged down in a war they could see no chance of winning. For that reason they decided to attack the rest of Asia and seize all the raw materials they could lay their hands on. The idea was to pretend the war was about liberating Asia from imperialism; in fact the Japanese just imposed their own brutal imperial rule on their fellow Asians.

Ordinary people in Asia suffered terribly during the war:

- **Starvation:** In many of the areas they conquered, and especially in China, the Japanese confiscated food for their own use and left the people to starve.

- **Rape:** The Japanese used a policy of rape to enforce their rule. The worst example was at Nankin in China, where thousands of Chinese women were systematically raped by Japanese soldiers. The Japanese also forced women to become 'comfort women' – prostitutes – for their soldiers.

- **Fighting and bombing:** The Pacific islands that the Japanese and Americans fought over were virtually destroyed and the inhabitants' homes with them. Tokyo suffered appalling firestorms from American bombing that actually killed more people than the atomic bomb raids. The people of Hiroshima and Nagasaki paid a terrible price when their cities were destroyed by American atom bombs and thousands died later from radiation sickness.

Communist take-over in China

In 1949 Mao Tse-tung's Communist Party seized control in Peking (see the Introduction for info about how Chinese names are rendered in English) and proclaimed the People's Republic of China (PRC). Result: Crisis, because the United States said the old government, which had fled to the island of Formosa (modern-day Taiwan), was the only true Chinese government and Mao's regime was illegal. Not that Mao worried: He just got on with sending help to every Asian communist movement he could find. You can read more about what Mao was up to in China in Chapter 16.

Prior to the Second World War, the Americans liked to think of Asia as their special part of the world. Americans were responsible for opening up Japan to the West (though by the Second World War they were probably wondering if doing so had been such a great idea) and China was an important base for American missionaries. When Mao Tse-tung seized power in China in 1949, US Senator Joseph McCarthy declared that America had 'lost' China and

American communist traitors were to blame (Chapter 15 covers Senator McCarthy and his interesting ideas). In fact, most Americans assumed that communist China would be in the pocket of the Soviet leader, Joseph Stalin, or 'Uncle Joe' as Americans called him during the war. Stalin shared this assumption. Big mistake. Mao and the other Asian communist leaders had no intention of taking orders from Moscow. Uncle Sam and Chairman Mao would fight it out for control of Asia.

The Korean War

Korea was split in two at the end of the war, with communists controlling the north and a pro-Western government in the south, both of them claiming the right to rule the whole country. In 1950 the North Koreans invaded the south and nearly conquered it, but the United States persuaded the United Nations to send help. The UN forces defeated the North Koreans, but then they invaded North Korea, which was just what Mao had warned them not to do. A huge Chinese army invaded and drove the UN forces back to the original border. The Korean War committed the United States to resisting the advance of communism throughout Asia. (Chapter 10 has more on the Korean War.)

The Vietnam War

The Vietnam War was one of the defining conflicts of the twentieth century, partly because it pitched a superpower against a tiny country that the Americans should've been able to crush before lunch, and partly because of the fierce controversy generated by American tactics and their effects on the people of Vietnam. Yet by the end of the century Washington had established friendly relations, and even a trade agreement, with communist Vietnam. So what was the Vietnam War really about? To answer this question, go to the later section, 'Apocalypse Now – Vietnam'.

Tigers or pussy cats?

By the 1990s the Asian countries seemed to be dominating the world economy, particularly as they specialised in producing the sort of hi-tech equipment on which the modern world has come to depend. But much of this success was an image: A few people were making a lot of money but behind the computers and fast cars the people of Asia still lived in utter poverty. Many of these 'Asian tiger' economies depended heavily on foreign loans and investment and in 1997 the cracks suddenly opened. Thailand found itself heading into bankruptcy and as its currency went into freefall, the market began to lose faith in the other Asian economies. South Korea and Indonesia virtually collapsed and others, such as Hong Kong, Taiwan, and the Philippines, were badly hit. Some governments were actually brought down by the crisis, such as that of General

Suharto in Indonesia. By the twenty-first century it was clear that the real Asian tigers were the two giants who'd survived the 1997 crash almost unscathed: India and the rapidly changing China (to find out why it was rapidly changing, see Chapter 16).

Japan – the Rise of the Rising Sun

Probably the most remarkable success story in post-Second World War Asia was Japan. No one expected that defeated, humiliated Japan would become an economic superpower, but it did.

Before the war Japan was a strange mixture of ancient and ultra-modern. The country had state-of-the art industry and military technology, but was still governed according to the medieval samurai code. The Japanese believed the emperor was a god and that they owed him absolute loyalty. This sense of loyalty was why the Japanese fought so fiercely, even against overwhelming odds. Some Japanese soldiers, cut off from news from the outside world, carried on fighting the war for years, still true to their oath of loyalty to the emperor. Even after the atom bomb attacks on Hiroshima and Nagasaki, the Japanese government still talked about carrying on the war until the emperor finally intervened and went on the radio to announce to his people that these new weapons meant the war had taken a turn which was not necessarily to Japan's advantage – which must be the understatement of the century.

The Court of King MacArthur

Japan began the post-war era under American occupation. The Supreme Commander of the Allied Powers (SCAP) was General Douglas MacArthur, who had made his name defending the Philippines against the Japanese in 1942. MacArthur soon showed he could be just as imperious as any emperor. When people asked if he would visit Emperor Hirohito, MacArthur replied that the emperor should visit him, and he did too. Japan had serious food shortages, so MacArthur arranged for American food aid. In return, he brought in some big changes:

- ✔ **The emperor was no longer a god.** Instead he became a British-style constitutional monarch, with an elected parliament running the country.

- ✔ **The army and the secret police were disbanded.** Japan was allowed to have a small army but for defensive purposes only. Japan declared it would no longer send troops abroad, not even for peacekeeping missions.

✔ **Large landed estates were broken up into small farms that peasants could buy.** This policy was to create a class of landowners – small landowners but landowners all the same – who wouldn't want communists trying to take their land off them. MacArthur's policy worked: The Japanese peasants became strongly anti-communist.

✔ **Old-style nationalists and fascists were sacked.** This included civil servants, lecturers, and teachers. As a result, Japanese students became very left-wing, which wasn't quite what MacArthur had intended.

The Allies held a series of war crime trials, like the Nuremberg Trials in Germany. Japan's wartime leaders, including the infamous General Tojo, were hanged. Japan also made an important decision. As it faced up to the terrible after-effects of the atomic bombs over Hiroshima and Nagasaki, the Japanese government decided to have nothing whatever to do with making, deploying, using, or even holding nuclear weapons, and they stuck to it.

Making a killing from killing

At first the Americans wanted to keep Japan as a rather backward, rural country, an nice easy market for American business. But in 1950 the Korean War broke out. The Americans needed lots of military equipment and they needed it fast. The Japanese knew how to grab an opportunity when they saw one: They could produce the hardware and get it to the front line more quickly than American firms. Soon American GIs were heading into battle in Toyota trucks and Japanese firms were revising their economic forecasts upwards.

When the Korean War was over, the Japanese moved into civilian transport and hardware. Japanese cars and motorbikes sold all over the world and by the end of the 1960s, Japan was the world's biggest shipbuilder. The Japanese also moved into niche markets such as electronics and hi-fi. By the end of the century, you could ride a Honda or a Mitsubishi motorbike, drive your Nissan car, play CDs on your Sanyo music centre, or listen to your Sony Walkman.

What was the Japanese secret? Discipline. The working day in a Japanese factory began with physical jerks and the company song. Trade unions were weak and strictly controlled and workers committed their lives to the company just as soldiers had sworn loyalty to the emperor during the war. By the 1980s Japanese companies were even setting up factories in the West.

The country that came in from the cold

Japan finally emerged from the shadow of the war in the 1960s. Japanese goods won a reputation for being cheap and reliable. In 1964 Japan became the first Asian country to host the Olympic Games and they proved a triumph, especially the state-of-the art gymnasium building. Four years later the Japanese writer

Kawabata Yasunari won the Nobel Prize for Literature. In 1970 Japan hosted the phenomenally successful Expo '70, the world exhibition of technology and trade, which showcased just what a hi-tech success story modern Japan had become.

Japan became a vital American ally in the Cold War and began to adopt elements of American culture. Japanese schools were remodelled on American lines and some even took up baseball. Rocky periods did occur: Major anti-American riots broke out in the 1950s after Japanese fishing catches were contaminated by radiation from American nuclear tests at Bikini Atoll in the Pacific, and left-wing students were often very anti-American. But most Japanese enjoyed the benefits of their close relationship with their old wartime enemy.

Korea – One Country, Two States

When the Korean War ended (see Chapter 10 for the details), the country was still divided into two states near the 38th parallel. These two states developed in very different ways.

North Korea – there ain't nothin' wrong with me

North Korea kept true to its hardline communist principles. In 1958 Kim Il-Sung took control and set about industrialising the country in a series of seven-year plans. He needed to borrow heavily to finance this industrialisation, so North Korea ended up deeply in debt. That Kim spent lavishly on the military and on a huge personality cult based on himself didn't help. He cut North Korea off from contact with the outside world so that by the time he died in 1994, it was an island of old-style communist dictatorship under an all-powerful leader. After Kim's death, his son Kim Jong-Il seized power and carried on the way his father had ruled. By now Korea was deep in economic crisis and famine – some experts reckon that two million people may have starved. The Chinese persuaded Kim to go and meet the South Koreans and accept food aid from them. He did, but he made it clear that doing so didn't mean North Korea would be changing anything else.

South Korea – nor me

South Korea was a big economic success story, like Japan (see the preceding section). Thanks to American aid it became a major financial centre and one of the world's leading producers of computers and information technology.

The trouble was that South Korea's idea of human rights and democracy took time to catch up.

Until 1960 the country was led by Syngman Rhee, who hated communists and thought the Korean War should never have stopped. He had no time for that democracy lark and banned protest and free speech and sent troops in to break up demonstrations. That he and Kim Il-Sung were such enemies was rather ironic, because they had a lot in common. Finally, in 1960 his electoral fraud was so blatant that South Korean students rose up and toppled his government, but the military seized power the following year under General Park Chung Hee. South Korea stayed rich but repressive until General Park was assassinated in 1979. In the chaos that followed, South Korea finally had to bow to international pressure and start introducing a few basic democratic freedoms because they were afraid that otherwise they might lose the right to host the 1988 Olympic Games. Since then South Korea has become more democratic, though the threat of military rule is never far away.

Apocalypse Now – Vietnam

Vietnam had been part of the French colony of Indo-China, which also included Cambodia and Laos. The Japanese overran Indo-China during World War II but ran into fierce Vietnamese resistance, especially from the communist Viet Minh, led by Ho Chi Minh. After the war the French thought they could simply move back in and carry on ruling as if nothing had happened, but they'd reckoned without Ho. The Viet Minh dominated the north of the country, so in 1946 Ho declared North Vietnam an independent state. The French reckoned this was all part of Ho's plan to take over the whole of the country, and they were right. But when the French rushed troops to crush North Vietnam, the Viet Minh proved just as effective against the French as they had been against the Japanese. In 1954 they finally surrounded the French at the Battle of Dien Bien Phu and forced them to surrender.

After they lost at Dien Bien Phu the French finally pulled out of Vietnam (see Chapter 11), which left South Vietnam vulnerable to a communist take-over. The Americans, fearing that if South Vietnam fell other countries in Indo-China would be bound to follow, decided to send help to South Vietnam. Sending help soon came to mean sending troops. Okay, officially they were 'military advisers', but their advice basically consisted of launching an attack on enemy positions and saying 'See? And that's how you take out an entrenched position. Next week: House clearance with hand grenades.' Without quite realising what was happening, America had drifted into a war.

The South Vietnamese government at the time, led by President Diem, was repressive and corrupt – not a good advertisement for Western democratic values. Diem was very intolerant of Buddhism, which was a bit tricky in a largely Buddhist country. Some Buddhist monks set themselves on fire in protest against the repression, until by 1963 even the Americans agreed that Diem would have to go. They stood by while Diem was toppled and murdered in a coup.

Then in 1964 the USS *Maddox* reported that it was under attack from North Vietnamese jets in international waters in the Gulf of Tonkin. Congress immediately passed the *Gulf of Tonkin Resolution*, formally authorising President Johnson to commit troops to Vietnam. This was war: Official.

In fact, the Gulf of Tonkin resolution was almost certainly based on a mistake. The *Maddox* had already been attacked in North Vietnamese waters during an earlier South Vietnamese naval raid. A couple of days later the *Maddox*'s radar reported a major North Vietnamese naval force coming towards it: The captain radioed to Washington and President Johnson presented his resolution to Congress. We now know that the *Maddox* never sighted a single North Vietnamese ship, that no shots were fired at it, and that what the radar operator picked up could just as easily have been interference caused by freak weather. Which just goes to show you should always check your references.

The battle for hearts and minds

The Americans soon found that this war wasn't a straightforward South v. North affair:

- **The North Vietnamese Army (NVA):** Highly professional and led by General Giap, who had defeated the French at Dien Bien Phu.

- **The Viet Cong (VC):** *South* Vietnamese communists who had fought against Diem's government and were just as happy fighting the Americans. The VC wore black pyjamas and hid out in the villages of the South Vietnamese countryside, operating from a network of underground tunnels, which made it almost impossible for the Americans to find them except by getting information out of the locals. Usually by force.

- **The Khmer Rouge (Cambodia) and Pathet Lao (Laos):** These were communist guerrilla forces in the neighbouring countries. They helped the Viet Cong by keeping open a supply line from North Vietnam which ran through their countries and was known as the *Ho Chi Minh Trail*. The Americans could bomb the Ho Chi Minh trail, but doing so meant spreading the war beyond Vietnam.

- **The South Vietnamese Army (SVA):** The SVA was never as well equipped as the American army, which didn't matter as long as the Americans were there, but it mattered a great deal when US President Nixon announced his policy of *Vietnamisation* – handing the fighting over to the South Vietnamese. Or, to put it another way, you're on your own now, buddy.

The helicopter came to symbolise the Vietnam War. The Americans used it to send patrols deep into the jungle to seek out the VC hideouts and to evacuate the wounded. The downside was that going everywhere by helicopter made it much harder for the Americans to make contact with the ordinary Vietnamese; the VC, who stayed on the ground (and sometimes under it), could mix with the villagers and listen to their concerns and fears. In the end, the war was going to be won by whoever won the hearts and minds of the people, and the helicopter wasn't the best way to do it.

The Americans bombed enemy bases in North Vietnam but they couldn't bomb Viet Cong bases without killing large numbers of South Vietnamese civilians. Using chemical weapons was the solution, especially _napalm_, a sort of inflammable jelly used in flamethrowers, and _agent orange_, a poison that destroyed the jungle cover to reveal the Viet Cong bases. Unfortunately, both chemicals caused horrific injuries among South Vietnamese civilians, which didn't do much for the Americans' image in South Vietnam.

The Vietnam War happened just when television news had perfected the sort of reporter-on-the-spot style we're used to today. TV news and newspaper magazine supplements were also able to show combat and injuries in close-up detail. Historians still argue about exactly what effect this coverage had on public opinion in America, but it certainly shocked TV viewers and newspaper readers around the world and made it much harder for the Americans to claim that their methods of fighting were justified.

Two events in 1968 highlighted the Americans' difficulties:

- ✔ **Tet (Chinese New Year) Offensive:** The Viet Cong launch attacks all over South Vietnam, including in the capital, Saigon. The Americans are caught off guard at first but soon recover and defeat the attackers. _But_ the TV coverage seems to show the Americans pinned down and losing, so many people still think the Tet Offensive was an American defeat.

- ✔ **My Lai massacre:** An American patrol led by Lieutenant William Calley kills all the inhabitants of a South Vietnamese village called My Lai. Calley was court martialled and pleaded that he and his men were suffering from the strains of conflict. Calley was sentenced to life imprisonment but later had his sentence cut.

In 1968 Republican Richard Nixon won the presidential election and set about planning to pull American troops out. He started handing responsibility for the war over to the South Vietnamese, and in 1970 he opened peace talks with the North Vietnamese in Paris. In 1973 the Americans finally pulled out. But Nixon had a bit of unfinished business to deal with first: Cambodia.

Cambodia's terrifying Year Zero

Cambodia was ruled by Prince Sihanouk, who managed to be both king and prime minister. Sihanouk was facing a communist rising led by the Khmer Rouge, so to win the communists over he allowed the NVA and the VC to operate from inside Cambodia. President Nixon and his Secretary of State, Henry Kissinger, decided to teach Sihanouk a lesson. In 1969 they launched massive bombing raids on Cambodia, and the following year they backed a coup that replaced Sihanouk with a pro-American government that promptly declared war on North Vietnam. So much, thought Nixon, for Cambodia.

Not so fast. In 1975 the Khmer Rouge toppled the Cambodian government and seized the capital, Phnom Penh. The Khmer leader, Pol Pot, announced 'Year Zero': The country would return to the sort of rural peasant society it used to be. Pol Pot forced the entire population of the cities out into the countryside to work. He had thousands of teachers, doctors, lawyers, and other professionals shot, and whole villages were massacred. You can gain an idea of the sort of madness that gripped the country in the film *The Killing Fields*. Today we reckon that some 1.7 million people were murdered under Pol Pot's appalling regime. Ironically, the country that finally stopped him wasn't America but communist Vietnam.

Vietnam: The endgame

In 1975, two years after the Americans pulled out of Vietnam, the NVA invaded the south again and reached Saigon. Panic-stricken South Vietnamese, especially those of Chinese origins (the Vietnamese hated the Chinese), fought desperately to get onto the last helicopters evacuating US embassy staff or set out in small home-made boats for Hong Kong or anywhere else that would take them. Some of these 'boat people' made it to the West, but many died before they could get there.

The new Vietnamese regime unified the country, renamed Saigon after Ho Chi Minh (who had died in 1969), and locked up its opponents. Vietnam soon quarrelled over territory with China, which launched a short invasion in 1979 to put the upstart little country in its place. After that event Vietnam turned to China's enemy, the Soviet Union, which probably wasn't such a great idea as the Soviet economy was getting into deep trouble by the 1980s.

However, the Vietnamese were able to strut their stuff in Cambodia. In 1978 they invaded, overthrew Pol Pot's disgusting regime, and set up a puppet government of their own. Unfortunately, the United Nations said that, appalling though it had been, the Khmer Rouge government was the legitimate government of Cambodia and the situation wasn't resolved until 1991, when the two sides agreed that Prince Sihanouk should come back as king and the Vietnamese would go home. Pol Pot was sentenced to death *in absentia* (meaning he wasn't there) but he died in exile and his Khmer Rouge killers got an amnesty. Sadly, history doesn't always have a neat ending.

In 1992 Vietnam developed a new constitution which allowed a lot more freedom. The Americans lifted their trade embargo in 1994, restored diplomatic ties, and in 2000 President Clinton arrived for an official visit. As the two countries signed a trade agreement in 2001 they must have wondered what all the fighting had been for.

India and Pakistan: After the Raj

Gandhi had great hopes of a proud, independent India that would set a new and higher moral example to the rest of the world. But Gandhi was assassinated in 1948 by a Hindu who was furious that the country had been partitioned, and many of Gandhi's dreams for India seemed to die with him. (Chapter 11 explains why India was partitioned into India and Pakistan.)

India: Voting and violence

India's first prime minister was Jawaharlal Nehru, leader of the Congress Party, which had led the country to independence. Nehru experimented with turning India into a democratic socialist state, and he even flirted with the idea of an alliance with the Soviet Union. He certainly needed friends, given these skirmishes India found itself in:

- ✔ **War with Pakistan over Kashmir (1948–9).** UN intervenes and partitions Kashmir between India (which gets most of it) and Pakistan (which gets a bit of it). India and Pakistan both claim all of it.

- ✔ **Border war with China (1962).** India loses and has to give up part of Kashmir to China.

- ✔ **Second war with Pakistan over Kashmir (1965).** Deadlock.

The dispute over Kashmir became more deadly as India and Pakistan both developed nuclear weapons. Not until the 2000s did the two countries calm down and agree to share the province peacefully. Watch this space.

Nehru died in 1964 and in 1966 his daughter Indira Gandhi (no relation to the Mahatma Gandhi, though it didn't do her any harm for people to think so) became prime minister. She was a tough cookie: When war broke out between the two halves of Pakistan in 1971, she joined in to help East Pakistan break away to become Bangladesh. When people accused her of electoral fraud in 1975, she simply declared a state of emergency – which from her point of view it was, I suppose – and locked all her critics up.

The tragedy of Bhopal

On 3 December 1984 poisonous gases leaked out of the Union Carbide plant at Bhopal. Some 2,500 people died that day and another 50,000 suffered terrible lung disease as a direct result. The gas leak was one of the worst non-political disasters of modern Indian history, but getting proper compensation for the victims through the American courts proved almost impossible. Welcome to the post-colonial, neo-colonial corporate world.

These developments made Mrs Gandhi unpopular, and in 1977 the unthinkable happened: Congress lost the election. Three years later, though, she was back, as tough as ever. By now, different ethnic groups in India were trying to set up their own states, and she used strong-arm tactics to put them down. In 1984 she sent troops in to attack Sikh extremists who had seized the Golden Temple in Amritsar, the holiest shrine in the Sikh religion. Shortly afterwards she was assassinated by her own bodyguards. Who were Sikhs.

After Mrs Gandhi, Congress was never able to regain the hold it had once held on Indian public life:

✔ **1984:** Mrs Gandhi is succeeded by her son, Rajiv.

✔ **1987:** Rajiv Gandhi sends troops to Sri Lanka to help put down the Tamil Tiger rebels.

✔ **1991:** Rajiv Gandhi is assassinated by a Tamil Tiger sympathiser.

The 1990s saw the rise of extreme Hindu nationalists, especially the Bharatiya Janata Party (BJP), who steadily won more votes until, in 1998, they took office. The BJP has tried to eradicate memories of the colonial past, renaming cities (Bombay became Mumbai, Calcutta became Kolkata, and so on) and rewriting the history books, but it has also encouraged violent attacks on Muslims. In 2002 Hindus massacred Muslims in the state of Gujarat, the BJP heartland. Shock at the violence helped Congress win the 2004 election, which installed Manmohan Singh, India's first Sikh prime minister.

Pakistan: A model military Muslim state

Despite all its troubles, India was still a democracy (see the preceding section); Pakistan has been ruled by a succession of generals with a few periods of democratic rule in-between the military coups. In 1973 Zulfikar Ali Bhutto was elected Pakistan's first civilian prime minister, but even he depended on army support, and although he did much to modernise the country, he didn't have widespread support. He resorted to such blatant vote rigging to win the 1977 elections that protests erupted on the streets and the army decided to get rid of him.

General Zia ul-Huq took control and two years later Bhutto was hanged. His daughter Benazir entered politics determined to avenge her father's death and bring down Pakistan's military rule. She was twice elected prime minister, in 1988 and 1993, and each time she was accused of corruption and dismissed. She went into exile to campaign for a return of democracy in Pakistan. This, however, was not going to be easy:

- ✔ Pakistan is an Islamic state, which in 1991 introduced Islamic (shariah) law. Shariah law lays down a set of religiously-based precepts and penalties, including stoning or beheading for adultery and amputation for theft, so its introduction didn't help the task of reinstating democracy.

- ✔ Pakistan became a front-line US ally when the Soviet Union invaded Afghanistan in 1980 and again after the US invasion of Afghanistan in 2002. The situation in Afghanistan, with Muslim fighters slipping back and forth across the border, kept Pakistan in a permanent state of tension which didn't encourage the holding of multi-party elections.

In 1999 General Pervez Musharaf launched yet another military coup in Pakistan. He became a key supporter of the US war on terror, which made him vulnerable to attack from the Islamic militants in his own country. His response was to suspend the constitution, hold on to power, and crack down on opponents and critics. Like any other military dictator, in fact.

Other South Asian countries

India and Pakistan had no monopoly on political problems in the South Asian region. Some of their smaller neighbours could give them a good run for their money in the violence and military dictatorship stakes.

Bangladesh

Bangladesh was originally East Pakistan, but it had little in common with the western half of the country a thousand miles away on the other side of India. In 1971 East Pakistan declared independence and with Indian help it was able to defeat the West Pakistani forces and set itself up as the independent state of Bangladesh. However, Bangladesh has suffered badly from natural disasters and famine: Severe floods in 1974 led to a state of emergency and a military coup. Since then Bangladesh has lived with a combination of military rule, poverty, and hunger.

Sri Lanka

Sri Lanka was the old British colony of Ceylon, which became independent in 1948. The people are divided between the majority Sinhalese and the minority Tamils, and they don't like each other. The Sinhalese pursued a policy of nationalism, keeping the Tamils down, until in 1976 the Tamils formed the

Tamil Tiger guerrillas to fight back. The fighting with the Sinhalese has been very brutal. They signed a ceasefire in 2002 but the fighting began again only two years later.

Nepal

Nepal doesn't actually exist just to supply sherpas for mountaineers and Gurkhas for the British army. It was a feudal kingdom which gave its people few human rights except the right to live in poverty. In 1959 the Nepalese tried to set up a multi-party constitution, but King Mahendra staged a coup the following year and took power back into his own hands. Opposition to the king was led by the Nepalese Congress Party, which won the election King Birendra felt obliged to call in 1990. By then, however, more and more Nepalese were turning to the Nepalese Maoists, who were running a guerrilla campaign to overturn the monarchy. Later, in 2001, it seemed as if Crown Prince Dipendra might have saved them the trouble when he burst in on his family and shot them all with a machine gun, including himself. But his uncle Prince Gyanendra succeeded and set about the family tradition of suppressing all critics and opposition.

Burma

The Japanese set up a puppet government in Burma but it was soon clear that they intended to rule the country entirely for their own benefit. Aung San U served in that puppet government but he quickly turned against the Japanese and formed the government that oversaw the end of the Japanese occupation and negotiated independence for Burma. Unfortunately he didn't live to see Independence Day because he was killed in a violent coup led by his rival U Saw. In 1962 the Burmese military seized control and they have held it ever since. Aung San U's daughter, Aung San Suu Kyi, formed the National League for Democracy which won the 1990 elections, but the military government took no notice: They put her under house arrest and have kept her there ever since. Aung San Suu Kyi won the Nobel Peace Prize and has become an international symbol of protest against military rule, not just in Burma but around the world, but so far the Burmese government has shown no sign whatever of bending to international – or Burmese – opinion and reintroducing democracy.

South East Asia

South East Asia is the area which comprises Thailand, Vietnam, Malaysia, and Indonesia. This region witnessed some of post-war Asia's worst warfare and internal repression.

The King and I – Thailand

Until 1939 Thailand was the ancient kingdom of Siam. The country was never colonised by the Europeans, but they controlled it nonetheless, mainly by dominating the Siamese king.

The musical *The King and I* is based on the memoirs of Anna Leonowens, a nineteenth-century English teacher who worked for a while at the Siamese court. The film was banned in Thailand because it took so many liberties with the truth. Her memoirs are not a very reliable historical source. No, she didn't single-handedly westernise Thailand and nor did she teach the king to waltz!

Some Siamese wanted the country to become more democratic, but the army wanted a dictatorship and in 1932 seized power and set one up. In 1939 the anti-Western Marshal Phibun took over, changed the country's name to Thailand ('land of the free' – nice irony, Marshal), and joined in the Second World War on the Japanese side. Not such a good idea: Phibun was overthrown at the end of the war, but he came back in 1947 and seized power again; Thailand remained a military dictatorship until 1973. The Americans turned a blind eye because Thailand supported them in Vietnam and even sent troops to fight alongside the US forces. The Thais have toppled their military governments a couple of times, in 1973 and in 1991, but the military have always been able to seize control again.

United we stand! Er, I said United we stand . . .

The Americans' big success in the Cold War in the 1950s was NATO, the North Atlantic Treaty Organisation, an anti-communist alliance of European and American states. Washington thought doing something similar in Asia would be a good idea, so in 1955 SEATO was born: The South East Asia Treaty Organisation. SEATO had eight members, only two of whom, Thailand and the Philippines, were actually in South East Asia; the others were Australia and New Zealand (okay, they were near South East Asia), Pakistan, Britain, France, and the USA. The alliance looked strong, especially as the British and French were busy testing their atomic weapons in the region, but when the Americans went to war in Vietnam and called on SEATO to help, most of the members suddenly remembered something really urgent they had to go and do. Which did not involve getting embroiled in Vietnam. Thailand, Australia, and New Zealand sent a few troops, but SEATO had proved a broken reed. It folded in 1975.

Meanwhile the actual South East Asian nations had been getting their own organisation going, the Association of South East Asian Nations (ASEAN). ASEAN was a trading organisation rather than a military alliance, and it had its ups and downs according to changes in the world economy in the 1980s and 1990s, but by the end of the century it was still going and it included all the nations of the region. Which was more than could be said for SEATO.

People power in the Philippines

The Philippines began the century as a US colony (see Chapter 2) and the whole country was geared towards growing goods for the American market. America finally granted the Philippines their independence in 1946, but the Philippines had to sign a free trade deal with Washington, let the US keep its naval bases on the islands, and give American citizens the same economic rights as Filipinos. In 1965 Ferdinand Marcos was elected president on a Philippines-for-the-Filipinos ticket, but being a staunch anti-communist, he soon changed his tune and kept in with Washington. Unfortunately Marcos was a lot better at spending money on his cronies than he was at running the economy: His wife Imelda spent a fortune on a massive collection of designer shoes. By the 1970s the country was heading deep into debt and people were protesting on the streets. Marcos's solution was to call in the army, declare martial law, round up opposition leaders, and send them into exile.

By the 1980s even Marcos couldn't ignore the economic crisis: He turned to the World Bank and the International Monetary Fund for a loan but they demanded big economic reforms. By now even the Americans were keeping their distance from Marcos, but he still didn't get the message.

When the opposition leader Benigno Aquino came back from exile to stand for election, Marcos had him murdered as he came off the plane. Filipinos were outraged, and Benigno's widow, Corazon, became the leader of all the groups opposed to Marcos's tyranny. Marcos tried to catch his opponents out in 1986 by suddenly announcing an election (on American prime time television, would you believe!) and rigging the result; unfortunately Mrs Aquino declared that *she* had won, and most foreign observers agreed with her. Marcos said no, *he* won and he had himself installed as president to prove it. So Mrs Aquino had herself installed as president too. So there.

In the end US President Ronald Reagan offered Marcos safe haven in the US if he conceded defeat. Marcos took Reagan's offer, though he looked like he was chewing a wasp, and the Filipino people burst into the presidential palace to celebrate – 'people power' they called this historic moment.

Corazon Aquino was a popular leader but she wasn't very experienced. She got the Americans to close their naval bases, but couldn't solve the country's economic problems, nor could she put down the breakaway independence movement by the Muslim Moro rebels. Her successor Fidel Ramos signed a deal with the rebels but it broke down, and his successor, a former film star called Joseph Estrada, was forced out of office on charges of corruption.

Malaysia: The rubber band

Malaysia was a federation made up of former British colonies, including Malaya, Sarawak, and Singapore. The native Malays despised the country's large Chinese and Indian communities, especially after China became communist in 1949 and it had looked as if Malaya's Chinese would try to force the country to do the same. The British and Malays had fought a long campaign against the Malay Chinese communists before independence, and after independence the Malays still tried to keep the Chinese and Indians under strict control by a policy of blatant racial discrimination. Tensions grew and the situation became so dangerous that in 1969 the government declared a state of emergency.

Meanwhile, Malaysia was rapidly becoming one of Asia's 'tiger' economies on the strength of its tin and rubber production. Under President Mahathir Bin Mohamad, Malaysia became one of the fastest growing economies in Asia, but at a price: Mahathir didn't believe in free speech and had the Malaysian opposition leader imprisoned. Even Mahathir couldn't stop the growth of the fundamentalist Pan Islamic Party, however. By the end of the century, Malaysia and Indonesia were both important centres of Islamic fundamentalism.

Singapore: Going it alone

The great port of Singapore had been a centre of British power in the East until it fell rather humiliatingly to the Japanese in 1942. Singapore joined the Malaysian federation in 1963 but the anti-Chinese discrimination laws were so severe that Singapore, three-quarters of whose population was Chinese, decided it would be better off going it alone, so it became an independent state in 1965. Singapore has been a big economic success story, another of the 'Asian tigers', especially when it managed to win some of the Western investment that had previously gone to Hong Kong, after it reverted to Chinese possession in 1997.

Live dangerously: Live in Indonesia!

From 1949 to 1968, Indonesia was led by the somewhat eccentric Achmed Sukarno. Sukarno had led Indonesian resistance against the Japanese during the war and he then forced the Dutch to go home. His favourite hobbies were military parades and locking people up. He decided democratic government was boring – all those fiddly elections – so he had a much better idea: It was called 'guided democracy' and to play you just did whatever Sukarno said. Personal dictatorship is another name for this idea.

Thanks to Sukarno's incompetent handling of the economy, the people of Indonesia were going hungry, but he just had protestors arrested and declared a new campaign to take people's minds off their problems. In 1963 he picked a fight (officially a 'confrontation') with Malaysia and sent guerrilla troops over the border into Sarawak, but since Britain, Australia, and New Zealand all sent help to Malaysia, the Indonesian army found itself bogged down in a war it couldn't win. Not to worry: 1964, Sukarno declared, was to be 'The Year of Living Dangerously', when Indonesia would challenge the power of the West. That challenge meant locking even more people up (for demanding nasty Western things such as democracy and food supplies, you see).

Sukarno certainly did live dangerously: He survived one assassination attempt because a man fired the whole magazine of a pistol at him. And missed.

Thank you, Mr Sukarno, we'll let you know

By the middle of the 1960s the different parts of the federation had decided it was time to get out: Sukarno stopped the Moluccans and Javans from getting away but the people of Aceh and Iryan Jaya (the western half of Papua New Guinea which the Dutch transferred to Indonesia in 1962) kept up a guerrilla campaign for years. In 1965 the Communist Party tried to stage a coup, even mutilating and killing six high-ranking generals, but they didn't unseat Sukarno. He then launched a terrifying counter-attack, shooting hundreds of thousands of 'red sympathisers': It was one of the worst outbreaks of indiscriminate slaughter of the twentieth century. Sukarno was completely out of control. In 1966 the army forced him to hand over his power to General Suharto, who ruled Indonesia for the next thirty-two years.

The events of 1965–6 in Indonesia are so murky, with various groups double-crossing each other, that historians still argue about exactly what happened. It seems probable that the American and other Western intelligence services played a role by encouraging the communists to strike, then encouraging the anti-communist bloodbath that followed. At any rate, Sukarno had become an embarrassment to the West, and the CIA was only too pleased to help Suharto remove him.

On Boxing Day 2005 Indonesia was one of many Asian countries that suffered from a devastating tsunami (enormous wave). The worst-hit area was Aceh, which had been battling for independence from Indonesia for thirty years. This disaster finally prompted the Indonesian government to grant Aceh the self-government it had fought for.

Beware strangers in paradise

Indonesia is one of the biggest Islamic countries in the world, and was bound to be caught up in the conflicts that followed the 9/11 attacks on New York and Washington. In October 2002 Islamist terrorists blew up a night club on the holiday island of Bali, killing 202 people, many of them Australian tourists. This event was a sign that Indonesia was right up there with Pakistan and Afghanistan on the front line of President Bush's War on Terror.

East Timor

East Timor was a Portuguese colony until 1975 when the Portuguese withdraw. Hardly had the islanders taken down the bunting, however, than General Suharto of Indonesia ordered an invasion. He said he wanted to stop a communist take-over; the people of East Timor reckoned he just wanted their land. The Indonesians set up a brutal regime, shooting or imprisoning anyone who opposed them, especially East Timor's large Christian population. The people responded with a guerrilla campaign, which just brought even more savage reprisals. The rest of the world called on Suharto to pull his men out of East Timor but he took no notice. After he was overthrown in 1998 Indonesia and Portugal agreed to let the people of East Timor decide on their own future and guess what? They voted to become independent. This obviously came as a great surprise to the Indonesians, who responded with another round of savage repression until the United Nations stepped in, sent a peacekeeping force, and organised free elections. Which voted in the East Timor nationalist party known as Fretilin, which wanted – have you guessed yet? – independence. East Timor finally won its independence in 2002, only twenty-seven years after it was first granted by the Portuguese.

The Wizards of Oz and the Orcs of New Zealand

Australia and New Zealand emerged from Britain's colonial shadow in the post-war years and came forward as independent states on the world stage. They had to work out their relationship with that other ex-British colony, the United States, and with their South East Asian neighbours. They also had to decide whether or not they still wanted to be ruled by a British monarch living on the other side of the world.

Fair Australia advances

Australia had always been as British as tea and toast until relations with the mother country came under increasing strain in the two world wars. The Australians blamed British commanders for their heavy losses at Gallipoli in the First World War, although more British and French troops lost their lives there than Australians, and in Singapore in the Second (see Chapter 3 to find out about Gallipoli and Chapter 9 for details on Singapore).

After the Second World War, Australia began to make friends with the Americans, signing defence agreements and even dropping the pound sterling in favour of the dollar. The British queen was still the Australian Head of State, however, and after prime minister Gough Whitlam failed to get his budget approved by the Australian Senate in 1975, the Governor General exercised his royal authority and sacked him, which even pro-British Australians thought was going too far. Britain had already turned its back on its Commonwealth trading partners by joining the European Economic Community in 1973, forcing Australia to start developing trading links with its neighbours in South East Asia. Perhaps it was time to drop the royal link: Australia certainly dropped 'God Save the Queen' for 'Advance Australia Fair'. Even prime ministers like Bob Hawke and Paul Keating began talking of setting up an independent republic, though no one could agree on what this should actually look like, so when Australia held a referendum about it, the people voted to keep the Queen. Strewth.

Monarchy or no monarchy, Australia was becoming less British, in fact less white. Since 1901 the government had denied full citizenship rights to Aborigines and had operated a White Australia policy to keep out undesirable (non-white) immigrants. Even white people were barred if the government didn't like their politics; in one famous case, a Czech communist was refused entry because he failed the language test – in Scots gaelic! Under Sir Robert Menzies, however, Australia developed a modern system of education and social security and dropped its racist citizenship rules. By the end of the century, more immigrants were arriving from Asia and eastern Europe – some of them even made it into Australia's, er, gritty and realistic soap operas like *Neighbours* – and an anti-immigrant party led by Pauline Hanson made headlines by calling for a return to traditional Australian values. Australians were having to decide what sort of a nation they wanted to be.

New Zealand

New Zealand is not Australia. Twentieth-century Kiwis were less keen than the Australians to dump Britain and take up with America. For most of the post-war period, New Zealand politics was dominated by conservative parties. Even when radical prime ministers Jim Bolger and David Lange started to talk about dropping the monarchy, they still kept their distance from US policy.

New Zealand adopted an anti-nuclear stance and refused to let nuclear warships into its ports. The government was furious when Greenpeace's ship *Rainbow Warrior*, which had been monitoring Western nuclear tests in the Pacific, was destroyed in Auckland harbour by the French secret service in 1985. By the end of the century, New Zealand had adopted a system of proportional representation which made it difficult for any political group to dominate. By then, however, the rest of the world had discovered the extraordinary beauty of New Zealand's spectacular landscape, thanks mainly to Peter Jackson's epic films of J. R. R. Tolkien's *Lord of the Rings* trilogy.

Chapter 15

Disneyland: Post-War America

*H*istorians – and not just American ones – have called the twentieth century *the American century*. That title doesn't simply reflect American power, it also means this was the century when the whole world, even countries who opposed or hated America, adopted American culture and technology, bought (or copied) American goods, and tried to share in the American dream.

Land of Dreams – Fifties America

'When you wish upon a star,' runs the Walt Disney song, 'Your dreams come true.' America was founded on dreams and the American Dream, the idea that anyone can make it big, is what kept the country going through the good times and the bad. In 1955 Walt Disney even created a dream-come-true kingdom at Disneyland in California. Children and adults could meet their favourite characters and go on rides based on moments from the films. Everything was clean, wholesome, all-American family fun. Welcome to fifties America.

Fifties America was basking in the wealth and security it had won in the war. American factories had built the tanks and ships that beat Hitler and now the whole world was buying American. America hadn't been bombed or invaded so it didn't have the sort of reconstruction problems other countries faced. In fact America was busy sending aid to Europe and Asia and establishing economic links all over the world. Meanwhile at home, all-American boys and their dads went fishing and all-American girls and their mums baked apple pie and the sun shone and everyone smiled and felt very lucky to be living in the greatest country on God's earth. Nothing could possibly go wrong.

Or could it?

Yabba Dabba Doo!

If you want to get a picture of how fifties America thought of itself, catch a few episodes of *The Flintstones* (it first aired in 1960, but the idea developed from the fifties into the following decade). The joke is that Fred and Wilma are from the stone age but really they're suburban fifties Americans, with a neat house, friendly neighbours, and a smart car. Americans enjoyed TV comedies like *I Love Lucy* or the *George Burns and Gracie Allen Show* that added a little sparkle or craziness to suburban life without in any way challenging or subverting it.

All-American presidents

Being president of a mighty superpower that is going through a period of unprecedented prosperity might sound like a dream job, but America's problems both at home and abroad proved challenging enough for the two men who led the country through the fifties.

- **Harry S. Truman (Democrat) 1945–53:** Tough anti-communist. Stood up to Stalin at the Potsdam conference in 1945 and issued the *Truman Doctrine* saying the US would help any country fighting communism. He organised UN help for South Korea in 1950, though he had to sack the megalomaniac UN commander General Douglas MacArthur before he could start the Third World War. Truman outlawed racial discrimination in the armed forces and started looking into civil rights, but the Korean War left him exhausted. He retired after the 1952 presidential election.

- **Dwight D. Eisenhower (Republican) 1953–61:** Known as 'Ike'. Allied Supreme Commander in the Second World War. He promised to sort out the Korean War and he did. He didn't sort out much else, though: His presidency saw the first big clashes over civil rights. Everyone liked Ike but he developed a reputation for being old and tired. He served his two terms as president and left the White House in 1961.

Reds under the beds!

In 1949 Americans got scared, for two main reasons: First, China became communist; second, the Russians exploded an atom bomb. Most Americans believed that communism was an evil force that would destroy all that was good about the American way of life, so these events were very scary. Where was Superman when America needed him? And then a man stepped forward to save America from the reds. Senator Joseph McCarthy of Wisconsin.

Are you now or have you ever been a pathological liar?

McCarthy, who claimed he'd been a tail gunner during the war (he hadn't), told Americans to be Very Afraid: He had a list of 205 card-carrying communists working within the State Department. When journalists pressed him for details, McCarthy said okay maybe not 205 but definitely 81. Well, call it 57. It was definitely lots of them, honest. No, he couldn't give any names (most journalists doubted he had any to give and they were right), so he started accusing General George C. Marshall, the man responsible for organising economic aid to post-war Europe, of standing by while Stalin took over eastern Europe and Mao took over China. That proves the Reds are in the State Department, said McCarthy. Well, doesn't it? Incredibly, many Americans believed him: They were scared of communists and McCarthy was telling them just what they wanted to hear.

People often assume that McCarthy's accusations were false. Most were, but not all: Some of the people he accused were communists, or had been. Alger Hiss, a State Department adviser who was prosecuted by the young Richard Nixon, certainly was a communist and may well have been passing papers to the Soviet Union. But the number of active traitors was always very small: Being a communist or communist sympathiser and a loyal American was perfectly possible (and legal). McCarthy could never see this.

McCarthy chaired the Senate Permanent Investigations Sub-Committee (not the House Un-American Activities Committee – that piece of information might win you a bet one day), where he bullied and shouted at witnesses, not caring (well, actually quite pleased) that he was destroying their reputations and careers along the way. People found guilty of having been members of the communist party were usually sacked and blacklisted. Many Hollywood directors and screenwriters hauled in front of McCarthy had to use pseudonyms to get any sort of work afterwards. McCarthy finally went too far when, on national television, he started claiming the US army, busy fighting the communists in Korea, was riddled with traitors. The viewing public saw through his lies and his support collapsed.

In the way they bullied people into confessing and accusing others, McCarthy's hearings bore a resemblance to Stalin's show trials (see Chapter 4 to find out about those). After Arthur Miller wrote his play *The Crucible*, which was apparently about the seventeenth-century witch trials at Salem but was really about McCarthy, it became common to refer to the McCarthy hearings as 'witch-hunts'. Just remember, though, that no one who went before McCarthy was hanged, shot, or sent to a labour camp.

In 1953 Julius and Ethel Rosenberg were found guilty of passing nuclear secrets to the Soviet Union and condemned to agonising deaths in the electric chair. The Rosenbergs thought that helping the Soviet Union to get nuclear weapons would make the world fairer and safer. Ironically, the American and Russian governments eventually agreed that the world was safest when both sides were armed to the teeth, but it was too late to help the Rosenbergs.

Fridges speak louder than war

The Cold War was so taken up with talk of war and nuclear confrontation that it was easy to lose sight of the question it was meant to be about: Were people happier under communism or under capitalism? In theory, the Soviet Union was the workers' paradise, but the Americans asked why so many workers seemed to want to escape from paradise to the Big Bad Capitalist West. Soviet premier Nikita Khrushchev was confident that communism would win: 'We will bury you!' he declared, and many Americans were scared that he might just be right. The communists had pushed the US out of North Korea in the Korean War (see Chapter 10 for the details), taken over North Vietnam, and would probably take over the rest of South East Asia (choose between Chapters 10, 11, and 14 for the details), and in 1959 they took over the Americans' favourite holiday island of Cuba (see Chapter 13).

But then in 1959 Mr Khrushchev and his wife dropped in on an exhibition of American life at the US embassy in Moscow and were shown a typical American kitchen, with a fridge and all mod cons. The Russians, who were used to kitchens where you only got electricity every other month and where fridges were reserved for high party officials, were amazed – Mrs Khrushchev kept trying out all the gadgets. But her husband was convinced the whole thing was a capitalist trick: Surely only the rich could afford this sort of luxury? But Vice President Richard Nixon assured them that this was how ordinary Americans lived. We call it capitalism, he added, ever so slightly gloating. The Khrushchevs went off in a huff and two years later Khrushchev oversaw the building of the Berlin Wall to stop anyone else heading west in search of a fridge.

Beep-beep-beep – Ha! Ha! Ha!

Americans got a shock in 1957 when the Russians beat them into space with *Sputnik*, the world's first space satellite. Khrushchev took every opportunity to rub the Americans' noses in it – 'Beep beep: Stick that in your fridges!' – and Americans had to get used to the idea of a communist beeping device passing directly overhead. Perhaps the time was ripe to get rid of kindly old Ike and get someone a bit more dynamic in the White House.

Blue suede shoes

For young Americans the fifties ended in 1956 when Elvis Presley recorded 'Heartbreak Hotel'. The song went to number one in the charts and created rock and roll virtually overnight. The record industry liked the way he mixed country with rhythm and blues; young people liked how he looked and sounded. Nervous TV executives, worried that his gyrating hips might shock the Bible Belt, told cameramen to shoot him from the waist up. Elvis carried on recording hits through the sixties – one of very few stars to succeed in both decades – but his real importance is that he provided young people with an icon they could relate to – and their parents couldn't.

The long fight for civil rights

The fifties American dream could sound pretty hollow to Americans who didn't fit into the image of white church-going suburban America. Many black Americans, descendants of Africans brought over as slaves in the eighteenth and nineteenth centuries, lived in poverty and even those who didn't had to cope with racial insults and violence. Conditions were worst in the former slave-owning areas of the South, where many white Americans liked to think that white supremacy was part of God's plan. They had all sorts of clever ideas for keeping their African American neighbours in their place:

- **Strict segregation:** Public spaces such as parks, cafes, cinemas, theatres, buses, and waiting rooms, even churches had 'blacks only' and 'whites only' areas and these rules were strictly enforced. Black and white Americans lived in different parts of town and sent their children to blacks-only or whites-only schools.

- **Unequal education:** Southern state governments made sure that blacks-only schools got a fraction of the money they spent on schools for whites. 'Black' schools had fewer books and resources and their teachers got paid less. Any bright African Americans who wanted to go to college in the South could forget it: They had to go to the integrated colleges in the northern states – if they could afford it.

- **Deny voting rights:** African Americans had enjoyed equal voting rights since President Lincoln emancipated the slaves in 1863 but the southerners had worked out ways to stop them exercising those rights. State laws imposed special voting tests designed for black voters to fail, such as asking them 'How many bubbles are there in a bar of soap?' or getting them to read out a passage of difficult text and then saying they'd pronounced it wrong. African Americans who managed to vote were sacked from their jobs or had their State food aid stopped or – and all too often this was the preferred method – they ended up dead.

- **Violence and intimidation:** Any African American who stepped out of line was liable to be murdered and all-white juries were happy to acquit anyone who got accused of the crime. Fourteen-year-old Emmet Till was murdered and his body thrown into the Mississippi for saying 'Bye, baby' to a white woman in a shop; war veteran Lamar Smith was shot in broad daylight in front of a white crowd for organising black voting in Lincoln County, Mississippi. No witnesses came forward and no one was ever tried for his murder.

I like to be in Am-err-icA!

In 1957 a sizzling new musical opened on Broadway called *West Side Story*. It updated Shakespeare's *Romeo and Juliet* to fifties New York, shining a pitiless spotlight on the downside of the American dream. Instead of feuding Montagues and Capulets, the show had warring gangs, the all-white Jets and their deadly enemies, the Puerto Rican Sharks, disillusioned with the racism and poverty they found on New York's West Side. In the lively Latin number 'America' the Sharks and their girls argue about whether or not life is better in their new homeland. 'Buying on credit is so nice!' sing the girls. 'One look at us and they charge twice!' the boys answer. This musical was a sign that problems of poverty and racial violence were by no means confined to America's black community, nor even to the Deep South.

Separate cannot be equal – official

President Truman had made a start on the civil rights issue by outlawing segregation in the armed forces and government service and setting up a commission to report on racial discrimination in the rest of society. The real kick-start, however, came from a little girl called Laura Brown, who in 1954 brought a case against her local school board in Topeka, Kansas. She argued that having to go to a 'black' school when she lived round the corner from a perfectly good 'white' school was demeaning and harmful, even though (this was Kansas, not the Deep South) the two schools were both equally good. The law seemed to be against her: The 1896 *Plessy v. Ferguson* case had established that separate schooling was allowed under the constitution as long as it was equal in all other aspects, but her counsel, Thurgood Marshall, argued that the very idea of having to go to a 'black' school suggested that Laura was somehow not good enough for the 'white' one and that this notion was psychologically damaging. The Supreme Court agreed and ruled that racially segregated schooling was unconstitutional.

This ruling didn't mean that racially segregated schools suddenly disappeared, however. Southern states dragged their feet and raised as many objections to the change as they could and the Supreme Court had to rule a second time to declare all segregation illegal. In 1957 white students and parents barred the way to a group of black students trying to enrol at the Central High School at Little Rock, Arkansas and screamed abuse at one, Elizabeth Eckford, who defied them and walked into the school. When the State Governor Orval Faubus called out the National Guard to keep the black students out of the school, President Eisenhower sent in federal troops to protect the students and enforce the Supreme Court's ruling.

Pictures of white mobs screaming hate at black students played straight into the hands of America's communist enemies, who accused the United States of blatant hypocrisy in claiming to stand for human rights when it couldn't even defend them for its own citizens.

The son of a preacher man – Martin Luther King

Martin Luther King's father, 'Daddy' King, was a Baptist preacher who believed in keeping your head down and thanking God for your blessings. His son, Martin Luther King Jr, didn't see life that way, which is why in 1955 he was approached by the leaders of the black community in Montgomery, Alabama to help with a problem that had arisen on the town's buses. Rosa Parks, an official of the National Association for the Advancement of Colored Peoples (NAACP), had been arrested for refusing to give up her seat on a bus to a white man. The black community were going to boycott the city's buses in protest and they wanted King to lead them. King proved a powerful speaker (well, he was a preacher) and after a year of the boycott, with people walking or sharing taxis rather than travel on segregated buses, the bus company, which depended heavily on its black passengers, finally gave in and desegregated its buses. King became a national hero.

Don't hit back!

King was a devout Christian and he campaigned according to Christian principles of non-violence. He drew inspiration from the way Gandhi had used non-violence to highlight the brutality of British rule in India and win over world opinion (Chapter 11 tells you more about how Gandhi managed it). King was under no illusions about the violence he was up against: Many of the bus boycotters had been arrested and beaten up. But he taught his followers not to hit back or even defend themselves, no matter what was done to them. He even sought out the most brutal local police chiefs to challenge knowing that the more the police used violence, the more public and international opinion would swing round behind the case for civil rights.

Both Eisenhower and the president who followed him, John F. Kennedy, had to approach civil rights with great care. If they appeared to be bullying the southern states – as some people thought Eisenhower had done at Little Rock – they could lose support from voters who feared their own states might be next. The civil rights fighters were going to have to keep a careful eye on the political situation if they were to win the White House round.

Crazy Time – The Sixties

America's high hopes came crashing down during the 1960s, which began with the election of the young, popular President Kennedy and ended with Americans walking on the moon. But in between America saw assassinations, violent clashes over civil rights, and the long drawn-out agony of Vietnam.

JFK

1960 was presidential election year and it had an interesting new twist. The two candidates, Richard Nixon for the Republicans and John F. Kennedy for the Democrats, went head to head in a series of TV debates. People who heard the men on radio didn't think there was much to choose between them but people who watched on TV preferred Kennedy: He was young and good looking and he obviously knew how to charm a TV audience; by contrast, Nixon looked awkward and he didn't smile much. The election was close: Kennedy won by just 0.1 per cent, but it was enough. 'The torch has been passed,' he declared in his inaugural address, 'to a new generation.' He and his beautiful wife Jackie held court at the White House, inviting poets, artists, and musicians: It was nicknamed 'Camelot' after the fabled court of King Arthur. After the tired years of Eisenhower, Americans could look forward to a glittering future. Or so they thought.

King of the New Frontier

For Americans the 'Frontier' didn't just mean the Wild West: It symbolised any big challenge that would sort out the all-American men from the all-American boys. Kennedy talked of addressing poverty and providing proper health care as America's 'New Frontier'. Unfortunately Congress wasn't in pioneering mood: It thought the New Frontier was too expensive and would allow the government to interfere too much with the states. It rejected the whole package. Back to the drawing board, Jack.

Foreign affairs . . .

Kennedy's record in foreign affairs was mixed:

- ✓ **Authorises the Bay of Pigs invasion of Cuba, 1961.** Anti-Castro Cubans invade Cuba to topple his regime. They'd planned with Eisenhower's administration. Kennedy inherited the plan and gave it the go-ahead. Bad idea: The invasion flops. Chapter 13 explains why.

- ✓ **Quarrels with Khrushchev in Vienna, 1961.** The two men meet for a constructive summit conference but end up arguing fruitlessly about the merits of capitalism and communism and just irritating each other. Not such a great idea.

- ✓ **Cuban missile crisis, 1962.** Depending on your point of view, Kennedy either stood courageously firm against the Russians or he recklessly brought the world to the brink of nuclear war. Chapter 10 has more on the crisis.

- ✓ **Visits Berlin and sees the Wall, 1963.** Good move: The Germans appreciate his support (they appreciate it even more when he gets his German slightly wrong so that 'I am a Berliner!' comes out as 'I am a doughnut!'). For more on the Berlin Wall, see Chapter 18.

Kennedy was also responsible for committing the United States to defending South Vietnam, which didn't prove such a good idea either.

. . .and domestic affairs

Kennedy presented a squeaky-clean family image but all was not as it seemed. J. Edgar Hoover, head of the FBI, knew about Kennedy's affair with Marilyn Monroe and he tried to use this information to blackmail the president into softening his liberal policies. Mind you, Kennedy wasn't above using dirty tactics himself. When US Steel wanted to put its prices up against Kennedy's wishes, the president called in the FBI to look out dirt on the US Steel bosses and carry out interrogations of journalists in the middle of the night.

Dallas

Kennedy went to Dallas, Texas in November 1963 to try to build up his support in the important southern states, though looking through some of the local leaflets attacking him (he was too northern, too Irish, and too Catholic for southern tastes) he reckoned he was heading into Nut Country. So it proved on 22 November when Lee Harvey Oswald took aim and shot him.

Yes, Lee Harvey Oswald did shoot JFK. The plaza wasn't a pheasant shoot full of gunmen on grassy knolls taking pot shots at the presidential car. As so often in history, the simple explanation is the right one, but if you believe the conspiracy theories, nothing written here will change your mind.

Partly because of the way he died, Kennedy became an international hero. For many years afterwards people could say exactly where they were when they heard the news of his assassination. More recently, historians have been much more critical of him. Revelations about his private life have tarnished the image, but more serious is the accusation that he didn't actually achieve much for America's poor or blacks or even for America's allies abroad. But American politicians were still conjuring up his image to boost their electoral ratings in the 1990s and beyond, so Camelot hasn't entirely vanished.

Civil rights or Black Power?

By the time Kennedy arrived in the White House in 1960, young blacks were becoming impatient for progress on civil rights. They decided to take action:

- **Lunch counter sit-ins:** Black students sat at whites-only lunch counters and waited to be served. They had a long wait, and many of them got beaten up or arrested (and frequently both).

- **Freedom rides:** Inter-state buses were still segregated once they reached the south, so black and white civil rights campaigners staged 'freedom rides', boarding the buses in the north and sitting defiantly together all the way to the buses' destinations in the south. White mobs attacked many of the buses and beat the freedom riders with metal bars while the police stood by and watched.

Martin Luther King joined in the lunch counter sit-ins and got himself arrested for his pains. While he was in prison, Kennedy, who was standing for election, phoned Mrs King to express his sympathy for her husband, so when Kennedy was elected, many civil rights campaigners thought, 'Great. Now we'll get some action.' Not so fast. Kennedy needed southern support to get his New Frontier plans through Congress (see the section 'King of the New Frontier' for details). That situation meant he could send federal marshals to protect the freedom riders but he couldn't afford to alienate southern senators by doing anything more. So King decided to turn up the pressure.

Marching for freedom

To pressurise Kennedy into taking some action on civil rights, Martin Luther King launched two of his most famous campaigns. The idea was to get maximum worldwide publicity, so he launched two very different kinds of march, one in the deep south, and one in Washington DC itself.

✔ **Birmingham, Alabama:** King organised a series of civil rights marches in the heart of the most racist, segregationist town in the south. Local sheriff 'Bull' Connor sent in police with fierce dogs and powerful fire hoses to attack the marchers (fire hoses are powerful enough to blast the bark off a tree, so using these was no empty gesture). People criticised King for putting schoolchildren at the head of the marches where they took the full force of the dogs and the water, but he knew the TV pictures of police attacking children would win people over and he was right.

✔ **March on Washington, DC:** To mark the centenary of emancipation from slavery, but really to tell Kennedy to get a move on and pass a civil rights bill, King organised a massive march on Washington, where he addressed the crowd whilst stood in front of the Lincoln memorial (a symbolic venue because Lincoln had emancipated the slaves in the nineteenth century). King's speech was a masterpiece. 'I have a dream,' he declared, 'that one day this nation will rise up and live out the true meaning of its creed: "We hold these truths to be self-evident; that all men are created equal".'

Civil Rights Act 1964

Kennedy couldn't just sit by and watch children being blasted by fire hoses or vast crowds listening to classic oratory just outside his window, so he started to draft a civil rights bill to guarantee equality under the law for all US citizens regardless of their colour. Kennedy was assassinated before he could pass this bill, but his successor as president, Lyndon Johnson, signed it into law in 1964. Instead of a Thank You card, however, all Johnson got from King was a complaint that the bill didn't mean diddly squat if black people couldn't vote. So King organised another set of marches in the jurisdiction of another not-very-bright redneck sheriff, this time at Selma, Alabama and the world watched news coverage of helmeted policemen baton charging the unarmed marchers. In 1965 President Johnson signed a voting rights bill into law to guarantee black Americans the same voting rights as white Americans. He probably wanted to add 'PS *Now* will you get off my back?' at the bottom.

Malcolm says: Shoot the dog!

Young blacks in the ghettos of America's cities thought Martin Luther King's non-violent tactics were stupid. They weren't interested in voting rights or who could sit where on a bus: They wanted an end to the poverty they were stuck in and they turned to a fiery young speaker called Malcolm X. Malcolm had been born Malcolm Little but on joining a Muslim group called the Nation of Islam, he learned that the surnames African Americans carried were imposed on them when their original African names were taken away from them by the slave owners. So, until he could find his true African name, Malcolm dropped 'Little' and substituted 'X'.

Malcolm X argued that marchers who were attacked by police with dogs should fight back and shoot the dog. But at which end of the lead?

Martin Luther King and Malcolm X represented two different approaches to the issue of equal rights and treatment for African Americans. Without King's campaign for equal rights, black Americans wouldn't be able to address the issues of poverty and justice Malcolm X highlighted.

Both men died violently. Malcolm X was murdered by the Nation of Islam (he'd fallen out with them); Martin Luther King was murdered by a white gunman at a motel in Memphis.

Black Power!

The most radical black movement was the Black Panthers, who carried guns and openly said they wanted to start a revolution in America. They set up self-help clinics and shops for black people in the poor areas of Los Angeles, but their leaders were all either killed or arrested in a big shoot-out with the police. People still talked of Black Power but it was overtaken by other issues, especially Vietnam.

Dance like a butterfly, sting like a bee

One of the most effective role models for African Americans in the 1960s and 1970s was Muhammad Ali, born Cassius Clay and the greatest boxer in the whole history of the world. At least he said he was, and I suppose he ought to know. At first Americans weren't sure they liked this cocky young boxer who was always boasting about how good he was. When he joined the Nation of Islam, changed his name, and refused to be drafted into the US military, white America was decidedly unamused: Ali was stripped of his heavyweight title and imprisoned. But gradually, as he won the big stage-managed fights with Joe Frazier and George Foreman and delighted press conferences by reading his poems about how he would soon be reducing his opponent to pulp and leaving him to the cleaners to scrape up, he won America – and the world – over. Later in life he fell victim to Parkinson's Disease, but he had done more than almost anyone else to change America's perception of its black citizens.

I have a dream too and this ain't it: LBJ and Vietnam

No one had expected Lyndon Johnson to become president. Kennedy had chosen the big Texan as his vice president as a way of winning over southern voters who would be put off by Kennedy's own northern, Catholic image. After Kennedy's death, Johnson was sworn in on the plane out of Dallas with Jackie standing beside him, still wearing the blood-stained outfit she'd worn in the fateful motorcade.

People underestimated Johnson. He was no hick but an intelligent and thoughtful statesman. He had big plans, especially for America's poor. He wanted to create a Great Society, a bit like a European welfare state, and to declare War on Poverty. Sadly, he had to put the Great Society on hold while he waged a very different war. In Vietnam.

Kennedy should take the blame for getting into Vietnam in the first place, when he sent thousands of US troops to 'advise' the South Vietnamese on how to fight their communist neighbours (Chapter 14 has the details on what the fighting in Vietnam was all about). Johnson didn't feel he could duck the commitment Kennedy had made to defend South Vietnam. The situation became a nightmare for Johnson, and here's why:

- **Jungle fighting:** The North Vietnamese and Viet Cong had bases deep in the jungle where it was very difficult for the Americans to find them. The Americans lost thousands of men in search and destroy missions without gaining any very obvious military advantage.

- **Bombing:** The US poured bombs onto North Vietnam, onto Cambodia, and onto the jungles of South Vietnam. All this tactic seemed to do was kill thousands of civilians and created a storm of controversy at home and around the world. Protestors would gather at the White House gates and chant 'Hey! Hey! LBJ! How many kids did you kill today?'

- **Protests at home:** TV news reports from Vietnam brought Americans onto the streets to protest against the war. Young people who could afford the fare and the hotel bills (that is, mainly kids from white middle-class families) skipped off to Canada to avoid being drafted to fight in it.

Historians can't decide on exactly how far the protests at home affected the outcome of the war. The US forces were actually doing well and defeating many of the big communist offensives, but to TV audiences at home the situation didn't look that way. It's important to remember that most Americans, especially older people, believed in what America was doing in Vietnam and supported the president, but it's also true that the protests made for bad headlines for Johnson at home and abroad and added enormously to the pressure he was under.

Woodstock

A wet weekend in August 1969 defined the youth culture of the sixties. The Woodstock Festival, held on farmland in upstate New York, attracted some 300,000 people, which was rather more than the organisers had catered for, but no one seemed to mind. The line-up included Crosby, Stills and Nash, The Who, and the psychedelic Jefferson Airplane; the facilities included mud, sex, drugs, rock 'n' roll. And mud.

In 1968, tired and drained, Johnson went on TV to announce that he would not seek, and would not accept, the Democratic nomination in the next presidential election.

Fly me to the moon

Ever since the Russians had put the first satellites and the first man into space, the Americans had been desperate to get up there too. John Glenn orbited the earth three times in 1962 but doing that wasn't enough. President Kennedy announced that America would send a man to the moon and bring him safely home again before the end of the decade. So put that in your pipe and smoke it, Ivan.

The moon programme was named *Apollo* after the Greek god of the sun. The Apollo missions gradually got closer to the destination, leaving the earth's atmosphere, orbiting the moon, and sending an unmanned module onto the surface, until, on 21 July 1969, Apollo 11 landed on the moon and Neil Armstrong and Buzz Aldrin set foot on the surface. And they planted the Stars and Stripes – America had the first inter-planetary empire.

The public lost interest in moon landings until, in 1970, Apollo 13 suffered serious engine problems. The world was gripped by the fate of the three trapped astronauts until they finally managed to splash down safely in the Pacific Ocean. The first sign that anything was wrong was when the astronauts radioed Mission Control 'Houston, we have a problem'. The second sign was when someone was heard saying 'Beam me up, Scottie'.

America in the Seventies

After the roller-coaster ride of the sixties (refer to the preceding 'Crazy Time – The Sixties' section), Americans were hoping for a more settled decade. After all, 1976 would bring the two hundredth anniversary of the Declaration of Independence. The seventies certainly produced some classic American films, like *Taxi Driver* and *The Godfather*, but in public life the decade brought a series of humiliations: The Watergate scandal, the less-than gripping presidency of Gerald Ford, and the agony of the Iran hostage crisis. This was going to be a difficult decade.

Tricky Dicky

Republican Richard Milhouse Nixon won the 1968 election and immediately looked for an exit strategy from Vietnam. He did not mean giving in, though. Nixon increased the bombing and kept up the pressure on the North Vietnamese to persuade them to negotiate. He also authorised massive bombing of Cambodia, which had been giving help to the North Vietnamese and their Viet Cong allies. So the protests at home continued. In 1970 National Guardsmen fired on protestors at Kent State University, Ohio and killed four of them. Student protestors now openly burned the American flag and defied the government. Vietnam was tearing America apart.

Finally, talks opened in Paris between Nixon's Secretary of State, Henry Kissinger, and the North Vietnamese. The fighting wound down and in 1973 the Americans pulled out. The agreement was that North Vietnam would leave South Vietnam alone, but no one believed that would happen and it didn't. In 1975 the North Vietnamese invaded again and this time they took the whole country. Look at the outcome any way you like: America had lost.

My fellow Americans, the party's over

Nixon came into office determined to balance the books. He thought Johnson's Great Society (see the earlier section) was just an excuse to spend money America couldn't afford, so instead of setting up aid programmes he announced big cuts in government spending. To make things worse, in 1973 the price of oil went through the roof (this happened around the world and Chapter 17 explains why), which meant Nixon had to try to keep inflation – and American pay packets – under strict control. On the whole, Nixon was successful and the American people seemed to appreciate it. Certainly they re-elected him in 1972 by a huge majority.

China in your hand

Nixon made a huge breakthrough in foreign policy. The two communist super powers, Russia and China, had fallen out and become deadly enemies. So Nixon played the classic game of divide and rule and made friends with China. As a young man he'd helped prosecute 'traitors' who had supposedly helped Mao Tse-tung come to power in Beijing; now Nixon travelled to China and shook hands with Chairman Mao in person. Historians agree that this trip was a momentous event, and it completely changed the power politics of the world. The US president's visit kick-started China's re-engagement with the outside world; Nixon also got China's support for his policy of withdrawing gracefully from Vietnam. Well, okay, cutting and running if you prefer.

A pinch of SALT

Good relations with China helped Nixon brush Vietnam under the carpet and talk tough to the Soviet Union. The two sides finally started talking about limiting the number of nuclear missiles they had pointing at each other. No, not getting rid of any – do try to keep up – just not producing quite as many new ones. The talks were called SALT – Strategic Arms Limitation Talks – and they were the first sign that reaching a thaw in the Cold War might just be possible.

Well, I'm not a crook. Okay, maybe I am

Everyone remembers Nixon for one thing: Watergate. What happened was that a gang was caught breaking in to bug the Democratic Party headquarters in the Watergate hotel and office complex in Washington – hence the name of the scandal. At first it looked like the work of a rogue dirty tricks brigade, but one of the men wrote to the judge in the case saying that the president had known all about it. Two reporters on the *Washington Post* smelled a story and started digging. They struck gold with a mysterious source they nicknamed 'Deep Throat', who confirmed that a massive cover-up was in operation and that the trail led right to the White House. Nixon angrily denied it, but soon the police vans started arriving for some of his closest aides and the world learned that Nixon had secretly taped White House discussions. The courts demanded the tapes and after a long tussle the White House handed them over. They were dynamite.

The White House tapes had long blank passages that had obviously been wiped, but the parts that survived were damaging enough. Nixon was clearly heard shouting in the foulest language demanding that the whole affair be covered up. He had a choice: Stay and be impeached or walk. He walked.

Some historians say that Nixon's presidency shouldn't be defined by Watergate, claiming that it overlooks his real achievements at home and abroad; others say Nixon was a shady character who brought it on himself.

After Nixon and Watergate

After Watergate, the seventies didn't bring much good news America's way:

- ✔ **President Gerald Ford** issued a pardon to Nixon and saw America through its bicentennial celebrations but couldn't solve America's economic crisis.

- ✔ **President Jimmy Carter** kept up the SALT talks with Russia, negotiated a deal between Israel and Egypt, and demanded that other countries respect human rights. No one took much notice.

- ✔ **The nuclear plant at Three Mile Island, Pennsylvania** overheated and threatened a nuclear catastrophe. Luckily the emergency was prevented but it was a close call.

✔ **Iran** had an Islamic revolution that toppled the Shah and turned the country into America's Enemy Number One. Iranian students stormed the US embassy in Tehran and took the staff hostage. President Carter could do nothing about it.

The Eighties, Reagan, and the End of the Cold War

Former film actor Ronald Reagan was elected president in 1980 by an America tired of the well-meaning but weak Carter White House. People joked about Reagan's short attention span and hazy grasp on detail but he did a lot better than people expected and the people loved his style. He brazened it out when sources revealed he'd been backing the Contra guerrillas fighting the socialist government of Nicaragua with the profits from illegal sales to, er, Iran and got away with it (see Chapter 13 for more about Nicaragua).

Reagan abandoned Carter's talk of détente (easing of tension) with the Soviets: He called them the 'evil empire' and massively expanded America's stockpile of nuclear missiles. The Soviets tried to keep up but their economy was feeling the strain and Reagan raised the stakes still higher with 'Star Wars', officially the *Strategic Defence Initiative*, a system of killer satellites in space. With Russia facing bankruptcy, the new Soviet leader Mikhail Gorbachev agreed to meet Reagan and talk. The two men got on famously and went further than anyone had expected: They agreed to scrap the whole missile programme. Suddenly the Americans and Russians ditched their Cold War posturing and became best buddies. Reagan's successor, George Bush, declared the Cold War over and a New World Order about to begin.

So I guess Ronald Reagan had the last laugh.

Chapter 16

Red on Red: Russia and China

. . . .

In This Chapter

▶ Tracing the rise of Mao Tse-tung

▶ Watching (in disbelief) as China splits from Russia

▶ Taking cover from Mao's Cultural Revolution

▶ Joining in with Gorbachev's changes in Russia

. . . .

*R*ussia and China were the communist superpowers of the post-war world. Nothing could stop them turning the whole world communist if they wanted to it seemed, and they appeared to be planning just that. But by the sixties these two communist superpowers had fallen out and were preparing for war – with each other. Why did Russia and China follow such different paths? And why did Russia – but not China – collapse?

Comrades? (Maybe)

Communism was based on the ideas of the nineteenth-century German thinker Karl Marx (Chapter 4 has an outline of his thoughts). Central to communist thinking was the idea that workers were brothers and sisters, *comrades*, to use the usual communist term. Communist countries usually did away with titles like 'Lord' and 'Lady', even 'Mr' and 'Mrs' (they thought these terms too bourgeois and middle class), and referred to everyone as 'comrade' – much more egalitarian. Don't get the idea, however, that these comrades were always comradely with each other. Communist comrades were just as capable of stabbing each other in the back as any bourgeois capitalist Mr or Mrs. The two leaders of the communist world, Russia's Joseph Stalin and China's Mao Tse-tung, smiled for the camera and kept up comradely appearances, but behind the smiles they and their countries were soon deadly rivals in the leadership of the communist world stakes.

Wicked Uncle Joe

Stalin had wormed his way into power in Russia in the 1920s by the simple method of appointing most of the membership of the Russian Communist Party and then keeping them loyal to him (Chapter 4 has all the details). He was utterly ruthless and had thousands of Russians, including some of his oldest Bolshevik comrades, arrested and shot. He shot so many army officers that the Red Army couldn't resist the Germans when they invaded in 1941, and Stalin was very lucky that they didn't take Moscow. But that minor detail didn't stop him shamelessly presenting himself as the Wise Leader Who Guided Russia Through the War. The Western Allies helped in this charade by presenting him as cuddly 'Uncle Joe'. (He could indeed be very friendly and cuddly to children, but he never let that stop him from having their parents shot.)

This white-washing of Stalin's image and contributions was so successful, in fact, that if you'd asked a communist anywhere in the world immediately after the Second World War which country and which individual they most admired, you'd have got a very clear answer: The Soviet Union and its leader, Joseph Stalin. For communists, Stalin was the only true hero to emerge from the war. According to them, Russia, not the capitalist Western Allies, had broken the power of Hitler's armies and had suffered most from his appalling rule. One communist partisan in Yugoslavia said he didn't mind the Germans bombing his country because each bomb dropped meant there was one less dropped on Russia. Okay, he probably didn't have many friends, but communists all around the world would have understood his point of view.

By 1945 Stalin was so powerful that the Western Allies could only stand by and watch as his troops took over the countries of eastern and central Europe, got rid of their pre-war governments, and put communist governments in their place. Stalin made sure that these governments obeyed orders from Moscow. He was the undisputed leader of the communist bloc and he loved it.

Stalin only had two challenges to his position to worry about:

- ✔ **Marshal Tito:** Josip Broz (codename 'Tito') and his communist partisans had liberated Yugoslavia themselves and Tito wasn't suddenly going to start taking orders from Stalin now that the war was over. Stalin was furious and declared that he only had to wag his little finger and Tito would fall (apparently he wagged the wrong finger because Tito was still in power long after Stalin had died).

- ✔ **The American atom bomb:** President Truman had warned Stalin at the Potsdam Conference that the United States had the atom bomb (he didn't actually add 'So don't try any funny business' but that's more or less what he meant). Stalin didn't need to worry, though. Communist sympathisers in Britain and America were busy passing atomic secrets to the Russians, so that Stalin was soon able to catch up with the Americans.

Historians (and spies) have long wondered how the Soviet Union was able to build atomic weapons. Stalin's agents were getting hold of Western atomic secrets, but Russia also had a first-class atomic weapons team, including Andrei Sakharov, Russia's 'father of the hydrogen bomb'. We now know, from material in the Soviet archives, that Stalin and Lavretii Beria, head of the secret police, simply didn't trust Soviet scientists, and insisted they build Russia's atom bomb the same way their spies were reporting that the Americans built theirs. Sakharov and his teams had more success pursuing their own ideas on the hydrogen bomb – the Soviet bomb was probably developed before the American one and certainly had a more efficient design – but the Russians liked to give the impression that they got all their atomic expertise from spies in the West, just so they could see the expressions on the CIAs' faces.

The Soviet atomic programme took a terrible toll of human life. Safety measures for the workers were almost non-existent and thousands died from radiation sickness. Sakharov himself became so sickened by the nuclear arms race that he turned against nuclear weapons entirely and became one of the Soviet Union's leading dissidents and peace campaigners.

Stalin may have been powerful but he was still paranoid about enemies. He had thousands of people rounded up and sent to the huge Soviet network of labour camps known as the *gulag*. His pet hates: Doctors, Jews, the city and people of Leningrad, people who looked at him in a funny way. Even high-ranking Soviet officials (in fact, *especially* high-ranking Soviet officials) were scared stiff of 'the Boss'.

And then, in 1949, Stalin really did get a new and powerful rival when Mao Tse-tung seized power in Peking and set up the People's Republic of China.

Mao Tse-tung – new kid on the bloc

China was enormous but it was also backward, corrupt, and weak. In the nineteenth century the Western powers had bullied China into accepting imports of opium (yes, back then drug smuggling was actually Western government policy!) and forced her to open up her ports to Western trade. During the Second World War the Allies pretended to treat the Chinese leader, Chiang Kai-shek, as an equal partner but China still had to do what the Western powers, especially the USA, told her to.

Once Mao and the communists had seized power in 1949, all that was going to change.

Translating Chinese characters and pronunciation can be difficult for westerners, and sometimes the 'Western' version of a Chinese name doesn't sound much like the original. The Chinese capital always used to be called 'Peking' in the West, but 'Beijing' is much closer to the Chinese pronunciation and eventually came to be the version people use nowadays. Pronouncing people's names is the same, except that not all the new versions are in wide use yet. Strictly speaking, Mao Tse-tung should be Mao Zedong, Chou En-lai should be Zhou Enlai, and Chiang Kai-shek should be Jiang Jieshih, but if you're not used to the changes you could find the new versions confusing. I stick to the versions in use at the time of each event.

So who exactly was Mao?

Mao's family were peasants, like millions of others in China, but the lad didn't fancy pushing a plough all his life so he ran away to school. He did well and got a job in Peking University stamping books. There he picked up one on Marxist theory and started reading. He liked it.

Mao agreed with Marx's analysis of capitalist society (Chapter 4 can fill you in on this) but he could see a major snag as far as China was concerned. Marx was writing in nineteenth-century Europe, which had a huge industrial working class. But China was an almost entirely agricultural country and its people weren't industrial workers but peasants. Marxists saw peasants as class enemies who just wanted to make a tidy profit from their farms, but Mao thought he could turn China's peasants into a revolutionary class. In 1921 Mao helped set up the Chinese Communist Party, though his peasants-are-revolutionaries-too ideas meant he was given a hard time by his more orthodox comrades.

The Long March

China had overthrown the emperor and become a republic in 1911, but the new Nationalist Chinese government led by Chiang Kai-shek had no time for communists. Neither did China's warlords, local gangsters who ruled most of the Chinese countryside. The communists set up a soviet (a communist governing council) in Jianxi province in southern China, but Chiang Kai-shek closed in on it with his troops. In January 1935, the communists decided trying to defend Jianxi was hopeless: They had to break out and head north. Their objective: The northern province of Shaanxi, 5,000 miles away. They called this journey north *The Long March*.

The Long March to Shaanxi was the defining event in forming the Chinese Communist Party and in putting Mao in charge of it.

- ✔ **The communists had to fight all the way:** Chiang's Nationalists and local warlords attacked constantly and the communists lost thousands of men. The experience gave the ones who made it a strong sense of bonding.

- ✔ **The communists weren't happy with their leaders and Soviet advisers:** Instead they turned to Mao, because he had better ideas on how to fight off Nationalist attacks.

✔ **Mao enforced strict discipline to make sure his men treated the local peasants fairly:** Chinese peasants were used to government troops making off with their food and animals without paying for them, so it came as a nice change when the communists arrived, asked nicely before they took anything, and paid for it too. Mao knew he had to win over the hearts and minds of China's peasants, and the Long March was his chance to do it.

The Long March became an epic episode in the history of the Chinese Communist Party. At one point the Nationalists removed the planking from a river bridge, so the communists had to fight their way across it just using the bridge's chains. Some 86,000 people set out from Jianxi in January 1935 and less than 20,000 made it to Shaanxi in October. But once they got there, Mao was able to set up a strong base and defy Chiang Kai-shek to bring it on.

All hands on deck! We can kill each other later

In 1937 the Japanese invaded China, so Mao and Chiang put their own war on hold while they both turned to fight against this new enemy. The communists concentrated on guerrilla fighting, which was just as well as the one time they tried a big offensive it was a disaster. Mao was also able to use the war to strengthen his personal hold on the communists:

✔ **Thousands of volunteers arrived to join the communists:** They didn't know much about communism, so Mao set up special classes where they could learn all about it. *His* version of communism, of course.

✔ **Mao trained a special class of combat leaders called 'Cadres':** Cadres made a special study of Mao's writings and they were utterly loyal to him. Mao took particular care to discourage cadres from thinking for themselves.

✔ **Mao took care of the peasants in his area:** He imposed strict caps on rents to stop greedy landlords exploiting the war to get rich, and he reorganised schools to allow students time to work in the fields.

Meanwhile, things weren't going quite so well for Chiang and the Nationalists:

✔ **Soaring inflation:** The Japanese controlled the industrial cities so the Nationalists didn't have any way of creating wealth. The government ended up deep in debt and with prices going through the roof.

✔ **Famine:** The Nationalists took hold of the peasants' food stocks, but they would only pay a fixed price for them. With inflation at over 200 per cent, many farms folded and the peasants went hungry.

✔ **Problems with the Allies:** Chiang had a gift for alienating people who were meant to be on his side. The Americans sent General 'Vinegar Joe' Stilwell to work with him, but Chiang ignored Stilwell's advice. He also refused to send any help to the British fighting the Japanese in Burma. In 1944, just when all the other Allies were finally beating the Japanese, Chiang took them on in a major campaign – and lost.

Made in Taiwan

In 1895, the Japanese annexed the Chinese island of Taiwan (also known as Formosa) and they held onto it until 1945. Taiwan seemed the perfect haven for Chiang Kai-shek and his followers after Mao won the civil war in 1949, and they headed there in huge numbers: Approximately *one million* mainland Chinese crossed over to Taiwan with Chiang. The communists did try attacking Taiwan, but they got badly beaten: This was one corner of China that would be forever Nationalist.

Chiang soon showed what he thought of the Taiwanese: He imposed martial law and banned all political parties other than his own Kuomintang. He wasn't interested in Taiwan except as a base for getting back to the mainland.

The United States recognised Taiwan as the only legitimate government of China until the 1970s, when President Nixon visited China and the US finally came round to recognising Peking.

Chiang kept up his tough grip on Taiwan until his death in 1975, but his son Chiang Ching-kuo loosened up and allowed a bit more freedom. Result: Taiwan took off as a major financial centre and manufacturer of cheap goods whose handles come off. Chiang Ching-kuo appointed Lee Teng-hui, a real live Taiwanese, as his vice president, and in 1988 the Taiwanese people elected him president in their first free elections. Just in time for the end of the century, the world had a little bit of democracy 'Made in Taiwan'.

Combined, these factors meant that when the war was over, Chiang was dangerously short of friends both at home and abroad, which was bad news because he was soon going to need every friend he could get.

China in your hand

Right at the end of the war, the Soviet Union declared war on Japan. The Russians rushed troops into Manchuria, and in 1946 they handed the whole area over to Mao and the communists. US General Marshall arrived to try to arrange a peaceful settlement between the two sides but no one was interested. They were preparing for war.

Chiang attacked first. Nationalist forces tore through the communist heartlands in northern China and forced Mao's men to retreat. But Mao had reorganised the army as the *People's Liberation Army* (liberating China from Big Bad Chiang, that is) and his army commander Lin Biao proved very good at launching guerrilla raids every time Chiang thought he'd won. By 1948 the PLA was on the offensive and in January 1949 it finally took Peking. Chiang and his followers headed for Taiwan, and Mao announced that China was now the *People's Republic of China*.

The Mao and Joe show

At first the Russians were delighted with Mao's victory over Chiang Kai-shek, but the Americans were aghast. Washington had supported Chiang and China was an important base for American missionaries. The United States insisted that Chiang's government on Taiwan was the only legal government of China and managed to persuade the UN to give China's seats to Taiwan. The Russians were furious and walked out of the UN in protest. Not such a great idea: They weren't there in 1950 to stop the UN sending troops to Korea (Chapter 10 has details on the Korean War).

Capitalist invaders – keep out or else!

When the Korean War started, Mao watched events closely: North Korea borders China, and he was worried that if the Americans won in the south they might follow it up by invading the north, and if they won there, what was to stop them deciding to get rid of the 'illegal' regime in Peking while they were at it? Quite. So Mao warned the UN that they could do what they liked in South Korea but the moment they stepped over the border into North Korea, the People's Liberation Army would fall on them like a ton of bricks.

President Truman warned the UN commander, General Douglas MacArthur, that under no, repeat no, circumstances was he to cross into North Korea. MacArthur, who had full, repeat full, confidence in his own judgement, took no notice and charged into North Korea almost to the Chinese border. Result: Thousands of Chinese troops poured into Korea and drove the UN troops back. Mao claimed that the Chinese had risen up spontaneously in righteous anger at this capitalist threat to their land (no one actually believed him, but it sounded good).

Marxism the Maoist way

Mao knew that the key place for building communism in China wasn't in the factories, as in Russia, but in the countryside. To do that, the Chinese would have to tick off a few items on their 'Things To Do' list:

- **Kill the landlords:** Landowners were hauled before special People's Courts and charged with exploiting the peasants for their own gain. Most of them were shot and their land was distributed to the peasants.

- **Give the peasants land:** Peasants all got a share in the local landlords' estates. Most of them promptly sold it and pocketed the profit. The Russians thought their behaviour confirmed all they'd ever thought about peasants.

- **Industrialise fast:** Mao copied Stalin's fast-track industrialisation scheme by planning everything centrally and imposing impossibly heavy production quotas. The Russians sent hundreds of technical experts to help the Chinese industrialise the Soviet way.

- **Collectivise the land:** Having only just given land to the peasants, Mao then took it off them. China's villages were reorganised into big collective farms which took their orders from Peking.

Mao also copied Stalin's technique of having thousands of people killed. Mao turned on 'counter-revolutionaries', corrupt (= not communist enough) cadres within the army, and China's remaining capitalists. Somewhere between 500,000 and 800,000 people were killed in these purges, though the rich capitalists usually had to pay crippling fines: Their money was much more useful to the regime than their deaths.

The Russians still weren't convinced that Chinese peasants were a revolutionary class, but they were generally happy with the way Mao's regime was shaping up. Mao, however, wasn't at all thrilled by developments in Russia.

Breaking up is hard to do – the big split

Communist China and the Soviet Union should have been close allies, but by the 1960s they were deadly rivals, hardly speaking to each other except in threats. This section explains why.

All change at the top

The problems began when Stalin died in 1953. Immediately, the leading members of the Politburo, the ruling council of the Soviet Union, started manoeuvring to seize power. What they were all scared of was that Lavrentii Beria, the ruthless head of the NKVD, the Soviet secret police, would get the top post, so they plotted together and had him shot for treason. None of them trusted the others, so instead of having one man in charge they had two: Georgi Malenkov as prime minister and Nikolai Bulganin as his deputy. Within a couple of weeks, however, Nikita Khrushchev had used his position as General Secretary of the Party to force Malenkov to step down. From then on Khrushchev and Bulganin ruled together. Then, in 1956, at the twentieth congress of the Soviet Communist Party, Khrushchev did the unthinkable: He launched a savage attack on Stalin.

I always knew that Stalin was a bad 'un

Khrushchev's attack on Stalin was in a 'secret' speech to the congress (it was secret because no reporters were present, though news of the speech soon leaked out). He denounced Stalin for his personality cult and for ruling Russia by terror, having thousands of loyal communists shot or imprisoned simply because of his own paranoia. The delegates were stunned. They'd been brought up to look on Stalin as a sort of god. Like everyone else, they'd imagined that if Stalin only *knew* what the secret police were up to, he'd soon put things right. Learning that Stalin knew all about the NKVD's actions perfectly well because he'd ordered them came as a profound shock. But if Khrushchev said Stalin knew, it must be true. Mustn't it?

Suddenly, it was open season on Stalin. People started smashing his statues and pictures; they even removed his embalmed body from the Red Square mausoleum, where it had lain in the place of honour next to Lenin. Never again, the Russian leaders declared, would they allow anyone to create a personality cult as Stalin had.

Western leaders were delighted to hear of Khrushchev's speech because they thought it meant Khrushchev was rejecting Stalin's hardline attitude towards other countries. But when the Hungarians rose up in 1956 in protest against control from Moscow, Khrushchev sent tanks into Budapest to crush them. De-Stalinisation didn't mean Russia had gone soft.

After his 'secret' speech, no one could challenge Khrushchev's position as the leader of Russia. In 1958 he edged Bulganin out of the picture and took power on his own. But he didn't set up his own personality cult and he had to treat his Politburo colleagues carefully. If he ever put a foot wrong they could get rid of him, and he knew it.

That's what comes of too much free speech: Mao's reaction

The rest of the world may have liked Khrushchev's attack on Stalin's posthumous reputation (see previous section) but Mao was appalled. He thought Krushchev was playing into the hands of the West and, in any case, Mao couldn't see anything wrong in establishing a huge personality cult and having thousands of innocent people killed: These were some of his own favourite hobbies. Mao thought the de-Stalinisation programme that followed the speech showed that Khrushchev was removing the Soviet Union from the true path to socialism. From now on China would work out its own way to socialism, without Russian help.

These boots were made for banging on the table

Not every day does a major world leader slip off his shoe in the United Nations General Assembly and bang it on the desk shouting out 'No! No! No!' but that's just what Khrushchev did in 1960 when the Philippine delegate accused the Soviet Union of imperialism in eastern Europe. Khrushchev wanted to make his rather different opinion clear, and he certainly did that. He always said he got his rough and ready manners from his peasant background and they could certainly make him a difficult guest. On his disastrous 1959 visit to America, he shouted angrily to his hosts, 'We will bury you!' He meant that Russia would out-perform the American economy, but the Americans thought he was threatening to blow them all up – perhaps because they wouldn't let him visit Disneyland (for 'security reasons' they said). 'Nyet' (pronounced knee-yet) is the Russian word for 'No' and after his UN performance it became Khrushchev's international nickname.

At least you don't have to worry about what to wear

One of the most striking features of communist China was that everyone wore plain blue overalls. Even the People's Liberation Army had the same uniform for everyone, regardless of ranks. Mao himself wore a plain suit that buttoned up to the neck. The idea was to abolish all signs of individuality (that was, like, so bourgeois) in favour of reflecting the collective will of the Chinese people. Unfortunately, the collective will of the Chinese people was a trifle, er, *boring*.

In 1957 Mao decided to broaden his ideas by encouraging China's intellectuals to speak out. 'Don't be shy,' he said, 'let a hundred flowers bloom!' Be careful what you wish for. In newspapers and on posters economists, writers, and journalists tore into Mao, denouncing him for not following orthodox Marxism and generally deciding he couldn't lead the country out of a paper bag. Mao had never been much of a fan of intellectuals, and this confirmed his low opinion of them. He cancelled the hundred flowers campaign and had all the people who'd criticised him locked up.

China's great leap backward

In 1958 Mao announced a bold new departure that would show the world that China had worked out the proper way to apply Marxist principles in practice. He called this plan the *Great Leap Forward*. It was a disaster.

Instead of a Soviet-style industrialisation programme, the Great Leap set up thousands of self-sufficient communes – rural villages with a bit of industry attached. No private property or family meals: Everything was to be done and held in common. Even sleep was rationed to six hours every two days, which is less than half what the body needs, especially for heavy outdoor work. Peasants had to plough in the new official 'close planting, deep ploughing' way dreamed up by some technocrat in Peking. Result: The grain harvest plummeted. The government was imposing massive grain quotas with terrible penalties for failing to meet them, so people just doctored the figures and hoped for the best.

Not content with ruining the harvest, Mao also forced peasants to undertake industrial steel production with little home-made (and completely useless) backyard blast furnaces, which meant chopping down every tree they could find to feed the wretched things. Result: The country's natural irrigation was wrecked and created devastating floods. Peasants had to spend so much time trying to get their furnaces to work that they couldn't look after the fields properly, so food production collapsed completely. Result: Famine. Something like *thirty million* people starved in Mao's Great Leap Forward.

By 1961 even Mao recognised he had a disaster on his hands and he had to import grain from Canada and Australia while the Russians looked on saying 'I told you so'. The other members of China's Politburo began to think the time might be right for a change of leader.

World communism – now in two exciting varieties!

The Russians were furious about the Great Leap Forward (see the preceding section, 'China's great leap backwards'). They said Mao should have listened to them; Mao said he wasn't going to take any lessons from Russia and anyway Khrushchev was too soft on the Americans.

'Well, at least I'm not planning to provoke the Americans into nuclear war by attacking Taiwan,' retorted Khrushchev.

'Huh,' said Mao, 'The atom bomb's a paper tiger. The Americans will never use it.'

So Khrushchev called Mao another Stalin and an ultra-leftist (which is a strange accusation to make against a communist leader!) and Mao called Khrushchev a bourgeois revisionist, which in communist circles was like calling into question the virtue of your mother. 'That does it!' said Khrushchev and he recalled all the economic experts Russia had sent to China. The Chinese clearly hadn't been listening to them anyway.

The tragedy of Tibet

The remote mountain kingdom of Tibet had its own distinctive culture and identity. In 1913 Tibet's spiritual leader, the Dalai Lama, took advantage of the overthrow of the Chinese emperor to declare the country independent, but the Chinese still regarded it as Chinese territory. In 1950 Chinese troops tore into the country to 'liberate' it – from the Tibetans, presumably. Nine years later the Tibetans staged a rising but the Chinese crushed them.

The Dalai Lama had to flee to India and the Chinese were so furious with the Indian government for sheltering him that in 1962 they attacked and captured Indian territory along the border. Since then the Chinese government has continued to threaten any government that receives or helps the Dalai Lama. As China has become richer and more powerful, Western governments have started keeping the Dalai Lama at arm's length.

Pulling out her economic experts was the equivalent of Russia withdrawing its ambassador: The action was a sign that goodwill between the two communist giants had broken down. The *Sino*(Chinese)*–Soviet split* was now complete. In the 1960s China and the Soviet Union stopped pretending they were friends and took very different paths towards establishing communism.

The split between Russia and China actually turned into a short war in 1969 over a disputed island, Zhen bao, in the Ussuri river. This situation was very dangerous, as both sides had nuclear weapons and China had no allies. The Russians started provoking trouble all along the border and the Chinese realised they'd have to negotiate a settlement. This negotiation was a sign that, big and strong though China was, she still needed friends.

Cultural Revolution in China

After the disaster of the Great Leap Forward (see the earlier section 'China's Great Leap Backwards') Mao's rivals on the Politburo decided he needed to retire. His main enemies were:

- Liu Shaoqui
- Deng Xiaoping

Liu and Deng encouraged a public campaign criticising Mao for leading China into economic disaster and for encouraging a huge personality cult saying how wonderful he was.

Mao's allies were:

- Lin Biao, an old comrade from the Long March
- Chou En-lai, Mao's right-hand man on the Long March – and Lin Biao's greatest rival
- Jiang Qing, a former film star and Mao's ultra-loyal fourth wife

The two sides in Chinese politics were squaring up for a fight. They spent the first half of the sixties hurling insults at each other.

One of the forms of criticism that really got under Mao's skin was a play called *Hai Rui Dismissed From Office*, written by the historian and deputy mayor of Peking, Wu Han. The play was based on an episode from Chinese history in which the hero, Hai Rui, protests to the emperor that the poor peasants are having their land taken off them and are being forced to live in communes and take orders from Peking. (Sound familiar?) The emperor is furious with Hai Rui and dismisses him from office, just as it says on the tin. Mao was furious too, as the play was clearly a not-very-subtle attack on his Great Leap Forward.

You're just a number in my little red book

During Mao's propaganda war with his enemies on the Politburo, he published a little pocket-sized, red-bound collection of his own memorable quotes and sayings. It was called *The Thoughts of Chairman Mao*, though everyone called it the 'Little Red Book'. You could keep this handy book in your breast pocket and take in a thought or two at the bus stop or while taking a breather from beating up reactionary bourgeois revisionists in the street. The thoughts weren't particularly profound: 'If you don't sweep in the corner, the dust won't go away on its own' or 'Classes struggle. Some classes win and some classes lose' (you don't say?), but they fired up the young Red Guards of the Cultural Revolution, who seemed to consult the book about any decision they had to make, including what to eat tonight and how to find their way to the station.

Mao got Wu Han's play slated in a review and accused Wu of being a right-wing revisionist: A very serious accusation. Wu was forced to confess in public that his script stank and that Mao was right and he would never dare do anything like that again and could he go home now, please? But Mao and his allies hadn't finished yet. They were going to unleash a storm over China so terrifying that no one would dare criticise Mao ever again. This policy was to be called the *Cultural Revolution.*

Cultural terror and the Red Guard

In 1966 Mao's wife Jiang Qing took over the Cultural Affairs Committee of the People's Liberation Army, got her opponents sacked, and set in motion the Great Proletarian Cultural Revolution. Mao and Jiang Qing declared that China was still riddled with bourgeois counter-revolutionaries and traitors (= people who didn't agree with Mao), especially teachers, lecturers, and the educated professional classes. Lin Biao called on China's young people, whether in school or in university, to rise up and hunt down the traitors.

Not every day do schoolchildren get the go-ahead to humiliate their teachers and China's young people leapt at the chance. They formed themselves into the *Red Guards*, fanatically loyal to Mao, who arranged for them to have free rail passes to travel to Peking and stage massive parades in Tianenmen Square, brandishing his Little Red Book and calling for the destruction of China's enemies.

When Mao unleashed his Red Guards on the country they tore China apart:

> ✔ Teachers, lecturers, party officials, and even Politburo members were tortured and humiliated. The Red Guards forced them to parade in public wearing dunces' caps with details of their 'crimes' written on them.

> ✔ Works of art and historical relics were smashed and the Red Guards burned any books that didn't follow the Maoist line, to 'cleanse' China of any trace of 'bourgeois' attitudes.

> ✔ Ordinary people were encouraged to denounce their neighbours as class traitors and bourgeois revisionists. It was wise to denounce your neighbour before your neighbour denounced you.

The Red Guards were completely out of control. The country, especially the cities, fell into anarchy. Schools and universities were shut and the economy ground to a halt. The rest of the world looked on in horror as China descended into self-destructive chaos.

Chou En-lai urged Mao to rein the Red Guards in. Chou realised that the Cultural Revolution was doing appalling harm to China's outside image and was creating bitterness that would take years to heal. Workers and peasants were already forming their own committees to oppose the Red Guards and restore order. Finally, in 1968 Mao gave in. He ordered the People's Liberation Army to move in against the Red Guards.

The Cultural Revolution slowed right down after 1968, but it never quite ended until Mao's death. Mao's opponents, Liu Shaoqui and Deng Xiaoping, were both forced off the Politburo and Mao's authority was complete. But somewhere between half a million and a million people were killed during the Cultural Revolution, and the scars it left in people's minds lasted for years: Jung Chan's memoir *Wild Swans* tells the story of its devastating effect on three generations of women in her family.

The Cultural Revolution showed that China wouldn't be changing policy as long as Mao was alive. He regularly went swimming in public, even in China's polluted rivers, to show that he was fit and strong and would be around for a good while yet.

An American president in Peking

In 1972 US President Richard Nixon and his Secretary of State Henry Kissinger visited China and met Mao. Mao's Cultural Revolution (see previous section) had only recently been denouncing everything Western, so this meeting with a pair of anti-communist American Republicans took the world by surprise, to say the least. But in fact the visit made perfect sense:

> ✔ The US would soon be pulling out of Vietnam and badly needed a new friend in Asia. Who better than China?

> ✔ China needed a friend in its long stand-off with the Soviet Union. Who better than the US?

> ✔ The US had played China at ping pong and the Chinese wanted a return match.

Nixon's visit was a great success. The US recognised Mao's government, stopped pretending Taiwan was the legal government of China, and agreed to let the People's Republic take China's seat at the United Nations. The door was open for China to pursue closer links with the West if it chose to. But would it?

After Mao

Mao died in 1976 and immediately a bitter power struggle got going between the radical 'Gang of Four', led by Mao's widow Jiang Qing, and the modernisers, led by Deng Xiaoping:

✔ The modernisers (or, if you were one of the Gang of Four, the 'pro-Western bourgeois revisionist traitors') wanted to continue the links with the West that the Nixon visit had opened up.

✔ The Gang of Four (or 'dangerous lunatics who want to plunge us all into chaos again' if you supported the modernisers) wanted to go back to the good old anarchy of the Cultural Revolution.

The modernisers won. The Gang of Four were arrested and sentenced to long terms in prison, where Jiang Qing eventually hanged herself. Not many wept.

China immediately began to import Western goods and to allow people to voice criticisms of Mao. In 1980 Deng finally made his way to the top and opened China to foreign investment. By the end of the century China was poised to become an economic superpower.

Hong Kong: One country; two systems

In 1987 Deng Xiaoping arranged with the British prime minister Margaret Thatcher that Britain would hand back Hong Kong in 1997, when its 99-year lease on the New Territories ran out. The British were concerned for the future of the Hong Kong Chinese under undemocratic Chinese rule and then realised that in 99 years they had never quite got around to introducing democracy into Hong Kong themselves. So the last British governor, Chris Patten, hurriedly set up a legislative assembly with free elections.

The idea was to embed the assembly so that the Chinese would not be able to get rid of it later. The Chinese were furious with Patten and made it clear they would not tolerate democracy in Hong Kong after 1997. On the other hand, the Chinese had no intention of dismantling Hong Kong's phenomenally successful capitalist system: China needed the money too much. 'One country; two systems' they called it, though for hardline Maoists 'blatant hypocrisy' would have been a better name.

Not everything in China had changed, though. In 1989, as the Soviet bloc began dismantling and the Berlin Wall came down (see the next section 'Meanwhile, Back in the USSR . . .'), Chinese students set up a huge camp in Tianenmen Square in Beijing (as Peking was now known in the West). Excited about the prospect of communist countries becoming more free, they called for democracy in China. But Deng Xiaoping wasn't about to tear down the communist regime he'd spent his life trying to set up. Before the horrified cameras of the world, he sent tanks into the square to destroy the students' camp and had democracy campaigners arrested and imprisoned. The decadent Russians could do as they liked: China was staying communist.

Meanwhile, Back in the USSR . . .

The Soviet Union experienced a long period in the sixties and seventies when it suppressed free speech ruthlessly while its economy slowly disintegrated. But in the 1980s Mikhail Gorbachev forced some long-overdue reforms past the aged stick-in-the-muds of the Politburo – and brought the whole Soviet system crashing down.

Thank you, Mr Khrushchev, and good night

Nikita Khrushchev, who'd emerged as leader of the Soviet Union by 1960 (see the earlier section 'I always knew that Stalin was a bad 'un'), enjoyed taking a tough line with the United States. He broke off talks with the Americans when a U2 spy plane was shot down over the Soviet Union in 1960, and he backed Cuba's Fidel Castro when President Kennedy backed the disastrous Bay of Pigs invasion the following year (see Chapter 13). In 1961 he built the Berlin Wall to stop East Berliners slipping away to the decadently high wages and stable economy of West Berlin, and the following year he risked global destruction when he tried to put nuclear missiles on Cuba. The Cuban missile crisis brought the world closer than it had ever been to all-out nuclear war and at the end of it, Khrushchev had to withdraw his missiles and promise never to try such a thing again (Chapter 10 has the scary details of this event).

The Politburo in Moscow couldn't decide which was worse: Losing to the Americans or Khrushchev's folly in provoking the crisis in the first place. Khrushchev was losing friends fast. He tried sacking more ex-Stalinists, but that just turned the army and police top brass against him (they were all ex-Stalinists). Then he told Russia's collective farms to drop what they were doing and grow maize, whether it was suitable for the land or not. Mostly, it wasn't. 'Enough!' said the Politburo. In 1964 they went in to see Khrushchev and told him to clear his desk. He did and retired to write his memoirs. He was lucky: In Stalin's day, he'd have been shot.

Mr Brezhnev's doctrine

The man who took over from Khrushchev (see previous section) was Leonid Brezhnev, a steady-as-she-goes politician, less erratic than Khrushchev and less brutal than Stalin. He wasn't weak, though: He enforced communist rule ruthlessly, clamping down on anyone, however eminent, who spoke out against the Soviet system. The *Brezhnev Doctrine* gave the Soviet Union the right to intervene in the internal affairs of other socialist countries if they seemed to be departing from the socialist line, and in 1968 he sent tanks into Prague to crush the attempt by the government of Czechoslovakia to allow more freedom of speech and give communism a human face.

The fate of dissidents, famous and otherwise

People who protested against Brezhnev's, er, interesting approach to human rights were known as *dissidents*. They included some very eminent people:

- **Alexander Solzhenitsyn:** Novelist who spent eight years in the gulag for criticising Stalin and wrote a book, *One Day in the Life of Ivan Denisovitch*, describing what it was like. In 1970 Solzhenitsyn won the Nobel Prize for Literature, but doing so cut no ice with Brezhnev, who had him arrested and exiled for writing *The Gulag Archipelago*, telling the history of the Soviet labour camp system.

- **Andrei Sakharov:** Prominent nuclear physicist who helped develop the Soviet Union's hydrogen bomb. But Sakharov spoke out against human rights abuses in the Soviet Union and in 1975 his work won him the Nobel Peace Prize. That international recognition didn't stop Brezhnev sending Sakharov and his wife into internal exile in Gorky, a one-horse town deep in the sticks, where they were cut off from communication with the outside world.

Solzhenitsyn and Sakharov were lucky: Less well-known people were sent to labour camps up in the Arctic regions of Siberia, or were committed to mental asylums. The official line was that the system was so perfect that anyone who spoke out against it had to be crazy. If anyone protested that they were sane and the system was crazy, then it proved they were crazy and should be locked up. But anyone who agreed that they were crazy clearly was and needed to be locked up. So you lost either way.

What is dat samizdat?

Printing *samizdat* literature (the name is a rather complicated pun on *Gosizdat*, the state publishing house, meaning 'DIY Publishing House'), which was secretly run off on little printing presses in garages and back rooms, was the only way to speak out against the regime. Samizdat literature was passed around among dissidents or left lying around for people to pick up and read. Doing so was a risky business, though, as the penalties for reading or even possessing samizdat literature were severe.

It's the economy, Comrade Stupid!

Brezhnev put so much effort into controlling free speech that he didn't keep his eye on the Soviet economy, which was rapidly going down the pan. The system was corrupt and inefficient. Shopping in Russia was a major undertaking: People queued for hours if they heard a rumour that a loaf of bread had been seen in the window. The shops were empty because food was left rotting beside the fields as no one had provided any transport to take it to the towns. Everyone was on the take and often the only way to get goods was on the black market. The Russian rouble was so weak that towns had special shops selling tourist tat, I mean beautiful souvenirs (mostly tuneless balalaikas and Russian dolls) simply to build up Russia's reserves of foreign currency.

What, Russians wondered, was the government spending its money on? The answer was:

- **Space exploration:** The Soviet Union had put the first satellites, dog, man, and woman into space (not all together, you understand) but all this heroic endeavour hadn't actually benefited the Soviet people.

- **Arms:** The Soviet Union was trying to keep pace with the Americans in the nuclear missile stakes, but the effort was driving the country towards bankruptcy.

Then in 1980 Brezhnev ordered the invasion of Afghanistan (Chapter 17 explains why). The Afghans fought a long guerrilla campaign and the war became a nightmare, killing thousands of young Russians and with no end in sight. Russia simply couldn't go on like this.

Gorbachev's Russian revolution

In 1985 Mikhail Gorbachev became Soviet leader and decided to tackle Russia's problems head-on. He began by encouraging people to speak openly about what was wrong, both now and in the past. This *glasnost* (openness) meant Russians could at last find out from the archives exactly what crimes the regime had committed in the past. The bodies of many of Stalin's victims were dug up and given a decent burial. The next stage of Gorbachev's revolution, perestroika, was trickier.

Perestroika

Perestroika (restructuring) meant cutting State subsidies and opening the Soviet economy to the full effects of the market – free enterprise or, as it is also known, capitalism. Russians used to having jerry-built flats and useless cars provided by the State at knock-down prices were taken aback, and the changes certainly produced a lot of hardship at first. Gradually, however, as Western firms began opening branches in Russia and quality goods began appearing in the shops, Russians came round to the change, but they didn't thank Gorbachev. The reason? Because Gorbachev's policy of reform led to the collapse of the communist bloc and of the Soviet Union itself.

In 1985 Gorbachev met US President Ronald Reagan for the first of three meetings. The two men found, to their amazement (and everyone else's) that they could agree to start destroying their stockpiles of weapons. The Cold War was coming to an end. In that case, though, why shouldn't eastern Europe share in Gorbachev's policy of glasnost and perestroika? People in Hungary and Czechoslovakia and East Germany started demanding an end to communist rule and instead of sending tanks to crush them, the Soviet government announced that each country could do as it wished. So, first Hungary opened its borders to the West, and then, in November 1989, the East German authorities opened the Berlin Wall. A wave of revolutions swept across eastern Europe, bringing the communist regimes crashing down. You can read more about these revolutions in Chapter 18.

Oops, THAT wasn't supposed to happen

Gorbachev found himself caught between two rival groups:

- ✔ **Radical reformers led by Boris Yeltsin:** They wanted a lot more change and they wanted it fast.

- ✔ **'Old Guard' communists in the army and Politburo:** They wanted to stop Gorbachev bringing in any more changes before the whole country collapsed.

In 1991 the Old Guard struck. They arrested Gorbachev at his holiday home in the Crimea and announced they were staging a coup. But Boris Yeltsin got up on a tank and called on Russians to defend the government. The White House (not the Washington one, the Russian parliament building) became the symbolic place for all those who wanted change in Russia. The public supported Yeltsin, the coup collapsed, and Gorbachev came back to Moscow.

But the coup had shown that Gorbachev was no longer in charge. The different nationalities of the Soviet Union were demanding their own freedom and Yeltsin wanted to give it to them. The Soviet Union would have to go, to be replaced by a *Commonwealth of Independent States.* Gorbachev was horrified: He was a convinced communist and he hadn't intended anything like this. The Ukrainians, Belorussians, Estonians, Latvians, Lithuanians, Armenians, Georgians, Azerbaijanis, and Uzbekistanis all began to go their own ways and set up their own independent (though not always very democratic) states (see Chapter 19 for more on this). On Christmas Day 1991, Gorbachev resigned. A week later the Soviet Union ceased to exist.

Part IV
To the Millennium

'You're tired!?! — We're all tired and
we'll all be glad when this century's over
but it's only 1915!!'

In this part . . .

Medieval people thought the year 1000 meant the end of the world. Twentieth-century people looked forward to the year 2000 with a mixture of excitement and nervousness. No one was expecting the world to end, though they were expecting all the computers to crash, which was almost as bad. The Cold War was over; the new world order would mean peace and international harmony. Wouldn't it?

Technology certainly suggested it would. These were the years of the Internet, of instant messaging all around the globe. Communications brought the world closer together than it had ever been. Moreover, it was the Asian countries, so long at the mercy of the rest of the world, who were now making the running.

But it was painfully clear that some of the century's problems simply wouldn't go away. The end of the Cold War brought no peace in the Middle East, where militant Islam would soon emerge as the biggest challenge to world peace in the new century. The last decades of the twentieth century saw scenes of famine and even genocide.

These were the confident years, when the twentieth century turned its back on its own past and looked to the future. These were also the years when the twentieth century needed to know a bit more about its own history.

Chapter 17

Muddle in the Middle East

. . . .

In This Chapter

▶ Looking on as Israel battles its neighbours

▶ Watching as Lebanon falls apart

▶ Witnessing peace deals and *Intifadas*

▶ Tracing the rise of militant Islam

. . . .

*T*he troubles of the Middle East have gone through many phases, with
different conflicts in various parts of the region. The longest-running
conflict, however, and the one which has proved most difficult to solve, is the
tug-of-war between Jews and Arabs for control of the ancient land of Palestine.
This chapter explains why this land of deserts and valleys became so unstable
and why its conflicts have come to dominate the peace of the world.

Strictly speaking we shouldn't talk of the 'Middle East'. That term's a throw-back
to the days when Europeans thought of the region simply as the land in the
middle that they had to cross to get to their empires in Asia. 'West Asia' is the
proper geographical term, but no one says that. We're probably stuck with
'Middle East' for some time yet and that's the term I use throughout this chapter.

When Israel was in Egypt's Land

Chapter 11 explains how in 1947 the British were forced by international opinion
and Jewish terrorism to hand Palestine back to the United Nations to be divided
into Arab and Jewish states. The State of Israel was set up in 1948 but its Arab
neighbours refused to accept it and tried to strangle the new state at birth.

Ever since Israel joined in Britain and France's ill-fated plot in 1956 to invade
Egypt and seize the Suez Canal (see Chapter 11), Egypt's leader, Colonel Nasser,
had led the Arab states in plotting to find a way to wipe Israel off the map.
Nasser wanted to unite the Arabs in a single Arab super-state. He managed to
get Syria to join Egypt in a United Arab Republic, though it only lasted a couple
of years. But even if he couldn't get the Arabs into one state, he reckoned he
could still get them to act together – against Israel.

In this early period of Israel's existence, its main enemies were the neighbouring Arab states. After Israel defeated the Arab states in 1967, the Palestinians took the lead with an international terrorist campaign.

Six days that shook the world

In 1967 the Arabs thought the time had come to crush Israel once and for all. First, Israel's economy was in trouble and its prime minister, Levi Eshkol, was looking old and tired. The Arabs thought that with a bit of help from them, the whole state might collapse. Second, The Arabs were trying to act as one people. Nasser was enthusiastic about 'Pan-Arabism', the idea of having one huge Arab state. So was the *Ba'ath* party, the Arab nationalist movement that had taken power in Syria and Iraq. What better for uniting the Arabs than a massive attack on Israel?

The initial attack

In April the Syrians started shelling northern Israel but the Israeli Air Force struck back hard. In May, Nasser got his troops into position and told the UN to withdraw its peacekeeping force from Sinai. Doing so was like sending Israel a message saying, 'Dear Israel, We are planning to attack you through Sinai as soon as the UN troops are out of the way. Thought you'd like to know. Love, Nasser.' The Israelis, who had excellent intelligence reports on the Egyptian forces, decided to get their retaliation in first.

There's black gold in them thar dunes

Until the internal combustion engine was invented most people's image of the Middle East was deserts and camels, but once geologists found oil under the desert sands early in the twentieth century that all changed. At first the Arab kings didn't always fully appreciate quite how valuable this black stuff was and many Western oil firms were able to negotiate very favourable terms. But by the 1950s the Arabs were fully aware of what an asset they were sitting on, and in 1960 they joined together to create the *Organisation of Petroleum Exporting Countries*, or OPEC to its friends. OPEC's job was to co-ordinate prices and production targets to avoid the industry being dominated by the West, especially the United States. In 1973 and 1979 OPEC deliberately raised oil prices and cut supplies in order to hit at Western countries for being too pro-Israel, but no one gets rich by not selling things, so this state of affairs didn't last. When the Arab countries started fighting each other in the 1980s, OPEC became less and less important.

The Israelis strike back

Early on the morning of 5 June 1967 the Israeli Air Force, flying fast and low so the Egyptian radar defences wouldn't pick them up, attacked the Egyptian Air Force while it was neatly laid out on the ground. The Israelis kept up wave after wave of the attack, destroying the aircraft, bombing the runways, and then zooming in again just as the Egyptians were clearing up and trying to get a few planes into the air. The Egyptians didn't know what to do: Their Commander-in-Chief was in a plane which didn't dare descend in case the Israelis shot it down, and the Egyptian Air Force Commander was stuck in traffic. It really wasn't Egypt's day. And it wasn't over yet.

The Israelis headed home to rest and refuel and then at lunchtime they headed off for Jordan and Syria and bombed their air forces into the ground too. They even bombed airfields in far-away Iraq, which had sent planes to attack Israel. Finally, in the evening the Israelis headed back to bomb the Egyptians again before calling it a day. The Israelis reckoned no one would've dared tell Nasser just how many planes he'd lost in the morning, so he wouldn't have given orders to move them out of harm's way. They were right.

The Israelis had effectively won the war on that first day, and the ground fighting had hardly started. Over the next five days the Israelis attacked in all directions, into Sinai and Gaza in the south, into the Golan Heights along the border with Syria in the north, and into the West Bank of the Jordan where they captured the ultimate prize – the city of Jerusalem.

Who won or lost what: A tally

By the time the UN passed a resolution calling for a ceasefire, the Israelis had captured 26,000 square miles of Arab territory:

- Sinai – captured from Egypt
- The Gaza Strip – captured from Egypt
- The West Bank – captured from Jordan
- The Golan Heights – captured from Syria

The Arab states were stunned. To lose on one front was bad enough, but to lose on all three was a disaster. The Arab League met in Khartoum to decide what to do. They came up with a defiant triple 'No':

- *No* peace with Israel
- *No* recognition of Israel
- *No* negotiations with Israel

Which sounded impressive except that they had *no* way of defeating Israel either.

The mass murderer in fluffy slippers

In 1961 Israeli agents swooped on a tall, balding, bespectacled man in a suburb of the Argentinian capital, Buenos Aires, bundled him into a car, and smuggled him out of the country. He was Adolf Eichmann, the former SS officer who'd helped organise the 'Final Solution', the Nazi policy of extermination of Jews. In 1944 he'd been personally responsible for sending the Jewish population of Hungary to the gas chambers. Eichmann was put on trial in Jerusalem for mass murder. Everyone was expecting to see a dashing figure in his black SS uniform; in fact Eichmann turned out to be an ordinary little man in a cheap suit. In his cell he wore a cardigan and fluffy zip-up slippers as if he'd put his feet up after a hard day at the office. For the writer Hannah Arendt, Eichmann summed up the 'banality of evil'. More worryingly, his appearance suggested that anyone could end up a mass murderer if the circumstances were right.

The trial helped Israelis, especially the young, to get a sense of what Jews had gone through in the Holocaust, and why keeping the Israeli nation safe and strong was so important.

The Arab states strike back

Israel's amazing triumph in the Six Day War (see the earlier section 'Six days that shook the world') didn't mean the fighting ended. The Egyptians were determined to get Sinai back and they kept up the pressure, launching small-scale attacks and raids, to try to wear the Israelis down. The tough, no-nonsense Israeli prime minister, Golda Meir, struck back with bombing raids deep into Egyptian territory. To make things worse, Egypt was supported by the Soviet Union, so the Americans were nervous about giving Israel a blank cheque to do whatever she liked in case doing so sparked a nuclear war. Nasser died in 1970 and by 1973 the new Egyptian leader, Anwar Sadat, sensed that Israel's position wasn't as strong as it looked, so he got in touch with the Syrians. 'Payback time for the Six Day War,' he told them. Was Syria up for it? 'You bet,' said Syria.

The Yom Kippur War

On 6 October 1973, Yom Kippur, the Jewish Day of Atonement and one of the holiest festivals of the Jewish year, the Egyptians and Syrians attacked. The Egyptians pushed into Sinai; the Syrians attacked in the Golan Heights. This time it was the Israelis who were caught on the hop and the Arab forces pushed them right back. The Israelis soon got their breath back, though: They retook the Golan Heights and shattered the Egyptians in a massive tank battle in the Sinai desert. The Soviet Union threatened to intervene to stop Israel completely destroying the Egyptians, the United States went on nuclear alert, and finally the two sides agreed to a ceasefire. The Israelis had won but the Arabs had given them a good run for their money.

No help? No oil!

The Arab states felt that one of the main reasons they'd lost the Yom Kippur War was because the West had been so solidly behind Israel. Whether it was because of European feelings of guilt about the Holocaust or the strength of the Jewish lobby in America, the West seemed to have decided that the Israelis were the good guys and the Arabs were the bad guys. So in 1973 the Arabs decided to apply a little pressure to help Western countries see things from their point of view. The Arab oil-producing countries suddenly raised their prices to Western countries by an incredible 70 per cent. Saudi Arabia cut its production and refused to sell any oil at all to the United States or the Netherlands, Israel's strongest allies in the West. Result: Chaos.

- ✔ Huge queues at petrol stations
- ✔ Western countries had to restrict petrol supplies and even drew up plans for rationing motorists
- ✔ Supplies of all other goods were disrupted because freight transport had to be restricted to save fuel
- ✔ Western countries looked round desperately for alternative sources of oil
- ✔ A bicycle became the must-have of 1973

Strangely enough, faced with this onslaught on their oil supplies, Western countries did start to change their tune and agree that maybe the Palestinians had a point after all, and every question has two sides to it, and maybe they'd been a bit hasty in backing Israel quite so strongly. Funny, that.

Egypt and Israel make peace: Icicles seen in Hell

Egypt after 1973 was a country with big problems. It had lost its oil fields in Sinai after the 1967 war (see the earlier section 'Six days that shook the world'). During that war, the Suez Canal had been so littered with sunken ships and unexploded bombs and shells that it had had to be closed, and no one knew when it would reopen. Shipping companies had started using other routes and were building supertankers that would be too big to use the canal when it reopened anyway. Since oil and the canal represented Egypt's main sources of income, these were serious losses. The Egyptian president, Anwar Sadat, realised that Egypt couldn't hope to sustain the sort of expenditure that an arms race with Israel would involve. Egypt desperately needed American aid to solve its economic problems so Sadat wisely sent home all the Soviet advisers his predecessor Nasser had engaged. But Egypt wouldn't get any American help while it was still at daggers drawn with Israel. That situation meant Egypt would have to think the unthinkable: Make peace with Israel.

Making peace would mean talking with the new Israeli prime minister, Menachem Begin. Begin was an old terrorist leader from the war against the British and he was just as tough on Israel's Arab enemies. But even Begin was taken aback (and very wary) when Sadat got in touch suggesting they talk. But his suggestion was no trick: In November 1977 the world watched in disbelief as Anwar Sadat, Israel's arch-enemy, travelled to Tel Aviv and addressed the Knesset, the Israeli parliament.

The following year US President Jimmy Carter seized the chance to invite both men to his country retreat, Camp David, to talk peace and do a bit of fishing. The informal setting worked. The three men agreed that:

- Egypt would recognise and establish full and normal diplomatic relations with the State of Israel, and accept its right to exist

- Israel and Egypt would make a permanent peace

- Israel would cut its troops in the West Bank and the Golan Heights

- Israel would withdraw its troops from Sinai, dismantle its settlements there, and gradually hand Sinai back to Egypt

- Begin and Sadat would negotiate terms for an autonomous Palestinian state in Gaza and the West Bank

The Camp David agreements earned Begin and Sadat the 1978 Nobel Peace Prize. Would they bring peace to the whole Middle East? Er, no. In 1981 Sadat was assassinated by men from an Islamist faction of his own bodyguard, disgusted with his 'betrayal' of the Arab cause. For the Middle East, such violence was business as normal.

Palestine: Two into One Won't Go

The Israelis proved tougher than anyone had expected, defeated the Arabs, and even took over the area the UN had designated as a Palestinian homeland while the Arabs were nursing their wounds and wondering quite what had hit them (see the earlier section 'When Israel was in Egypt's Land'). So the Palestinians, like the Jews before them, were a people without a home, living as refugees in the neighbouring Arab countries. Now it was their turn to dream of regaining their homeland.

War'n'terror – the PLO

The Palestinians hadn't been sitting around waiting for the Arab states to liberate them: They'd set up a whole set of rival liberation movements of their own. You could choose from:

- ✔ The Palestine National Liberation Movement (Nationalist)
- ✔ The Popular Front for the Liberation of Palestine (Marxist)
- ✔ The Democratic Front for the Liberation of Palestine (Democratic)

In 1964 the *Palestine Liberation Organisation (PLO)* was formed to try to unite these different groups. It was soon dominated by the Palestine National Liberation Movement, also known as *Al Fatah*, which carried out terrorist attacks on Israel from its bases in Syria and the West Bank, though it never quite controlled the even more radical Popular Front for the Liberation of Palestine (PFLP). After the Six Day War (see the earlier section 'Six days that shook the world'), the PLO had to clear out of the West Bank and move to Jordan. From there they planned a series of terrorist attacks designed to put pressure on Israel and win publicity for the Palestinian cause.

The Arab states soon learned that the PLO were difficult and dangerous guests. They virtually set up a state within a state in Jordan, operating their own law and police force. King Hussein was afraid that they'd try to take over his kingdom completely.

The Dawson's Field hijacking

The PFLP's most spectacular attack was a mass hijacking of three international airliners in 1970, designed to force the British, German, and Swiss governments to release PLO terrorists captured during previous hijacking attempts. With 56 hostages' lives at stake, the three governments gave in and released their prisoners. The PFLP then blew up the three airliners in front of the world's press at Dawson's Field in Jordan. The hostages weren't on board, though no one knew this till a bit later.

A very black September

The Dawson's Field hijacking (see previous section) was the last straw: Within days King Hussein of Jordan declared martial law and sent the Royal Jordanian Army in to destroy the PLO bases. After a week of heavy fighting the king's men won: the PLO had to pull out and move to Lebanon, where they caused even more trouble (see the later section 'The Killing Grounds of Lebanon').

The PLO were very bitter about the Jordanian action and called it 'Black September' in memory of the month in which it happened. One radical PLO group actually called themselves 'Black September' and vowed to get revenge. In 1971 they assassinated the Jordanian prime minister. The following year they scored their most spectacular coup when they attacked the Israeli team at the Munich Olympics.

An Olympic gold for murder

Black September's most dramatic attack was at the 1972 Olympic Games in Munich, where they burst into the quarters of the Israeli team, killed two of them, and took nine more hostage. A tense stand-off followed as the terrorists demanded the release of 200 Palestinians held in Israel and safe passage out of Germany. The Israelis refused the demand but the Germans offered to fly the terrorists and their hostages to an Arab country. Then, at the airport, the German police opened fire. All of the athletes, four of the terrorists, and one policeman were killed in the gun battle that followed.

The Munich attack showed how ruthless some of the Palestinian groups were; it also made Israel more determined than ever to defend itself and to crush the PLO.

Yasser Arafat

The PLO's leader was Yasser Arafat, the man who'd set up Al Fatah back in 1956. Arafat liked to present himself as a man of action, always wearing military uniform and even carrying a pistol when he addressed the United Nations General Assembly in 1974. But despite his terrorist image he preferred to work through negotiation; many of the rival Palestinian liberation groups within the PLO got fed up with him and said he wasn't militant enough, though most Israelis thought he was, thank you very much.

To his followers within the PLO Arafat was a hero, standing up fearlessly for the Palestinian cause on the world stage. In 1974 he persuaded the Arab League and the United Nations to recognise the PLO as the only legitimate voice of the Palestinian people. But Al Fatah's rivals within the PLO, and some historians too, thought Arafat was seriously overrated. Under him the PLO kept getting expelled from front-line countries like Jordan and Lebanon, ending up in Tunisia, which isn't exactly round the corner from Palestine. The peace deals he negotiated in Oslo and Washington didn't last, and even the Palestine Authority he helped set up crumbled when the Israeli army came and shelled it to pieces. A mixed record, then.

The Intifada – shaking Israel off

Israel was determined to keep the lands it had taken in the Six Day War (see the earlier section 'Six days that shook the world'). It had given Sinai back to Egypt, but it wasn't planning to give up the West Bank, the Gaza Strip, or the Golan Heights. Keeping these lands didn't just mean planting an Israeli flag: The builders arrived and started building settlements for Israelis to come and live in – not tents but proper housing estates, with driveways and bus stops and local shops and schools. Israel was treating the occupied territories as if they were just normal parts of the country. The idea was to make the Israeli presence in the occupied territories so permanent that moving them out would be impossible. European countries had done much the same whenever they moved their borders – which they often did.

By the 1970s and 1980s Jewish immigrants were arriving from Russia, where the communist regime had continually persecuted them. Many of these new arrivals settled in the 'new' territories of Gaza or the West Bank and they expected their new government to stand by them. Israeli governments who were tempted to compromise with the Palestinians had to remember the hard-liners among their own population.

The United Nations repeatedly told Israel to clear out of the occupied territories, but Israel took no notice. Neither governments nor terrorists could make the Israelis budge. So the young Palestinians decided to see what they could do with a few stones.

Remember the story of David and Goliath? The boy David killed the mighty Goliath with a single stone from his sling. Perhaps the Israelis should have remembered that story, because in 1987 young Palestinians in Gaza took to the streets and started throwing stones at Israeli soldiers. Now here's a dilemma: If people are throwing stones at you, does that mean they're armed? And should you fire back?

History, maybe unfairly, has usually been on the side of the stone throwers. In 1770 a crowd in Boston threw stones at some British soldiers, the soldiers fired back and have been blamed for a massacre. In Northern Ireland in the 1970s youths got stone throwing down to a fine art: British soldiers had to fight back with baton charges and rubber bullets, which looked just as bad in the press. The problem is that if the soldiers retaliate they appear to be attacking unarmed people. On the other hand, if people are throwing stones at you, you've got to do *something*. But what?

The Israelis decided to open fire on the stone-throwers. But every time Israeli soldiers opened fire, it provoked another outburst of stone throwing, either in Gaza or in the West Bank. In one of the worst incidents, Israeli soldiers killed 17 Palestinians on Temple Mount in Jerusalem. The stone throwing even got a special name: *Intifada* ('the shaking off'). Israel had a full-scale crisis on its hands.

When Israel had been defending itself against Arab attacks, the West had sympathised with the underdog; now, television footage of Israeli soldiers firing on 'unarmed' youths made the underdog appear to have become a very nasty bully.

A little peace? The Oslo Accords

Yitzhak Rabin, the Israeli defence minister in charge of the army fighting the Intifada, was the first to realise that Israel was fighting a war it couldn't win. In 1992 he became prime minister and with his foreign minister, Shimon Peres, Rabin made it clear he was ready to talk. The government of Norway stepped in to help. It invited the Israelis and the PLO to Oslo where, in 1993, they drew up a set of agreements to make peace. They'd have signed them too, only US President Bill Clinton didn't want to miss a photo opportunity, so he invited them to sign the Oslo Accords in Washington. So it was that on 13 September 1993, on the White House lawn and with Clinton spreading his arms out behind them, the Israeli prime minister Yitzhak Rabin and the PLO leader Yasser Arafat shook hands.

The Oslo Accords were followed by a second agreement called 'Oslo B' and the Gaza–Jericho agreement. Taken altogether, here's what they said:

✔ The PLO recognises Israel and accepts its right to exist. Which, for the PLO, was quite an admission.

✔ Israel recognises the PLO as the legal representative of the Palestinian people. Which was not going to be easy for most Israelis to swallow.

✔ Israel recognises that the Palestinians have the right to an autonomous homeland, which is to be in Gaza, Jericho, and some parts of the West Bank. This wasn't easy for Israelis to swallow either.

✔ Israel agrees to start withdrawing its forces from the West Bank. A new Palestinian security force would take over. The Israeli West Bank settlers weren't going to like that one bit.

The Oslo Accords were the biggest breakthrough in the Middle East since Sadat and Begin had met at Camp David (see the earlier section 'Egypt and Israel make peace: Icicles seen in Hell'). Like them, Rabin, Peres, and Arafat all shared the Nobel Peace Prize. And just as had happened with Sadat, an assassin saw to it that the plan was wrecked. On 4 November 1994 Yitzhak Rabin was shot by an Israeli extremist as he was coming out of a huge rally for peace. How's that for irony?

Normal service is resumed

Some Israelis regarded the assassinated Rabin (see previous section) as a martyr; others thought he got all he deserved. In 1995 Israelis elected the hardline Binyamin Netanyahu prime minister. He dragged his heels over implementing the peace deal as much as he could, saying the Palestinians were not to be trusted. They'd set Gaza up as a state of sorts, called the

Palestinian National Authority, but it wasn't really national and it didn't seem to have much authority. Despite massive injections of cash, mainly from Europe, its economy was falling apart, the Palestinian police detained people without trial, and the whole system seemed to be mired in corruption. Worse, terrorists were still operating from within the National Authority area, and the Israelis said the Palestinian police were doing nothing about it. In 2000 a second Intifada broke out. This time Hezbollah (the Lebanese militant group; see the later section 'The Army of God') got involved, providing the Palestinians with weapons, as did a radical Palestinian group called *Hamas*, who thought the PLO had gone soft and was never going to get anywhere. The peace process seemed to be going into reverse.

In 2002 Israel began a massive assault against the Palestinian National Authority. Yasser Arafat found himself under siege in his headquarters in Ramallah. He was already a sick man and in 2004 he died in hospital in Paris. The peace deal he and Rabin had negotiated in Oslo was dead too.

The Killing Grounds of Lebanon

Lebanon in the 1960s was the Middle East's playground: A sunny holiday destination where tourists could enjoy the sandy beaches or watch the world go by in one of the French-style cafes in its fashionable capital city, Beirut. By the 1970s, however, Lebanon was torn apart in a vicious and complex civil war and Beirut had been reduced to rubble.

From Lockerbie to Libya

On 21 December 1988 a Pan American flight from London Heathrow to New York blew up over the small Scottish town of Lockerbie. All the passengers and crew were killed and so were 11 people on the ground. Suspicion surrounded all America's enemies in the Middle East, especially Iran and Syria, but in the end the finger pointed at Libya's erratic dictator, Colonel Gaddafi. Gaddafi had a long history of supporting anti-Western terrorist groups: Staff at his London embassy had even opened fire on a demonstration in the street, killing a policewoman. In 1986 the US Air Force bombed Tripoli, killing one of Gaddafi's children. Was Lockerbie his way of hitting back?

The British demanded the extradition of two Libyan agents and got the United Nations to impose sanctions on Libya until Gaddafi agreed to hand them over. Ultimately he did, though only one of them was convicted and some people still doubt he was involved. Very slowly, Libya began to improve relations with the West and stopped backing terrorists and Islamic fundamentalists. Gaddafi even had a visit from the British prime minister Tony Blair, though that may have been punishment enough. For both of them.

Lebanon had been part of Syria, but when the French took Syria over after the First World War they separated Lebanon from its neighbour and set it up as a separate autonomous republic in 1926. Lebanon's population is comprised of three groups which set it apart from other Middle Eastern countries:

- **Maronite Christians:** An ancient Christian sect who made up about half of the Lebanese population until the 1960s.

- **Muslims:** Drawn from the orthodox Sunni group and the Shi'ite sect. By the 1960s Lebanon's Muslims were growing in numbers – fast.

- **Druzes:** A Muslim sect who grew out of the Shi'ite tradition but had developed some rather oddball ideas of their own. Most Muslims didn't accept them as Islamic at all.

The different religious groups in Lebanon all claim to be larger than their rivals. The issue is so sensitive that no one has dared hold a religious census in the country since 1932. Whatever the result, one group or other would almost certainly claim the count had been rigged. What we do know is that the Christian proportion of the population decreased during the twentieth century, but beyond that it is much harder to get accurate statistics.

In 1943 the different groups in Lebanon worked out a power-sharing constitution that gave most power to the Christians. Doing so made sense because the 1932 census suggested the Christians were in the majority and they certainly tended to own most of the country's wealth. However, by the 1960s the Muslim population was growing at such a rate that they overtook the Christians to become the biggest group by far. Once the (Muslim) PLO moved its base to Lebanon in 1970 after it was thrown out of Jordan, the Lebanese Muslims started demanding changes: They wanted the constitution altered to give most power to them. The PLO supported the Muslims, but the Christians were afraid of what would happen if they gave up their power, so they said no. Both sides started acquiring guns. Then in 1975 Christian militia attacked a bus carrying Palestinians. It was war.

Who's killing whom?

The Lebanese civil war was pretty confusing because it had more than one side and groups changed sides:

- Christians, Muslims, and Druzes all fought against each other but they didn't all fight all the others all of the time. Two deadly enemies who were always against each other were the pan-Arab Muslims, who wanted an Arab super-state, and the right-wing *Phalange* Christian movement.

- The Syrians, who didn't trust the PLO as far as they could spit, were worried that the Palestinians were setting up bases along their border, so they sent troops in to help the Christians (who were fighting the Palestinians – do try to keep up) so as to keep the Palestinians concentrated in the south, along the Israeli border, where they couldn't threaten Syria.

- In 1978 the Israelis, who didn't want the PLO along their border, invaded to help the Christians (who were fighting their enemies the Palestinians, remember). This development meant that Israel and Syria, who were deadly enemies, had actually been fighting on the same side! The UN told Israel to get out, so they did and a UN peacekeeping force moved in.

- In 1980 the Syrians turned *against* the Christians (because the Christians were being helped by the Israelis. See? The whole situation's simple really).

Through all of this chaos, the PLO had been getting stronger in the south and were launching missile attacks into Israel. The Israelis hit back by launching bombing raids into Lebanon, but doing so wasn't enough to stop the attacks. So in 1982 Israel launched a massive full-scale invasion of Lebanon. They overran the south of the country and reached Beirut. The PLO had to pack up quickly and clear out. The Lebanese, who were thoroughly fed up with the Palestinians taking over their country, welcomed the Israelis with open arms.

Israel had won yet another crushing victory over its enemies. But then the Israelis made their fatal mistake. They decided to stay.

Lebanon's camps of death

The Israelis were hoping to turn Lebanon into a sort of puppet state, but the Lebanese hadn't waved goodbye and good riddance to the PLO only to be taken over by the Israelis. Then the Israelis found themselves linked to one of the most shameful episodes to come out of Lebanon's already terrible civil war.

On 14 September a pro-Syrian group blew up the Lebanese Christian president-elect, Bashir Gemayel. Gemayel had been regarded as a hero to Lebanese Christians, and some of them decided to take terrible revenge. Four days after the assassination, Christian militia arrived at two Palestinian refugee camps at Sabra and Shatila and shot everyone they could find. The Israelis, it was revealed, had deliberately stood by and let them do it. The Israeli defence minister, Ariel Sharon, resigned. Israel's image as the Liberator of Lebanon was well and truly destroyed, just when it was about to face its deadliest enemy yet.

The Army of God

A new group on the Lebanese scene decided to drive Israel and all westerners out of Lebanon once and for all. Called *Hezbollah* (the 'Army of God'), it was inspired by the Islamic Revolution in Iran (see the later section 'Islam – the New World Revolution'). Hezbollah wanted to set up an Islamic republic in Lebanon and wipe Israel off the map, not just because it was occupying Palestinian land, but because it believed that Jews were the enemies of God. For the first time the Israelis found themselves up against an enemy as fierce and determined as they were themselves.

As Lebanon collapsed into anarchy, a multinational peacekeeping force arrived, though finding much peace to keep was difficult. Hezbollah, who didn't want westerners around the place, launched a series of devastating suicide bomb attacks against the peacekeeping forces' headquarters: 239 people were killed in just one bomb blast at the American military HQ. The peacekeepers hurriedly pulled out. In 1985 the Israelis themselves finally acknowledged defeat and withdrew.

With the Israelis and the PLO both out of the picture, the Lebanese them-selves had to try to restore some order and stability to their country. In 1990 General Aoun of the Christian militia seized the presidential palace and declared himself president. But the Muslims and their Syrian backers didn't want him: Their man, Glias Hrawi, formed his own government and the two men spent most of the year arguing over who was in fact president, until in October General Aoun finally gave way.

Lebanon was much more stable in the 1990s and managed to rebuild some-thing of its national pride and confidence. Lebanon's new challenge was how to prevent the Syrians trying to dominate the country as the Palestinians and Israelis had done in the past.

A hostage to fortune

Seizing Western hostages was a favourite Hezbollah tactic. The Archbishop of Canterbury's special envoy, Terry Waite, had managed to negotiate the release of Western hostages in Libya and Iran, so in 1987 the Archbishop sent him to Lebanon to see what he could do there.

Not much, as it turned out, because he was kidnapped himself by Hezbollah, who were suspicious of the way the Americans had used him in their rather shady arms deal with Iran. They kept Waite prisoner until 1992.

Islam – the New World Revolution

In the 1970s the Middle East seemed to be turning its back on its traditional way of life. Oil-rich Arabs drove flashy cars and spent their evenings at the casino, having a few very non-Islamic drinks. Shops sold Western music and Western fashions. Women left their veils at home and walked out in fashionable jeans and t-shirts. Traditional imams in the mosques could only shake their heads in disapproval. History, apparently, was against them.

But history was about to go into sharp reverse. Starting in Iran.

Iran: The fundamentalist things apply

The Islamic Revolution that brought down the Shah of Iran in 1979 changed the whole direction of the Middle East. Instead of a dispute over who should own Palestine, Middle Eastern politics became a cultural battle about the role of Islam throughout the world.

The shah must go on

The dynasty of shahs who ruled twentieth-century Iran wasn't that ancient. In 1923 Reza Khan became prime minister and three years later he overthrew the shah and had himself crowned Reza Shah Pahlevi. Reza's regime was strongly pro-Nazi (he changed the country's name to 'Iran' ('Aryan') to please Hitler), but in 1941 the British and Russians got rid of him and put his son, Muhammad Reza, in charge. However, the new shah quickly learned that real power lay with the popular Iranian nationalist leader Muhammad Mossadeq. In 1953, the two men tussled for power and Mossadeq seemed so firmly entrenched that the shah fled the country. At that point his friends the Americans stepped in: The CIA staged a coup which overthrew Mossadeq (he spent the rest of his life in jail) and put the shah back on his throne.

This time the shah kept power firmly in his own hands. He sent troops to crush the attempts by the Kurds and Azerbaijanis to break away, and Savak, his dreaded secret police, kept close tabs on anyone suspected of disloyalty. He was particularly tough on those who objected to the way Iran was becoming increasingly Western. In 1963 he launched the 'White Revolution', a big drive to spread Western ideals such as rights for women and education for all and eradicate traditional Islamic culture. One of the many people who were arrested and exiled for opposing this revolution was an up-and-coming Islamic scholar called Ayatollah Ruholla Khomeini.

This country is now under new (divine) management

Khomeini settled in Iraq, where he called not only for the shah to be overthrown but also for a complete rejection of Western culture. He said Iran should go back to its Islamic roots and govern itself by Islamic law. In comparison to the shah's repressive regime, many Iranians found they liked what they were hearing. In 1978 the Iranians persuaded Iraq to kick Khomeini out, but he just moved to Paris and carried on his campaign from there. By then protests against the shah had got out of hand; in 1979 he was forced to flee and Ayatollah Khomeini flew in from Paris to take charge.

What followed was a strange sight for the twentieth century: A popular revolution taking a country straight back to the Middle Ages:

- ✔ Iran became an Islamic republic. High ranking clergy were in charge, with Ayatollah Khomeini in overall charge for life.

- ✔ Western music was banned (and Country music wasn't exactly approved of). Women were to wear Islamic dress and lose many of their civil rights.

- ✔ Strict *Sharia* (Islamic) law was to be applied, including execution for adultery and cutting off the hands of thieves.

- ✔ Anyone who opposed these changes was to be executed too.

- ✔ Khomeini declared death to America! He referred to the United States as the 'Great Satan', an evil power out to destroy all Muslims.

Iran went through a period of terrifying chaos. Thousands were killed on the Ayatollah's orders. In November 1979 Iranian students took his anti-American message to heart by storming the American embassy in Tehran and taking the staff hostage. The Ayatollah may not have ordered the snatch, but he certainly refused to do anything to get the hostages released, despite calls of protest from all over the world. US President Jimmy Carter authorised a dramatic James Bond-style rescue attempt, but mechanical difficulties and bad luck caused the commanders to abort the mission, which then ended in a fiery crash between two of the aircraft involved . Just to rub the humiliation in, the Ayatollah finally released the hostages just as Carter left office in 1981.

After the hostage crisis Iran tried to improve relations with the West, but in 1989 *The Satanic Verses* by the Indian-born British author Salman Rushdie appeared, attacking aspects of Islam. The Ayatollah passed a *fatwa* sentencing Rushdie to death and calling on Muslims all over the world to assassinate him. Western governments protested at this attack on freedom of speech; Muslims protested at this attack on their faith. The Iranian revolution had become a worldwide confrontation between Islam and Western culture.

Better know your Shia from your Sunni

Like Orthodox Christians and Catholics in the Christian Church, Islam is divided into two main groups, and they don't usually get on. Most Muslims are *Sunni*, from 'sunna' meaning 'custom' or 'how to behave'. The Sunni believe that they follow in the correct tradition of Islam handed down directly by the Prophet Muhammad and his successors. The Shia say that the line of succession went through the wrong people and that it should have gone through Muhammad's cousin and son-in-law, Ali. The issue may seem somewhat arcane to outsiders, but this dispute between Muslims is every bit as serious as the splits within Christianity. Every year the Shia celebrate the martyrdom of Ali's son Husain with a re-enactment of his death and a bloody ceremony where the men cut their heads with knives and allow the blood to stream down them, as a sign of their devotion to their faith. As the West would very soon learn, this was not a faith to trifle with.

Note to self: Don't invade Afghanistan even if they ask you

The Kingdom of Afghanistan spent much of the twentieth century playing hard to get. In the 1920s and 1930s it switched between being a Western-style state and going back to its traditional style of rule and it spent the Cold War getting help from both sides without actually committing itself to either. In 1978 a communist group within the army seized power but the members all ended up fighting each other. Babrak Kemal took power himself in 1979 but he needed more support. He asked the Russians for help.

In December 1979 the Soviet Union invaded Afghanistan. Immediately all the warring groups stopped fighting each other and banded together to fight the Russians. Like the Americans in Vietnam, the Russians had all the latest military hardware, but they couldn't defeat the guerrillas fighting on their home ground. The Russians stayed in Afghanistan for ten long, unhappy years, losing thousands of men, until eventually in 1989 they pulled out.

The Americans did all they could to help the Afghans fight the Russians. They sent arms and money to the *Mujahidin*, the Islamic 'Holy Warriors' who were resisting up in the hills. Unfortunately, when the Russians pulled out in 1989, the Afghans didn't all become instantly pro-American. Instead, the different groups resumed the in-fighting that the Russians had so rudely interrupted, so that by the early 1990s the country was in chaos.

The nearest Afghanistan had to a pro-Western group was the *Northern Alliance*, but they were losing ground to the militant Mujahidin. By 1996 an extreme Islamic group called the *Taliban* had taken over most of the country. They turned Afghanistan into an Islamic republic along the same lines as Iran. They didn't just force women to give up their jobs and cover up in public: They completely banned all aspects of Western culture and executed thousands of people who objected to their brutality.

The Taliban had two main sources of support:

- Income from the international drugs trade
- Osama Bin-Laden and the Al-Qaeda network

The Americans were kicking themselves: They'd helped turn Afghanistan into a major international headache. For America, mainly.

Ba'ath Ba'ath – Black Sheep

Not all Arab states became Islamic republics. Some followed a radical new creed called *Ba'athism*. Ba'athism ('renaissance') began in Syria in the 1940s as a movement to drive foreigners out of the Middle East and set up one pan-Arab state. It was a secular creed, which borrowed many ideas from socialism. Like the Nazi or Communist Parties, the Ba'ath Party insisted on unquestioning obedience and it set its leaders up as all-powerful dictators.

Arabs tended to like Ba'athist ideas in theory but not necessarily in practice: Egypt and Syria joined together as one state in 1958, but the union fell apart four years later. Syria, however, stuck to the Ba'athist ideal. The other country which took the Ba'athist path was Iraq.

Syria: President Assad's kingdom

The Ba'ath Party seized control in Syria in 1963 and from 1970 the country was ruled by the Ba'athist army commander, General Assad. Assad ruled with a grip of iron: Businesses were nationalised and critics and opponents locked up. Assad was particularly ruthless with religious opposition: He crushed an Islamic fundamentalist revolt against his rule in 1982.

Assad's neighbours couldn't rest easy either: He did his best to turn Lebanon into a Syrian puppet state and he made no secret of the fact that he couldn't stand Saddam Hussein and the Ba'athist government of Iraq. When the PLO were abandoning terrorism for the negotiating table, Assad provided a base for the Palestinian terrorist Abu Nidal to launch attacks against Israeli and Western targets, but when Syria's Soviet support collapsed in 1989, Assad tried to open up links with the West. By and large, the West was not impressed.

Iraq: The republic of fear

The Ba'ath Party took control in Iraq in 1968. In some ways, Ba'athism was very good for Iraq: It modernised, gave much greater freedom to women, and turned itself into a strong, Western-style state. The West wasn't convinced, though, because the Iraqis nationalised the oil industry, taking it out of the hands of Western companies. However, the military commander, General Saddam Hussein, was gradually taking more power into his hands and in 1979 he took over the presidency. He ruled by terror, using the army, the secret police, and members of his own family. On one occasion he sat in a Ba'ath Party meeting calmly smoking a cigar as his men dragged delegates who had criticised him outside to be shot.

Saddam Hussein played on the fact that Iraq had some of the richest reserves of oil in the world; unfortunately, the oil fields were mostly in the Kurdish lands in the north and the Shia lands in the south. Neither group felt at home in Saddam's Iraq and both wanted out of it: The Kurds wanted their own state and the Shia wanted to join with Iran. Saddam's response: Full-scale military attack, even using poison gas.

There ain't room in the Middle East for both of us: Iran v Iraq

Iran and Iraq represented the two opposite extremes of Arab states: Iran was a fiercely Muslim state, Iraq was a fiercely anti-religious, secular state. In 1980 Iraq took advantage of the chaos in Iran to try to seize disputed land on the border (see the earlier section 'This country is now under new (divine) management' to find out why Iran was in chaos). At first the Iraqis caught the Iranians on the back foot, but Iran swiftly recovered and fought back, and the war soon became a long slog, more like the trenches of the First World War than the hi-tech late twentieth century. The fighting finally stopped in 1988, mainly because each side was exhausted, and Saddam had his eyes on an easier victim. What had each side gained from eight years of war? Precisely nothing.

Iran was America's great enemy in the 1980s, and the Americans reckoned that Iran's enemy, Iraq, must be their friend. So Washington kept Saddam Hussein well supplied with weapons and anything else he needed to fight the war. (The Americans were also secretly selling arms to the Iranians, but that's another story – see Chapter 15.)

Pick on someone your own size! The war for Kuwait

In the 1980s OPEC reached an amicable agreement with the West to lower oil prices. Cheaper oil would hit Iraq badly unless Saddam could somehow corner the market. So he cast his eye on the neighbouring state of Kuwait – small, vulnerable, defenceless, and sitting on some of the world's largest reserves of oil. In August 1990 the Iraqi army invaded Kuwait, drove the emir into exile, and announced that henceforth Kuwait was a province of Iraq.

Iraq had been claiming Kuwait long before Saddam Hussein came on the scene. The Iraqis said the British had carved it out of Iraqi territory when they ruled the region; in fact, Kuwait had been an autonomous land, with its own ruling house, since the eighteenth century.

Saddam miscalculated badly in Kuwait. He assumed that his friends, the Americans, would just tut tut loudly and let him off, but instead President George Bush Senior and British Prime Minister Margaret Thatcher denounced his action and arranged for a United Nations force to liberate Kuwait. (Saddam holding all the westerners in Kuwait hostage didn't help his cause.) Saddam boasted that he would win the 'Mother of All Battles' but in the event the coalition forces walked all over his men in a couple of weeks. The Iraqis set fire to the Kuwaiti oil fields in a fit of sour grapes, creating an ecological disaster for the whole region. Saddam's days appeared numbered. And then the UN forces stopped.

President Bush stuck to his mandate: The UN had said he could liberate Kuwait, but it hadn't said anything about toppling Saddam Hussein. This development was bad news for the Shia and Kurds, who had risen up in rebellion expecting coalition forces to be arriving at any moment. Instead they got the Iraqi army arriving in force, and they always enjoyed killing people who couldn't fight back. The UN forced Saddam to accept a no-fly zone over Kurdistan and imposed a set of sanctions to try to force him to grant a few basic human rights, but many people in the West, especially around the White House, thought that they'd missed a golden opportunity to get rid of a very nasty dictator.

Postscript

The coalition forces who liberated Kuwait (see previous section) operated from bases in Saudi Arabia. After the war, the United States kept its troops on Saudi territory. The sight of American soldiers riding around the Prophet's homeland was too much for one wealthy Saudi citizen already sickened by the corruption of the Saudi royal family – one Osama bin Laden. In 1988 Bin Laden had become head of a network of Islamic fundamentalist guerrillas fighting against the Russians in Afghanistan where, of course, the Americans had kept him and his men well supplied with arms and ammunition. But now Bin Laden reckoned the Americans had gone too far: The presence of their troops on Saudi soil, he decided, was a deadly insult to all Muslims and his network would avenge it. What was his network's name? Al Qaeda.

Chapter 18

Europe Rides Again

. . . .

In This Chapter

▶ Watching western Europe recover and flourish

▶ Seeing the European Union grow

▶ Weighing up different ideas on how to run a country

▶ Tracing the rise and fall of the communist bloc

. . . .

*N*o one driving round the bomb sites and destruction of Europe's cities in 1945 could have imagined that it would ever recover. No sooner had the fighting ended than the continent was cut in two by the Cold War. Yet western Europe did recover, and pretty quickly too, to become a high-tech economic powerhouse. Eastern Europe meanwhile was in the grip of communist dictatorship and falling farther and farther behind the West. When the Cold War was over, Europeans had some painful readjustments to make.

Sunrise in the West

Western Europe recovered quickly after the war because of American economic aid. Known as *Marshall Aid*, it was named after General George C. Marshall who organised it. The main idea was simply to help Europe get going again, but supplying aid was also a good way for America to win friends and, presumably, influence people. For this reason the Soviet Union wanted nothing to do with Marshall Aid and told all the countries it controlled in eastern and central Europe not to accept it either. So western Europe recovered much more quickly than eastern Europe. Western Europe kept its lead over the East right up to the end of the century.

C'mon, c'mon, let's get together

Thanks to Marshall Aid, western Europe was able to brush itself down and get going again. But the western Europeans also saw the advantage of working together more closely. The old days of the European Great Powers were well and truly over, but together the Europeans might still be able to play their part on the world stage.

After the Second World War, Europe was divided in two by the wartime Allies. Western Europe was tied to the United States and in central and eastern Europe the Russians installed communist governments that would take orders from Moscow. Germany and Berlin were both divided down the middle. Chapter 10 has the details on how Europe was divided in the Cold War and the tensions it produced.

The destruction from the Second World War was much worse than the First World War: All over the continent towns and cities had been bombed into rubble and people were stranded hundreds of miles from their homes. The whole continent was shattered.

Many people thought the two world wars showed what happened if you let nations follow their own paths and their own narrow self-interests. If nations acted together for a change, wouldn't it mean no more wars? The victorious Allies had already set up the United Nations Organisation; why not have a United Nations for Europe?

In 1949 representatives of different European states met in Strasbourg and set up the *Council of Europe* dedicated to upholding peace and human rights in a continent that had been pretty careless with both. The Council of Europe set up a *European Court of Human Rights*, which soon played an essential role in upholding human rights across the continent. But the member states made sure that the Council of Europe only had the power to advise them, not to force them to do anything they didn't want to do. Not quite such a step forward, then.

Before the Second World War most Europeans thought entirely in terms of their own country; after the war people thought much more in terms of Europe as a whole. Some people worried that their countries would lose their special sense of identity, but the idea of building some sort of European identity was definitely becoming more widely spread.

What else can you build with coal and steel? The European Community

If you have to rebuild a continent shattered by war, a great deal of construction work will be necessary and in the 1940s that meant using a lot of coal and steel. Three men thought this necessity might be an opportunity to build something rather bigger and longer-lasting than houses or factories. France's Jean Monnet and Robert Schuman and West Germany's Konrad Adenauer signed an agreement to pool their two countries' coal and steel resources. This agreement was significant because disputes between France and Germany had been at the root of both world wars. If these two old enemies could start working together, it might mean an end to European wars.

That's enough butter, thank you

The most controversial aspect of the EEC was its policy on farming and food production. It paid farmers generous subsidies to produce large quantities of butter and milk, regardless of whether or not the market wanted them. Result: Farmers filled whole warehouses with food that couldn't be sold. These 'butter mountains' and 'wine lakes' were a scandal, when other parts of the world didn't have enough to eat. The EEC's refusal to change the subsidy system that had produced this surplus in the first place made the situation even worse. When the EEC became the European Union, its rules said that member states had to stop subsidising their own producers and bring in EU subsidies instead. That was too much for the Norwegians, who repeatedly rejected the idea of joining the EU.

The agreement was called the *European Coal and Steel Community (ECSC)*, which suggested that the three men had rather wider visions for where it might lead. Sure enough, four other European countries soon joined in – Italy, Belgium, Luxembourg, and the Netherlands. Before long they asked themselves, 'Why pool only coal and steel? Why not trade freely in everything?' So in 1957 they signed the Treaty of Rome turning the ECSC into the *European Economic Community (EEC)*, known to its friends as the 'Common Market'.

The EEC started simply as a free trade club but the Treaty of Rome spoke of creating an 'ever closer union'. Over the next forty years that's exactly what the EEC did.

The muscles of Brussels

The EEC set up its headquarters in Brussels, though it also had a base in Strasbourg and had to decamp there once a year to keep the French happy. It set up a Council of Ministers to make decisions and a European Parliament to advise them (but not to pass laws – no one wanted a rival for their own national parliaments). Brussels was also the headquarters of the EEC's atomic energy agency, Euratom. As the EEC countries began to flourish in the 1960s and 1970s, Brussels became a major international political centre.

I say, that looks fun! Can we join?

Churchill had spoken passionately in favour of the Council of Europe and had even called for a United States of Europe, but he'd never considered Britain being part of it. The British were wary of the EEC and set up their own European Free Trade Area with the Austrians and Scandinavians but it never matched the EEC's success. Eventually the British decided to ask to join the EEC, even though doing so would mean dropping all Britain's special trading links with the Commonwealth. France's President de Gaulle was having none of it. 'Non!' he declared, 'England is not a part of Europe: She is, 'ow you say?'

Boom bang-a-bang (not to be confused with Ding ding-a-dong)

One of the most exciting technological developments of post-war Europe was meant to be Eurovision, a continent-wide (make that a western-half-of-the-continent-wide) TV service binding nations together in a celebration of European culture and heritage. Er, *right*. In fact the only aspect of Eurovision that has ever come to general notice has been its annual song contest, famous for such cultural treats as over-the-top costumes and songs with catchy titles like the two in the title of this sidebar (I promise you, I did not make those up). Most of the original countries have got so used to Eurovision that they hardly take it seriously any more but the newer states of central and eastern Europe take it very seriously indeed and mount impressive spectacles with fire and troupes of dancers leaping about to the thumping beat, all interspersed with traditional shepherds' bagpipes from their country's picturesque hills. The voting always brings out all the worst of Europe's national prejudices so that people all over the continent can enjoy giving their ancient enemies *nul points*. The Eurovision Song Contest is frankly bizarre – kitschy, compulsive, and sometimes even quite musical, but definitely bizarre.

A stooge for ze Americans. She come in over ma dead bodee!' He was right too: De Gaulle died in 1970 and Britain finally joined in 1973. Some Britons have spent their lives since then trying to get Britain out again.

In 1967 the EEC dropped the 'Economic' from its name and in 1992 it changed to *European Union*, which made its political agenda crystal clear. It also took on new members, including Ireland (1973), Denmark (1973), Greece (1981), and Spain and Portugal (both 1986).

Most countries joined the EEC because they got subsidies and near-full employment. However, they only gained these benefits because the big countries subsidised the smaller ones, as Britain's prime minister Margaret Thatcher, no great fan of the European Community, never tired of pointing out.

Refining the EC

Before decisions were taken within the European Community all countries had to agree, which was fine when it only had six members, but wasn't such a good idea when more members joined. Once the Cold War was over the states of central and eastern Europe would want to join too. You couldn't run such a huge union if every member had a veto, so the EC (EU from 1992, remember) took steps to strengthen Brussels and make it harder for any individual state to hold things up:

 ✔ **1986 Single European Act:** Creates a single market with complete freedom of movement for goods, money, and people. Decisions on the market to be taken on a majority vote: Say good-bye to the veto, lads.

- ✔ **1992 Treaty of Maastricht:** Changes the European Community into the European Union, with a common foreign and security policy (not that that worked in practice) and closer co-operation on justice and police matters. It also gives greater powers to the European Parliament and draws up plans for a single European currency.

- ✔ **1999 Single European currency:** The first international currency since ancient times, though the Eurocrats come up with a very boring name for it: The euro. Most member states (though not all) opt to join it.

Yes, but who pays for all this?

Western Europe recovered from the Second World War thanks to American handouts. Some Europeans thought that they could go on living on money provided by the State. Others had different ideas.

Social democracy the Swedish way

The Scandinavians led the way in this thinking. Sweden developed a social security system with education, health care, child care, and a whole range of other benefits all provided by the State. Taxation provided the money to pay for it all. The Swedes were rather proud of their system and liked to hold it up as an example for other countries to follow. Not all countries went quite as far down the road of State intervention as Sweden, though, and by the 1990s the Swedes were running into serious cash-flow problems. In 1995 the Swedes finally gave in and joined the European Union.

Socialism-lite

In the rest of western Europe two main political groups fought for their vision of the future:

- ✔ **Socialists:** Wanted the State to be responsible for as much as possible, certainly all social services and preferably the essential industries as well. The State should provide pensions and benefits for all and should step in to protect workers' jobs when firms got into difficulty.

- ✔ **Christian Democrats:** These were Conservative political parties in Germany and Italy, though other right-wing groups thought the same way. They wanted to preserve some elements of capitalism, but they were happy to work with the socialists and to support a big State-run sector of the economy.

This strange hybrid of socialism-lite with a dash of capitalism was peculiar to Europe and for a long time this approach seemed to work very well. In the 1960s western Europeans enjoyed almost full employment, high wages, and financial security and felt rather superior to the State-run system in the communist bloc and the State-runs-nothing system in America.

We'll keep the sort-of-red flag flying here: Eurocommunism

Communists played a crucial part in resisting the Nazis during the war and they hoped to take power after the war: In France the communists nearly did. Communists regularly stood for election across western Europe, and in some areas they did very well. The Italians regularly elected communists to their regional councils and the city of Bologna had a communist council for years. But these 'Eurocommunists' didn't try to set up a secret police or send people to labour camps. They worked within the democratic system and didn't try to tear it down. Above all, they didn't take orders from Moscow. They were disgusted with the way the Russians had crushed the Hungarians and Czechs when they'd tried to show a bit of independence (see Chapter 10 to find out what this was all about) and they were determined to work things their own way.

Market forces

By the 1980s the Christian Democrat idea of getting chummy with the left was beginning to wear a bit thin. The Italian Christian Democrats were caught up in a series of corruption scandals and were even accused of being in cahoots with the Mafia. But the country which knocked the old left–right consensus on the head was Britain.

British Labour and Conservative governments had proved utterly incapable of controlling the powerful trade unions, who paralysed the country with strikes so often that other Europeans talked of strikes as the 'British disease'. In 1979 the British elected a doctor who took drastic measures to cure the British disease: Margaret Thatcher. She passed laws to break the power of the unions and she sold off whole sectors of the State-run economy to private investors. She wanted a completely free market and she had no patience with anyone, trade union or European Union, who stood in her way.

Mrs Thatcher's philosophy – low taxes and keep to what you can pay for – won her three elections. Other Europeans disliked the way she tried to force her ideas on them but by the 1990s more of them were coming round to her way of thinking.

Hang up the uniform, General

Some European states took a bit of time to wake up to the fact that they were living in a continent that was meant to be a shop window for democracy. These included:

- ✔ **Spain:** General Francisco Franco ruled Spain from his victory in the Civil War (see Chapter 5 for the details) until his death in 1975. Franco worked closely with the Catholic Church to keep Spain a strict one-party dictatorship, though when the economy started going downhill, he had to allow more of a free market economy than he would've liked. When he died, the monarchy took over again under King Juan Carlos.

Cyprus

Cyprus was a tricky problem that nearly caused a war between two NATO members, Greece and Turkey. Cyprus was Greek until the Turks conquered it in the sixteenth century: Both sides' descendants still live on the island. The Greek Cypriots fighting to get the British out (see Chapter 11) wanted 'Enosis' – union with Greece. But the British wanted to set up an independent Cyprus where they could station some of their troops, so that's what they did. In 1974 the Greek government tried to take Cyprus over but the Turks sent their troops into the northern, Turkish part of the island and declared it a separate state. Only Turkey recognises 'Turkish Cyprus', but Greece gave up its claim to Cyprus when it entered the European Union.

- ✔ **Portugal:** The first Portuguese republic had been a fairly chaotic affair until 1926 when the military staged a coup. Antonio Salazar set Portugal up as a fascist state and ruled as its dictator from 1933 to 1968 when he had a stroke. Salazar kept Portugal agricultural, backward, and poor, and nearly bankrupted the country by fighting to keep hold of its African colonies (see Chapter 11). In 1974 the military staged another coup, this time to get rid of the dictatorship and move Portugal towards democracy.

- ✔ **Greece:** Greece had suffered a terrible civil war after 1945 between monarchists and communists: The monarchists only won with massive American help. Then the Greeks argued about the rights of the crown and the rights of the army until in 1967 a gang of Greek colonels seized power for themselves. The colonels weren't very good at governing, but they were very good at imprisoning and torturing people. In 1974 they tried to seize hold of Cyprus but lost, which brought their government crashing down and created a democratic republic in its place.

Not everyone was happy to move towards democracy. In Spain in 1981 some officers tried to close down the Spanish parliament and set up another military government, but King Juan Carlos held firm and the coup was beaten. All three countries were rewarded for their commitment to democracy by being admitted to the European Union.

All countries great and small

Despite all the talk of European unity the different countries of western Europe developed in some very diverse ways.

France

France spent the first fifteen years after the war afraid that it was going to have another revolution. The wars in Indo-China and Algeria divided opinion in France so deeply that by 1960 the French were expecting revolution and invasion (by the French Algerians) at any moment (see Chapter 11 for lots more on what was causing all this angst in France). France's Fourth Republic didn't give anything like enough power to the president to deal with this sort of emergency, so the French turned to General de Gaulle and said he could redraft the constitution any way he liked. So he did (creating France's Fifth Republic, still going today), giving lots of power to, well, himself. De Gaulle saw France through the boom years of the sixties but he was badly thrown when French students rioted in 1968 and resigned the following year.

Gaullism carried on under Georges Pompidou and the very lordly Valérie Giscard d'Estaing, who always gave the impression he found having to speak to the plebs a chore. In 1981 the French decided to take him down a peg or two and elected the socialist (and, as it turned out, equally lordly) François Mitterrand, a wily old bird who completely ran rings round the Gaullist leader, Jacques Chirac. Mitterrand kept France dependent on its system of State subsidies, which stored up lots of economic trouble for Chirac when he finally succeeded Mitterrand in 1995.

West Germany

That's the Federal Republic of Germany but 'West Germany' for short. Its first chancellor, Konrad Adenauer, was a remarkable man who did much to help Germans recover from the stigma of the war and become accepted again on the world stage. Adenauer realised that West Germany must stick close to America, a lesson also learned by the mayor of West Berlin, Willi Brandt, who went on to become chancellor. Brandt was the first West German leader to start talking with East Germany to try to relax some of the tension, though no one expected the conversations to lead anywhere. His rather dashing successor, Helmut Schmidt, steered the country through the effects of the Arab oil embargo (see Chapter 17 for the lowdown on this) but he lost support when he allowed the Americans to station long-range missiles on West German territory and was forced out of office.

Italy

The Italians' system of proportional representation led to a string of coalition governments, not all of which lasted longer than a wine gum, yet somehow the system – and the country – survived. The Italians achieved a difficult balancing act between communism, socialism, and Catholicism, made more difficult and dangerous by endless strikes and a campaign of left-wing terrorism by the Red Brigade (see the 'Terrorism' section later in this chapter). The veteran prime minister Giulio Andreotti was charged with corruption and links with the Mafia, which rather summed up Italy's problems by the 1990s.

Britain

That's the United Kingdom of Great Britain and Northern Ireland or the 'UK' as the country's generally known nowadays. The British surprised the world in 1945 by voting against Churchill and for the Labour Party, who promptly nationalised the major industries and introduced a welfare state, including a free health service for all. The Conservatives soon accepted these changes, but neither party was able to control the militant trade unions who, by the 1970s, were regularly paralysing the whole country with nationwide strikes.

Meanwhile Britain seemed to be the big exception to the western European economic miracle: In 1976 it even had to apply to the International Monetary Fund for a loan. Mrs Thatcher's Conservative governments in the 1980s turned the picture round, however, crushing the unions after a bitter year-long battle with the miners, selling off nationalised industry, and stopping government subsidies: If an industry couldn't pay its way, it had to go under even if doing so meant massive unemployment until the economy adjusted. Thatcherism hit the old industrial areas very hard: Factories and mines closed and thousands of people found their whole way of life suddenly disappearing. In time, these areas would adjust to the new IT and service industries that were replacing the old heavy industries, but this change was very painful.Britain's economy was forging ahead at last, but it was leaving a lot of very angry, disillusioned people in its wake.

Belgium, the Netherlands, and Luxembourg

Known as 'Benelux' for short, these three small countries became more important thanks to the European Union. Brussels got both the EU and NATO headquarters and little Luxembourg got the European Court of Justice and the Secretariat of the European Parliament, as well as more banks than it knew what to do with. Hosting these organisations didn't make either country very interesting, though. The Netherlands had social problems arising out of large-scale immigration from their former colonies in Asia and the most liberal drugs and pornography laws in Europe. Much more interesting.

Street fighting man

Western Europe seemed to have it all – money, fast cars, big houses, money – but underneath the prosperous facade a lot of anger was simmering.

Campaign for Nuclear Disarmament (CND)

The Campaign for Nuclear Disarmament began in Britain in the 1950s as a protest against American nuclear missiles being stationed there, but the movement soon spread to other countries. Thanks to nuclear accidents such as Three Mile Island in Pennsylvania and Chernobyl in the Soviet Union, the anti-nuclear campaign also opposed the use of nuclear power for peaceful purposes. Some nuclear protesters went further than just marching and broke into American nuclear bases to do what damage they could before the guards got them.

Student riots

Students in the sixties and seventies gained a reputation for protest marches, usually against the Vietnam War or General Pinochet's regime in Chile (see Chapter 13 to find out what they had against him). Most governments shrugged their shoulders and took no notice, but in 1968 students in Paris rioted against the government of General de Gaulle and seemed to come close to bringing him down. He actually left the country briefly, though he soon came back and unleashed the dreaded riot police, who dealt with the students and have patrolled French campus corridors ever since.

Terrorism

Prosperous capitalist western Europe threw up a variety of different – and very deadly – terrorist groups. These included:

- **The Baader–Meinhof gang:** West German anti-capitalist gang led by Andreas Baader and Ulrike Meinhof. They attacked American military installations and other symbols of the triumph of capitalism, killing six people before they were rounded up. Baader and Meinhof committed suicide in prison.

- **The Red Brigade:** Italian group with a similar agenda to the Baader-Meinhof gang. Their greatest coup came in 1978, when they captured the former prime minister, Aldo Moro, and left his dead body in a car parked halfway between the headquarters of the two main parties. The Italian police eventually managed to turn the tables on the Red Brigade, mainly by persuading members to turn informer.

- **The Provisional IRA:** That's the Provisional Irish Republican Army. The IRA campaigned against the British presence in Northern Ireland. They killed hundreds of people in Northern Ireland but their most spectacular coups were a series of bomb attacks in mainland Britain, including one that came within an ace of killing the prime minister, Margaret Thatcher.

- **ETA:** ETA stands for Euzkadi ta Azkatasuna (Basque Territory and Freedom). It campaigns for independence for the Basque territory in the Pyrenees between France and Spain. It specialises in assassination and in 1973 it managed to kill the Spanish prime minister Carrero Blanco, though it just led Franco's government to take savage reprisals.

Nowhere was safe from terrorists. In 1986 the Swedish prime minister Olaf Palme, who had actually demonstrated against the Vietnam War while prime minister, was shot. His assassin was never found so we still don't know why.

No-no NATO

The western Europeans were key players in NATO, the Western alliance the Americans put together in 1955, but some countries had an uneasy relationship with it. De Gaulle pulled France out of NATO in 1966, preferring to rely on France's own independent *Force de Frappe* (strike force); Greece pulled out for a while after democracy was restored in 1974; Spain kept its own independent forces when it joined in 1982. Until the Cold War ended, being in NATO meant having US nuclear missiles stationed on your territory, which inevitably led to big protest marches. The Germans were particularly dubious about NATO: If it came to war, they'd be in the front line.

Western European governments were generally very pro-NATO but they were wary of being dictated to by the Americans.

In 1975 NATO leaders and leaders from the Warsaw Pact met in the Finnish capital, Helsinki, and drew up a set of agreements which laid down:

- ✔ **A warning system to stop little incidents starting a nuclear war by accident:** Most people were probably alarmed to discover that no one had thought of putting this in place before.

- ✔ **Co-operation in economics and technology:** Though this didn't extend to helping each other with their ballistic missiles.

- ✔ **A commitment to human rights:** From now on countries that ignored human rights could be held to account.

Eastern Promises, Promises

Eastern and central Europe were controlled by the Soviet Union, which rejected American Marshall Aid in favour of putting its trust in the communist system. The rest of the Soviet bloc didn't get any choice in the matter: It had to go along with it.

The Soviet response to the European Union was *Comecon*, a sort of trading and industrial union of all the Soviet bloc countries. Essentially it worked as a supersize planned economy: Instead of just planning the Soviet economy from Moscow, Comecon planned the whole of the communist bloc's economy, laying down what each country should produce. Planning everything centrally, however, led to widespread corruption and inefficiency. The Soviet media always liked to show TV footage of Western workers on strike or unemployed, so as to contrast their situation with the full employment, high wages, and guaranteed housing workers in the Soviet bloc enjoyed thanks to State subsidies. The reality, however, was chronic over-manning, with no incentive to expand or even change. Eastern Europe fell badly behind the West in scientific and technological development.

We caught him telling the truth, sir

All governments use spin and propaganda and all politicians can be caught out avoiding the truth, but life in the Soviet bloc was based on a regime of systematic lying. Eastern European governments censored all expressions of opinion, and even bugged the homes of prominent people to check up on what they were saying in private. Government news programmes would announce endless lists of statistics which were supposed to prove that production was breaking all records and that life in the communist bloc was better than anywhere else. Schoolbooks were altered to present the official point of view, especially about history and culture. People growing up in eastern Europe learned how to give the 'correct' answer to questions, while always reserving judgement in case it later turned out they'd been told a pack of lies.

The impulse to lie was so ingrained that the Soviets even started denying that major events such as Stalin's death or the Chernobyl nuclear disaster had happened. For this reason Gorbachev began his campaign of reform by encouraging Russians, and the rest of the Soviet bloc, to speak openly and to face up to the truth. Chapter 16 gives you the lowdown on Gorbachev's changes.

You don't want to mix with them westerners, comrade

Countries in the eastern bloc controlled travel very strictly. Foreigners visiting the East could expect to be followed and watched and to have a 'minder' attached to their group. Eastern bloc citizens could almost never travel to the West. Official permission had to be given to leave their countries, and it was generally granted only for travel to another communist country. Sports or cultural groups travelling to the West had to have a minder from the secret police to keep tabs on the group members and prevent them from mixing with westerners.

You fools! You let him get away!

Even secret policemen are human, and some very prominent figures, including the Russian ballet stars Rudolf Nureyev and Mikhail Baryshnikov, the Czech tennis ace Martina Navratilova, and even Stalin's own daughter, Svetlana, all managed to give their minders the slip and defect to the West. Defecting was a very dangerous business, though: The authorities at home never let families travel to the West together, so defectors really had to be prepared to leave everyone they loved behind. Even worse: The authorities often punished the families of defectors. Doing so helped discourage others from getting the same idea.

Despite the risks many people were willing to try to escape to the West. Some of the most ingenious attempts were made in Berlin by people trying to get through 'Checkpoint Charlie', the most notorious crossing point between East and West Berlin. People tried tunnels, hot air balloons, and bizarre hiding places in impossibly small cars to try to get across. Some tried the most direct way – by running – but many were shot trying to cross no-man's land between East and West. The eastern bloc countries were ruthless in making sure the workers stayed in their workers' paradise.

Please sir, I want some more (freedom, that is)

The people of eastern Europe didn't just sit back and let their governments trample on their freedoms:

- **East Berlin 1953:** Workers demonstrate against the slow pace of economic recovery. *Measured response of the Soviet government*: Sends in tanks and crushes the demonstrations.

- **Hungary 1956:** Government of Imre Nagy allows freedom of opinion and releases political prisoners. Also announces that Hungary will leave the communist military alliance, the Warsaw Pact. Oops. *Measured response of the Soviet government*: Sends in tanks and crushes the Hungarians.

- **Czechoslovakia 1968:** Government of Alexander Dubcek allows freedom of opinion and releases political prisoners. Doesn't say anything about leaving the Warsaw Pact. *Measured response of the Soviet government*: Sends in tanks and crushes the Czechs.

Ironically, Dubcek had actually cleared his reforms with Moscow first, but the other eastern European governments were scared that their own people would get ideas from the Czech example so they were determined to stop it. Soviet leader Leonid Brezhnev was having second thoughts anyway, so he welcomed this invitation to show a bit of force.

One eastern bloc leader stood by the Czechs in 1968. Nicolae Ceausescu of Romania spoke up in support of Dubcek, which made many people in the West think that maybe he was a bit of a liberal himself. Bad mistake. Ceausescu soon proved one of the most brutal and repressive of the eastern bloc's many brutal and repressive dictators.

All Change! All Change!

By the 1980s, the communist states of eastern Europe had strayed a long way from their Marxist ideals. Instead of being workers' paradises where everyone worked for the common good in a spirit of equality and comradeship, they'd become corrupt and inefficient dictatorships, with an inner elite living very well while the great majority of the people had to make do without even the most basic consumer goods. The economic inefficiency was so acute that only the far-from-inefficient machinery of State repression prevented popular uprisings. So when Soviet leader Mikhail Gorbachev started loosening up the State's grip on free speech and allowing people in eastern Europe to speak their minds, the people's anger and resentment finally boiled over.

Poland: The cracks show

Poland provided the first sign that the eastern European regimes might not be able to go on keeping their people down forever. The Poles had a history of giving their communist masters grief: Polish workers had staged major protests in 1956, and in 1970 they forced President Gomulka to resign by coming out on strike.

Most Poles found a less dramatic way of defying the regime: By going to church. Poland remained defiantly Catholic, despite all the communist regime could do to discredit the Church. In 1978 Poland's Catholics got a massive boost when the Archbishop of Krakow, Karol Wojtila, was elected Pope John Paul II. No sooner had he settled into the Vatican and chosen new curtains than he was back in Poland for a state visit. No one's saying the pope was the only cause of what happened next, but he was certainly a major cause of it.

In 1980 workers in the Lenin Shipyard in Gdansk came out on strike in protest at the poor living conditions and lack of freedom in Poland. (Savour the irony for a moment, of workers at a shipyard named after Lenin, coming out on strike in protest *against* a communist government. If you're not sure why you should find this ironic, have a look at Chapter 4.)

The strikers were led by an electrician called Lech Walesa, who sported the heavy moustache Poles always admire in their leaders. Walesa announced that the shipworkers were launching a new trade union to be called Solidarity, open to any workers in any industry who wanted to stand up for freedom in Poland. *Measured response of the Polish government:* Solidarity was banned and the government introduced martial law.

But this time the military didn't get away with using violence. Solidarity continued underground, the rest of the world applied economic sanctions to Poland, and Lech Walesa won the 1983 Nobel Peace Prize.

Solidarity didn't bring the Polish government down, but it did provide an important sign to the Soviet leader Mikhail Gorbachev that the old days of just sending in the tanks were over.

And they all lived happily ever after?

Mikhail Gorbachev's coming to power in the Soviet Union in 1985 signalled the end for the eastern bloc (see Chapter 16 to find out more on Gorbachev and his changes in Russia). Gorbachev knew he would have more than enough to do holding Russia together: He had no intention of trying to prop up the eastern Europeans. He announced that they must each find their own way forward, without help from Moscow.

In 1989 anti-communist revolutions took place all over the Soviet bloc, with communist governments collapsing all over eastern Europe:

✔ **Hungary:** Had been more liberal than the rest of the bloc since 1956 anyway. Opened its border with the West, whereupon thousands of East Germans suddenly decided they'd always wanted a holiday in Hungary, and started selling off pieces of the barbed wire barrier as souvenirs.

✔ **East Germany:** Had its fortieth birthday celebrations spoiled by major protests in Leipzig and huge numbers of East Germans suddenly deciding to go to Hungary to visit the border. In November, the government opened its own borders, including the Berlin Wall. The world watched in disbelief as crowds of people climbed on top of the Wall and started hacking the hated thing to pieces.

Romanian holiday

Romania was a good example of the sort of conditions that led the people of communist Europe to turn against their leaders. Romania's leader, Nicolae Ceausescu, had set up a personal dictatorship and personality cult while his people starved. He also started a programme of 'systematisation', which meant bulldozing peoples' villages and forcing them into ugly, half-built concrete blocks. He kept the country under firm control through the *Securitate*, the secret police. But he handled repression better than he did industrial development and by 1982 the country was deep in debt. To balance the books, Ceausescu simply exported everything Romania produced, leaving nothing much in the shops for ordinary Romanians to buy. The country was returning virtually to a barter economy and the people were living in Third World-style poverty and squalor. Meanwhile Ceausescu and his wife Elena lived very comfortably and appointed members of their family to important positions throughout the country. In 1989 the people's anger finally boiled over and brought the hated regime crashing down.

✔ **Czechoslovakia:** Pulled down its own communist regime a few days after the Berlin Wall fell. The event was so peaceful it was called the 'Velvet Revolution'.

✔ **Bulgaria:** Protests on the street forced its veteran dictator, Todor Zhivkov, to resign.

✔ **Romania:** When news reached the capital, Bucharest, that the army had killed peaceful demonstrators in the town of Timisoara, the crowd stormed Nicolae Ceausescu's communist party headquarters while he was still addressing them, and he had to escape by helicopter. The *Securitate*, the secret police, kept up a fierce gun battle against the army (who had switched sides) before they were finally overcome and Ceausescu and his wife were tried and shot.

The countries of eastern Europe became democracies, and their peoples were hoping that the future would bring the sort of freedom and prosperity they imagined existed in the West. The Germans got the first taste of this new life, when West German Chancellor Helmut Kohl virtually frogmarched his East German counterpart into a reunification of the country in October 1990. From now on, eastern Europe would be taking its cue from the West.

Chapter 19

New Order: Wrapping up the Twentieth Century

....

In This Chapter

▶ Discovering post-Soviet Russia – and friends

▶ Witnessing the collapse of Yugoslavia

▶ Following the tragedy of Rwanda

▶ Greeting the Millennium

....

*W*hen the Berlin Wall fell in 1989 US President Bush announced a 'New World Order' of international harmony and trust. People looked forward to the exciting new millennium with confidence and hope. Certainly the 1990s put the long-running conflicts in South Africa and Northern Ireland more or less to rest. But in Africa and Europe they also brought back horrors everyone thought had gone for good. As the century drew to a close and the Millennium loomed, much in the world had changed, but much had stayed the same.

After the Wall Is Over

The fall of the Berlin Wall led to big changes across eastern Europe. Not all these changes went smoothly. The communist system was based on an all-powerful State controlling every aspect of its citizens' lives, including their education, their work, where they lived, and even where they could go on holiday. The economy was entirely State-directed and controlled. Moving from this system to a capitalist system where you made your own fortune, or went down, without the State getting involved, and where you were free to speak your mind without worrying about who was listening, wasn't going to be easy. Westerners didn't always help the process either, by rubbishing the old system that people in eastern Europe had spent their lives trying to make work. East Europeans soon got the idea of working within a capitalist system, but learned that capitalism had its downside as well. Perhaps it's not surprising that within a few years of the fall of the Berlin Wall, people could still be heard saying resentfully that life in the old system hadn't been *all* bad.

When did the century end?

Just as historians like to talk of the nineteenth century going on really right up to the First World War (see Chapter 2 to find out why they think this), so historians are already pointing out that the twentieth century didn't really end in 2000: It ended either a bit earlier than that or a bit later, depending on your point of view. The two significant dates are:

✔ **10 November 1989:** The day the Berlin Wall came down and everyone knew the Cold War really was over.

✔ **11 September 2001:** Also known as 9/11, the day the World Trade Center came down. 9/11 quickly became the defining sign that a new century had arrived.

But if you want to get technical and go simply by the millennium dates, the twentieth century ended at midnight on the night of 31 December 2000. So all those Millennium celebrations at the start of the year 2000 were a year too early!

Rubble, rubble – rebuilding Germany

As soon as the Wall came down West Germany's Chancellor Helmut Kohl started talks with his East German opposite number Lothar de Maiziere about reuniting the country. Kohl was a big man who looked as if he might eat the diminutive East German leader for lunch, which was rather how East Germans came to feel about the whole process of reunification.

A single Germany was proclaimed on 3 October 1990 and the cleaners had hardly started sweeping up the streamers and balloons when the whole eastern half of Germany went out of business. Thousands of former East Germans found themselves out of a job; meanwhile West Germans started realising they'd have to foot the bill for rebuilding the East. Learning to become one people again for the 'Ossis' and 'Wessis' (easterners and westerners) would take time.

The two Germanys had to get permission from the old wartime Allied powers, the United States, the Soviet Union, Britain, and France, before they could reunite the country. Not all of the Allies were sure that they wanted a massive united Germany in the heart of Europe, especially when Chancellor Kohl started talking about extending Germany's eastern frontier into Poland, prompting unhappy memories of how the Second World War had started (see Chapter 9 if you're not sure about this). Britain's Margaret Thatcher even convened a special meeting of history specialists to brief her on united Germany's track record (their verdict: Not good). But ultimately nothing could stop the drive to end forty years of division and suspicion and put Germany together again.

Secrets and lies

The dreaded East German secret police, the *Stasi*, had kept detailed files on the population. If you've seen the 2007 film *The Lives of Others* you'll have an idea of how they went about bugging private houses and apartments. After reunification, many people in former East Germany demanded to see exactly what was in their files. Often they found that their closest friends and colleagues had been systematically reporting on them for years. Perhaps some things are best left unopened.

I like driving in my car (it's not quite a Jaguar)

Nothing summed up the change that swept across the newly reunited Germany better than the fate of the East German Trabant car. Actually 'car' is a rather generous description of this vehicle that appeared to be made of plastic and had a rather less powerful engine than the average lawnmower. Imagine a garage of full-sized toy cars and you've got the general idea. Even so, getting a 'Trabbi' was the big dream for people in East Germany, and the process was no joke: You had to apply to the authorities and wait sometimes years before you got to make your choice from the dazzling range of officially approved colours: Light blue, slightly lighter blue, very light blue – or beige.

After reunification the Trabbi became a cult item. Young westerners liked to drive them (they liked the irony), Trabbi races were held, and Trabbi films were shown at the cinema. The ultimate status symbol for people in East Germany had suddenly become a national joke.

Russian roulette and the end of the USSR

Russia was led in the 1990s by Boris Yeltsin, the charismatic president of the Russian Federation. Yeltsin's path – and Russia's – was determined by two rather different coup attempts: The August coup in 1991 and the October coup in 1993.

1991: The August coup

Old-style communists, fed up with Soviet leader Mikhail Gorbachev's reform programme sending the Soviet Union down the pan (see Chapter 16 to find out why they thought this), had Gorbachev arrested at his holiday home in the Crimea and seized power themselves. Number one reform fan Boris Yeltsin climbed on a tank and told everyone to gather at the White House (the Russian Parliament building) to defy the coup plotters and stand up for change. They did, the coup collapsed, and Yeltsin became such a hero he forced Gorbachev to resign and took over the government himself.

The August coup persuaded the non-Russian republics within the USSR that they wanted out. Yeltsin recognised their independence and, since the Soviet Union now had nothing to be a union of, on 31 December 1991 he formally dissolved it. (For details of the various republics that sprang up, see the 'Break-away republics' section later in this chapter.) Yeltsin did try to set up a *Commonwealth of Independent States* to replace the old Soviet Union, but this idea was like the governor of a gulag (labour camp) expecting released prisoners to keep in touch and the idea didn't last long.

Getting the old centrally planned, hopelessly corrupt, and inefficient Soviet-era economy to adjust to a capitalist market economy was bound to create chaos as real prices (as opposed to 'Don't-worry-the-State-will-pay prices') kicked in. Sure enough, the rouble became worthless, inflation rocketed, and so did poverty and unemployment. Russia seemed to be heading back to a barter economy. The old-style communists and Russian nationalists in the Supreme Soviet and in the Congress of People's Deputies decided, 'Enough already! Yeltsin must go!'

1993: The October coup

The plotters' cue came when Yeltsin sacked his obstructive, anti-reform deputy president, Rutskoi. When the Supreme Soviet and the Congress of People's Deputies objected, he replaced them with a Duma and a Senate (both good pre-Revolution non-communist names) and gave himself lots more power. The Supreme Soviet and Congress of People's Deputies tried to sack him, but Yeltsin, who had the Russian army on *his* side, simply besieged them inside his old headquarters, the White House (the Russian parliament building, remember). He sent the troops to storm the building, and 148 people were killed in the fighting.

Defeating the October coup made Yeltsin's position a lot stronger, though world opinion was alarmed at the bloodshed. The Russians were more concerned about how long it was taking to get any of the famous benefits from this democracy idea – a few basics in the shops would be nice. No matter how angry they got, though, Yeltsin was always able to deflect their anger away from him. For instance, he won the 1996 presidential elections mainly by cutting the price of vodka. Otherwise, he just sacked whoever was prime minister at the time (he got through prime ministers the way most of us get through hankies) and carried on.

The difficult times that hit Russia and the old Soviet republics after 1990 made a lot of Russians look back wistfully to the past. Some missed the anti-Semitism and authoritarian government of the tsars, but many more wanted to go back to the good old days when Stalin was in the Kremlin and everyone else knew their place – in the gulag, mostly.

By 1998 Yeltsin's health was so bad (nearly as bad as the Russian economy's) that he quickly sacked a few more prime ministers and handed power over to his protégé, the scary Head of Russian Intelligence, Vladimir Putin.

The president is indisposed . . . as a newt

Boris Yeltsin was a colourful character, with a rather alarming tendency to throw off his jacket and party in public. Doing so probably wasn't such a great idea for a man with a serious heart condition, though it was the result of his whole-hearted support for the ancient Russian right to drink yourself under the table. Even the Irish, not a people exactly unfamiliar with the bottle, were taken aback when Yeltsin arrived on a state visit to Dublin so blotto he couldn't actually emerge from the plane. On the one hand, Russians quite liked this 'Man of the People' hard-drinking image; on the other, they felt Yeltsin's antics were demeaning. Russians didn't like not being a superpower any more, and Yeltsin's behaviour just rubbed their noses in it.

Break-away republics

When the Bolsheviks staged the Russian Revolution (see Chapter 4) they seized control of the Russian empire as well. The tsars had taken over huge areas of eastern Europe and central Asia, and under Lenin these all became Soviet Republics too. But once the Soviet Union fell apart, many of these republics decided perhaps it was time they went home now, made their excuses, and declared themselves independent. Regaining independence did not always proceed smoothly:

- ✔ **The Baltic:** Lithuania declared itself independent in 1990. Russia sent in troops to stop them, but then Latvia and Estonia did the same and in 1991 the Russians finally accepted the situation. Latvia and Estonia denied full citizenship rights to Russians living within their borders, saying they only settled to 'Russify' the countries and swamp the original people. Which was true, though whether that justified denying them citizenship was another matter.

- ✔ **The Caucasus:** Georgia, Armenia, and Azerbaijan all got their independence in 1991. Former Soviet Foreign Minister Edward Shevardnadze took over in Georgia but he couldn't control the corruption and disorder and was caught out rigging elections and deposed in 1993. Armenia and Azerbaijan started fighting over the disputed area of Nagorno Karabakh. The fighting stopped in 1995 but the dispute goes on.

- ✔ **Eastern Europe:** Ukraine declared independence in 1991 and insisted the world stop saying 'the Ukraine' as though the country were something found in a toolbox. The government of Ukraine wanted to develop a liberal economy with links to the West but the pro-Russian communists in the Ukrainian parliament did everything they could to block it. Result: By 1998 the country was nearly bankrupt. Belarus stuck to Soviet-style policies and even revived the Soviet-era flag: Was declaring independence worth it? Moldova couldn't decide whether or not to unite with Romania (final answer: No) and got into fierce boundary disputes with Ukraine and Russia.

Now, about those missiles

The only trouble with a superpower imploding is that it tends to have rather a large number of nuclear warheads for the new small states to inherit. The West tried hard to ensure that the Soviet Union's old nuclear arsenal stayed in reliable hands, if Boris Yeltsin could be described in that way, and they sent weapons experts to advise on how the weapons should be dismantled and disposed of (answer: Very, very carefully). But the exact fate of the Soviet Union's nuclear arsenal remains a matter of concern to this day.

 ✔ **Central Asia:** Uzbekistan became a repressive one-party state. It set itself up as a model Islamic state, but massacring Turks (1989), maintaining a corrupt government, and using child labour to keep the country's vital cotton industry going was probably not the best way to go about it.

Dismantling the Soviet Union was supposed to help in setting up democratic governments, but all too often the presidents of these new states seemed to think that elections were more fun when you'd fixed the result in advance and that the busy modern head of state needs a busy modern secret police force.

Chechnya

Ask Russians and they'll tell you that Chechens are bandits and thieves; ask Chechens, and they'll tell you that they've been fighting to drive the Russians out of their land since the eighteenth century. Stalin's way of dealing with the Chechens was typically brutal: He deported the whole population to central Asia and they were only allowed back in 1957. In 1991 the Chechens declared independence, like everyone else in the Soviet Union, but rival Chechen warlords soon started fighting each other and the whole state sank into civil war. 'Told you!' said the Russians, who'd been doing all they could to encourage the fighting.

In December 1994 President Yeltsin ordered the invasion of Chechnya. Result: Disaster. The rest of the world condemned Russia and the Chechens were so good at ambushing Russian troops that Yeltsin was forced to pull out. Utterly humiliated, many Russians wanted a re-match.

In 1997 Chechnya, which is mainly Muslim, declared Islam the state religion. By then law and order had almost completely broken down and many local bandit groups were launching attacks over the border into Russia. So when Vladimir Putin took over in 1998, he decided to deal with the Chechens once and for all. In 1999 he launched a full-scale invasion.

The second Chechen war was very brutal. Both sides committed appalling atrocities, including torture. The Russians reconquered Chechnya and brought it back under Russian government, but Chechen terrorists hit back. In 2002 they took the audience and players hostage at a Moscow theatre and 130 of them were killed when the Russian security forces used gas to storm the building. In 2004 Chechens took a whole school hostage at Beslan and 331 people died in the gun battle that followed, including 186 children.

International opinion has often condemned Russian actions in Chechnya, but the Russian government says that its strong-arm tactics are all part of the global War on Islamist Terror. Not everyone is convinced.

Oh, East is West

In 2004 ten countries, eight of them from the former Soviet bloc, joined the European Union, which meant their citizens could travel within the EU looking for work. Suddenly western Europe was awash with polite and reliable Polish plumbers and bar attendants. Russia was relaxed about its former satellite states joining the EU, but it was much less happy about them joining NATO, which seven of them did in 2002.

NATO (the North Atlantic Treaty Organisation) was a Western military alliance formed in 1949 to oppose Soviet expansion; in 1955 the Soviet Union and its allies formed the Warsaw Pact to oppose NATO (see Chapter 10 for details). After communist rule collapsed in eastern Europe the Warsaw Pact folded, but the Americans kept NATO going: They thought it might come in handy if they ever needed to take military action without going through the United Nations.

The death of Yugoslavia

Yugoslavia in the 1990s saw the worst fighting in Europe since the Second World War. The conflict produced cruelty and atrocities on a scale no one would have believed possible in the last decade of the twentieth century.

One big unhappy family

Yugoslavia was made up of a number of different ethnic groups, including Serbs, Croats, Slovenes, Muslims and Albanians. By and large these groups lived in their own areas of Yugoslavia. Slovenes inhabited Slovenia up in the north near Italy and Switzerland; the Croats lived in a curiously-shaped region like a letter 'n' on its side; the Serbs lived in the southern region of Serbia, which had once been a separate state of its own; the Albanians lived in the southern province of Kosovo. The area where different groups overlapped was in the central province of Bosnia Herzegovina, which had Bosnian Serbs, Bosnian Croats, and a large community of Bosnian Muslims. These groups had developed very different cultures. The Slovenes and Croats were Catholic and used the Latin alphabet; the Serbs were Orthodox Christians and used the Cyrillic alphabet; while the Albanians had a language of their own. To find out how such a diverse group of people had all ended up in one country see the sidebar 'How did one country get into such a big mess'?

These different groups were all formed into one country under Serb leadership at the end of the First World War but underlying ethnic tensions remained, especially between the Serbs and the Croats. These tensions were made much worse in the Second World War, when the Croats helped the Germans to hunt down the Serb-led resistance. After the war Yugoslavia became a communist state under Marshal Tito, who managed to keep the ethnic tensions under control. They hadn't gone away, however, and after his death in 1980 they gradually worked their way to the surface again. By the end of the decade, Yugoslavia was poised to dive into terrible civil war.

The trouble began in the province of Kosovo. Most Kosovars were Albanian but the Kosovan Serbs ran the province and the Kosovan Albanians didn't like it. They started attacking their Serb neighbours, who said they'd get their big brother on to the Albanians and appealed to Serbia for help. The new Serbian leader, Slobodan Milosevic, responded by saying that Serbia would stand up for all Serbs, throughout Yugoslavia. In fact, he said Serbia ought to rule the whole of Yugoslavia, as they had in the old days (for that history lesson, see the sidebar 'How did one country get into such a big mess?'). That idea didn't appeal much to the Slovenes and Croats, who were already fed up with having to subsidise the poorer areas down south. If the Serbs were going to start talking about taking the country over, the Slovenes and Croats wanted out.

Kosovo was the site of the most important event in Serbian history, the 1389 Battle of Kosovo Polje where the Turks defeated the Serbs and conquered the whole kingdom. For Serbs, losing control of Kosovo would be like Americans giving up Plymouth Rock or Egypt losing the pyramids: Unthinkable.

A war in four parts

Yugoslavia fell apart in four very bloody stages.

War No. 1: Slovenia

When the Slovenes announced they supported the Albanians in Kosovo, the Serbs cut off all trade with them, which was silly since Slovenia had most of Yugoslavia's industry. In January 1990 Slovenia declared independence, and after a short, but bloody, war the Serbs had to let Slovenia go, muttering that they'd never liked the place anyway.

War No. 2: Croatia

In 1990 Croatia elected a new nationalist anti-Serb and anti-Semitic leader, Franjo Tudjman. Tudjman sacked all Serbs working for the government and introduced Nazi-style racial 'purity' laws to stop anyone who wasn't 'pure' Croat from driving or holding insurance. In 1991 Croatia declared independence.

How did one country get into such a big mess?

In the Middle Ages modern-day Yugoslavia was conquered by the Turkish Ottoman empire. The Turks offered easy terms (that is, no taxes) to anyone who converted to Islam, and some of the people in Bosnia Herzegovina did – the modern-day Bosnian Muslims are their descendants. Modern-day Slovenia and Croatia are the areas the Turks' Catholic neighbours, the Habsburg empire, managed to take over and they've remained Catholic to this day. The Christians who remained within the Ottoman empire belonged to the Orthodox Church: The modern-day Serbs and Macedonians are descended from them (if you're keen to know more – okay, if you're a bit lost – see *European History for Dummies* (Wiley)).

After the First World War both the Ottoman and the Habsburg empires collapsed. The Serbs, who had fought on the Allied side, said, 'Why not give the whole region to us?' and, essentially, the Allies did. The new 'Kingdom of Serbs, Croats, and Slovenes' was to be ruled by the King of Serbia. In 1928 he changed the country's name to 'Yugoslavia' ('Land of the South Slavs'), though he might as well have called it 'Greater Serbia', because that's what it was.

The Croats hated this new Serb regime. In 1934 the Croat *Ustashe* resistance group assassinated King Alexander on a state visit to France. When the Germans invaded Yugoslavia in 1941, these ethnic divisions came into the open:

✔ **The Croats** saw the invasion as a chance to get their own back on the Serbs. The Ustashe put on smart new uniforms and became a brutal pro-German militia.

✔ **The Serbs** set up a resistance movement called the *Chetniks* with a charismatic leader called Mihailovic to fight the Germans and get the king back.

✔ **The Communists** set up a *partisan* resistance group under Josip Broz (codename: 'Tito') to fight the Germans and the Ustashe. But they didn't want the king back, so they also fought the Chetniks. The Chetniks sometimes betrayed the partisans to the Germans.

The Western Allies sent help to Tito, so in 1945 he was able to take the country over. His partisans promptly massacred captured Croats and Chetniks for what they had done in the war.

After the war Tito set up a federal system in Yugoslavia where all the different ethnic groups could share power together: Any nationalist groups who tried to break the country up got stamped on mercilessly. He opened Yugoslavia to Western tourism and even private industry: He wanted to modernise the country and rid it of the old ethnic hatred. His approach seemed to work, but no one quite knew what would happen after Tito died in 1980.

The Croatian Serbs got together in armed groups called Chetniks to stop Croatia pulling away; the Croats revived the armed military group Ustashe that had been responsible for the assassination of King Alexander in 1934 (see the sidebar 'How did one country get into such a big mess?' for more on these events). Both sides committed appalling atrocities, but the Serbs had the upper hand because Milosevic and the Yugoslav army were both helping them. The Serbs besieged Vukovar and massacred its people and they even

bombarded the beautiful historic port of Dubrovnik. By the time the UN negotiated a ceasefire in 1992 the Croatian Serbs controlled a third of Croatia. The
Croats wanted it back.

Some of the best-known atrocities in the Yugoslav wars were committed by
Serbs against the other ethnic groups, but Croats and Muslims also committed appalling atrocities against Serbs. Don't think the fault all lies on one side.

On 15 January 1992, mainly under pressure from Germany, the European
Community recognised the independent states of Slovenia and Croatia. No
one argues much about Slovenia, but historians and commentators argue
fiercely over whether or not recognising Croatia was wise. Many think doing
so led directly to the bloodshed that followed.

By 1995 the Croats were much better organised. They attacked the Croatian
Serbs, retook the Serb-held land – and raped and shot as many Serbs as they
could find. Serbia had to grit its teeth and accept independent Croatia.

War No. 3: Bosnia-Herzegovina

Bosnia-Herzegovina's (that's the proper name, but from now on I'll call it
Bosnia for short) Serbs, Croats, and Muslims had always got on well together,
but once Slovenia and Croatia had pulled away, the leader of the Bosnian
Serbs, Radovan Karadzic, declared he *didn't* want Bosnia to go it alone. On
the other hand, the Bosnian Croats and Muslims didn't want to be a small
minority inside a vengeful Serbia: They voted for independence.

Slobodan Milosevic kept the Bosnian Serbs supplied with lots of very big
guns and they used them to bombard the Bosnian capital, Sarajevo, so savagely that the UN imposed sanctions on Serbia, and the EU and the United
States recognised Bosnian independence. The UN sent in peacekeeping
troops, but the Bosnian Serb commander, General Ratko Mladic, took no
notice: He even specialised in taking UN troops prisoner. Mladic's men
attacked the Muslim areas, killing, torturing, and raping as they went. TV
cameras showed emaciated prisoners in Serb concentration camps: The
situation seemed to be Nazi Germany all over again. Bosnia's Muslims fled in
panic to a series of UN Safe Areas where the UN troops would protect them.
Or so they thought.

As if they hadn't got enough to worry about, Bosnia's Croats and Muslims
now started fighting each other. The Croats shelled the ancient Turkish
bridge at Mostar, which linked the Muslim and Croat parts of the town, and
brutally forced Muslim prisoners into fuel tanks where many of them were
suffocated by the fumes. Muslim troops murdered and tortured Croat prisoners. The savagery in Bosnia went three ways.

Actually, we call it 'mass murder'

When Croatian Serbs bombarded the little Croat village of Kijevo, they gave the world one of the century's most disgusting phrases. The Serbs wanted the region to be entirely Serb and Kijevo stood in their way, so they systematically destroyed or deported its population and announced that the area had been 'ethnically cleansed'. 'Ethnic cleansing' or even just 'cleansing' became the standard term for deporting or slaughtering the population of a town or village simply on grounds of their race. It's probably too late to stop the use of the phrase now, but it provides a ghastly euphemism for mass murder (like the Nazis' 'Final Solution' for gassing people) and it should never have been accepted, still less used, by the world's press.

In 1995 the Serbs launched a series of savage attacks to win the war before the Americans imposed some sort of peace deal. Serb guns bombarded Sarajevo's crowded market place. Serb troops attacked the UN Safe Haven of Srebrenica and massacred the Muslims gathered there virtually under the eyes of the Dutch UN troops who were supposed to be protecting them.

The United States decided to act. NATO planes attacked Serb positions and the Americans stuck the leaders of Serbia, Bosnia, and Croatia in an air force base at Dayton, Ohio and didn't let them go till they'd reached a settlement.

The Dayton Accords said:

✔ Bosnia-Herzegovina is to be independent with two self-governing republics, a Croat–Muslim one and a Serb one called Srpska.

✔ The presidency is to rotate between the three ethnic groups.

And why, you may very well ask, couldn't they have done that from the start?

War No. 4: Kosovo

Everyone had rather forgotten about the tensions in Kosovo until Albanian and Serb Kosovars started fighting each other in 1997. Both sides began massacring as many of the others as they could find, though the Serbs had greater resources for doing so. In 1999 US President Clinton took time off from his busy love life (the nearby sidebar, 'A tale of two presidents', explains all) to order NATO air strikes first on Serb positions in Kosovo and then on the Serb capital, Belgrade (though their biggest hits were a crowded train and the Chinese embassy). In June 1999 the Serbs and Albanians finally agreed on an independent Kosovo. NATO troops went in to keep the peace – and discovered evidence of mass murder by both sides.

New Nations, New Dangers

The last decade of the twentieth century saw big changes, and tragedy, in Africa and the Middle East. The world watched in amazement as South Africa moved away from its repressive apartheid system towards true democracy – without provoking the bloodbath that had seemed inevitable for so long. Tragically, the little state of Rwanda was to more than make up for this lack of bloodshed by tearing itself apart in an orgy of massacre and genocide that shocked the world, while Robert Mugabe's government in Zimbabwe provided a case study of how to set up a personal dictatorship and reduce an entire country to poverty. In the Middle East, the United States was helping the Israelis and Palestinians to feel their way towards peace, little realising that it would soon face its most deadly enemy – al-Qaeda.

Somewhere over the rainbow – South Africa

By the 1980s the South African government was up against an international boycott of its goods and commerce, and strikes and election boycotts by opponents of apartheid at home (see Chapter 12 for more on the apartheid system and why South Africa had it). In 1988 Prime Minister P. W. Botha declared a state of emergency to deal with the strikers, but in 1989 he suffered a stroke and had to resign. The new prime minister was a very different character, F. W. de Klerk.

Votes for all

De Klerk was determined to find a peaceful way to initiate some genuine democracy in South Africa. He began by removing the ban on the African National Congress (ANC) and releasing political prisoners including, on 11 February 1990, Nelson Mandela. The whole world watched as Mandela walked to freedom, but turning South Africa round wasn't going to be quite so easy: de Klerk had to convince his own party and both he and Mandela had to win over the Zulu Inkatha Freedom Party, which wanted a separate Zulu homeland. Not until 1993 did all sides finally agree to set up a democracy with equal votes for everyone, regardless of colour.

South Africa's first ever democratic election took place in April 1994 – a hugely symbolic moment. Africans queued for hours to register for the right to vote for the first time in their lives. The ANC won the election by a landslide and Nelson Mandela became South Africa's first black president.

The rainbow nation

Mandela wanted to reassure all the peoples of South Africa that they would be valued equally. South Africa was to be 'a rainbow nation' of many colours, he declared (and his colourful shirts seemed to take this rainbow idea literally). President Mandela had some serious problems in his in-tray:

- ✔ **Crime:** South Africa had a very high rate of violent crime and democratic elections and racial harmony weren't going to change it.

- ✔ **The Zulus:** They were still demanding their own homeland.

- ✔ **Healing the wounds left by the apartheid system:** How could justice be done without reopening all the old wounds?

- ✔ The Spice Girls wanted to meet him

But building harmony wasn't going to be easy: Memories of the murder and torture carried out under apartheid were still fresh and painful. But the Archbishop of Cape Town, Desmond Tutu, came up with a bold idea.

Truth hurts

Archbishop Tutu set up a special *Truth and Reconciliation Commission*. Instead of just prosecuting everyone who had committed acts of brutality under apartheid, which would just have filled the country's jails and left people feeling angry and resentful, his idea was to bring accused and accusers together in an open courtroom and give everyone the chance to speak openly. If the accused recognised – in public – exactly what they had done wrong and declared their remorse, they would receive an amnesty. If they didn't, then they would be prosecuted to the full extent of the law.

Many people were sceptical about the Truth and Reconciliation Commission and felt very unhappy to see the men who'd murdered their loved ones walking free. But somehow Bishop Tutu's idea worked. It wasn't easy for former policemen and officials to admit to crimes, especially when they had to listen to the testimony of people they'd beaten or tortured. But these admissions helped South Africa come through the incredibly painful process of facing up to the past so that it could start dealing with the future.

No happy endings

Saying that once South Africa got democracy all its problems were over would be nice, but sadly it's not true. The crime rate soared and inflation was out of control. The Zulus kept up their pressure for a separate homeland. South Africa suffered from the terrible spread of AIDS throughout Africa, but wasn't able to do much about it because Nelson Mandela's successor, Thabo Mbeki, refused to believe the scientific evidence about how AIDS was transmitted. So, no happy endings: This is history, remember, not a film.

How to wreck a country: Zimbabwe

When Zimbabwe became independent in 1980, Robert Mugabe, leader of the Marxist ZANU party, was elected president (Chapter 12 has the details). At first Mugabe worked together with his opponents to get the country going on a democratic basis, but he became increasingly autocratic.

Zimbabwe's richest land and business was still in the hands of the white minority. Mugabe's government was up to its eyes in debt, so he sent his old veterans from the fight against white rule to confiscate white farms by force. When other countries said this approach was no way to reach a fair settlement of a genuine land reform issue, Mugabe said he wasn't going to be preached to by a bunch of colonialists and took no notice.

Meanwhile inflation was out of control and the people were living in dire poverty. Anyone who criticised Mugabe was arrested and beaten, including the Opposition leader, and many were tortured. The rest of the world condemned Mugabe and the European Union banned him from visiting its member countries; more importantly, the other African states condemned what he was doing to the long-suffering people of Zimbabwe.

Genocide: Rwanda

Until the 1990s most of the world was probably a bit hazy about exactly where Rwanda was. For the record, Rwanda was a Belgian colony and it became independent in 1962. Rwanda had two tribal peoples: the minority Tutsi, who had helped the Belgians run the country, and the majority Hutu, traditionally Rwanda's peasant farmers. Tutsis and Hutus didn't much like or trust each other. After independence the Hutus turned on the Tutsis (they'd been helping the Belgians, remember) and forced them to flee into Burundi and Uganda. From this position, the Tutsis formed the *Rwandan Patriotic Front (RPF)* to protect themselves against the Hutus. In 1990 the RPF tried invading Rwanda, but failed, which made things even worse for them, because President Juvenal Habyarimana (a Hutu and proud of it) started arresting any Tutsis he could find.

Who shot JH?

President Habyarimana badly needed money – for his army, mainly. The International Monetary Fund and the World Bank would only lend to him if he reached some sort of compromise with the Tutsi. Gritting his teeth, in April 1994 the president flew to a meeting in Dar-es-Salaam, where he agreed to take some Tutsis into his government. On his way home with the president of Burundi, his plane was blown out of the sky by a surface-to-air missile. Both men were killed. This event was the signal for the killing to start.

The Hutus blamed the Tutsis for the murder, but the evidence doesn't support this theory. The Tutsis had nothing to gain from killing Habyarimana – as events showed only too clearly. Most commentators agree that the assassination was probably the work of Hutu militia, angry with the president for making concessions to the hated Tutsis.

Days of slaughter

For months the special Hutu militia, the *Interahamwe* ('those who stand together') had been stockpiling machetes – cheaper than guns and no chance of shooting your own side by mistake. As soon as the assassination was announced, the Interahamwe started killing Tutsis and any pro-Tutsi Hutus, including the prime minister and her Belgian bodyguards. The Interahamwe forced ordinary Hutus to betray their Tutsi neighbours and kill them. Some Tutsis fled to their local churches for protection. The Interahamwe followed them there and some Hutu nuns and priests actually helped kill them.

In the hundred days that followed the president's assassination, something like *one million* Tutsis were massacred in Rwanda, nearly all with crude machetes. The world could hardly believe this massacre was happening in the 1990s, on the eve of the twenty-first century – but it was.

Hurting the Hutus

Over in Uganda, the (Tutsi) Rwandan Patriotic Front, horrified by the news from home, invaded Rwanda to save anyone who was left and to take revenge on the Hutus. Now it was the Hutus' turn to run. Virtually the entire Hutu population fled to hastily put-up refugee camps in Tanzania and Zaire. At one camp in Zaire 50,000 people died of cholera. The Interahamwe controlled the camps and took all the best pickings from the international aid effort for themselves.

President Mobutu of Zaire supported the Interahamwe, but in 1996 Laurent Kabila overthrew Mobutu. He wanted the Interahamwe out of Zaire and he wanted it now. The Interahamwe fled and the Hutus were free to return home.

Where was the rest of the world?

Where indeed. When the killing started the UN evacuated all foreigners – including nearly all of its troops. The Organisation of African Unity appealed to the UN to stay but the Americans didn't want another disaster like Somalia (see Chapter 13) so the UN had to make do with a small force. Small forces can't protect whole populations from being massacred, and this one was no exception. The film *Hotel Rwanda* gives you an idea of the horrors of the Rwandan genocide and the poor showing the UN made in trying to stop it.

In November 1994 the UN set up an international tribunal to deal with cases arising from the Rwandan genocide, but it was small and it worked very slowly. Like the rest of the UN's efforts, in fact.

A tale of two presidents

In 1992 Democrat Bill Clinton was elected US president. Clinton was the first president from the post-war 'baby boomer' generation and certainly the first to play the sax at his inauguration party. His wife, Hillary Rodham Clinton, was a professional lawyer who intended to be a very hands-on First Lady; though it soon transpired that her husband had been pretty hands-on with various young women, most notably a young White House intern, Monica Lewinsky. He narrowly avoided impeachment for lying about his affair and some people even said he launched the Kosovo bombing (see the 'War No. 4: Kosovo' section) to distract attention away from the scandal.

Clinton came into office with big ideas for social change in America, though most of his plans got shot down by Congress. He did, however, manage to balance the budget, a feat which had always escaped Ronald Reagan, and he had big successes abroad. He helped seal the peace agreement between Israel and the Palestine Liberation Organisation (see Chapter 17 for the details), between the different groups fighting in Bosnia (see 'The death of Yugoslavia' section), and between the Catholics and Protestants in Northern Ireland (see Chapter 7 and *British History for Dummies* (Wiley)).

In 2000 Clinton's vice president, Al Gore, ran for president against George Bush, governor of Texas and son of Clinton's predecessor, President George H. W. Bush. The election was very close and came down to a few votes in just one state, Florida, where the governor was Bush's brother Jeb. Florida declared Bush had won, but the Democrats complained that large numbers of Democrat votes were being discounted on highly dodgy grounds. The legal challenges looked set to drag on for months, but the Supreme Court called a halt to them, thereby handing the presidency to George W. Bush. Many commentators still claim that actually Al Gore won that election. If he had, bearing in mind President Bush's invasions of Afghanistan (2002) and Iraq (2003), the history of the world in the early twenty-first century could have been very different.

The Road to 9/11

Hopes for a peaceful New World Order were dashed only a few months into the new century by the 9/11 attacks on New York and Washington. Suddenly the whole world had heard of al-Qaeda, but no one knew much about them. Where did this conflict come from?

You've got the road map upside down!

In the 1990s Israeli, Palestinian, and American leaders all tried to resolve the long-running dispute about who should own Palestine, but however close they got to a deal, something always wrecked it.

- ✔ **1993: Yitzhak Rabin signs the Oslo Accords with Yasser Arafat agreeing to pull out of the West Bank** but in 1995 Rabin is assassinated by an Israeli opposed to any sort of deal with the Palestine Liberation

Organisation (PLO). The new prime minister, Binyamin Netanyahu, promptly builds lots of shiny new Jewish settlements on the West Bank.

✔ **1998: The Americans force Netanyahu to talk with the PLO** but in 1999 the Israelis simply remove him from office. New prime minister Ehud Barak withdraws troops from Lebanon, talks with the PLO, and generally seems far too willing to meet others half way, so in 2001 the Israelis throw him out and elect the ultra-hard-line Ariel Sharon instead.

✔ **2001: Sharon invades the Palestinian Authority area in the West Bank and bombards Yasser Arafat's headquarters in Ramallah.** Sharon's action was prompted by a second Palestinian *Intifada* (uprising – Chapter 17 has details on the first one) which had broken out in protest at his declaration that Jerusalem's Dome of the Rock and the al-Aqsa mosque, two of Islam's holiest shrines, would remain in Israel's hands forever. Sharon blamed Arafat (rightly) for organising the uprising, but although he could trap Arafat in Ramallah, he couldn't defeat the Intifada.

✔ **2003: US President George W. Bush announces a 'Road Map' to Peace**, with Palestine and Israel recognising each other and Palestine stopping the Intifada. Sharon and the moderate Palestinian leader, Abu Mazen, accept the concept, but the Israelis and Palestinians don't. No one knows why it's called a 'road map'.

✔ **2003: Sharon builds a concrete 'security fence' (that's a wall to you and me) to separate Israelis and Palestinians.** Its critics, including the UN, point out that the wall seems to have annexed some 40 per cent of Palestine's territory as well. Sharon's response: 'Does it really? That's handy.'

✔ **2005: Sharon pulls Israeli troops out of the Gaza Strip and demolishes Israeli settlements.** This action causes deep bitterness among the Israeli settlers in Gaza, some of whom have to be removed by force, but it enjoys the support of most Israelis. Shortly afterwards, however, Sharon is incapacitated by a massive stroke that leaves him in a persistent vegetative state.

At the start of the twenty-first century the problem of Palestine was as far from being solved as ever. The United States had been trying to get the two sides talking, but many Arabs thought the Americans were too pro-Israeli.

Wanted dead or alive – Osama bin Laden

Al-Qaeda ('the base' or 'the grid') is an international network of different Islamist terrorist groups spread across some thirty countries. The network grew out of the Mujahidin, the guerrilla groups who resisted the Soviet occupation of Afghanistan in the 1980s when the United States used to send the Mujahidin arms and money, but after the Russians left, and especially after the First Gulf War against Iraq (1990–1), the Mujahidin began to turn against America. This anti-American feeling developed partly because the US tended to support repressive Middle East regimes (including Saddam Hussein, until he invaded Kuwait), but mainly because US troops were stationed on the holy soil of Saudi Arabia, homeland of the Prophet Muhammad. (See Chapter 17 for all the relevant background.)

As the Taliban gradually won control of Afghanistan in the 1990s, they encouraged al-Qaeda to use the country as its base. The different groups within al-Qaeda saw different aspects of Western life, such as the freedom to criticise religious views, and elements of American foreign policy, such as supporting Israel and failing to protect the Muslims of Bosnia and Chechnya, as hostile to Muslims all over the world. So al-Qaeda began launching spectacular attacks on symbols of American power:

- **Bomb attack on the World Trade Center (1993):** six people killed, and over a thousand injured
- **Bomb attacks on the US embassies in Kenya and Tanzania (1998):** 224 people killed, mostly Africans
- **Suicide bomb attack on USS *Cole* (2000):** Seventeen killed

The West gradually learned to take al-Qaeda more seriously, until, on 11 September 2001, it launched its most spectacular coup: It hijacked four civilian airliners and crashed them into the twin towers of the World Trade Center, bringing them both crashing down, and into the Pentagon; the fourth plane, presumably aiming for the White House, crashed into the ground. '9/11' was the biggest terrorist attack in history and it stunned America.

War on Terror

President Bush immediately declared War on Terror, which initially meant war with Afghanistan. An American-led international coalition invaded the country, overthrew the Taliban, and installed a democratic government.

In 2003 President Bush started threatening Iraq, stating that President Saddam Hussein was storing weapons of mass destruction. When UN weapons inspectors said they couldn't find any evidence of these weapons, Bush, with Britain's Tony Blair beside him, went ahead and invaded anyway: Better safe than sorry. Bush also claimed that Saddam Hussein had supported al-Qaeda, which was unlikely, since Iraq was an aggressively secular state and Saddam had been persecuting Muslims for years, but the accusation helped sell the war to the American people.

The Iraq War quickly toppled Saddam: He was tracked down, tried, and hanged. The Iraqis got an elected government, but they also got a Mujahidin-style rising against the Americans and Brits which cost thousands of lives. As so often in the twentieth century, winning the war was much easier than winning the battles that followed. If only Bush and Blair had read this book.

Chapter 20

And the Living Is Easy – For Some

The twentieth century, especially its second half, saw bigger and faster changes in people's lifestyles than any century in history. Travel and communications meant that people could contact each other and travel much farther and more quickly than ever before. Long-held beliefs changed and so did the traditional roles of men and women. In the 1950s a strange moody, nocturnal animal called the teenager was discovered, grazing from kitchen fridges. This chapter rounds off the twentieth century by showing how it affected, well, you.

Techno Beat

Technological change didn't suddenly start in the twentieth century: After all, the nineteenth century saw a complete industrial revolution. But the twentieth century saw change happening much faster than before and reaching into everyone's everyday world. New products and inventions were only expected to last a few years before they went out of date, or just fell out of fashion. And thanks to television and the Internet, something that happened in one place could very quickly spread all round the world.

The mighty atom

Scientists had been working for years on atomic energy before the atom bomb was dropped on the Japanese city of Hiroshima in 1945 (see Chapter 9 for the details). The British scientist Lord Rutherford identified the atom and the Danish scientist Niels Bohr worked out how atoms move. The key to releasing the atom's enormous power lay in the way it either split (fission) or merged with another atom (fusion). Either way, doing so leads to a nuclear chain reaction that releases mind-blowing amounts of energy. Atom bombs work on nuclear fission, hydrogen bombs on nuclear fusion – and they both create a very, very big bang.

For war

Scientists working on nuclear energy didn't take long to realise that their work could be used for military purposes. Nazi Germany certainly realised the possibility and set up a programme to develop an atomic bomb; luckily, some of the leading German physicists in Nazi Germany, most famously Albert Einstein, were also Jewish and had managed to get out. As a result, American and British scientists were responsible for developing the first atomic weapons. The Cold War (see Chapter 10) kept them all in business for years to come.

And for peace

During the 1950s and 1960s the world felt as if it was living in the shadow of a nuclear war that might break out at any moment. But scientists were keen to show that nuclear energy wasn't just for making bombs. The energy it produced could be used to drive other machinery with enormous power. Producing electricity was the most obvious use. Electricity was generated in enormous power stations whose dynamos were run on coal: Old power stations have those huge chimneys for that reason. Most of the coal mined around the world didn't go onto people's fireplaces: It powered the generators that fed electricity to the light bulbs or the kitchen. But coal was messy and dirty and the job of getting it was filthy and dangerous. Nuclear power could drive a power station much more cleanly, more efficiently, and (the key consideration for many governments) at a fraction of the cost.

So the 1950s and 1960s saw a large number of nuclear reactors and power stations being built. Most people welcomed this new 'clean' source of energy.

Nuclear energy had one ever so slightly enormous drawback: It produced large quantities of highly radioactive waste, with a half-life (that is, the time it takes for half of it to decay) of hundreds of years. Throwing that lot in the bin with the newspapers and potato peelings just isn't possible. Nuclear waste has to be buried in vast sealed concrete storage dumps deep under the ground. And all nuclear facilities run the risk of leakages, as happened at Three Mile Island, Pennsylvania in 1979, or catastrophic explosion, as happened at Chernobyl, Ukraine, in 1985. That disaster helped spearhead a major youth movement campaigning against nuclear power in the 1980s.

More recently, attitudes towards nuclear power have changed. Risks from waste and leaks still exist, and terrorist attacks are a new danger, but many people have said that nuclear energy is a very environmentally-friendly form of energy, with an important part to play in reducing greenhouse gases and preventing global warming.

Be afraid. Be very afraid.

Some writers and filmmakers in the first half of the century tried to imagine what life would be like in the second half, and quite often the image they came up with was pretty scary:

✓ H. G. Wells imagined a journey in a time machine which saw the twentieth-century world being destroyed in a cataclysmic war. His novel *Things to Come* described London being destroyed in a terrifying air attack. (Wells also came up with *The War of the Worlds* about a Martian invasion of Earth, so you can see he was a real bundle of laughs.)

✓ Fritz Lang's film *Metropolis* showed a future high-tech world in which people were reduced to the level of cattle.

✓ Aldous Huxley's novel *Brave New World* imagined a future where the people were bred like animals by an all-controlling State.

✓ George Orwell's *Nineteen Eighty Four* was so scary that people spent the 1970s anxiously counting down the years. Orwell pictured a gloomy world where the State had complete control over people's lives, even their innermost thoughts.

What these dark predictions all had in common was *technology*. They all imagined that technology would transform people's lives and make them easier to control. Some people would say that they got that part right.

We're on the telly

Incredible though it may seem, when television started in the 1930s no one was sure that it would catch on. The image quality was very poor compared with the cinema, and no usherettes came round selling chocolates or ice creams. But in the 1950s, American TV produced comedies, westerns, and adventures which went down well with audiences all over the world. Other countries copied the format of American TV game shows and adapted them for their own audiences. By the 1960s television was well on the way to becoming a major part of Western domestic life, even among poorer people, and it was one of the main consumer goods that people elsewhere in the world aspired to.

Makes you think, doesn't it?

Television beat cinema hands down in documentaries and factual programmes. Cinemas showed newsreels before the main feature, short films about world events or about the olive harvest in Morocco, with a commentator – plus what sounded like a full orchestra – speaking over it, and you had to sit through it all and like it before they let you watch *Singin' in the Rain*.

Television, on the other hand, could have studio-based shows, interviewing important people and challenging their answers. Some of the interviewers became well-known characters in their own right. Talk shows and celebrity interviewers helped make the new medium seem more exciting and cutting edge.

The tragedy of the tests

In the 1940s and 1950s, when atomic weapons were still new, the nuclear powers held tests to check that their bombs actually worked and to measure their effects. The American and British governments tested their bombs on remote Pacific islands and deep in the outback of Australia (which shows what they thought of Pacific islanders and Australian Aborigines). They sent large numbers of troops to witness the explosions from what they reckoned was a safe distance. They were wrong. The troops were far too close and were given feeble protection, such as extra-strong sunglasses or being told to stand with their backs to the actual explosion. Many of these men later developed leukaemia and cancer as a direct result of the radiation they received witnessing these tests. Which shows what their governments thought of them, too.

It ain't real if it ain't on TV

Before television got going, most people could only see the world outside through cinema and the press; people who grew up after 1945 expected to see things on television first. Some of the landmark events of the second half-century, such as the Kennedy assassination, Vietnam, the moon landings, or the terrorist attacks on the Munich Olympics, were all played out on television.

Sometimes, television actually made events happen. King Juan Carlos of Spain and Boris Yeltsin in Russia both defeated military coups in their countries by timely appearances on television calling on people to defeat the plotters. Politicians agree that TV footage of Vietnam helped turn Americans against the war. To many people in the second half of the century, television *was* reality.

Some politicians latched onto this powerful new medium very quickly. Kennedy was a made-for-TV president and so was his old enemy, Cuba's Fidel Castro (see Chapter 13 to find out why they were such enemies). Older politicians had mixed reactions: France's President de Gaulle was very effective on television; Churchill tried it once, looked awful, and never touched it again. By the end of the century, though, no politician anywhere in the world could expect to succeed without being very adept at appearing on television.

We'll be back after the break

One novelty that started in American television was the ad break. Advertising became a sophisticated social exercise: Advertisers identified their different types of audience and what TV programmes they were watching and when, in order to sell to them more directly. Some very clever people worked in advertising: The novelist Salman Rushdie coined a famous slogan for advertising cream cakes at a time when dieting was all the rage: 'Naughty. But nice'.

TV adverts were so good for business that advertisers could afford to pay top stars huge sums just for reading one or two lines, even one or two words, in an advert. Actors love adverts.

See It Now!

The American broadcaster Ed Murrow made his name sending back reports from London during the Blitz in the Second World War. In the 1950s he fronted a ground-breaking TV show called *See It Now*, which nosed out the big stories and asked the awkward questions. In 1954 Murrow took up the challenge that the rest of America's press was ducking and denounced Senator Joseph McCarthy for his harassment of people accused of communist sympathies. You can see the show recreated in the film *Good Night and Good Luck* (that phrase was Murrow's sign off). *See It Now* pushed out the boundaries of what investigative TV could do and set a standard for TV around the world to match. Oh, and McCarthy wasn't able to refute Murrow's charges.

Television helped the second half of the century to develop a common culture around the world: People wore the same sort of clothes, listened to the same sort of music, and watched the same shows all over the world. In that sense we can say that television helped to make the world seem a smaller place. On the other hand, people sometimes accuse television of eroding traditional cultures and ways of life.

By the 1980s and 1990s broadcasters were beaming their signals down from satellites in space. Satellite TV channels could be sent into homes in many different countries, so satellite TV potentially was a very powerful medium. One of the leading satellite TV companies was Sky, owned by the Australian-born broadcasting billionaire Rupert Murdoch. Murdoch had already built up a newspaper empire for himself in Britain, Australia, and the United States; by the 1980s he was using his control of Sky to help persuade China to open up more to the rest of the world. Many people thought – and still think – that it was a bad idea to put so much power and influence into the hands of a TV executive.

The development of mass communications in the twentieth century placed more power in the hands of media tycoons than at any time in history. Some commentators argue that communications like TV, e-mail, and the Internet are forces for democracy and empowerment, allowing ordinary people all over the world to communicate with each other and to access vast stores of information in ways that were unimaginable only a few years ago. Others point out that this simply means that the big companies can control more people's access to information and ideas than ever before.

You spin me round (like a record)

If one invention can be credited (or blamed, if you prefer) with having created the twentieth-century teenager, it was the 45 rpm single record. Pre-war records were made of heavy vinyl, they turned very fast at 78 rpm, and you needed whole stacks of them to play any decent-length piece of music. The single was small, lightweight, and funky, and it was just long enough to hold a single hit song (plus the B side so you could hear what your pin-ups sounded like on a bad day). The single was perfect for parties, bedrooms, jukeboxes, and radio stations. Nothing marked out the cool young dudes from the saddo parents more than the great 45 v 78 rpm divide.

The age gap between parents and their offspring, especially those in their teenage years, was probably the biggest social difference between the second half of the century and almost every century that had preceded it. Pop music, more than anything else, was the thing that really created a global youth culture. The earliest pop music had a clean wholesome image, but in the 1960s pop – especially rock – developed its distinctive message of rebellion and defiance of the older generation and its values. The biggest bands, like the Beatles or the Rolling Stones, became enormously popular global phenomena – well, popular with young people anyway – and the more successful they were, the more outrageous their music, their image, and their lifestyles became. The 1970s took the rebellion still further with glam rock, heavy metal, and, if they didn't seem outrageous enough, punk.

By the 1990s, as the 1960s and 1970s generation found they had teenage children of their own, the musical age divide became less marked. The different generations listened to different bands but they were all part of the same pop culture. Middle-aged people even carried on wearing the same sort of fashions they had worn in their rebellious youth and in Britain pop and rock stars like Paul McCartney and Mick Jagger were knighted by the queen. Youth culture had been absorbed into the mainstream.

Planes, trains, and automobiles

The railways had allowed people to travel much greater distances than they had ever done before, and thanks to Henry Ford cars were much more affordable by the middle of the century than ever before. But transport was completely revolutionised in the post-war years in ways that even Ford hadn't anticipated.

Reach for the sky

'Hi. I'm Trudy. Fly me.' Pan Am airlines used that sort of advertising line in its sixties and seventies heyday. The idea, though, was that most people who saw the advert could never dream of flying Trudy or any of her equally pretty and inviting colleagues: Flying was for the rich businessman with an expense account – not for nothing were the beautiful people known as the Jet Set. Flying was exotic and exciting and definitely not for the hoi polloi. But that situation began to change in the seventies, as various airline entrepreneurs, led by Freddie Laker's 'Skytrain', looked at ways of opening up the sky to the people. By the 1980s people of even relatively modest backgrounds were flying off for foreign holidays and thinking nothing of it.

For hash get cash

A separate youth culture developed first in the States, mainly because young Americans were flush with cash so they could afford their records and clothes (and drugs): The sixties tended to swing much less in poorer parts of the world. But in the West, the meanie capitalist manufacturers and retailers of jukeboxes, convertible cars, hi-fi equipment, televisions, guitars, drum kits, amplifiers and recording equipment, posters, backpacking trips to India, leather jackets, paisley pattern cloth, hair ribbons, and small round spectacles all made a very tidy profit out of the anti-capitalist drop-out generation, thank you very much. And so did the drugs barons, man.

In theory, the phenomenal growth in air travel should have broadened travellers' minds and helped the mutual appreciation of different cultures. In practice, flying merely fuelled a tourist industry which kept visitors away from reality and gave them a carefully-crafted image instead. The only natives that most tourists met were the hotel receptionist and a group of folk dancers.

Engine trouble

For a long time the train seemed to be the great loser in the transport revolution. Diesel was replacing dirty old steam in most countries by the sixties, and trains were certainly useful; They just seemed rather *dull*. Trains were what you took to work each day; holidays increasingly meant packing up the car or heading for the airport. Not until the eighties, when electric trains such as the Japanese Bullet Train or the French TGV began to reach seriously fast speeds, did trains suddenly become sexy again. And when fears about global warming made flying something you had to do in private, between consenting adults, trains became the green way to get around.

You need wheels

Late twentieth-century cars developed in ways the pioneers of motoring could never have imagined. Driving became a way of life for millions of people around the world, and Sunday morning worship often took the form of kneeling before the family car and washing it. Cars even seemed to develop national characteristics:

- **Citroën (France):** Sleek, smooth, and streamlined, looked as if it might whisper 'you 'ave ze most beautiful eyes'.
- **Rolls Royce (Britain):** Grand and posh. And broke by the 1970s.
- **Chevrolet (USA):** Enormously long and flashy, built for driving down the freeway with the cover down, raising one's arms and whooping. Basically, 'I'm rich. I'm cool. Get outta my way.'
- **Volkswagen Beetle (West Germany):** A Nazi design that found a much more peaceful – and effective – way to take over the world.

> ✔ **Volvo (Sweden):** Square and sensible. And rather boring.
>
> ✔ **Mitsubishi, Toyota, Datsun, and so on (Japan):** Small, perfectly formed, steadily overtaking everyone on the outside.

You could argue that the biggest changes in motoring in the late twentieth century weren't so much in the cars as in everything else that cars need. Petrol stations stopped being places where you could loftily tell an attendant to 'Fill her up!' and became petrol self-service supermarkets. Motorways became enormous, with multiple lanes and huge, fiendishly complicated junctions. Road signage began to be standardised across countries so motorists could know exactly which rule they were ignoring. Motels were joined by 'drive-in' cinemas and 'drive-thru' fast food outlets. If you couldn't do it from a car, it wasn't worth doing.

Computers take over

The world's first programmable computer was enormous. Codenamed 'Colossus', it was built by British codebreakers in the Second World War to crack German codes. Films and TV programmes showed computers filling whole rooms, and the people who knew how to use them were always incredibly brainy. That image changed in the 1970s when IBM developed the *personal computer* – a piece of hardware that could sit on a desk. By the 1980s computers were moving out of the office accounts department and into the home. But the PC was still essentially a combination of a very clever calculator for doing hard sums and a word processor. The computer revolution occurred when Tim Berners-Lee launched the World Wide Web. Suddenly the world found it had a mind-bogglingly big superhighway running past its window (or, usually, its Windows) just waiting to be filled with information. On anything.

The full implications of the computer revolution took time to sink in. The Internet wasn't just an enormous public library: It became an information exchange, connecting people across whole continents. E-mail, which had begun as a way for geeks to exchange bad jokes, became the standard means of instant global communication. Suddenly everything from shopping at the supermarket to running the nation's defence forces could be done from a computer screen.

Information is power

Any politician or general knows that information is the most important weapon, and the computer revolution had created information banks beyond previous imagining.

The IT revolution is still going on, and the speed of change can leave us a bit breathless. You'll have your own thoughts and experiences, but from a historian's point of view, IT raises some very familiar issues about the way powerful people have always sought to control the less powerful. Where governments exercised control using secret policemen and prison camps; now technocrats with computer files wield power. The technology has changed massively: The motives and the dangers haven't changed one bit. Consider the following:

- ✔ **China cracks down:** When the Chinese government confronted pro-democracy campaigners in Tianenmen Square in 1989 (see Chapter 16), it tried to cut off the Chinese people from any information about what was happening by the usual means of censoring the press and blocking foreign TV and radio signals. But Beijing couldn't block satellite TV, and it couldn't stop fax machines working, so people in the outside world simply faxed outside news reports of what had happened to contacts inside China. By the turn of the century, though, China was an enormous emerging market which the big IT companies needed to do business with. The price? Internet giant Google had to agree to censor its Chinese version to omit any mention of the events of 1989.

- ✔ **ID data:** ID storage systems became so sophisticated that enormous amounts of personal information could be stored on a single microchip or on the magnetic strip on an ID card. But who held this information? Governments passed laws protecting data and privacy but microchips and data disks are physical objects and can be lost or stolen just like anything else. News reports all over the world began to carry stories of huge files of personal data being lost because some official had had a laptop stolen and computer-literate criminal gangs discovered just how easy it is to steal someone's identity – and their money – just by sitting down at a computer terminal.

Live long and prosper

Medical science made huge advances in the second half of the century (it did in the first half too, remember). The United Nations set up the World Health Organisation to co-ordinate efforts to combat some of the world's biggest killers and it has had some huge successes against diseases like smallpox and tuberculosis. The WHO sponsors vital research which has helped limit the effects of AIDS and made huge inroads into the treatment of cancer.

The result of medical advances? On the whole people are living much longer than they used to. In the past, people in their forties were regarded as old and sixty was a great age. Not any more. In the developed world, people who stay reasonably fit and healthy (not, of course, an option for many people in the developing world) can expect to be around to burden their great-grand-children. Medicine has also helped cut the infant mortality rate. More people living longer + more babies surviving infancy = one massive population explosion.

Ok gr8 cu l8er

Translation for older readers: 'OK, great. See you later.' Mobile phones began as the ultimate executive toy, a way of showing the world how very important you were and that you had to be contactable at every hour of the day or the world would stop turning. And even then, the important message usually consisted of the words 'I'm on the train!' shouted so loudly that the phone wasn't necessary in the first place.

What turned the mobile phone into the world's must-have was teenagers discovering the joys of texting. A whole new language was born, which left the older generation like, I mean, totally left out? LOL :) But the mobile phone also developed other uses: It could be a camera, a video camera, a small TV, or a computer – in fact, it had become a general communications device. A way of keeping tabs on people.

History has plenty of examples of population explosions and they always mean big changes. More mouths means more pressure on food and resources: The nineteenth century had to revolutionise agriculture and industry. Bigger populations often produce firm, hard-handed governments – Russia and China in the twentieth century have both found that out. And a population explosion has nearly always meant many more people at the bottom of the pile than at the top. We'll see in due course if the twenty-first century follows the same pattern, but every other century in history has.

The Times They Are A-Changin'

Not only technology changed lives in the late twentieth century. Attitudes and ideas changed enormously. Assumptions that had held good for centuries were suddenly questioned and thrown out with the rubbish.

Imagine there's no heaven

The big new ideas of the first half of the century, fascism and communism (you need Chapters 4 and 5 here), rejected belief in God, though some fascist regimes shared their anti-communism with the Catholic Church. Some historians argue that this rejection of religion was one of their greatest weaknesses: Certainly the churches were an important force in resisting Nazi rule and bringing communism down. The consumer world of the second half of the century didn't try to destroy or control religion: It just ignored it. In Europe, shops opened on Sundays, people ignored Church teaching on abortion and contraception, and fewer people bothered going to church on Sunday morning.

Suffer, little children

Nothing damaged the authority of the Church more than the revelation that priests in many different countries had long been engaged in the systematic abuse of children, and that the Church authorities had covered it up. This discovery wasn't just a case of a few rogue priests: The compensation bill faced by the Catholic Church in Boston, Massachusetts was so huge it threatened to bankrupt the diocese. Staunchly Catholic countries such as Ireland and Italy were shaken by the revelations that began to emerge in the 1990s. Hypocrisy is the kiss of death for any religion, and this was one of the worst scandals imaginable. Churches introduced changes and worked more closely with the authorities to try to stamp out child abuse in their schools and parishes, but for many around the world the damage had been done.

A very different picture developed in the United States, where evangelical religion became a significant force, especially in the Midwest. Billy Graham had led the way in the 1950s and 1960s, and by the 1970s and 1980s many evangelists had turned to television as a way of taking their message – and their appeal for funds – to a wide audience. No politician could ignore the 'Bible Belt' and Jerry Falwell's *Moral Majority* movement had a big influence on government under Ronald Reagan in the 1980s. Moral issues such as abortion and gay rights proved much more dangerous for American governments than for Europeans.

Outside the developed world, the Church has played two very different roles:

- ✔ **Leading the people in their fight for justice:** In South America and in Africa the Christian churches have been at the forefront of movements to spread education and healthcare and to oppose governments that rule by tyranny and force.

- ✔ **Helping dictators to oppress their countries:** Churches have also helped right-wing dictators in Spain, Portugal, and Vietnam on the grounds that they were standing up against the spread of communism.

Allah is Great

During the 1970s Islam seemed to be going the same way as Christianity: Sidelined by Western commercialism. That situation changed with the Islamic Revolution in Iran. Like all big revolutions, the Iranian revolution had an impact far beyond its own country: Muslims all over the world, including the growing Muslim communities in the West, took inspiration from Iran not to undermine Western society (though that was what the Ayatollah Khomeini hoped to do) but to stand up for Islam with a degree of pride and not to try to hide it away, as they saw more and more Christians doing with their faith. The result was that by the 1980s and 1990s, Islam was becoming a major force in world politics. And since the United States was the country the Ayatollah had identified as the 'Great Satan', this clash of religions and culture was always likely to see fireworks – as the first few years of the twenty-first century amply proved.

A woman's place

Look at adverts or photos from any time up to the sixties and seventies and you'll find it hard to believe how they portrayed women. The stereotypes were:

- **Housewife:** Servant. 'Here's your supper, dear.' Also willing dupe for washing machine salesmen.
- **Secretary:** Airhead.
- **Nurse:** Dolly bird; unless a senior nurse, in which case: Dragon.

These stereotypes didn't just exist in adland. Women earned less than men in the same jobs, they could be – and were – excluded from the upper ranks of professions and even from whole areas of work. In Britain women's railway tickets were stamped 'W' for 'woman'. Even more seriously, male-dominated legal systems found it hard to take violent crimes against women, especially rape, seriously: In fact, women who brought legal cases could often end up being accused of having brought the whole thing on themselves.

Burn those bras

The liberation of women – which is still far from complete – began in America in the late 1960s as a radical feminist movement. Angry protestors disrupted beauty pageants and defaced posters portraying women simply as sex objects. They symbolically burned their bras as representations of restrictive male control, while bemused men looked on wondering what all the fuss was about. This radical phase was vital to break down centuries of entrenched attitudes – and this was the situation in the developed West; attitudes were going to be even harder to change in some other parts of the world.

Pad those shoulders

By the 1980s women had moved away from the radical 'Women's Lib' phase and into the boardroom. Not yet into the top jobs – many companies operated a 'glass ceiling', ostensibly being entirely open to women but in fact restricting them to the lower levels – but they were on the inside. 'Power dressing' was fashionable, using big shoulder pads to make women look, well, male.

Can we get a better icon?

Women looking for powerful role models in the 1980s and 1990s could look up to singers such as Madonna or Cher (none of those male-dominated surnames conferred by a patriarchal society, you see) but the political world presented more of a problem. The most obvious figures were powerful women leaders like India's Indira Gandhi or Britain's Margaret Thatcher, but they weren't necessarily icons you'd want. Mrs Gandhi led a brutally repressive regime; some people say the same for Mrs Thatcher, but whatever you think of her politics, she hated feminists. Hillary Clinton was a good role model – tough, intelligent, and a wronged wife to boot. But everyone's favourite by a long way was Britain's Princess Diana, the beautiful, caring, jet-setting, doomed star of every magazine cover in the world. The women who launched the feminist movement in the sixties could never have dreamed that by the end of the century the woman most other women looked up to would be a fairytale princess in a tiara.

Let's talk about sex

Sex didn't actually begin in the 1960s, though you could be forgiven for thinking so. What did begin then was an openness about the subject and an acceptance that it was what people do. What didn't get going in the sixties was an acceptance of the consequences.

The starting point for the sexual revolution in the late twentieth century was probably the publication in 1948 and 1953 of two reports on American sexual behaviour by Professor Alfred Kinsey. Kinsey conducted detailed confidential surveys about sexual behaviour and came up with findings that shocked fifties America. Kinsey reported that various sexual practices that had always been thought of as bizarre, immoral, and the sign of a degenerate and perverted mind, were actually entirely common and mainstream. Or to put the matter simply: Most ordinary, normal, and respectable people have sex in many different ways and enjoy it.

Let it all hang out

What happened in the sixties was that free sex became part of the big youth revolution against the attitudes of their parents. Having sex and not feeling embarrassed or ashamed of it went with not being ashamed of listening to rock music or of not wearing a tie. The next stage was to get the rest of society to accept sex as part of ordinary life. The 'Permissive society' was the term used, which sounded rather grand but actually just meant a huge growth in strip clubs and porn magazines. Sales of old raincoats went up as well.

Gay people had a much harder fight for acceptance. Homosexual acts were illegal in many countries until the 1960s, and in some countries were (and are) punishable by death. In 1978 a gay San Francisco city official called Harvey Milk was shot and his killer received only a five-year sentence. Gay opinion in San Francisco was outraged and the case helped wake America up to the prejudice that existed against gay people. By the 1990s attitudes had become much more tolerant, but both the military and the Christian churches still found accepting equal rights for gay people impossible.

Maybe babies?

The sexual revolution couldn't have happened without the contraceptive pill. The Catholic Church condemned this pill and forbade Catholics to use it, though judging from the way Catholic family size began to decrease, even in Italy, not many of them listened. 'The Pill' seemed to give women control of their own bodies and to allow them to have sex as and when they chose without having to face the consequences. A different view is that the Pill allowed men to be even more irresponsible than usual.

Alongside the Pill, some Western countries began to legalise abortion in the sixties and seventies. This legislation was mainly a way of saving women from the horrors of 'backstreet' abortion, but by the 1980s and 1990s opponents of abortion were complaining that women were using abortion effectively as a form of birth control. This issue is a standard topic for college debating societies and the bitter controversy surrounding it shows no sign of dying down.

Oh, I hadn't thought of that

The sexual revolution may have been fun, but it had two unintended consequences:

- ✔ Many women complained that sex, and particularly pornography, turned them into toys for men and could lead to sexual violence
- ✔ AIDS

AIDS (Acquired Immune Deficiency Syndrome) began to appear among the gay community in America and had the medical world baffled. Much to the delight of the religious right, AIDS was nicknamed the 'gay plague'. But AIDS quickly moved into the rest of society, especially through infected blood. Still principally spread by unprotected sex, hetero- or homosexual, AIDS has reached epidemic proportions in Africa. Medical science has made enormous progress in stemming the impact of AIDS, but, as always, most of the money has gone on the strains most prevalent in the West; Africa gets much less money spent on its version of the disease.

North and South

In 1977 the former West German Chancellor Willi Brandt sat down to chair a special UN commission on the relationship between the developed world, which he called, broadly, 'the North', and what was then called the Third

World, or 'South'. The commission's reports pointed out that the different parts of the world depend on each other and that the wealthy North had to help the South not just when disasters happened but regularly. Brandt called on the developed world to devote part of its annual GDP to overseas aid. Some countries did so; a lot said they would but didn't.

The Brandt report was significant because it changed the way commentators and world leaders *thought*. Before Brandt, most people in the West thought of the developing world as a sort of irritant, always having disasters and asking for money. The Brandt report brought home to people in the West the idea that North and South are interdependent: What happens in the South affects what happens in the North and vice versa.

Destroying the planet

Environmentalists in the 1970s and 1980s concentrated on criticising pollution and the effect it was having on the environment, but by the 1990s the stakes were clearly a lot higher than polluted rivers. The world was using up energy and emitting carbon into the atmosphere at such a rate that it was eroding the earth's protective ozone layer, the only thing between us and the full force of the sun. The result was a change in the world's very climate and a growth in global warming. Some people tried to say that the idea of global warming was over-hyped but scientists are now in overwhelming agreement that this challenge is real and urgent.

Identifying the problem is a lot easier than solving it. People in the West are now much more aware of their 'carbon footprint' – the amount of carbon they produce every day through ordinary activities like driving to work or using dishwashers. Governments put out messages appealing to people to change their lifestyles and reduce their carbon emissions, but without much effect. Westerners show no sign of flying less frequently, even though the carbon impact of air travel is well-publicised and widely known.

Part of the reason for the lack of progress in the developed world is that people there are aware of the enormous impact on the environment of the emerging countries in other parts of the world, especially India and China. As these new economic giants start to get used to their new status, their peoples want to enjoy some of the perks of life that people in the West have enjoyed for so long, and that includes gas-guzzling cars, air travel, and homes full of carbon-emitting gadgets. Telling people in these countries that they have to hold back from enjoying their new-found prosperity was never going to be easy: Too often their response is 'Why should we?'

Governments signed up to promises at special 'Earth Summits' at Rio in 1992 and Kyoto in 1999 to try to reduce carbon emissions, but the United States held back and so did China, which was rapidly overtaking America as the world's biggest emitter of carbon. The 2007 summit at Bali nearly broke down until the United States finally gave way and agreed to sign up to targets for cutting carbon emissions. As so often in history, politicians take time to catch up with the real world and its problems.

To the New Millennium

Back in the tenth century, Europeans were fearful that the first Millennium would mark the end of the world. As the 1990s drew to a close the world awaited the Year 2000 with a similar mixture of excitement and trepidation: Scientists were concerned that the world's computers would succumb to the dreaded 'Millennium Bug' and stop functioning because they couldn't tell the difference between 1900 and 2000. Thankfully, that didn't happen. Celebrations were held around the world to mark the end of one century and one Millenium and the start of another, but when it actually arrived the new Millennium felt much like the previous one. People soon got used to writing dates beginning with '20' though no one could quite decide what name to give the first decade of the new century. The clothes and the cars of the first years of the new century looked much like those of the last years of the old one. Life, like history, carried on.

Part V
The Part of Tens

'Are we there yet?...
Are we there yet?...
Are we there yet?...'

In this part . . .

Time for some lists! Here you get the chance to lap up
my own personal preferences and prejudices and try
them out on your friends. You'll find my nominations for
the century's greatest iconic moments, most illustrious
international organisations, most important films, and
absolutely worst ideas. Read and enjoy.

Two health warnings, though. First, remember these are
just my ideas. You may disagree with every word I write
here: That's what freedom of opinion means. Just bear in
mind that I'm not claiming any special insight: The most
I'll say is that I think each example I've included has a
good case and is at the very least well worth considering.

Second, some of these examples will seem a bit 'heavier'
than others. Totalitarian dictatorship might seem a rather
weightier burden to carry than other people's chewing gum
habits. Not so fast. The little things in history, as in life,
can have the greatest impact. No one ended up in therapy
because they were worried about the future of constitutional government, but plenty of people get driven nuts by
the noise from next door or the latest rise in interest rates.
Politicians know this; the best historians know it too.

You're in the hands of a historian who knows.

Chapter 21

Ten Iconic Images

*M*any images can stay in the mind, but these iconic images have become a shorthand for the twentieth century itself.

The Titanic Goes Down, 1912

The fate of the British ship *Titanic* never loses its grip on our collective imagination. The ghastly sight of an enormous ship, which had seemed so powerful, so reassuringly *safe*, upending and disappearing into the sea leaving people alone in the vast ocean is enough to chill anyone's blood. The *Titanic* was a twentieth-century ship of fools, a floating microcosm of the class-bound society of the Western world, with its state ballroom and luxury cabins for the rich and cramped cabins for the plebs. Its owners arrogantly declared it 'unsinkable' and insisted that it race across the Atlantic brushing aside all warnings. The ancient Greeks used to say that those the gods wish to destroy, they first make mad. They'd have understood the *Titanic* story perfectly.

Find out more about the world of the *Titanic* in Chapter 1.

Your Country Needs YOU!

Mrs Asquith, wife of Britain's prime minister in the First World War, once said that Lord Kitchener might not have been a great man but he made a great poster. The famous British World War I recruiting poster issued in 1914 has been reprinted and imitated in different versions around the world ever since. Kitchener's staring eyes and pointing finger are a triumph of economy and for their time the poster was an astonishingly modern concept. But nowadays we also look at the poster with sombre hindsight. The young men who responded to its call were the same recruits who were sent over the top in the Battle of the Somme to be mown down by German machine guns. Kitchener didn't live to see this tragic outcome of his recruiting drive: He drowned in June 1916 when the ship he was on hit a German mine. He died; his poster lived on.

Find out more about the First World War in Chapter 3.

The Empire State Building

Standing 1,250 feet and 102 storeys high, soaring into the heavens like a cathedral spire, the Empire State Building symbolised America: Big, beautiful, and anyone could climb to the top. Built in record time, the ESB opened in 1931 to general amazement: *This* was what modern America could do! But even as the ESB went up, the Depression set in and many men who'd built it ended up living in shanty towns called Hoovervilles. In 1945 a US Army Air Corps plane crashed into the ESB, killing 14 people. Ironic, then, that when the ESB gave up its number 1 spot as the world's tallest building it was to the twin towers of the World Trade Center. But that's another story.

Find out more about America in the Depression in Chapter 8.

Auschwitz

Auschwitz's sinister railway arch stands in our consciousness like the mouth of hell. That railway track linked Auschwitz to every corner of Europe: Trains came from within Poland and from Italy, France, Germany, Norway, Czechoslovakia, Hungary, the Greek islands and the Channel islands: A continental railway network with a death camp at its heart.

All ages like to pride themselves on how far they've advanced from the barbarism of the past. At Auschwitz the Nazis recreated slavery on a biblical scale, complementing it with industrial-age mass murder. Auschwitz stands as an icon of the appalling things humans once did, and can easily do again.

Find out more about the Holocaust in Chapter 9.

The Mushroom Cloud

Before the *Enola Gay* dropped its atomic bomb on Hiroshima on 6 August 1945 no one had any idea of what a nuclear explosion might look like. The smoke rose to an enormous height and formed a sort of mushroom shape: It quickly became a symbol of the horrors of nuclear war. The hydrogen bombs and nuclear warheads developed in the 1950s were thousands of times more powerful than the Hiroshima bomb. Since then the world has lived in the shadow of the mushroom cloud. We're still under it now.

Find out more about the bomb and the Cold War in Chapters 9 and 10.

Marilyn Monroe

Born Norma Jean Mortensen, though she took her mother's name, Baker, she grew up fatherless, in and out of foster homes and orphanages. She married at sixteen, divorced, dyed her hair, and entered movies as Marilyn Monroe. But why did she touch the world so deeply? Perhaps it was her girl-next-door innocence alongside her anything-but-innocent sexuality. That image of her in *The Seven-Year Itch*, trying oh-so-demurely to hold her skirt down in the delicious updraft from an air vent, has it all. The press loved her looks, her teasing ('It's not true I had nothing on,' she said of one notorious photoshoot, 'I had the radio on'), her marriages (baseball player Joe DiMaggio and playwright Arthur Miller, of all people), and her lonely death, from an overdose (intentional? We still don't know), aged 36. A true icon.

Find out more about post-war America in Chapter 15.

The Vietnam Girl

You know her photo. Kim Phuc was the young Vietnamese girl, naked and screaming after a US napalm attack, in Nick Ut's 1972 Pulitzer prize-winning photo. That photo is the defining image of the Vietnam War. The sight of children suffering is shocking in any war, but she was in a *South* Vietnamese village: The Americans were on their side. President Nixon angrily tried to denounce the photo as a fake, but its authenticity was confirmed by a British news camera team, who filmed the whole thing. Kim went on to become an international peace activist. The burns on her body eventually healed; the scars inside never did.

You can find out more about the Vietnam War in Chapters 14 and 15.

Che Guevara

Che Guevara is probably more famous as a poster than for anything he did in real life. Alberto Korda's photograph of Che, rugged and unshaven in his revolutionary beret, is still showing on a student bedroom wall near you.

He was more tubby and less good looking than his photo, but so what? *That's how a true revolutionary should look.* Che helped Castro seize power in Cuba and sat in Castro's cabinet for a time before setting off to lead the revolution in Bolivia. The Bolivians shot him and paraded his bullet-riddled body for the photographers. That image isn't a pretty sight: Stick to the poster.

Find out more about Che Guevara in Chapter 13.

Neil Armstrong Walks on the Moon

Oh, yes he did.

When the Russians got the first satellites, the dog, man and woman into space (not all in the same ship, you understand) the Americans were badly shaken. John F. Kennedy reassured them that the US would send a man to the moon and back before the end of the decade. The Apollo programme built up through the decade until finally, on 20 July 1969, Neil Armstrong stepped onto the moon. The communication technology failed on the big day, and the lines he'd carefully prepared for the occasion were transmitted all wrong: 'That's one small step for (oops – missed out 'a') man; one giant leap for mankind.' The images of Armstrong and Buzz Aldrin on the surface of the moon seemed to embody hope and optimism for the future, but pretty soon moon landings became *so* last decade. Man on the moon was that rare thing – an icon that lost its power.

Find out more about post-war America and the space race in Chapter 15.

Tianenmen Square

As communist regimes toppled across Europe in 1989 students in China thought they too would be able to establish democracy. They flocked to Tianenmen Square in Beijing and set up a camp around a statue of the 'spirit of democracy'. And then the tanks moved in. The democracy movement was crushed, but not before a remarkable moment. A young man stood in front of a line of four tanks and forced them to stop. The world's press filmed it. When they tried to get past him, he got on his bike and stopped them again. It was a wonderful symbol of an individual standing up for freedom and stopping tyranny in its tracks. You won't see pictures of this famous moment in China – the government has made sure of that – but no government can ever suppress the truth for ever. Man 1: Tanks 0.

Find out more about communist China in Chapter 16.

Chapter 22

Ten Triumphs of Technology

In This Chapter

▶ Finding the gadgets that make life a little easier . . .

▶ . . . and finding some gadgets that might worry us just a bit

*T*he twentieth century was nothing if not the century of technology. We're so used to the power of technology to take away pain or carry us huge distances that remembering that life was ever different is difficult. Everyone has their own ideas of which have been the most significant technological breakthroughs. I've avoided some of the most obvious, like cars and planes, because I suspect we all know about the impact – for good and bad – that they've had on our lives. I look at this as a historian rather than as an engineer: These are just some of the technological breakthroughs of the twentieth century that had a big impact – sometimes surprisingly big – on the way people actually lived, and even on how they thought.

The Refrigerator

Never underestimate the power of food. Empires have been built – and fallen – on the search for food: Whoever controls the food supply controls the people. In 1959 Soviet leader Nikita Khrushchev and his wife were treated to an American display of economic and technical superiority at a trade fair where they could marvel at the latest designs of fridges. The Americans knew full well that such things were virtually unobtainable in Russia. Khrushchev knew this too. Throughout history, the simple, everyday objects that people really care about have had the most profound effects.

Until the nineteenth century if you wanted to keep food cool you had to keep an expensive ice house in the garden or invest in an insulated ice box, lined with tin or zinc (not cheap). Nineteenth-century inventors toyed around with various designs of refrigeration units but they ran on toxic gases so you kept your fridge outside if you had any sense, in case of leaks. In 1929, however, a bright spark at General Motors called Thomas Midgley came up with a non-toxic chemical compound that he called Freon. It worked and in the years after the Second World War homes all over the world began to install fridges run on Freon. It even ran air conditioning. Cool.

Don't break open the bubbly yet, though. Freon is made up of a number of chlorofluorocarbons, CFCs for short, which are now busily eating away at the earth's protective ozone layer. Not so cool.

Television

You might think television is an obvious choice, like cars or aeroplanes, but you could argue (and I do) that television had a deeper impact than either of those. I don't underestimate the importance of transport, but television actually changed the way people *thought* and saw the world around them. You could even say that television took the world back to the days before the printing press, when people thought and communicated visually, rather than through the printed word. Television created a world of people who *watch*.

Part of television's impact lies in the speed with which it took hold. In the 1930s and 1940s television was a novelty toy. In the 1950s people in the West began to latch onto it, and by the 1960s it was everywhere, even on the moon. The poorest households saw a television set as a necessity, not as a luxury. Television allowed people around the world to share in the same experiences, watching major events from the cosiness of their own homes: The Vietnam War, the Munich Olympics crisis, the fall of the Berlin Wall, Tianenmen Square, and Nelson Mandela walking to freedom were all TV events. Politicians dropped the ancient art of oratory in favour of the TV soundbite, and terrorists cannily learned to exploit the potential of TV news schedules: The 9/11 attacks, for example, were carefully planned so that the TV cameras were covering the first plane crash when the second one attacked. The people who control TV have become figures of global power, their every move watched nervously by the leaders of even the most powerful countries.

Nothing, not even the Internet, has done more to create a global universal culture than television.

Cats' Eyes

Some of the most important breakthroughs with enormous impacts on everyone's lives are the ones we hardly notice. I'd list street lighting here (think of the lives it must have saved around the world) except that it was a nineteenth century breakthrough; the twentieth century just substituted electricity for gas. But a small triumph in the same area of preventing death on the world's roads came one foggy night in 1933 when a Yorkshireman called Percy Shaw was saved from driving over a steep precipice by the reflection of a cat's eyes in his headlights. 'By gum,' thinks Percy, 'now that's an idea.' Being an inventive chap, he designed a reflective stud that lies flat in the road and shines in the headlights of an on-coming car. Simple, effective, and cheap. And almost certainly to be seen on a motorway near you.

James Callaghan decided that introducing cats' eyes was his most important achievement as British prime minister. Different versions are in use in different countries, and the new 'smart' cats' eyes can trigger red lights to stop oncoming vehicles. A small but genuine technological triumph which has probably kept *you* safe more times than you can count.

The Helicopter

Everyone knows the story of how the Wright brothers made the first powered heavier-than-air flight at Kitty Hawk, North Carolina in 1903 (if you don't, it's in Chapter 2). That was a massive technological breakthrough and no mistake, but I've included the helicopter rather than the plane here for rather different reasons. Planes can duck and weave, drop bombs or food parcels, and blast each other out of the sky, but they are still essentially a way of getting from A to B. Helicopters, because they can hover, move forwards or backwards, and don't need runways, can interact with the ground much more effectively than planes can. Helicopters can winch people off sinking ships or inaccessible mountainsides, airlift people from rooftops, carry troops straight into battle and whisk the wounded straight out again, search for criminals or monitor the traffic, and ferry blood supplies or human hearts, or even politicians canvassing for votes. Okay, that last one might not be such a plus.

Frenchman Paul Cornu made the first successful helicopter flight in 1907. Helicopter pioneers needed a powerful motor to lift the thing and a lightweight metal to make it out of – they hit on aluminium. Russian helicopter pioneer Igor Sikorski solved the problem of *torque*, which happens when the rotor forces the fuselage to rotate in the opposite direction to the engine, by introducing a tail rotor to counteract the torque and keep the copter flying straight. The helicopter's versatility, and the way it has been integrated into the lives even of people who *aren't* travelling, wins it a place in this list.

The Ballpoint Pen

If life were fair the credit for ballpoints would go to John Loud, who invented one back in 1888, but it didn't work very well and was never exploited commercially. Instead the laurels go to Laszlo Biro, a Hungarian journalist fed up with having to fill his fountain pen every five minutes only to see it tear up the newsprint paper he was using. He worked with a small ballbearing to control the flow of ink to the pen tip and got his breakthrough when the Royal Air Force commissioned his company to supply pens to pilots who found their fountain pens leaked at high altitudes. Biro patented and marketed his pens in Argentina through his company, Eversharp, where they attracted the notice of a sharp Chicago businessman called Milton Reynolds. Reynolds pinched the idea and marketed ballpoints in the US, where Biro didn't have a patent. The 1950s saw a veritable ballpoint war as more companies got in on the act and tried to sell cheap, messy ballpoints to the public, who soon got fed up with ballpoints leaking in their pockets and looked out their trusty fountain pens and bottles of ink.

Two companies rescued the ballpoint's reputation. In 1957 Biro sold Eversharp to the Parker pen company, whose reputation for high-quality pens helped get ballpoints accepted socially. At the other end of the market, the Frenchman Marcel Bich had introduced a cheap throw-away ballpoint in 1952. He chopped the *h* off his name and the Bic pen was born.

The world of pen nibs and inkwells seems like ancient history now, but it's a reminder of how expensive and how much *work* writing used to be. Biro's invention helped spread literacy to everyone, so it's appropriate that his name should have entered the English language and that his invention features here.

Satellites

Who'd have thought, when the Russians launched *Sputnik* in 1957, that satellite technology and humankind's conquest of space would end up with a little box in your car telling you to turn right at the next junction? *Sputnik* was a propaganda triumph for the Russians and certainly put the Americans' noses out of joint until they could start launching their own satellites. But it took a while before anyone could actually work out what these satellites could do. *Telstar*, a US–British–French collaboration (and that's remarkable enough on its own!) was the first communications satellite, launched in 1962 and capable of transmitting television pictures. By the 1970s NASA (the National Aeronautical and Space Agency) was launching *Landsats* that could transmit detailed pictures of the earth, which could then be used for anything from weather forecasting to crop management. Satellite photography has allowed us to map power usage around the world and more recently to track the progress of climate change.

The first satellites went up at the height of the Cold War and it didn't take long to exploit their potential for espionage. No need for agents furtively peeping from behind newspapers when the 'spy in the sky' can look over an enemy agent's shoulder and read the time from his watch. Now any of us can look up an address on the Web and see a detailed satellite photo of it. Ronald Reagan's 'Star Wars' proposal for a satellite system to destroy incoming nuclear missiles raised the stakes higher than the Russians could afford to go and played a crucial part in bringing the Cold War to an end.

The way in which satellite technology has come down from the stratosphere into our ordinary lives is why I place satellites on this list.

Heart Transplants

As the twentieth-century world put age-old scourges like smallpox and plague behind it, other diseases like cancer and heart disease took their place. I've included heart transplants here because they're a good example of the application of technology to medicine. People have long been used to the idea of seeking a remedy for illness in the natural world, but the idea of transplanting a human heart from one body to another, as you might replace an old car engine, still seems almost miraculous: It's the nearest we come to bringing people back to life.

The first successful human heart transplant was carried out in South Africa in 1967 by Dr Christiaan Barnard, and it provoked enormous excitement around the world. Unfortunately, these early transplants weren't very stable: Barnard's patient only lived another 18 days. Too often the recipient's body tissue simply rejected the new heart. Scientists worked on immunosuppressant drugs to overcome the body's resistance, and from the 1980s recipients began to live for significantly longer; the number of heart transplants began to climb again. Even children could receive heart transplants and in 1984 a baby girl in the US gained a few days' life with a baboon's heart. To say that we take heart transplants for granted is probably an overstatement, but the idea that they are possible is now well established in our minds. For that achievement alone heart transplantation deserves its place here.

Personal Computers

We depend on computers so much now that we can scarcely believe how much *effort* we used to put in to tasks that now take a click of the mouse. Modern computing can be traced back to the nineteenth century and its principles to the British wartime codebreaker, Alan Turing, but the big breakthrough came on 12 August 1981 when IBM released its new 'PC' – Personal Computer. The PC had a keyboard, a monitor, two floppy disk drives, and an operating system called MS-DOS designed by a company called Microsoft headed by one Bill Gates. A new world was born.

Time magazine made the IBM PC its 'Man of the Year' in 1981 as the full, mind-boggling implications of computing began to take shape. In fact IBM didn't particularly benefit from the breakthrough (anyone could design the hardware), but Microsoft did. Two years later a company called Apple bit back with its Macintosh computer, which still has its fans, but Microsoft, which in

1983 launched its Windows operating system (it nearly got called 'Interface Manager' – yawn), was unstoppable and remains unstoppable as I write this. On a Windows-powered PC.

Mobile Phones

No one objected to police walkie-talkies (okay, criminals weren't too pleased) yet somehow for a long time people resisted the idea of mobile telephones. Their acceptance wasn't helped by the first-generation models, launched in the early 1980s, which were huge and mainly designed for use in cars by loud-mouthed people with too much money. By the 1990s mobiles were much smaller and easier to use, so ordinary people bought them. People still worry about the effects of mobile phone masts in public streets and whether the phones themselves will frazzle our brains. I guess time will tell.

The impact that mobiles had took everyone by surprise. No one expected SMS text messaging to become so popular, nor that mobiles would be able to take pictures, show films, and operate as portable computers. And who could have predicted just how mad you could drive people by choosing an annoying ring tone? Above all, no one realised that mobile phone records would enable phone companies – and the authorities – to keep track of our movements. Still, you can always tell them – and everyone else – exactly where you are by shouting loudly into your mobile 'I'm on a train!' A qualified technological triumph, then.

Barcodes

Had barcodes remained a way of putting prices on goods in supermarkets, I wouldn't have included them here. But they've grown beyond their origins into one of the most important ways by which They keep tabs on Us.

A barcode is essentially a speedy identification system which can tap into a database. For example, supermarket barcodes identify an item and the database gives the price. But what if *you* are the item and the database carries your personal information? A passport barcode, for example, can give a border control guard instant access to huge amounts of information about any passenger just arrived off the plane. Even supermarkets are getting into the control game, using barcodes on their products and their own loyalty cards to build up profiles of their regular customers. Alongside the metallic strips and microchips on the plastic cards we all depend on, the barcode has done more than anything else to give the State, big business, and anyone else with access to the right technology the information they need to keep an eye on all of us.

Chapter 23

Ten Films That Made an Impact

. . . .

In This Chapter
▶ Films with a message, whether you agree with it or not
▶ Films that defined an era

. . . .

*N*o, this isn't my list of the top ten films ever made, nor are they necessarily my favourites, but these are films that, for some very different reasons, made an impact in the twentieth century. You might miss a few titles – *Citizen Kane* for example, which I find impresses film directors more than it does the rest of us, or *A Clockwork Orange*, whose main impact lay in getting banned. I've also missed out two important film brands, Disney and Bollywood. Nothing against either, but their impact has been more as a whole genre rather than through any individual film. Of course, you may disagree. Inevitably, the list is dominated by American films, but I've included a few reminders that the rest of the world can make influential movies too.

Birth of a Nation (D. W. Griffith, 1915)

Griffith's racist US Civil War epic is worth seeing as a document of its time, though it doesn't make comfortable viewing. Its central message soon becomes pretty clear: North and South (that's the white north and south, of course) could've been united in eternal friendship had it not been for those villainous blacks. And villainous the black characters certainly are in this film, plotting, scheming, and stealing women. In terms of history the film's bunkum, but it's an undoubted technical feat: Griffith was particularly skilful at recreating the panoramic battle scenes. *Birth of a Nation*'s long, so settle down with a sandwich, watch it through, and admire the camerawork and direction. And then go and have a bath.

Battleship Potemkin (Sergei Eisenstein, 1925)

Another silent epic, though from a very different ideological stable from Griffith (see preceding section). *Battleship Potemkin* tells the story of a naval mutiny during the 1905 revolution in Russia, though in more of a documentary style than the melodramatic style the Americans favoured. This film regularly features in directors' and critics' lists of the ten greatest films ever made, for its powerful close-ups of faces and the famous, much-copied scene where the Cossacks move in to shoot down the crowds on the Odessa steps. It was the first Soviet film to score a hit on the world stage and probably did more to spread the Soviet message than any number of Lenin's speeches.

All Quiet on the Western Front (Lewis Milestone, 1930)

This tale of how a young German soldier in the Great War gradually loses his innocent enthusiasm is still one of the most powerful anti-war films ever made. *All Quiet on the Western Front* was based on the novel by the German writer Erich-Maria von Remarque, who drew on his own experiences in the trenches. The film caught the anti-war mood of the time and was also significant, for an American film, in presenting the story from the German point of view. As you watch it, in fact, it soon ceases to matter which side the boys are on at all.

Despite its success, however, the film got left behind when the international mood changed. The Nazis banned it – and burned the book – and as the world moved closer towards war in the 1930s fewer people had time for an anti-war message. *All Quiet on the Western Front* is a powerful and moving film, but it couldn't change the world.

Triumph of the Will (Leni Riefenstahl, 1935)

The Nazis had an unerring instinct for spectacle-as-propaganda and they built a vast complex of arenas and parade grounds outside Nuremberg where they could stage their mass party rallies. In 1934 Leni Riefenstahl, Hitler's favourite filmmaker, got permission to make a film featuring the annual Nuremberg rally: The result was *Triumph of the Will*, unashamedly Nazi but a triumph of the filmmaker's art.

The Nazis, who didn't usually have time for go-ahead, feisty women, let Leni Riefenstahl film as and where she liked, so she stretched out on the ground for those shots from below of Hitler looking masterful, where you can see up his nostrils, and had herself hauled up a flagpole to film some of the march-pasts from above. The result is overwhelmingly powerful, much more so, in fact, than if you were present at the rallies themselves, which were very long, very tedious, and you couldn't see anything like as much as you could in the film. A disturbing masterpiece, but a masterpiece nevertheless.

The Wizard of Oz (Victor Fleming, 1939)

The munchkins weren't allowed to mingle with the rest of the cast and Judy Garland was seventeen, not a little girl of eight (and you wonder that she was so screwed up?). When Princess Margaret told her that *Somewhere Over the Rainbow* still made her cry, Judy replied, 'Ma'am, that song ruined my life.' But what about the film: Witches, wizards, cowardly lions – what's that all about?

Well, *The Wizard of Oz* isn't about Kansas or even Oz: It's about the Depression and how to get out of it. When it was being filmed, America was still in the grip of economic misery: The sandstorm that blows Dorothy's house away would have reminded a lot of people of the dustbowl that had devastated the American Midwest only a few years before. It was only natural that Americans should wish for 'somewhere over the rainbow' and for a great wizard (President Roosevelt, perhaps?) to come down and solve all their problems for them. But the message of the film is that, in the end, Americans must look within themselves for the courage – yup, and the heart and the brain – to solve their own problems. Because, be it ever so humble, there's no place like home.

Seven Samurai (Akira Kurosawa, 1954)

Kurasawa specialised in Japanese historical epics, with lots of banner-wearing horsemen galloping across the screen slashing at each other with swords, like *Kill Bill* at the races. This film tells of a group of samurai warriors who risk all to protect a defenceless village against a gang of bandits. If that scenario sounds familiar, it's probably because *Seven Samurai* was the inspiration for a famous American re-make, *The Magnificent Seven*.

Americans in the 1950s were understandably nervous of Japanese exports and culture so soon after the war, and anything about the samurai code was bound to spark off very uncomfortable memories: The samurai concept of honour lay behind the brutal treatment Allied prisoners of war had suffered at Japanese hands. However, *Seven Samurai* shows this code being attached to a much more noble cause. This film is also a powerful portrayal of ordinary people's despair in the face of forces they can't control. Okay, most people around the world saw the Yul Brynner version, but the original played an important part in the healing process after the war and is well worth seeing.

Psycho (Alfred Hitchcock, 1960)

Hitchcock's masterpiece probably didn't do too much for America's motel trade, nor for shower manufacturers come to that, but it worked wonders for psychoanalysis. As the increasingly disturbing whodunnit unfolds, we realise we are dealing with a dangerously unstable boy with a decidedly unhealthy fixation on his mother, though we don't realise the full horror until right at the end of the film (I won't say any more in case you haven't seen it).

Film buffs marvel at how Hitchcock breaks all the rules, killing off his glamorous star early in the film, twirling the camera round in a spiral to focus on her eye, but *Psycho* really reflects America's growing love affair with Freud. This is a film about the strange games played out in the mind and how we love to try to unravel them. No coincidence that in the traditional gathering-in-the-library scene at the end, it's not the detective who does the talking but a psychiatrist. America has never quite got off the couch since.

Dr Strangelove (Stanley Kubrick, 1964)

Actually, that should be *Dr Strangelove or: How I Learned to Stop Worrying and Love the Bomb*. Issued only two years after the Cuban Missile Crisis, this was Kubrick's blackly satirical response to the nuclear tension of the Cold War. The plot is simple, but horrifying: A crazed American general, convinced that the Russians are somehow weakening American manhood, launches an unauthorised nuclear attack on the Soviet Union. The US president and all his advisers gather in the underground war room, but are powerless to stop it and the world (and the film) ends in a nuclear exchange between the two superpowers to the accompaniment of Vera Lynn singing the Second World War favourite *We'll Meet Again*.

The film has some wonderful performances, not least from Peter Sellers, who plays three parts: the mild-mannered US president, an English RAF officer, and the eponymous ex-Nazi Dr Strangelove himself. The comedy goes from beautifully-crafted lines like 'Gentlemen! You can't fight in here: This is the war room!' to the final image of a gung-ho redneck astride the falling atom bomb he's managed to free from its moorings.

In the face of the threat of nuclear annihilation, filmmakers could either try grim reality or they could opt for satire of the blackest kind. When you watch *Dr Strangelove*, you see the ordinary citizen's response to the Cold War.

The Battle of Algiers (Gillo Pontecorvo, 1966)

Pontecorvo's masterpiece is a gripping exploration of terrorism and counter-terror at the height of the Algerian War, and it doesn't pull its punches: The opening scene shows an Arab prisoner being tortured by French paratroopers. Pontecorvo got the authentic documentary feel he wanted by using ordinary people – the paras' commander is one of the few parts played by an actor. That his sympathies lie with the Algerian rebels is obvious, but he doesn't flinch from showing the appalling consequences of their actions: The scenes where they blow up a series of cafes and bars full of young people are shocking and very bloody. But he also shows how the French respond by planting bombs in Arab residential districts and torturing prisoners with electric shocks; in one scene, French residents suddenly turn on a harmless old man in the street simply because he's an Arab. *The Battle of Algiers* is a brilliant and disturbing analysis of the way in which terrorism – on both sides – can corrupt a society, and is as relevant to the age of Iraq, Abu Ghreb, and Guantanamo Bay as it was when it was made.

Apocalypse Now (Francis Ford Coppola, 1979)

This is the war film for people who don't like war films. Or war. *Apocalypse Now* was Coppola's reworking of Joseph Conrad's *Heart of Darkness* for Vietnam, showing an idealistic young officer gradually learning the full horror of the war as he pushes ever further up river in search of the mysterious Colonel Kurtz, played by Marlon Brando. The film's full of helicopter imagery, from the opening shot of a ceiling fan in Saigon, and the sight of helicopters firing rockets at a Viet Cong village while playing Wagner's *Ride of the Valkyries* at full volume has become one of cinema's most famous set pieces. If you get the chance, see this film on the big screen for the full effect.

Directors turned to Vietnam as a way of exploring the soul of America itself. *Apocalypse Now* shows the corrupting nature of the conflict: One striking sequence, deliberately reminiscent of the scene at the US embassy when Saigon fell, shows GIs desperately clambering onto a rising helicopter, but not doing so for freedom or democracy: They just want to get at the *Playboy* models inside. At a time when the world was increasingly nervous about East–West nuclear confrontation, *Apocalypse Now* caught the height of the anti-war mood. It didn't last long, though: *Rambo* was just around the corner.

Chapter 24

Ten International Bodies that Made a Difference

In This Chapter

▶ Considering some world governments that worked and some that didn't

▶ Admiring NGOs working for peace, health, and justice

▶ Dealing in ideals, hopes, principles, oil – and woggles

*T*he nineteenth century created the nation state but the twentieth century was the era of internationalism. International bodies, some of them government-led, others, known as NGOs (Non-Governmental Organisations) independent of governments, crossed boundaries and sought to unite the world in a sense of common humanity. They're not saints: International bodies and NGOs are as open to failure, incompetence, or corruption as any other groups, but they have made a major contribution to the health, wellbeing, and liberty of the world. Here are some of the most important.

The International Committee of the Red Cross

The Red Cross has its origins in the nineteenth century, when Swiss Henri Dunant was shocked at the lack of medical aid for the wounded after the 1859 Battle of Solferino, but it came into its own in the twentieth century. The Red Cross is about a lot more than first aid: In 1864 it drew up the first Geneva Convention, binding signatories to proper treatment of prisoners of war and in the twentieth century the Convention was progressively extended to cover racial discrimination and hostage-taking.

The Red Cross hasn't been free of controversy: Its symbol raises uncomfortable memories of the crusades and the blind eye it turned to the Nazi concentration camps detracted badly from the good work it did for prisoners of war and refugees. But the Red Cross has continued to set an important example of neutrality and humanity for others to follow.

Scouting

The scouting movement was founded in 1907 by an eccentric upper-class British officer called Robert Baden-Powell (BP), who saw instilling a bit of manliness into the young as a way to save the British empire from going flabby. It soon proved to have a much wider appeal. For working-class children, scouting offered a wonderful escape from the backstreets into the outdoors and into a culture of comradeship where class or religion simply didn't matter. And you got to wear long shorts and a woggle.

Scouting quickly went international, with huge jamborees for scouts and guides from all over the world. Not everyone liked the marching and saluting, and the fascist and Soviet versions (dictators tend to ban scouting, which has got to be a good sign) were unashamedly military, but scouting has adapted and survived and is still going strong today. Not bad for a crusty old colonel of the British empire.

The League of Nations

Yes, I know the League proved a flop when it was unable to contain aggressive dictators in the 1930s (not that nation states did much better) but it still deserves a bit more consideration. For one thing, it did actually get off the ground, and it set a vital precedent as an international body that is above nation states. Ordinary people around the world were deeply committed to its ideals and set up local branches of the League of Nations Union to further its aims of peaceful collective action. And let's face facts: The League's record isn't so different from that of today's 'international community'.

The League saved countless lives by working out a system of shipping lanes and banning the then-widespread use of poisonous lead paint. Its actions set the vital precedent that safety standards should be decided by international law and not left to different countries to do as they liked. The International Labour Organisation, which protects the rights of working people and runs vocational training for workers and managers, survived the fall of the League and still flourishes today: In 1969 it won the Nobel Peace Prize. No one's calling the League a success story, but a body that made a difference? Emphatically – yes.

The United Nations

The UN's image has been so tarnished by failure and scandal in recent years that recalling the enormous optimism it evoked when it was launched is difficult. Everything about the UN, from the bold design of its building to the sky blue berets of its troops, suggested that *here* was a world government with teeth. If so, it's overdue for a visit to the dentist.

The UN has seen some famous set pieces, such as Soviet premier Khrushchev banging his shoe on his desk in the General Assembly and shouting 'Nyet! Nyet! Nyet!' (translation: 'No! No! No!') when the Philippines president referred to 'Soviet imperialism', Yasser Arafat addressing the UN on behalf of the Palestine Liberation Organisation, or US ambassador Adlai Stevenson presenting the Security Council in 1962 with photographic evidence of Soviet missiles on Cuba. UN peacekeeping forces have a very mixed record: They kept the warring sides apart in the Middle East but they stood by during the massacres in Bosnia and Rwanda in the 1990s. Perhaps the UN is seen at its best in the work of its agencies, the World Health Organisation, the High Commission for Refugees, and the endeavours of UNICEF to protect and support children all round the world from the effects of poverty or exploitation.

The European Union

Love it or loathe it, the European Union is the most successful of the twentieth century's many international regional organisations. The EU began with a hugely symbolic post-war agreement between France and Germany to help each other out with coal and steel and soon grew into a free trading community of six countries committed not just to dismantling trade barriers but to creating an 'ever closer union'.

As an economic community the EU was a great success, though its policy of farming subsidies rewarded overproduction and led, for a time, to massive surpluses of butter and wine. As new members joined, the community sought to become more of a political union, which caused problems, especially with Britain. By the early twenty-first century the EU covered nearly the whole continent and was operating the modern world's first successful international currency, the euro. The European Union certainly made a difference; I'll leave you to decide if it made things better.

The Campaign for Nuclear Disarmament (CND)

CND began in 1958 as a protest against the deployment in Britain of nuclear weapons, but its ideals, methods, and logo quickly spread around the world. In the 1980s it revived as the Cold War enemies deployed a new generation of missiles, and it spawned an international protest movement against nuclear power itself.

CND marches and rallies attracted huge numbers of people, especially the young, who became increasingly used to the idea of joining in global protest events such as Live Aid and anti-globalisation demonstrations. Historians disagree about what impact CND had on the military policy of either side in the Cold War – probably very little – but as an example of democracy in action and of ordinary people taking a stand against a policy with which they profoundly disagreed, it was of enormous importance.

Amnesty International

If you're a lawyer and think everybody hates you, remember Amnesty International, founded in 1961 by Peter Benenson, a British solicitor, and Seán MacBride, an Irish lawyer and politician. Amnesty campaigns tirelessly against torture and capital punishment and for the release of prisoners of conscience around the world. That's a *lot* of prisoners.

Thanks to Amnesty, ordinary people can have a real impact: Just sending a letter to a head of state or a postcard to a political prisoner shows that the world is watching and prisoners do sometimes get released because of these missives. Amnesty also takes governments to court and gets landmark legal rulings passed. The bad news is that Amnesty is needed at all; the good news is that it does make a difference.

Oxfam

Hunger and famine in wartime Greece led to the creation of Oxfam, one of the best-known relief organisations combating hunger and poverty throughout the world. The Oxford Famine Relief Committee was one of a number of such committees set up to raise funds for the Greeks but it then carried on after the war, raising money for other wartime refugees. In 1951 Oxfam moved outside Europe for the first time in response to a famine in Bihar in India.

Oxfam has provided the model for other relief agencies but its education work is just as important, showing people in the West that the developing world is not made up of faceless victims but of individuals with the same human dignity and feelings as people anywhere else in the world. Oxfam pioneered the charity shop as a way both of raising funds and spreading its message, and it also took a lead role in recycling waste. Few international organisations have had such a widespread and positive impact as Oxfam.

Organisation of Petroleum-Exporting Countries (OPEC)

OPEC began in 1960 as a self-help group of five countries – Iran, Iraq, Kuwait, Saudi Arabia, and Venezuela, who got together to harmonise their prices, production, and export strategies. As more countries joined in by the 1970s, OPEC began to take on the dimensions of a political power bloc, especially in the oil-rich Middle East. The Arab countries found they could use oil as a weapon against the oil-hungry West. In 1973, OPEC raised its prices and imposed an oil embargo on Western countries that had supported Israel during the 1973 Yom Kippur War, and took similar action in 1979 after the Iranian Revolution.

Since the 1970s OPEC's influence has declined. Western countries started producing their own offshore oil so they wouldn't depend on OPEC so much. Oil prices slumped in the 1980s, and as the world explores other forms of energy, even for cars, OPEC's grip on world affairs has loosened. OPEC was split when Saddam Hussein of Iraq attacked fellow-OPEC member Kuwait in 1990, essentially to grab hold of its oilfields.

OPEC's glory days are past, but in its time OPEC was a power in the world, a reminder that the big boys couldn't have everything their own way.

Greenpeace

Greenpeace began in Canada in 1969 with the call to 'Save the Whale' from being hunted to extinction and to stop Canada's annual seal cull; it played a key part in getting an international moratorium on whaling and boosting international sales of whale music.

Greenpeace soon moved on from whales and wide-eyed baby seals, though. In the 1980s it became a leading voice for those opposing the spread of nuclear energy and nuclear weapons, stressing the disastrous impact nuclear activity would have on the worldwide environment. In 1985 its flagship *Rainbow Warrior*, which had been disrupting French atomic trials in the Pacific, was blown up in Auckland harbour by the French secret services, but Greenpeace continued its campaigning, focusing increasingly on the wider environment. If the world is alert today to the threats posed by human activity to the environment, much of the credit lies with Greenpeace.

Chapter 25

Ten BAD Ideas

. . . .

In This Chapter

▶ Exposing tyranny, cruelty, exploitation, and crime

▶ Marvelling at flared trousers for men

. . . .

*F*rom banning alcohol to shoving people into high-rise tower blocks, the twentieth century was as capable of coming up with really bad ideas as any other. This isn't a definitive list by any means, but you get the idea.

Prohibition

Talk about the law of unintended consequences. No one in America expected banning the sale, production, and consumption of alcohol to lead to wholesale racketeering, mob violence, and corruption on an unprecedented scale, but really, when you see the smuggling industry that arises just from customs duties, it wouldn't have taken the greatest of minds to predict some sort of trouble if you took away people's tipples. Drunkenness was a major problem in America, and the anti-alcohol brigade had a very serious case, but complete prohibition wasn't the answer. On the other hand, without prohibition we wouldn't have all those gangster movies, so maybe it had its plus side.

Totalitarian Dictatorship

Dictatorship is nothing new – ask the Romans – but totalitarianism, in which everything is under the control of the State, was a twentieth-century innovation. That for most of the world's population, dictatorship, not democracy, was the norm for most of the twentieth century is a sobering thought. Dictatorship fans used to say how efficient it was – look at that: Another train on time – compared with boring old democracy with its endless elections and objections; in fact, historians often point out that much of dictatorship's efficiency is all façade and that behind the gleaming jackboots the government is often inefficient, badly organised, and corrupt. Totalitarianism has led to labour camps, oppression, murder, censorship, and aggressive war. Give me a few late trains any day.

Racial Segregation

Racial segregation reached its most finessed form in the twentieth century, with separate benches, toilets, schools, cafes, churches, cinemas, and heaven knows what else, according to the shape of people's noses or the colour of their skin. Quite apart from the injustice of it all, think of the *expense*.

Most racial segregation is quite open about the racial hatred that underpins it – 'The Jews are our misfortune' the Nazis taught German children in the 1930s – but sometimes, as with apartheid in South Africa, the authorities try to claim it is merely 'separate development' and all quite harmless. For this reason, the famous Brown case in Kansas in 1954 was such an important breakthrough. Little Linda Brown (well, actually her dad) took her local School Board to court not because her 'black' school was bad or under-funded – unlike most 'black' schools in America, particularly in the South, it was actually quite adequately funded – but because telling someone they can't come in to a school, or a cafe, or a cinema, or a toilet, because of the colour of their skin is demeaning and damaging, regardless of how good the alternative might be. She won.

The Domino Theory

The Domino theory that US President Eisenhower spoke of never had much logic to it. His idea was that if communism set down roots in one country (we're talking South East Asia here, but it could apply elsewhere), then others would 'fall' to it in turn, like a row of dominoes. This theory over-looked a number of vital differences between countries and dominoes. *Why* a country would turn communist just because the neighbours did was never quite made clear: Perhaps they imagined Thailand looking through its net curtains at Laos or Vietnam and saying, 'Oh look, they've got TV next door, *and* a new car, *and* they've instituted a Marxist-Leninist dictatorship of the proletariat. Right, we're getting all three first thing in the morning.' Tragically, this theory led America to rush troops to Vietnam and ultimately to extend its bombing to Vietnam's neighbours, Cambodia and Laos. *That* development turned people towards the communists and one of the results was Pol Pot's genocidal regime in Cambodia. Put the dominoes away and listen more carefully to the people.

Concrete Tower Blocks

They called them 'cities in the sky' and came up with exciting plans and drawings showing them soaring upwards like buildings in science fiction films. And then the planners and designers went home to their nice cottages and left the poor people who actually had to live in their creations to discover what life was really like up there in the clouds. What they found was more concrete than ethereal. People were stuck up at the top of huge blocks of flats, cut off from the grass or even the pavements where they'd previously walked and played. While mothers and elderly people had to cope with lifts that kept breaking down, young people on these soulless estates turned to drugs and crime, enlivened by the occasional riot, adding a sense of violent menace to the already bleak atmosphere. Social housing is a major priority for governments all round the world, but the concrete cities of the post-war years illustrate just how to take a problem – and make it worse.

Chewing Gum

If you've ever had to prise hardened gobbets of chewing gum off the underside of a school desk, you'll understand why I hate the stuff with every fibre in my body. The sight of someone's jaw masticating is stomach-churning enough, and when they're speaking to you, it's just plain rude. But worse than the chewing is what people do with it. The makers tell you to wrap finished gum in the silver paper it came in and dispose of it carefully. What most people do is drop it on the ground for others to walk in: Usually me. Scraping the ghastly stuff off your shoe is bad enough, but when you think of where it's been . . . Although chewing gum was invented in the nineteenth century and may well help people concentrate on their work, its proliferation must rank as one of the lowest points of the twentieth century.

Plastic Wrapping

You need some plastic wrapping to keep food fresh, of course, but the packaging industry didn't stop there. Everything was to be wrapped in cellophane before it could possibly be allowed to pass into a customer's hands. Initially consumers protested at the sheer waste of it all and, presumably, the added costs, but in more recent years we've become a lot more aware of the environmental impact of producing the stuff in the first place, only for it to go straight in the bin (you can't yet recycle plastic wrapping). At long last retailers are beginning to wake up to the issue, producing biodegradable plastic bags or even cloth ones, but plastic wrapping carries on as strong as ever. A good idea gone badly wrong.

Esperanto

Oh dear. If you're an Esperanto speaker you'll be asking 'Kiel vi povas fari tion al mi?' ('How could you do it to me?'). After all, the idea of Esperanto is to bring people together in a common language with no irregular verbs, where you don't have to remember if 'table' is masculine or feminine, and to enable enthusiasts to write letters to newspapers (but not in Esperanto, curiously) saying how much better the world would be if everyone spoke it. Well, I'm sorry ('Mi beda ras'), but I don't buy it. You can create a communications system from scratch, but language is a lot more than that: It's part of a people's cultural heritage, part of who they are, and if you tell them 'Your language is no good; learn this one' (and many rulers through history have done just that), you're effectively rejecting their culture and identity. When you learn a language you are also learning about the people who speak it; Esperanto is mother tongue to no one. Nice thought; bad idea.

Sequels

Sequels stink. At least the early days of cinema employed a bit of imagination: *Bride of Frankenstein* instead of *Frankenstein II*. More recently, filmmakers have shown as little creativity in their titles as they have in the contents. *The Godfather II* was an exception, an intelligent and gripping film, as powerful and well crafted as the first, but *The Godfather III* wasn't. If a film works, that's because it's well written and crafted, with its own natural flow and shape. Endlessly recycling the same characters and the same basic idea is just lazy and does the audience a disservice. (I explore this idea further in my next book, *Twentieth Century World History for Dummies II*).

Flares for Men

Not for nothing are flares a distress signal. Sailors have long treasured their bell-bottom trousers, but at least they had the decency to wear them at sea. This particular form of horror first hit land in the 1920s in the form of 'Oxford bags'. The fashion didn't last, but returned in the 1970s, growing to ever bigger proportions until air was circulating up and down men's trouser legs and the pavements shone from being swept by the cuffs of thousands of pairs of frayed jeans. Drainpipe trousers returned in the 1980s, when the flares tendency went through the body and emerged at the other end in the biggest hairstyles seen since the eighteenth century. The 1990s brought blessed relief, until some fool came up with the idea of seventies retro and flares came back again. Just bear in mind, you can look intelligent, witty, urbane, handsome, and well dressed, or you can wear flares. Not both.

Index

FOR DUMMIES®

Do Anything. Just Add Dummies

UK editions

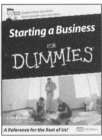

FOR DUMMIES®

Do Anything. Just Add Dummies

HOBBIES

Poker
978-0-7645-5232-8

Knitting
978-0-7645-5395-0

Drawing
978-0-7645-5476-6

Also available:

Art For Dummies
(978-0-7645-5104-8)

Aromatherapy For Dummies
(978-0-7645-5171-0)

Bridge For Dummies
(978-0-471-92426-5)

Card Games For Dummies
(978-0-7645-9910-1)

Chess For Dummies
(978-0-7645-8404-6)

Improving Your Memory
For Dummies
(978-0-7645-5435-3)

Massage For Dummies
(978-0-7645-5172-7)

Meditation For Dummies
(978-0-471-77774-8)

Photography For Dummies
(978-0-7645-4116-2)

Quilting For Dummies
(978-0-7645-9799-2)

EDUCATION

Psychology
978-0-7645-5434-6

The Koran
978-0-7645-5581-7

Anatomy & Physiology
978-0-7645-5422-3

Also available:

Algebra For Dummies
(978-0-7645-5325-7)

Astronomy For Dummies
(978-0-7645-8465-7)

Buddhism For Dummies
(978-0-7645-5359-2)

Calculus For Dummies
(978-0-7645-2498-1)

Cooking Basics For Dummies
(978-0-7645-7206-7)

Forensics For Dummies
(978-0-7645-5580-0)

Islam For Dummies
(978-0-7645-5503-9)

Philosophy For Dummies
(978-0-7645-5153-6)

Religion For Dummies
(978-0-7645-5264-9)

Trigonometry For Dummies
(978-0-7645-6903-6)

PETS

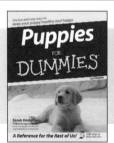

Puppies
978-0-470-03717-1

Dog Training
978-0-7645-8418-3

Cats
978-0-7645-5275-5

Also available:

Aquariums For Dummies
(978-0-7645-5156-7)

Birds For Dummies
(978-0-7645-5139-0)

Dogs For Dummies
(978-0-7645-5274-8)

Ferrets For Dummies
(978-0-7645-5259-5)

Golden Retrievers
For Dummies
(978-0-7645-5267-0)

Horses For Dummies
(978-0-7645-9797-8)

Jack Russell Terriers
For Dummies
(978-0-7645-5268-7)

Labrador Retrievers
For Dummies
(978-0-7645-5281-6)

Puppies Raising & Training
Diary For Dummies
(978-0-7645-0876-9)

FOR DUMMIES®

The easy way to get more done and have more fun

LANGUAGES

978-0-7645-5193-2

978-0-7645-5193-2

978-0-7645-5196-3

Also available:

Chinese For Dummies
(978-0-471-78897-3)

Chinese Phrases
For Dummies
(978-0-7645-8477-0)

French Phrases For Dummies
(978-0-7645-7202-9)

German For Dummies
(978-0-7645-5195-6)

Hebrew For Dummies
(978-0-7645-5489-6)

Italian Phrases For Dummies
(978-0-7645-7203-6)

Japanese For Dummies
(978-0-7645-5429-2)

Latin For Dummies
(978-0-7645-5431-5)

Spanish Phrases
For Dummies
(978-0-7645-7204-3)

Spanish Verbs For Dummies
(978-0-471-76872-2)

MUSIC AND FILM

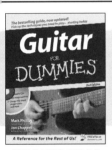
978-0-7645-9904-0

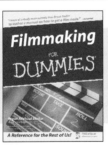
978-0-7645-2476-9

978-0-7645-5105-5

Also available:

Bass Guitar For Dummies
(978-0-7645-2487-5)

Blues For Dummies
(978-0-7645-5080-5)

Classical Music For Dummies
(978-0-7645-5009-6)

Drums For Dummies
(978-0-471-79411-0)

Jazz For Dummies
(978-0-471-76844-9)

Opera For Dummies
(978-0-7645-5010-2)

Rock Guitar For Dummies
(978-0-7645-5356-1)

Screenwriting For Dummies
(978-0-7645-5486-5)

Singing For Dummies
(978-0-7645-2475-2)

Songwriting For Dummies
(978-0-7645-5404-9)

HEALTH, SPORTS & FITNESS

978-0-7645-7851-9

978-0-7645-5623-4

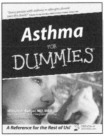
978-0-7645-4233-6

Also available:

Controlling Cholesterol
For Dummies
(978-0-7645-5440-7)

Diabetes For Dummies
(978-0-470-05810-7)

High Blood Pressure
For Dummies
(978-0-7645-5424-7)

Martial Arts For Dummies
(978-0-7645-5358-5)

Menopause FD
(978-0-470-061008)

Pilates For Dummies
(978-0-7645-5397-4)

Weight Training
For Dummies
(978-0-471-76845-6)

Yoga For Dummies
(978-0-7645-5117-8)

FOR DUMMIES®

Helping you expand your horizons and achieve your potential

INTERNET

978-0-470-12174-0

978-0-471-97998-2

978-0-470-08030-6

DIGITAL MEDIA

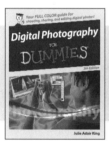

978-0-7645-9802-9

978-0-470-17474-6

978-0-470-14927-0

COMPUTER BASICS

978-0-470-13728-4

978-0-470-05432-1

978-0-471-74941-7